Searching for
The New France

Searching for
The New France

Edited by
James F. Hollifield
and George Ross

Routledge
New York and London

Published in 1991 by

Routledge
An imprint of Routledge, Chapman and Hall, Inc.
29 West 35 Street
New York, NY 10001

Published in Great Britain by

Routledge
11 New Fetter Lane
London EC4P 4EE

Copyright © 1991 by Routledge, Chapman and Hall, Inc.

Printed in the United States of America

Library of Congress Cataloging in Publication Data

Searching for the new France / edited by James F. Hollifield and George
   Ross.
      p. cm.
   Includes bibliographical references and index.
   ISBN 0-415-90249-5. — ISBN 0-415-90250-9 (pbk.)
    1. France—Politics and government—20th century. 2. Social
change. 3. Political stability. 4. Gaulle, Charles de, 1890-1970-
-Influence. I. Hollifield, James Frank. 1954- . II. Ross,
George, 1940- .
DC369.S38 1991
320.944—dc20   90-22790

British Library Cataloguing in Publication Data
Searching for the new France.
  1. France, history, 1958–
  I. Hollifield, James *1954–* II. Ross, George, *1940–*
  944.083

  ISBN 0-415-90249-5
  ISBN 0-415-90250-9 pbk

We dedicate this book to the memory of

Georges Lavau, 1918–1990

a great friend, colleague, and tireless
scholar of French politics and society.

Contents

Abbreviations   ix

Preface   xiii

Introduction: Janus and Marianne
                 George Ross   1

Chapter One: Governing the Economy in the Face of
                 International Challenge: From National Developmentalism
                 to National Crisis
                 Alain Lipietz   17

Chapter Two: The Institutions of the Fifth Republic
                 Stanley Hoffmann   43

Chapter Three: Towards a Centrist Democracy?
                 The Fate of the French Right
                 Martin A. Schain   57

Chapter Four: The French Left: A Tale of Three Beginnings
                 Jane Jenson   85

Chapter Five: Immigration and Modernization
                 James F. Hollifield   113

Chapter Six: In Search of the Etat Providence
                 Douglas E. Ashford   151

Chapter Seven: Trade Unions, Unemployment, and Regulation:
                 1962–1989
                 René Mouriaux   173

Chapter Eight: Educational Pluralism in the French
                 Fifth Republic
                 John S. Ambler   193

Chapter Nine: Where Have All the Sartres Gone?
                   The French Intelligentsia Born Again
                     George Ross   221

Chapter Ten: The Foreign Policy of the Fifth Republic:
                   Between the Nation and the World
                     A. W. DePorte   250

Conclusion: Still Searching for the New France
                     James F. Hollifield   275

Bibliography   299

Index   321

Contributors   331

Abbreviations

ANPE	Agence Nationale pour l'Emploi
APEL	Association pour l'Ecole Libre
APLE	Association Parlementaire pour la Liberté de l'Education
ASA	allocation supplémentaire d'attente (supplementary unemployment benefit)
ASSEDIC	unemployment compensation
CDP	Centre Democratie et Progrès
CDS	Centre des Démocrates Sociaux
CERES	Centre d'Etudes, de Recherche et d'Education Socialistes
CES	Collèges d'Enseignement Secondaires
CFDT	Confédération Française Démocratique du Travail
CFTC	Confédération Française des Travailleurs Chrétiens
CGC	Confédération Générale des Cadres
CGP	Commissariat Général du Plan
CGT	Confédération Générale du Travail
CIASI	Comité Interministériel pour l'Amènagement des Structures Industrielles
CIR	Convention des Institutions Républicaines
CNAL	Conseil National d'Action Laïque
CNIP	Centre National des Indépendants et Paysans
CNPF	Conseil National du Patronat Français
CNRS	Centre National de la Recherche Scientifique
DGD	Dotation Globale de Décentralisation
DPM	Direction de la Population et des Migrations

FEN	Fédération de l'Education Nationale
FGDS	Fédération de la Gauche Démocrate et Socialiste
FLN	Front pour la Libération Nationale (Algerian)
FN	Front National
FNB	Fédération Nationale du Bâtiment
FO	Force Ouvrière
FONDA	Fondation pour la Vie Associative
IGAS	Inspection Générale des Affaires Sociales
MRG	Mouvement des Radicaux de Gauche
MRP	Mouvement Républicain Populaire
OFPRA	Office Française de Protection des Réfugiés et Apatrides
ONI	Office Nationale d'Immigration
PCF	Parti Communiste Français
PR	Parti Républicain
PS	Parti Socialiste
PSU	Parti Socialiste Unifié
RI	Républicains Indépendants
RPF	Rassemblement du Peuple Français
RPR	Rassemblement pour la République
SFIO	Section Française de l'Internationale Ouvrière
SGEN	Syndicat Général d'Education Nationale
SGI	Société Générale d'Immigration
SIVP	Stages d'Initiation à la Vie Professionelle: youth-oriented, sub-minimum wage jobs program
SMIC	Salaire Minimum Interprofessionel de Croissance (minimum wage)
SNCF	Société Nationale des Chemins de Fer
SNES	Syndicat National des Enseignements de Second Degré
SNE-Sup	Syndicat National de l'Enseignement Supérieur
SNI	Syndicat National des Instituteurs
SONACOTRA	Société Nationale de Construction de Logements pour les Travailleurs
UDC	Union du Centre
UDF	Union pour la Démocratie Française
UDR	Union des Démocrates pour la République

UNAPEL	Union Nationale des Associations pour l'Ecole Libre
UNEDIC	Unemployment compensation
UNEF	Union Nationale des Etudiants de France
UNI	Union Nationale Interuniversitaire
UNR	Union pour la Nouvelle République
URC	Union des Républicains de Centre
URP	Union des Républicains de Progrès pour le Soutien du Président

Preface

The essays in this book represent a collective effort by ten scholars to examine the extent of the political, social, and economic changes that have overtaken France over the past three decades. We began this project with the objective of placing these changes into historical perspective, and we took the essays of an earlier volume, *In Search of France,* edited by Stanley Hoffmann, as a model for our inquiry.[1] The contributors to that work focused their attention on the twentieth-century crises and upheavals that transformed France from a world power to a more modest European state, struggling to find a new political identity. Indeed, the authors were writing in the shadow of the Algerian War, which resulted in the demise of the Fourth and the founding of the Fifth Republic.

As the title to the current volume indicates, we believe France continues to struggle for a political identity, even though war and crisis are fading memories. The Fifth Republic has survived intact for three decades, thus defying early critics who predicted instability and new crises of legitimacy. Yet France in the 1990s, like Europe itself, seems to be at a crossroads. Having successfully modernized its economy along the classical lines of industrial capitalism, creating in the process a mass-based consumer society, France is again faced with difficult choices. Although the range of choices is less daunting than those faced by earlier regimes—the republican consensus is not threatened, and monarchy and empire are no longer viable options—the quality of French democracy, economic productivity, and cultural and intellectual life are at issue. For the time being, a choice seems to have been made with respect to France's role in the world: Gaullist dreams of national grandeur have receded in favor of an interdependent, European path of development. But the decline of Gaullism has raised once again the issue of the political and social identity of the nation. Likewise, economic modernization seems to have created at least as many problems as it solved. The challenge for the authors in this book is to interpret the changes that have occurred over the past three decades, to place them in historical perspective, and to weigh the alternative explanations for change in specific areas of French life.

Apart from the dedicated group of scholars who contributed to the book, many other colleagues deserve thanks. The book grew out of a conference that was held at Brandeis University in May 1988 under the auspices of the Center for International and Comparative Studies. We should like gratefully to acknowledge the support of the Center, Robert Art, its director, and the staff who helped us to plan and run the conference. In addition, we received early support and encouragement from Ioannis Sinanoglou and the Council for European Studies, which provided us with a workshop grant. The discussants and panel chairs from the conference, some of whom are acknowledged by the individual authors in this volume, helped us to refine our arguments and analyses. Finally, several individuals at Brandeis and Routledge must be given recognition for the special role they played in bringing this project to fruition: the editors at Routledge, Jay Wilson and Cecelia Cancellaro have shown great patience and perseverance, as we struggled to mold this work into a coherent volume; Jennifer Franco, a doctoral candidate in politics at Brandeis, was very helpful in the organization and running of the conference; and one individual, William Field, also a doctoral candidate in politics, has given generously of his time and lent his intellectual talents to the editing of the book. To him, in particular, we are especially grateful.

James F. Hollifield
George Ross
May 1990   Brandeis University, Waltham, Massachusetts

Note

1. Stanley Hoffmann, ed., *In Search of France* (Cambridge, Mass.: Harvard University Press, 1963). The contributors to this book included Stanley Hoffmann, Lawrence Wylie, Charles Kindleberger, Jean-Baptiste Duroselle, Jesse Pitts, and François Goguel.

Introduction: Janus and Marianne

George Ross

> . . . Rarely has Marianne so strongly resembled Janus.
>
> —Stanley Hoffmann
> 1963[1]

Reflections on "Marianne's" elusiveness are still appropriate. *Plus ça change . . . plus c'est la même chose?* Not at all, as the essays that follow demonstrate! Nearly a quarter-century ago the authors of *In Search of France* reflected on a France that was at a clear turning point. The early 1960s seemed to be a moment of conclusions as well as beginnings: France was closing down its empire, its population was growing, its economy modernizing, its political institutions and discourses were changing, and it had begun a quest for a new place in a new international setting. France had to be "sought" anew because it faced a multiplicity of fundamental choices. What had been would almost certainly be no more. What was *becoming* was less clear. The "stalemate society"—Stanley Hoffmann's justly famous characterization of Third Republic France—that had maintained the French in a situation of historical suspended animation, was at an end, and a dynamic new "modern" France was taking shape. Marianne could be equated to Janus because not even the most far-sighted specialists could be quite certain what this new France would turn out to be.

Searching for the New France is a volume that does for France in the 1990s what *In Search of France* did for the 1960s. Specialists from different disciplines discuss the quarter-century that France has lived through since the early 1960s. In analyzing the past and projecting trends into the future, the essays make clear that France today is as Janus-like as it was in the 1960s. But the uncertainty of these essays is of a different quality altogether. The passage from "stalemate" to "modernity" twenty-five years ago was seen as the opening of a bright, new—if uncertain—future. A quarter-century later France's prospects engender no such optimism. Were our authors to be asked to supply an adjective to modify uncertainty, the majority of choices would range from "gray" to "ominous."

1

France in the 1960s: Anticipating Modernity

To many visitors in the late 1950s France still seemed "eternal," quaint, imbued with a certain timelessness. American tourists might have fallen in love with the *Grand Hotel du Napoléon*—which, in reality, was very small, with minuscule rooms stuffed with ancient armoires and toilets *à l'étage*—and luxuriated in the *coq au vin* with burgundy wine served at the local restaurant. The hotel didn't look like the Howard Johnson's in Kansas City and the restaurant—well, it certainly beat local fare at home. And everything was very inexpensive. Indeed, contrasts provided the mental snapshots. The countryside teemed with real peasants, often using technologies that Kansas had long since left behind. Cities, including Paris, were ill-equipped. Public transportation was antiquated, symbolized by art-nouveau metro stations and buses with balconies that might have been used to ferry *poilus* to the trenches during the First World War. Plumbing, even when it had migrated indoors, had an ageless quality, and woe to those not forewarned about the paucity of paper goods. The plethora of bakers, butchers, and candlestick-makers had its charm, but where were the supermarkets? The private automobile was just becoming accessible to ordinary French families, in the process bringing terror to an antiquated highway system. Television had just appeared, an extraordinarily effective medium for General de Gaulle's press conferences. But its few brief hours of daily broadcasting on one network were a far cry from "what we have at home." And try to make a telephone call!! The France of Marcel Carné's *Hôtel du Nord* and Jean Renoir's *La Règle du jeu* was still alive.

By the early 1960s modernization was in the air, however. Somehow, despite the political chaos of the Fourth Republic and perpetual colonial warfare, the French economy had been sneaking into the *trente glorieuses*.[2] The metro began to modernize. *Autoroutes* began to parallel the clogged *Nationales*. Innumerable cranes filled city and suburban skies, building innumerable new apartment houses, with modern plumbing, in which innumerable migrants from the countryside would soon live. Jacques Tati's *Mon Oncle* was a transition figure. Jean-Luc Godard's *Pierrot le Fou* was in the wings. What was the leading tourist attraction in France in the first years of the 1960s? Not the Louvre, not Versailles, but the new *aérogare* at Orly airport where on weekends French people, by the tens of thousands, observed modernity, embodied and symbolized in the Caravelle, taking off and landing. By the time *In Search of France* appeared, take-off away from the economic "stalemate" had been successfully negotiated and landing in a new consumerist, mass production, urbanized, televised, and motorized France was assured.

Most observers of France at the time believed, however, that France was different and unlikely to modernize "like the others." As Charles Kindleberger concluded, it was neither the market nor French capitalists that counted, but rather "new men" and "new attitudes."[3] France's economic take-off was accomplished largely *despite* a notoriously risk-averse business class. A handful of very clever and determinedly modernist high civil servants had manipulated reforms from the Resistance, the Marshall Plan, and various levers that the state had acquired to intervene in economic life to make everyone else—a conglomeration that included capitalists, workers, merchants, peasants, and politicians—change despite themselves, often without even being aware what was happening. Indeed, important analysts like Andrew Shonfield in his landmark *Modern Capitalism* presented France's state-led and "indicatively planned" rush to modernization as an inherently superior, more rational and rapid way to do things than relying on the market.[4] France, he thought, had abandoned its backwardness to become a beacon and vanguard.

It was obvious that this economic modernization would be unable to work its full magic without profound political changes. Powerful residues of the Third Republic's institutional stalemate had helped paralyze the Fourth Republic, and in 1962 it was really too early to tell whether the Fifth Republic would be able to uproot them. Born in a quasi-coup in 1958, the new Republic brought General de Gaulle to power bearing important constitutional ideas about strengthening the executive in ways that would clarify, and perhaps amplify, the central state's economic roles. De Gaulle managed to cobble together a heterogeneous coalition of "new men"—technocratic modernizers, both in the state and in business—and many of the social groups who stood to lose most from the resolute modernization that these "new men" had in mind. What would result from this? Masterful shrewdness plus genuine charisma allowed de Gaulle to navigate the complex last years of the Algerian War without losing his political footing. But by the end of the war in 1962, when *In Search of France* went to press, de Gaulle's Republic was turning to face the more "normal" tasks of promoting economic growth, managing social change, and redefining France's place in a postimperial world. Several authors feared that the bad habits and political cantankerousness of the French might reappear.

Here as well there were reasons to be optimistic, however. Direct elections to the new presidency, the result of an autumn 1962 reform, promised to strengthen the executive even further. General de Gaulle's charisma was a personal gift, by definition nontransferable to successors. Direct presidential elections might work to institutionalize a certain amount of automatic charisma at the relative expense of party politicians and narrower interests. If a strengthened executive was one positive prospect, new partisan political coherence might be another. The 1962 elections showed movement towards a Right-Left polarization that, if it continued, could create a predictable political debate allowing the electorate clear choices.

The constitutional and political future was nonetheless cloudy. What would happen in the Fifth Republic if and when the president and parliamentary majority differed? What if the conservative elements in de Gaulle's coalition were able to overrule or block the modernizing "new men"? What would happen to modernization if the Left turned out to be more than rhetorically anticapitalist? Despite such doubts, there were grounds for optimism. If political institutions began to work better, economic and social modernization might be facilitated. One could then hope that the meliorative and healing effects of economic and social change would, in turn, help out politically.

On the social front such limited optimism was harder to maintain. In the *beaux quartiers,* old-fashioned bourgeois superiority and paternalistic authoritarianism thrived in better-off families, upper-level educational institutions, and companies. In the parts of town, smoldering working-class anger infused with a heavy accent of *ouvriérisme* and class hatred produced periodic explosions. Rural France was beautiful and the *Village in the Vaucluse* was undoubtedly a wondrous place to visit, but it was horribly backward.[5] And if one liked museums to satanic mills, all one needed do was to wander the back streets of Roubaix, Valenciennes, or Maubeuge. For that matter, trying to get service in a bank, a post office, or a university library was sufficient reminder that sociologists were onto something in their discussions of persistently troublesome, and quite unmodern, French authority relationships. Although educational institutions were fast being flooded by the postwar baby boom, schooling was still overwhelmingly elitist and literary in outlook. Moreover, hordes of young people crowded into a room designed for small numbers in the seventeenth century could make even the magnificent Sorbonne look Shabby: new facilities were desperately needed.

Problems abounded, but there was widespread agreement in the early 1960s that economic growth might provide ways in which to resolve them. If French society looked odd and rather unreformed—perhaps even "blocked" in ways—people were confident that rising incomes would make new choices possible and shake off the habits of "stalemate." Consumer capitalism would homogenize lifestyles and dampen the effects of social hierarchies. People would become more urban and urbane, mobile and well-schooled, and live in class-mixed environments. They would get information about the world more from the media than from relatives and neighbors, and thus become more moderate and tolerant. The number of educationally credentialed white-collar and professional workers would increase, gradually imposing a model of middle-class achievement on French mores. In time, the many barriers and provincialisms, so long the fuel of various wars among the French, would break down. That was what modernization could do.

France's international position in 1962 was at a turning point as well. After the disgrace of defeat and Vichy, France emerged from World War II determined to rebuild its national dignity, only to see this determination founder in Cold War and colonial warfare. The end of the Algerian War was thus both the end of the road for French colonialism and the symbolic beginning of a new search for international prominence. General de Gaulle, full of plans for the future, initially led this quest. Prior to the final agony of the Fourth Republic, France had made a commitment to building the European Economic Community (EEC). The new

Common Market seemed to provide an ideal setting for France to wean itself from the false securities and uncompetitive product mixes of empire and protectionism. Even General de Gaulle abandoned his anti-Europeanism, reasoning that a *Europe des Patries* could become a factor in overcoming the domination of France by the superpowers, which had developed from Yalta and the Cold War.

The Fourth Republic had left another present for the General. An independent French nuclear deterrent—the *bombinette,* as *le Canard Enchaîné* labeled it in the early 1960s—could give a new identity and mission to the disillusioned military forces returning from Algeria and thereby help guarantee political stability. Even more important, it might allow new leverage toward independence from the United States, enabling France to reestablish some part of the national dignity for which the Resistance had striven but which had disappeared with the Cold War. And, finally, it was yet another impressive symbol of France's economic modernization.

Restoring *grandeur* was the Gaullist objective. State-led economic modernization was a prerequisite to renewed French standing in the world and, in addition, was technologically essential to give France the wherewithal for military modernization. In reciprocal fashion, military modernization would stimulate civilian technological advance and economic modernization. As France came to a new importance in the world, acting in Europe by developing close ties with the West Germans, the French themselves would change, become proud again.

Taking the Pulse of a New France

Very little worked out as anticipated. Much of the problem lay with the assumption, widespread in the early 1960s, that the great twentieth-century transformation was from "premodern" to industrial social orders. A "premodern" society—really, one that had not yet adopted American-style consumerist capitalism—involved the perpetuation of all kinds of backward habits. "Modern industrial society" was Americanized mass consumption, mass education, burgeoning middle classes, political pluralism, and cooperation between capital and labor in production. Once a society became definitively modern in industrial ways its basic parameters would henceforth be relatively constant, even as the whole system worked to produce greater and greater abundance. Thus, from the vantage point of the early 1960s the issue for France was either "breaking through" to modernity or declining.

We now know the fatal flaw in this reasoning. Modernity is not something that a society achieves once and for all, a magic plateau where older problems disappear and new ones are more easily managed. Virtually all of the essays in this volume underline the enormous irony of what has really happened to France in the last quarter century. The ruse of history was that there was no magic plateau at all: indeed, the contours of the new environment were extremely difficult to decipher. Instead, modernity turned out to be built on shifting sands and to provide only a treacherous footing.

Nowhere was this truer than in the economic realm, as Alain Lipietz's essay shows. The state-led Gaullist trajectory for catching up worked very well until the mid-1970s. France invested, produced, urbanized, motorized, consumerized, and "supermarketized" with alacrity. As a result, much of the Third Republic quaintness that our 1950s tourist photographed was bulldozed under. France's economy grew very rapidly, even compared with other advanced capitalist societies, its international trading position improved, per capita incomes went up, and lifestyles changed dramatically.

But modern times turned sour. In the 1970s stagflation appeared, growth levels declined, and unemployment shot up. Worse still, the usual 1960s remedies—state intervention, massive public works programs (nuclear electricity, telephones), demand stimulation—did little to stop what looked increasingly like a downward spiral. Private-sector investment virtually ceased, productivity improvement slowed, and French industry started to fall behind again. The unpleasant revelation in all this was that the French miracle had not been all that miraculous. During the boom, France had benefited from a relatively beneficent international trade setting in which there had been space for almost everyone's products. This setting disappeared, beginning in the mid-1970s, and France's comparative weaknesses reappeared. French capital, which had basked for years in the reflected glow of the technocrats' achievements, once again looked risk-averse and un-innovative. Governments were often unable or unwilling to act with the foresight and energy that the situation demanded, and when they did try to be decisive they often made matters worse, largely because the battery of statist economic-policy tools that Shonfield had heralded as everyone's future became progressively less effective. Nowhere was this clearer than in the early 1980s, when the Left came to power. The new circumstances seemed to dictate tactics of decentralized restructuring, "flexibility," rapid response to changing markets, and entrepreneurial agility—tactics diametrically opposed to those which the Left brought to the situation. An enormous *crise de conscience* followed as the Left, and the French more generally, rejected *dirigisme* and began a quest to "rediscover the market."

The evolution of French institutions and political life was no less surprising. As Stanley Hoffmann shows, the Gaullist constitution worked—surviving the departure of the general himself—largely because with direct election the power and presence of the president never ceased to grow. The constitution also proved itself to be much more flexible than most observers had anticipated. For its first twenty-three years the stability of the Fifth Republic had been premised on the perpetuation of presidents and parliamentary majorities of the same political coloring. *Alternance* in 1981, when a president and parliamentary majority of the Left were elected for the first time, quite successfully destroyed this myth. *Alternance* also demonstrated, beyond the remarkable resilience of Fifth Republic institutions, that the constitution had gradually and subtly seduced virtually everyone in French political life into loyal support. Between 1986 and 1988 there came yet another permutation, *cohabitation* between a Left president and a Right parliamentary majority.

General de Gaulle and his team, perhaps without being aware of it, had written a constitution *à géometrie variable* that allowed flexibility of democratic representation and a strong president. A number of clouds hung over this success story, however. There were, for example, some easily conceivable, perhaps even likely, "geometric" institutional patterns that might not have such felicitous consequences. *Cohabitation* in 1986–88 involved unique circumstances and unique personalities, but different results would have been easy to envisage. Sustained occupation of the Elysée by a president of a different political stripe from the parliamentary majority, for example, might eventually weaken the executive and substantially increase the importance of parliament, moving the Fifth Republic much closer in practice to the Fourth.

Moreover, however flexible, the Fifth Republic immeasurably "personalized" French politics, and the prognosis for such personalization must be mixed. General de Gaulle was the pioneer as ever, deliberately presenting himself as representing the nation over and above specific interests. François Mitterrand did more or less the same thing in 1988. Contrasting these two approaches more closely is striking, however. De Gaulle combined charisma with a sharp-edged and purposive national agenda. Mitterrand combined charisma with an agenda that was strategically blurred, avoiding strong proposals altogether, in order to occupy the electoral Center. Perhaps, after a decade of angular and somewhat ineffectual programmatic confrontations, this was indeed what the French wanted. But it may also be that focus on personality has come to be tied, in normal "modern" circumstances of sophisticated polling and television campaigning, with just such blurred agenda personalization. Voters may seek someone for whom they feel personal sympathy rather than an agenda. Major elections then become periodic media rituals around which elites maneuver policies in a relatively unconstrained way. Moreover, serious public debate over essential issues is downplayed, and, in time, the quality of political culture is lowered.

From the vantage point of 1962 it was safe to project a solid Right-Left polarization of France's partisan debate. Institutional changes obliged the multiplicity of parties and fragments to present "united fronts" on both sides, fronts that would give the electorate clear program choices. A Right coalition claiming to derive legitimacy and ideas from General de Gaulle and the Gaullist Resistance proposed a strong executive and state to promote a modern, capitalist France aspiring to international *grandeur*. The Left bloc, claiming its own reformist Resistance legitimacy, proposed a social-democratic France, again with a strong state but with less stress on the executive, promoting policies to redistribute authority and income. On both sides, various partisan bits and pieces were ,refractory. On the Right were those nostalgic for empire and those who favored modernization for everyone but themselves. On the Left was the pro-Soviet and "revolutionary" Communist Party. Prevalent views on modernization were comforting, however, since they predicted confidently that such vestiges from the past would shape up or die.

For a while, something like this logic did seem to be at work. Martin Schain's essay on the Right shows its limits, however. During the tenure of the General himself, Gaullism did bring many of the disparate elements of the Right together into an electoral coalition, but the process never led to a genuine conservative party. Fragmentation was papered over by logrolling and alignment behind the president. This arrangement continued under Pompidou but began to fade in the 1970s. "Clans" and separate, rival organizations emerged around the 1974 presidential elections, followed in the later 1970s by growing disagreement among different segments of the Right about program. By the 1980s any expectation that economic modernization and presidentialism might produce a unified Right had been completely dashed. Instead there existed a bewildering variety of messages, usually attached to ambitious *presidentiables,* indicating profound disagreements about principles and strategy. There were neoliberals à la Thatcher and Reagan, populists flirting dangerously with dark social anxieties about security and immigration, old-line Gaullists trying to patch together various propertied groups, and Christian Democrats who believed in social solidarity and the welfare state. Had the Right been ambushed by its own institutional creations, hence the fissiparous nature of factional rivalries around the presidential candidates that had appeared? Had it been swept away by the paradoxical consequences of its successes, particularly in the economic realm? Were even deeper trends at work? Whatever the answers here, when tried and true approaches ceased to work, rather than finding substitutes, the Right gave way to cacophony. Moreover, the emergence of the racist Front National (FN) created enormous new strategic and electoral problems, problems that cast a pall over the Right's future.

As Jane Jenson shows, the Left failed to conform to the vision of the "modernizers" quite as much as the Right. A Left divided by the Cold War began the 1960s as if it had internalized the injunctions of political modernizers. Progress toward a workable coalition was gradual and complicated, but successful, as demonstrated by the 1972 "Common Program for a Left Government." Ultimately, after considerable coalitional difficulty, the Left won power in 1981. The 1980s showed, however, that for *this* Left, electoral success was its own undoing. Once in power, the Left's programmatic and ideological coherence collapsed very quickly. The problem was that it then could find few convincing substitutes.

The logic of Fifth Republic partisan bipolarization *had* created two distinct blocs with different policy programs on offer, with the Left proposing its own distinct, somewhat strident, variant on social democracy—albeit a 1945 model. Then, in time—and here the cross-cutting mechanisms of presidentialism must be considered—all of this broke down, leaving the Socialists seeking ways to occupy the Center-Left and the Communists out of the picture altogether. Many observers greeted the decline of ideological rhetoric and Communist power as good things. But what kind of representation would come out of a Socialist party that seemed ever more devoted to cliquish struggles over the succession to President Mitterrand? Moreover, there was a problem of numbers. A Socialist candidate could win a presidential runoff. Yet by themselves the Socialists had nowhere near the number of votes needed to win a parliamentary majority. Finally, one voter out of three still used the ballot to protest—whether voting for Communists, the rising Greens, or the dreaded Front National (many of whose voters had once voted for the Left)—and there were ominous signs of rising levels of abstention and indifference.

The matter of immigration brought together issues of national tradition, institutions, economics, the state, and partisan politics to provide excellent illustrations of how a resolute search for one version of modernity might lead to unexpected destinations. French industrialization had traditionally used immigration as an essential source of labor supply, then relying on tried and true "Republican" methods to turn immigrants into French citizens. There were no "hyphenated" French. One came to the Lorraine from Italy to work in the steel mills, and one's children became French, thanks in large part to schooling. The economic modernization of the *trente glorieuses,* carried out despite chronic labor shortages, drew in millions of new immigrants. The combined effects of the beginning of a 1970s economic downturn and political change in the 1980s made it clear that older Republican formulas might no longer work. Non-Europeans, especially North African Muslims, appeared much less assimilatable than earlier European immigrants. The emergence of a particularly virulent stream of French xenophobia and racism was both a consequence and cause of this.

James Hollifield's essay discusses these complicated matters. Neither the mainstream Right nor the traditional Left has been able to respond creatively to the needs of France's new immigrant population, nor have they been able to offer alternatives to contain and channel the social discontent that has eventuated in racism and support for the Front National. The problem goes far beyond the collapse of ideological schemas that for decades had helped aggregate diverse interests. Deep republican assumptions about the French state, what it is and does, and what it means to be French have been challenged.

Our 1960s colleagues addressed social issues by writing about "the grass roots" and "bourgeois France." The intervening quarter-century has been socially turbulent far beyond anyone's expectations. Beyond the issue of immigration just discussed, rural France has been transformed, cities have been renewed, the workplace has been redesigned, leisure has taken on new contours, the life-cycle has been modified (more schooling, less work, changed marriage and childrearing patterns, the institutionalization of the *troisième age*), and France's general occupational structure has been altered. All of this makes it virtually impossible today to define, let alone study, objects called "grass-roots" and "bourgeois France." Now a wide range of social and cultural phenomena—about which the best specialists and observers felt confident in discussing a bare twenty-five years ago—have been transformed beyond all recognition. The French have come to resemble other Europeans vastly more than they once did, while, simultaneously, there is greater differentiation inside France. Four discrete areas illustrate this: social policy, industrial relations, the educational system, and the evolution of the intelligentsia.

The evolution of French social policy, unlike virtually everything else discussed in this volume, is straightforward, as Douglas Ashford describes. Economic growth and modernization during the *trentes glorieuses* led to an expansion in social programs within outlines largely set out in post-Liberation years. In the first year or two after 1981 the Left tried to expand social programs despite difficult economic circumstances, but mainly to produce more of what already existed, and by 1983 this attempt had foundered, along with the Left's broader economic package. What followed looked much like what had gone before, with the evolution of social policy marked by schemes of tinkering and creative financing to meet continuing deficit problems, without much modification of underlying structures.

Beneath this straightforward story there was an even more essential continuity. As opinion polls throughout the 1980s repeatedly showed, while the French might be willing to contemplate important changes in relations between state and economy, they had little desire to see such changes have a negative impact on their welfare-state systems. They were profoundly attached to their *protection sociale* and welfare state. This attachment, in turn, has played an important political role, among other things making any full-blooded Thatcherite neo-liberalism virtually impossible. It also gave the Socialists some semblance of programmatic self-presentation when their ideology and program collapsed after 1982–83.

The story of French industrial relations, which René Mouriaux tells through the lens of employment, looks straightforward as well. In the early 1960s, French unions were comparatively weak in members, organizational and mobilizational power, and shop-floor legal prerogatives. They were, if anything, even weaker in 1990. The virtually full employment that existed on and off throughout much of the *trente glorieuses* had occurred largely despite, rather than because of, the unions. One can confidently assert the same thing about the high unemployment of the 1980s. Appearances are misleading, however. In between 1962 and 1990, industrial relations in France had been on a veritable roller coaster. After Algeria, the 1960s brought intensifying industrial conflict, rapidly rising trade-union strength, and eventually, after the monumental strikes of 1968, a period of important reform of labor relations. Steps were then taken to make French industrial relations somewhat more like those in other European societies. Economic downturn and the beginnings of restructuring in the later 1970s, combined with the effects of Left political divisions, weakened unions and undermined some of the effects of earlier reforms. The fate of Left reformism toward labor after 1981 was symbolic. A series of measures designed to strengthen workers and unions in the workplace, and especially to beef up their contractual position at firm level, functioned largely to benefit employers. In fact, the French system of industrial relations failed to "modernize" in the way 1960s specialists had expected. The irony was, however, that by 1990 most specialists had long since discarded 1960s conventional wisdom on such matters. In many countries, not simply France, the relative power of labor was in decline, and systems of industrial relations were in profound flux.

In the 1960s, the one thing that any society like France, in which a substantial postwar demographic boom and economic modernization occurred virtually simultaneously, would have been expected to do was to introduce large changes in its educational system. And indeed, as John Ambler's essay shows, this did occur. Ambler's chosen vantage point, the politics of educational policy, provides a particularly good angle on the various contradictions and shortcomings of the changes that followed, however. Educational expansion in France has been fraught with periodic crises, including gigantic explosions in May–June 1968 and January 1986, explosions that had direct effects on French politics more generally. Moreover, the process moved forward without really attenuating France's two-tier system of higher education. Although there has been a substantial increase in schooling in general, and although the percentage of each cohort pursuing higher education has risen, certain young people are still diverted at a very early age into the rarified and exclusive schools that produce France's ruling elites, while everyone else goes to second-rank, often ill-equipped and crowded institutions.

Controversies in the 1980s, prompted by Socialist efforts to act out a century-old republican and *laïc* educational reform agenda revealed not only how much time had passed this agenda by, but also how much trouble had developed for French primary and secondary education. Educational reform was as much at the center of France's social agenda in 1990 as it had been in 1960. The modernizers who had believed in the 1960s that educational change to respond to the needs of a "modern" society was largely a matter of facilities and expanded access had clearly been wrong. Whether France's educational policy-makers in the 1990s, confronted with all sorts of entrenched interests, social problems, and financial constraints, would do any better than their predecessors was less than clear.

George Ross provides another approach to social matters in his discussion of the evolution of the Left intelligentsia. This has not been simply a cultural decoration to populate cafés, fill bookstores, and attend faculty meetings. Taking seriously a self-definition dating at least from the Dreyfus Affair, if not earlier, the French Left intelligentsia has seen itself as the creator of universal, liberating ideas that, given sufficiently energetic missionary efforts, might become the future of ordinary people. Quite as important, this self-defined mission was not a delusion. Left intellectuals have made a substantial political difference, particularly since the early 1960s. This story is one of dramatic change, first of the rise and intensification of strident radicalism and then, by the 1980s, of retreat towards liberal modesty. Here, it might be argued that one of the important things that really did make France distinctive in the early 1960s, the unusually large role of intellectuals in the definition of key public moral and political debates, may have changed by the 1990s.

We have left France's international position until last, to be discussed in Anton DePorte's essay. Even in the early 1960s, De Gaulle's strategy of reconstructing French *grandeur* received mixed reviews, both inside and outside France. Moreover, the General clearly failed to achieve many of his own most important goals.[6] His formula of combining French economic modernization, Franco-German cooperation in the EEC, and an independent French nuclear deterrent simply did not grant France enough new power to make much of a dent on the post-Yalta order. During the 1960s France proved enough of a gadfly-irritant to anger American leaders and stimulate anti-French feelings in the United States, and the French were able to play a more active and influential international role than any other European nation (particularly in formerly colonial areas), but the essential outlines of the Cold War world remained unchanged, and by the 1970s there was a clear decline in Gaullist orientations and a slow but sure reintegration of France into the NATO world. Brezhnevite muscle flexing in the aftermath of Vietnam and West European peace movements stimulated this process even more under François Mitterrand in the early 1980s, despite a great deal of initial nationalist rhetoric to the contrary.

The story would have been simple to tell had it ended in 1985. An overambitious Gaullist France had faced constraints from deep structural realities and had then turned toward a more conventional posture. However, many of these structural realities themselves evaporated in the crucible years of 1989 and 1990. In the uncertain new context, some of France's new initiatives have been very important indeed. Beginning in 1984–85, Mitterrand and Jacques Delors, the new president of the European Commission set out a new European trajectory towards "1992." At the core of their strategy was the notion that French politics and politicians would ally with West German economic strength to promote fuller European integration. The collapse of "existing socialism" in 1989 made the future of this strategy quite unclear, but it still provided one of the few clearminded and dynamic elements in the new post-Yalta European environment. The new uncertainty flowed from the relative lack of resources of French politics in a Europe faced with a politically and economically reunited Germany.

Postmodernization?

It is fashionable these days to employ a conceptual vocabulary of "posts"— "post-Fordist" in the production realm, "postmaterialist" in the ideological, "post-Marxist" in the political, and "postmodern" to refer to virtually anything from architecture to apparel. Let us coin yet another variant. France in the 1990s has reached a moment of "postmodernization." What do we mean by this? Within virtually every dimension that our essayists discuss, France has changed fundamentally. "The stalemate society" is something that now exists only in old movies and in the memories of senior citizens. Yet change has not brought France to the magic, tranquil plateau that the modernizers saw as the end result of modernization. One conclusion of the complex story told in *Searching for the New France* is that if in the 1960s France had energetically stepped onto the train to modernity, by the 1990s it had to face the fact there was no longer any such station on the railroad.

But what station did France ultimately reach? Before turning to the specific answers that our essayists propose, let us make a few brief suggestions. In general, the processes of change that France had embraced by the early 1960s brought with them not only promises confirming the desirability of modernity, but also more covert tendencies leading to the eclipse of one France and the creation of another, quite different France. The first France had a strong identity and geographical and cultural boundaries, and was a society whose "grass-roots" national character and culture could be clearly defined and, more important, experienced by the French and observers alike. France has not disappeared, of course, far from it! But *this* France may no longer exist.

France in the 1990s is experiencing an identity crisis. Only the smallest dimension of this can be attributed to failures to modernize. Indeed, as most of our essays show, French society did quite a good job in achieving the objectives that it set out to achieve. To a much greater degree the crisis has occurred because many of the modern ways of doing things that were belatedly, and sometimes painfully, learned have turned out to provide inadequate responses to the current situation. This is particularly true in economic matters, the discursive and programmatic content of political life, educational policy, immigration policy, and a number of other essential issue areas. The dilemmas of postmodernization go even deeper than this, however. As France, like its advancing capitalist neighbors, did move forward decisively and successfully over recent decades, frontiers of all kinds—economic, political, social, cultural—between the "new" France that emerged and the various worlds around it became more and more blurred. Indeed, both for those who live in and for those who study this new France, what it now means to be French "at the grass roots," culturally, is much less clear.

Recent decades have involved a profound redistribution between the "national" and the "international" for virtually all societies. The idea of modernization was that through the appropriation of advanced knowledge, technologies, ways of looking at the world, and ways of cooperating socially a specific backward France would become a specifically modern France. What happened instead was that modernization pushed the economy, culture, polity, and governments into a maelstrom of international flows. As this happened, even larger bits and pieces of the country's multiple destinies began to elude its direct control.

To the degree to which economic modernization was successful, to take one example, France was more and more implicated in an ever more competitive expanding international market. Its firms had to become European or global while an increasing amount of the economic activity carried on in the Hexagon itself was coordinated from the outside. To take another example, to the degree to which France became committed to a degree of currency stability within the EEC through the European Monetary System in an increasingly trade-integrated Europe, it lost an important margin of domestic macroeconomic policy autonomy. Strategies leading to comparatively high levels of inflation, unduly low interest rates, or chronically high commercial deficits, which might have been possible earlier, became so costly in the new Europe that they could not be undertaken at all, a lesson that the Left learned to its chagrin in the early 1980s. Moreover, efforts to maintain employment and, perhaps, to restructure threatened economic sectors like steel and coal mining through subsidies and statist voluntarism had developed into a complete zero-sum game by the later 1970s. Governments that attempted to do such things borrowed resources from more central sectors to keep up with what was proceeding apace elsewhere, causing France to fall further behind. In quite another realm, despite nationalist cultural bluster of all kinds, by the later 1980s it had proved to be virtually impossible to do anything but capitulate to the rampant internationalization, and particularly the Americanization, of the mass media. And, needless to say, we could go on listing examples.

General de Gaulle wanted to lead a chronically stalemated France away from its self-limitations and self-defeating political and cultural propensities toward renewed *grandeur*. He foresaw an economically, militarily, and culturally stronger France emerging from the efforts that he so fervently enjoined his fellow citizens to undertake. History's irony was that the very changes for which the General so eloquently proselytized could not possibly lead to the results that he desired. Instead, they transformed France into a middle-sized European society ever more implicated in a multiplicity of transnational arrangements and processes for which Gaullist categories of independence and self-confidence seemed less and less appropriate.

Let us rejoin, ever so briefly, the foreign tourists we met earlier. Recall the images that they brought with them from their visit to a provincial city in the later 1950s. They stayed at the *Grand Hotel Napoléon,* which, belying its name, was quite small and owned by a M. and Mme. Dupont who were perplexing to the degree to which they were simultaneously solicitous and authoritarian. They settled into their tiny room with *lavabo* and tried to decide which little bristrot awaited their evening's pleasure, straining their eyes reading the *Guide Rouge* under a naked light bulb hanging from the ceiling. Now, in 1990, they return to the same provincial city, grandchildren in tow. The *Grand Hotel Napoléon* is still there, "But the prices, my goodness, it's much cheaper to stay in Kansas City." Chances are, however, that the place to stay in town is now the *NovoSofitel,* a large new white building that is a Gallicization of standard Sheraton architecture, "just like in Kansas City." They can still find that favorite little restaurant from thirty years ago, even though they now have to worry a lot about whether they can afford it. But what do they notice while walking toward it, thanks to the clamor of their grandchildren? A full range of *Flunches, Quikburgers,* and other assorted fast-food outlets. Aha, France has been taken over by the Americans, they conclude. In some ways they are correct. Modernity has brought consumerist Americanization while simultaneously preserving some of the old France—the quaint restaurant now has a computerized cash register, while, in the kitchen, a microwave quietly does its work. But what they discover, with a bit of further investigation, is that the "American-international" hotels, fast-food emporia, sporting-goods stores, and software outlets, all shiny chic and new-looking, are actually French. Moreover, they are often parts of a far-flung international empire controlled by French business interests. Thus our friends can easily make reservations to stay in another French-owned and operated *Novosofitel* in Helsinki or, perhaps, Heidelberg. And their grandchildren, who, like most very young Americans, are rather conservative in their dietary habits, might want to wolf down hamburgers from *Quik* or *Flunch* in both places, once again French-owned and operated.

Modernization to achieve *grandeur* was an illusory quest. The world for which France tried to remake itself was reconstructing its own parameters at the very same time. France is unquestionably quite a bit less like it was a quarter-century ago and rather more like its neighbors. Together they are all somewhat less in control of the various mechanisms and resource exchanges that once encouraged their own illusions of *grandeur.* Where France stops and the rest of the social, economic, cultural, and political world begins is now very hard to predict. What our American tourists discovered in superficial ways had a more profound significance. France has modernized to become a participant in a wide range of international flows. Its "postmodernization" quest must now be to maximize its presence and leverage over these flows while becoming ever more dependent upon them.

General de Gaulle would be appalled at the unintended consequences of his dedicated crusade. France is no longer "steadfast and unchanging." France is Europe and Europe is France. Moreover, Europe itself is but one important region of the international market and culture. French success is contingent on its ability to be a player in all of these realms. One dimension of France's future drama will, of course, be its capacities to generate such success. It will not come automatically. The other important dimension is that such success, if it can be engineered, is certain to make France even less the France of old.

Notes

1. Stanley Hoffmann, et al., *In Search of France* (Cambridge, Mass.: Harvard University Press, 1963).

2. "Thirty Glorious Years" is a term borrowed from the title of Jean Fourastié's important book, *Les Trente glorieuses, ou la Révolution invisible de 1946 à 1975* (Paris: Fayard, 1979).

3. Charles Kindleberger, "The Postwar Resurgence of the French Economy," in Hoffmann, et al., *In Search of France,* p. 156.

4. Andrew Shonfield, *Modern Capitalism* (Oxford: Oxford University Press, 1965).

5. Rural France is marvelously described in Lawrence Wylie's classic ethnography, *Village In The Vaucluse* (Cambridge, Mass.: Harvard University Press, 1957).

6. See Jean Lacouture, *De Gaulle,* vol. 3, *Le Souverain* (Paris: Seuil, 1986).

1

Governing the Economy in the Face of International Challenge: From National Developmentalism to National Crisis

Alain Lipietz

> A nation is a soul, a spiritual principle. . . . It presupposes a past but is
> constituted in the present by one tangible fact, consent, a clearly enunciated
> wish to continue life together. The existence of a nation is a plebiscite which
> recurs every day. . . .
>
> —Ernest Renan

April 24, 1988. After the first round of the presidential election France was divided into two, as usual. From another angle, however, it was cut into three as well. On the Left the Socialist candidate had 34 percent. On the Right were two moderate candidates, one with 20, the other with 16 percent. The two blocs were fighting over the center in the almost total absence of a mobilizing project, with the possible exceptions of technological change and Europe. The third part, divided between the two extremes of the political spectrum, announced its refusal of this soulless consensus. The Left of this part was fragmented, with a Communist Party desperately defending old *acquis sociaux* and reduced to 7 percent and, at about the same level but divided, the alternative and ecologist forces. The frightening surprise came from the extreme Right—14.5 percent of the vote went to Le Pen and his party of fear, exclusion, racial hatred, and irrational fantasy. A quarter-century after Gaullist stabilization, the end of colonial warfare, and the great outburst of enthusiasm about modernization, a French political world that everyone thought had "grown up" to transcend great "ideological" debates had come apart to expose an acute new national identity crisis.

Some observers would respond by claiming that on the "big issues" like defense, institutions, and the role of the state, the disagreements that had divided Right from Left in the 1965 presidential elections, had disappeared. My hypothesis, in contrast, is that the bedrock of national consensus constituted by the "plebiscite of daily life" had never been stronger than in this earlier epoch, when powerful Left forces struggled against the forms and rhythms of growth managed by the Gaullists. Today's ideological silence, interrupted—and so energetically!—by racist clamor and "law and order" demagoguery, does not demonstrate positive consent. On the contrary, it reveals an absence of common consensus on the fundamental values against which one might measure secondary disagreements. "The old is dying while the new has yet to appear . . . a dusky dawn when morbid symptoms will appear," as Antonio Gramsci noted.

It is impossible to do complete justice here to such a profound crisis. Instead, I would like to propose certain methodological tools and then illustrate them qualitatively as a way of exploring domestic and international state-economy relations over recent decades. Thus, I would like first of all to introduce a set of concepts derived from what has been called the "French regulation school."[1] In the two parts that follow, I will show, once again qualitatively, how these concepts can enlighten us about the transition from a regime of a relative consensus to a multidimensional crisis. More precisely, I will explore "the old that has died"—and that had dominated the *trente glorieuses*—and the causes and processes leading to crisis. The fourth and final part will review the efforts—really, the successive failures—to transcend this crisis that have created the present situation.

I. Tools for Studying State-Economy Relations

Questions about "state-society" or "state-economy" relations cannot be answered in the same ways for every type of society. At the very least it is necessary that, in the society in question, the economic sphere of "civil society" should be already autonomized, independent from the other social relationships of power, endowed with external boundaries and related to social relationships of power that are explicitly designated as political (the formation of norms and laws, the "monopoly of legitimate violence," etc.). This is certainly true for capitalist market economies, where organization of production is predominantly delegated to firms that hire wage-earners and sell commodities. For France in 1962 one must also add to the picture a still large sector of small-commodity production in agriculture, commerce, and the crafts.[2]

Even in this case the distinction between the economic and the political is not completely clear, however. Mediation between commercial interests, capitalists, and wage-workers seems to occur through money. But property rights over wealth and even the existence of money itself presuppose institutionalized political compromises. Moreover, firms themselves are the locus of struggles that are microsocial forms of politics—struggles over working conditions and wages that are politically constrained from outside the realm of the economy. There is thus a "political sphere" that extends beyond the state apparatus strictly defined.

The reproduction of a capitalist merchant economy articulated to a sector of small-commodity production does not occur automatically. Conditions for production and income distribution change over time, as do alternative preferences concerning the social use of what is produced. However, it is important to recognize that for prolonged periods these processes seem to be compatible and that, as a result, accumulation and economic growth do not suffer major crises.

This kind of congruent compatibility among production norms, distribution, and social utilization can be called an *accumulation regime*. Any such regime is itself constructed upon general principles of work organization and technology use that we propose to call a *technological paradigm*.

An accumulation regime involves observable macroeconomic regularities that guide economic actors. The behaviors of agents would nonetheless still be threatened by radical uncertainty about future coherence, other things remaining equal. There is thus a need for predictable intervention by regulatory mechanisms. A *mode of regulation* thus includes the implicit or explicit norms, institutions, compensatory mechanisms, and methods for circulating information that serve as the permanent mechanisms adapting individual behavior and anticipation to the broader logic of the accumulation regime, mechanisms that work, in particular, on wage formation, modes of competition between firms, and methods for creating money and credit. A mode of regulation serves practically as a "map" to guide individual agents so that the deeper preconditions for balanced accumulation and reproduction can persist.

The creation and consolidation of a mode of regulation depends on the political sphere. Neither the market nor the wage relationship can on its own create and enforce respect for money, property rights, or security in social life. Such matters lead us into a realm of sociopolitical struggles and "truces," into a realm of *institutionalized compromises,* the equivalent in the political sphere of what competition, workplace conflicts, and the accumulation regime are in the economic. Social groups do not engage in endless struggle. Whatever the magnitude of conflict among interests, and however great inequality may be, over long periods these groups constitute a nation within which power relations persist without major confrontation, implying a stable system of domination, alliances, and compromises among social groups—a *social bloc.* Such a social bloc is *hegemonic* when it can gain legitimacy for arrangements that work in its favor as being also in the interest of the nation as a whole. Renan's "plebiscite" can in this way be tacitly repeated every day.

Within a social bloc the positions held by different groups are unequal.[3] Dominant groups can achieve their own fundamental interests and impose their own conceptions of socioeconomic development. Their allies, even those without a primary role in domination, can also achieve some basic goals through the hegemony of the bloc as a whole. "Relay" groups, which may occupy quite subordinate positions, may play essential roles in demonstrating the felicitous nature of the bloc's global compromise in their lives or through the authority delegated to them, in particular in the management of the most-dominated groups (whose interests are, in fact, satisfied the least, but who nonetheless must be sufficiently taken into consideration to produce the consent needed to avoid a day-to-day resort to brute force). All of this comes down to the fact that, in a hegemonic bloc, that part of a nation whose interests are not taken into consideration at all must be very small.

There is a certain triangular coherence between the "hegemonic bloc," "accumulation regime," and "mode of regulation." The basis for reproducing the hegemonic bloc is the existence of an accumulation regime that can satisfy social needs and the demands of different bloc components—including dominated groups. In its turn, the mode of regulation—upon which the existence of an accumulation regime depends—is nothing more than an ensemble of *habituses*[4] and institutionalized compromises struck during the processes constituting the bloc, one that can persist only to the degree to which the bloc itself supports it. It is also quite important to know how legitimate "interests" come to be defined. What principles of justice are invoked by the different groups engaged in struggle within the bloc? Here it is necessary to invoke a "universe of political discourses and representations" in which individuals and groups recognize themselves and express their identities, interests, and divergences.[5] Indeed, the very existence of a hegemonic bloc will depend upon the creation and consolidation of this "universe." The mode of structuring legitimate identities within the universe of political discourses is the "societal paradigm." When a paradigm is hegemonic, the vast majority of individuals see themselves as active, engaged members of a society who can anticipate specific advantages from such membership and are willing to assume duties and responsibilities toward it such that, even if in conflictual ways, the hegemonic bloc can reproduce itself.[6]

This particular approach is different from the various reductionist traditions, Marxist and/or individualist, that endow agents with interests defined by the "universal laws" of mercantile wage-based economies and that, once the balance of power determined by the initial distribution of property is taken into consideration, are reconciled through a more or less unequal equilibrium of power and wealth. A capitalist economy will not always work in the same way. It can articulate itself to another form of production, for example. The ways in which agents enter economic relationships and behave depend upon a mode of regulation that varies over time and from country to country. Moreover, political equilibria, the explicit or implicit compromises that allow forms of regulation to persist, themselves emanate from a hegemonic bloc that in its turn is the product of specific historical evolution. Finally, the way in which individuals and groups conceive of their identities and interests inside a societal paradigm bloc are cultural inventions that are simultaneously produced by, and the battlefield of, ideological struggles.

Thus the mutual accommodation of each of our four elements—which we might label a "model of socio-economic development"—is a quasi-miracle. Once it occurs, this accommodation tends to consolidate itself, allowing us to speak of it as an "ex-post functionalism." But it may also be undermined by specific internal contradictions and/or by what was excluded by, or develops external to, the model, i.e., what it ignored or rejected as it consolidated itself. We can therefore hypothesize the incidence of two types of social conflict. There will first be struggle about issues of equity, and about the empirical reality of the distribution of advantages internal to the same paradigm that the hegemonic bloc is supposed to guarantee within the accumulation regime. This type of struggle, directed against "infringements"—"anomalies" or "backwardnesses"—within the legitimate realm, will seek fuller implementation of distributive justice or the improvement of regulatory mechanisms. The second type targets the hegemonic paradigm itself in the name of another paradigm altogether involving other interests and another conceptualization of social life, past or future, implying another accumulation regime, different forms of regulation, and the constitution of a very different social bloc. Thus the intensity of open conflict—strike days or electoral militancy, for example—may not in itself be an index of the weakness of basic consensus: such struggles could be of the first kind. Conversely, apparent consensus between political forces in a situation where not much mobilization occurs may indicate the absence of any sense at all of what is just or of what one might mobilize about. And because society hates a vacuum, we see the coming of monsters—"morbid symptoms," in Gramsci's words.

What about the state in this? If by "state" we mean "the apparatus that society gives itself to prevent social groups from destroying one another in endless struggle,"[7] one can easily see that the state is an actor in the accumulation regime through taxation, productive activity, expenditures, a direct force of economic regulation, and, more broadly, the guarantee of certain regulatory forms. It is also a locus for the "condensation" and management of the social compromises that constitute a hegemonic bloc, ultimately in coercive, if "legitimate" ways, and the place where the universe of political discourse, as defined by the hegemonic social paradigm, is expressed.

Such are the "functions"—*cum grano salis*—of the state vis-à-vis a national society, what Delorme and André call the "internal state."[8] This state can be more or less "circumscribed" or "inserted" in relationship to the economic sphere. Even in the case of a capitalist state, which is maximally circumscribed by the economic, as in idealized representations of British capitalism in the nineteenth century, at the very least the state retains the tasks of insuring the reproduction of a stable currency and property relationships—the "functions of public order"— to which one should add the activities needed to ensure the reproduction of the general material conditions for capitalist production: infrastructures and so on. In the dominant postwar model of development, in contrast, the state was particularly "inserted." But the state has yet another "function," since it is charged with managing interactional conditions between the national society and other nations. National defense is the most obvious dimension of this "external" state, but the international economic dimension has acquired more and more predominance over internal regulatory activity in the recent period.

II. Fordism à la française[9]

Imperial France ended for good in 1962. Attention then focused on the Hexagon and its international setting. Some basic choices had nonetheless already been made. Like the rest of the advanced capitalist world, France had embraced a Fordist developmental model and opted for the construction of Europe. We will first consider the major characteristics of Fordism as an accumulation regime, and then evaluate its French specificities, an approach that allows us to raise the issue of international challenges for the first time. Next we will review the configuration of France's hegemonic bloc and societal paradigm in these years in order to outline the disequilibrated and voluntaristic character of the "French miracle."

1. The Fordist Model

Fordism was the accumulation regime that emerged after the Second World War in answer to contradictions raised by revolutions in the "technological paradigm" of the first half of the twentieth century. Taylorism and mechanization had intervened at the level of the forms of production, primarily in industry but in agriculture as well. Taylorist principles separated "intellectual" tasks—research and development, engineering, the scientific organization of production—as much as possible from "manual" labor, which increasingly became the de-skilled execution of pre-set tasks. Fordism added a technologized design of work itself that incorporated collective knowledge. It created a dichotomy between the "methods office" and the "assembly line." The very rapid gains in productivity that followed posed the issue of effective demand in acute forms. The Fordist accumulation regime thus featured rapid rises in per capita investment and consumption, which allowed the system to offset the productivity gains created by this technological paradigm in what might be called "intensive accumulation centered on mass consumption."

In terms of the mode of regulation, Fordism needed to stabilize the wage relationship so that productivity gains would be shared between capital and labor; Fordism also needed income predictability. Structures for collective bargaining, the welfare state, and social legislation were thus devised. Fordism next needed specific relationships between firms and banks—in particular those that facilitated the institution of "administered prices"—that would allow firms to undertake a continuing transformation of the technological apparatus without perverse consequences. It also needed a specific form of monetary creation—credit emitted by banks under the control of a Central Bank—which closely followed the economy's evolution. Finally, it demanded a massive increase of the state's regulatory role in the economy, principally through management of wage relationships, monetary emission, and, only secondarily, a discretionary budgetary policy. Other classical components of the interventionist state—planning, industrial policy, policies shaping the development of agricultural structures, trade protection—grew in importance. The reader will recognize in this catalogue of state missions and capacities to influence economic circumstances in order to guarantee mechanisms of Fordist regulation that which is currently—and incorrectly—labeled "Keynesianism."

2. The Specificities of French Fordism

French Fordism was initially distinguished by its imported nature and voluntarism. The *grands commis*—high civil servants—who came out of the Resistance, and the American Marshall Plan advisers who came slightly later, inherited a France and, more important, a hegemonic bloc that had been defeated. Profoundly marked by the Commune of 1871, the Third Republic bloc had made industrial growth a secondary priority, had limited the state's economic role—except to protect corporatisms and run the customs system—and had excluded the working class from progress. It had been a "bloc of possessors"—industrialists-merchants-peasants and savers—that sought above all to defend property rather than to promote free enterprise. Its hopes were for some kind of quasi-Malthusian "social tranquility." Modernization efforts after 1944 thus came almost exclusively from high civil servants who were supported by those social forces, principally wage-workers, that had been pushed aside until the defeat of 1940.[10]

The dominant technological paradigm of the Third Republic was premised on the knowledge possessed by skilled workers, peasants, and craftsmen. The accumulation regime was primarily, if moderately, extensive. The internal mode of regulation was primarily competition, but there were numerous protected sectors—peasant agriculture in particular. Thanks to trade protection, the Meline laws from the beginning of the twentieth century allowed reproduction of a low-productivity peasantry, which as late as 1945 constituted forty-five percent of the active population. The societal paradigm was built on the identity of the "small property-owner-producer-citizen-soldier." Even the working class—including the Communist Party where it had a rural base—defended a Proudhonian ideal of "small property" and the dignity involved in being independent, *à son compte*.[11] There was opposition to *les grands,* but it was essentially a hostility to those whose success had not come from their own efforts.

Forces emerging from the Resistance saw this model as the basic cause of the defeat. A decisive break with it was necessary for progress to be possible, including technical progress, of course, which even the PCF equated with rationalization, Taylorism, and mechanization.[12] Social progress was equated with enough growth in popular purchasing power to guarantee full employment via demand expansion. Progress in the realm of the state involved guaranteeing collective interests against the ravages of uncontrolled individual competition. The three ingredients of the Fordist economic model—its technological paradigm, accumulation regime, and mode of regulation—were thus accepted as the foundation of a progressive compromise by the Left itself.[13] All that remained, to cite the general secretary of the Parti Communiste Française (PCF), Maurice Thorez, was to "roll up our sleeves." But even this would be insufficient to the task without a hegemonic social bloc and a stabilized societal paradigm.

The problem was the elites. Regrouped primarily in the Centre National des Indépendants et Paysans (the party of non-resisters) and in the Mouvement Républicain Populaire (the MRP, which was led by Christian Democratic resisters and officially supported General de Gaulle), they used all the power of inertia to block the coming of the new mode of regulation.[14] Nonetheless, that which counted—collective bargaining, the minimum wage, social security—had by 1946 been put into place by a "developmentalist" bloc of salaried groups and modernizing state technocrats.

To provide a motor for building the new model, the state was thus substituted for propertied elites, endowing the French mode of regulation with its specificities. In the realm of wage regulation, first of all, a centralized system developed that, rather than emerging firm by firm through a "diffusion of victories" like American "connected bargaining," was consolidated through legislation and administrative action.[15] The 1945 social security system was built in similar ways: if it emerged as an agreement between "social partners," it was managed, in fact, by the state (especially after 1964). Prices were "administered" as much by the state as by firms. The decentralization of credit creation did not occur until after 1967 and even then was regulated by the state through the nationalized banks. Most important, the state intervened energetically in building the productive apparatus itself through subsidies, nationalization, and planning, by 1967 producing a relatively full-fledged Fordist system. After 1967, planning began to fade, but very powerful state administrations or nationalized firms (the Direction Générale des Télécommunications, Direction des Armements, Commissariat à l'Energie Atomique, Electricité de France, Société National des Chemins de Fer [SNCF], and the like) perpetuated a "state entrepreneurialism" that controlled research and industrial development in high-technology sectors.

The consequences of this voluntarism were miraculous. An accelerated transition to Fordism occurred, one that lasted until 1968, rather longer than the consolidation of a conventional Fordist regime.[16] Formidable industrial and agricultural accumulation allowed France to equip consumer industries and the housing sector, and to establish conditions for an urban "American Way of Life" at the cost of an extraordinary dismantling of earlier spatial arrangements. Agriculture, pushed ahead by a "tractor revolution," found itself newly supervised through its integration into the food-processing industries. The number of peasants in the rural population had dropped to ten percent by 1968 because of an exodus from the land accompanied by an incredible housing construction effort and by movement of industrial and tertiary employers into the countryside.[17] Small independent urban workers were rather brutally pushed aside by salaried middle-strata workers either directly or through intergenerational change. Superimposed on the specific problems of Fordist regulation, therefore, were issues of articulating small-commodity production to capitalism.

What about France's international insertion? Paradoxically, the major "developmentalist" gamble constrained the sovereignty of the external state. Entrance into the EEC—of which Pierre Mendès-France, standardbearer of Fourth Republic developmentalism, disapproved and which de Gaulle initially opposed, along with the Communists and the old elites of the Centre National des Indépendants et Paysans (CNIP)—was imposed by the MRP and Socialists in 1957. Political considerations—Atlanticism in particular—played a role in the decision, but there was also a desire to disrupt resistance to modernization by "burning bridges" to any return to Third Republic-style Malthusian protectionism. At the core of this was confidence that statist voluntarism would be successful enough at adapting France's productive apparatus to allow it to compete internationally. The EEC was also relied upon—here the external state became partially *communitaire* turned back upon the internal state—to minimize the upheaval of agricultural revolution. General de Gaulle was finally won over to this outlook at the end of the 1960s.

The whole package deserves closer examination, however. French Fordism remained marked by the country's underdevelopment as of 1945. Fordism implied a strong engineering and machine-tool sector with a high percentage of skilled workers. Rather than moving in this direction, the French *patronat* continued to rely upon what seemed to be an inexhaustible reserve of unskilled labor flowing from the decline of rural population, the massive entry of women into the labor force, and immigration. It thus specialized in a kind of "bargain basement" Fordism for final assembly work that, when necessary, involved buying equipment from foreign producers. The unsophisticated system of industrial relations that resulted had its counterpart in the realm of inter-industrial relations where big firms tended to deal contemptuously with smaller, specialized subcontractors, often with the primary goal of keeping prices as low as possible. In other areas, as we will see, the integration of the traditional middle classes into the salaried workforce came at the cost of an overblown tertiary sector with strong inflationary implications.

Despite such weaknesses, French Fordism reached the 1970s in a favorable position in the international market, for two reasons. The state acted directly as a "traveling salesman" for French high-tech production tied to public purchasing. And regular currency devaluations were used to wipe out inflation differences with international competitors in those areas of low-priced industrial production where competitiveness depended upon cheap labor. Everything went well until 1973, however, because all EEC countries were following similar trajectories of rapid Fordist growth, creating a relatively unconstraining environment. This was even truer because countries retained important aspects of sovereignty, guarding the leverage needed to adjust exchange rates and to engage in an administrative protectionism through the judicious manipulation of norms and standards and via the imposition of national preferences in public purchasing.

3. The Unstable Hegemony of Developmentalism

Given the economic base, a hegemonic bloc appropriate to Fordism must be constructed around a productivist compromise between entrepreneurs and wage-earners, with engineers and technicians acting as important intermediary groups. The most plausible societal paradigm is that of a "salary-earning society"[18] in which guaranteed social protection and full employment are granted in exchange for accepting the hierarchy of technical competencies. This is what existed in Northern European countries, where social democracy had promoted a precocious institutionalization of Fordism. And this is precisely what Jean Monnet, Etienne Hirsch, and Pierre Massé—the *grand commis* technocrats of "the Plan" who developed the theory of "distributing the fruits of growth"—actually proposed. It was also a profound aspiration of both manual and "intellectual" salaried groups. In the 1950s, however, no majority existed for such a bloc. The *patronat,* peasantry, and independent urban producers, all loyal to the conservative "owner-producer" paradigm, rejected Fordism and its trade-union victories and social security. The instability of the Fourth Republic followed, as did the failures of the Mendès-France and Félix Gaillards.

The Algiers putsch in 1958 was a miraculous ruse of history. It brought to power a general steeped in the culture of an earlier era who would nevertheless lead France with an iron hand through decolonization and toward Fordist modern-ization. De Gaulle's simple strategy was to create a majority in the name of the old paradigm and to promote exactly the opposite of what this majority desired economically, while simultaneously disarming wage-earner opposition through achieving the things the Left parties desired, growth in production and mass consumption orchestrated by the state. The theme of *grandeur* allowed the market-ing of one product under the pretense that it was another. The Fordist bloc that emerged was thus rather wobbly. Its principal social base was in the trade-union and parliamentary opposition. Its directive core, high-state technocrats, used this opposition's mobilization to promote policies that ran against both the shorter-run interests of the dominant classes and the electoral base of the ruling party. This very party then progressively integrated centrist opposition into its ranks, groups like Giscard's Independent Republicans (a split-off from the CNIP).

Such an implausible political strategy would have been unworkable without institutionalizing appropriate modes of regulation and without some debasing of the Fordist societal paradigm. The story of the workers provides a first illustration of this, involving their paradoxical commitment to a paradigm while they simulta-neously struggled against those who were trying to make this same paradigm viable. Strongly committed to the ideological lead given by the Communists, the working class experienced its opposition to the Gaullist regime as a campaign against out-of-date private interests subordinated to American imperialist interests that were selling out the growth of productive forces and refusing to enlarge social benefits. The Gaullists responded by giving a nationalist, productivist, and statist twist to growth, one that often put the Communist leadership and the modernizing Left in embarrassing positions.

A second illustration is the *cadre's* saga, that of a social group that was able to build its own identity while participating in the larger movement toward the creation of a hegemonic bloc. "Dominated agents" of capitalist domination in the Fordist model, engineers and technicians, were the mediating group par excellence in a Fordist hegemonic bloc, the group that might identify itself with the liberal professions either as independent workers "collaborating" with management—their identity in the older paradigm—or as agents possessing delegated patronal authority. Luc Boltanski has shown how complicated cultural and institutional interactions touching the autonomy of pension systems and taxation led them toward a new self-definition as Fordist employees while they continued to demand an identity as liberal professionals and possessors of cultural capital.[19] The Gaullists encouraged the "meritocratic" dimension of this over its capitalist patrimonial side. The catchall category of *cadre* thus flowered, absorbing an important part of an older petit-bourgeois heritage while making successful claims to high status and income.[20] With all of the inflationary consequences that this brought, *cadre* became the vanguard of Fordist consumerism and, simultaneously, a high-priestly caste advocating the "scientific" legitimacy of both the hegemonic bloc and the technological paradigm. And this all happened with the warm approval of the Communists and with that of the bulk of modernist political sociology.

Our third story concerns the peasantry, which moved from one hegemonic bloc into another without changing its basic position. Small agricultural producers had a choice among three conceivable self-understandings—small owners, small entrepreneurs, or workers. In the old order the peasant saw himself as an owner opposed to the *partageux*. In the new Fordist order, confronted with new imperatives to equip themselves, go into debt, and integrate contractually into agrobusinesses, peasants might have reconceptualized themselves as "quasi–wage-earners." But cultural activists in the agricultural revolution, in particular the *Jeunesse Agricole Catholique,* were able to persuade them that they were "small, dynamic entrepreneurs." The state then stepped in. Huge cooperatives like *Crédit Agricole,* the largest bank in the world, helped them to sustain this vision. It was nonetheless essential to guarantee peasant incomes and debt payments, so the Gaullist state then prevailed upon the EEC to set up a vast system of agricultural price supports (rather than direct income subsidies). The management of this enormous regulatory apparatus tying small agricultural production to capitalism was delegated to the peasant organizations themselves. The consequence was a corporatistically organized peasantry right in the middle of Fordism,[21] one that was able to extract guaranteed-income parity from the rest of society. Ministers of agriculture, acting as the delegates of the French peasantry and often using the sometimes-violent peasant mobilizations to achieve their purposes, extracted subsidies from Brussels in support of this.

The Gaullist state thus built Fordism by keeping the social groups that ordinarily would have been its natural base out of power, and by supporting itself politically on social groups integrated into Fordism in corporatistic ways. French Fordist consensus thus was a product of corporatistic demands arbitrated by a technocratic state whose autonomy above civil society seemed maximal, a "quasi-Bonapartism."

III. Fissures

The first cracks in this complicated edifice came from the events of May 1968, which, beyond their economic effects, also constituted a crisis of culture, hegemony, and paradigms. Five years later, the face and "map" of France had changed. Among other things, the society had matured in the direction of social democracy. Ironically, the economic crisis of the 1970s, which came next, made this social-democratic option quite impossible, at least in any of its traditional forms.

1. The Triple Crisis of May 1968

The Debré-Giscard stabilization plan (1963) to moderate the disequilibria created by the Algerian War—which had been financed on credit—ended in a "Keynesian gap" (i.e., it did not provide enough demand stimulation) and consequent underemployment caused by working-class underconsumption. The 1968 strikes—the largest in history—liquidated a long backlog of demands and, by facilitating an upward surge in wages, propelled workers once and for all into a consumer society. The 1968 events were thus first of all a crisis *within* Fordist regulation.

The year 1968 was also a crisis of transition to Fordist regulation. The informal Grenelle agreements (May 27) crystallized a modern form of wage relationship, creating the SMIC and consecrating firm-level union rights in *Sections Syndicales d'Entreprise*. In broader terms, however, the mass revolt of the educationally credentialed *petite bourgeoisie* demonstrated the need to conclude an incomplete paradigmatic revolution: it was time to get rid of the archaic moral order imposed by Gaullism, to banish rural values, and to break with a quasi-Bonapartist state. Here the insufficient development of social democracy was paralleled by material difficulties. The university had always functioned as an apparatus to promote the traditional *petite bourgeoisie* into the liberal professions or the teaching corps.[22]

The mass university's new function of converting a propertied petite bourgeoisie into an intellectual one transformed it into a factory producing devalued degrees, causing untold student bitterness.

But protest against the exaggerated statism of French Fordism created space for an even more radical revolt, one that contested the very existence of the role of state and hierarchy in Fordism, even in its social democratic formulations. An irremediable divorce was thus consummated between the young and political forces of the Left that dreamed of—and actually succeeded in imposing in 1968—a more classical Fordism. In similar ways a number of strikes called the Fordist order in factories into question.

The years after May 1968 were thus paradoxical. Gaullist, then Pompidolian and Giscardian, ministers devoted themselves to applying the finishing touches to a truly Fordist and social-democratized institutional structure. The Right's electoral base continued to resist such things, demonstrating the existence of what Chaban-Delmas called a *société bloquée*. The "new society" of which the Right dreamed was proposed, from rather more legitimate sources, by the 1972 Left Common Program. Finally, at the "social base"—in the working class, tertiary sectors, and among youth—there developed a combination of a longing for Fordism's material benefits and an individualistic rejection of its excessive statism. All of this would have led to a Left victory in 1973 or, at the latest, 1974, but for the weight of the PCF, which allowed the Right to squeeze out a victory in 1974. The PCF's defection from the Left alliance in 1978 facilitated another narrow Right victory. The Left did not come to power, then, until 1981, when François Mitterrand proclaimed that "the sociological majority has finally become the political majority." It was nonetheless, economically and ideologically, too late. Fordism had entered crisis, both in France and internationally.

2. The Crisis of Fordism[23]

Fordism's technological paradigm ran out of steam first. Productivity growth began to decline despite ever-rising levels of per capita investment. The declining profitability that resulted led, in time, to a slowdown in accumulation itself. The need to absorb an abrupt rise in oil prices after 1974 aggravated the problems. Unemployment grew, but the safety net of the welfare state—unemployment insurance in particular—prevented cumulative depression. The welfare state itself was financed by the productive system, however, which meant that profitability was eventually touched, leading, as the 1970s went on, from growth to stagflation.

In the meantime, the accelerated internationalization in production and markets continued, spreading from advanced areas to the Third World. The integration that occurred clashed with the national character of regulation, in the EEC in particular. To ensure favorable commercial balances and high levels of profitability, especially in the second half of the 1970s, governments and business elites tried to squeeze down wages and the internal market. This policy of "beggar thy neighbor" culminated after 1979 in the victory of monetarism over Keynesianism that marked the end of Fordism's "Golden Age."

Converted to the Fordist paradigm along with the bulk of employers and editorial writers, Giscard d'Estaing and his prime minister Jacques Chirac responded to the 1974 oil shock as good Keynesians, attempting to stabilize effective demand and to avoid too abrupt a transfer of national income from profit to wages and oil rent. The unemployment insurance fund was shored up. Purchasing power grew, if more slowly than it had before. Efforts to maintain trade balances were pursued through devaluations and *grands contrats,* usually with state-subsidized engineering exports. At this point policy came out of an ignorance of the fact that the crisis originated from the supply side—a crisis of the industrial paradigm—and that internationalization would make it impossible to regenerate growth through Keynesian demand stimulation. The replacement of Chirac by Raymond Barre in 1976 was a declaration of failure.

IV. Improvizations and Failures[24]

Raymond Barre was undoubtedly the first to confront crisis by abandoning the Fordist paradigm, after 1978 in particular. After an attempt to "restore" Fordism after 1981, the Socialists in their turn retreated to a liberalism that the Right, after 1986, would attempt to consecrate in sterile dogmatism.

1. Barre: The Initial Liberal Offense

By freezing wages and liberating prices it was possible—at the cost of rising inflation—to stop the rise in purchasing power and permit a stabilization of investment while accelerating unemployment growth. In fact, this policy sketched out a new paradigm in which full employment would cease to be the goal. Henceforth, employment policy became an accounting balance. The ambition of achieving "equilibrated national growth" on French territory, the bottom line for the developmentalists, was abandoned. Firms were encouraged to reestablish profit margins without regard for national social consequences in order to stop the drop of profits in Gross Domestic Product, but in ways that led to increasing use of "anomic" employment patterns such as part-time and temporary work. Above all, the earlier logic behind France's international insertion was dropped. The "teeth" behind this were provided by the adoption of a policy of a "strong franc" tied to the Deutschmark in the European Monetary System. The *territorial* competitiveness of French firms was largely undercut, but possibilities for foreign investment were enhanced. The overall guiding concept was to place and maintain France in specific international market niches.

Declining research and development in technology plus the lack of a "postfor-dist" policy for restructuring the productive apparatus—in contrast to the situation in Japan, Germany, and Italy—quickly blocked development in the few medium-term competitive niches that France possessed, as later became clear. New policy approaches in industrial relations were nonetheless encouraged in documents like the Sudreau Report, but with few results. When Raymond Barre left power in May 1981, the franc was overvalued by twenty percent (at the 1977 parity of French buying power with the Deutschmark), unemployment was rapidly rising, France had a huge trade deficit, and it was well on the way to deindustrialization.

2. Mauroy I: The End of the Fordist Paradigm

The signatories of the 1972 Left Common Program came to power in 1981 carrying all their developmentalist baggage. They believed that it was essential to put the finishing touches on French Fordism by Keynesian demand stimulation and a structurally targeted industrial policy to reinforce national competitiveness. The election of Mitterrand to the presidency and a huge Left victory in the June 1981 legislative elections, giving the PS by itself a majority, seemed to give the Left virtually all levels of power. The PCF was brought into the new government for obvious sociopolitical reasons, but it was not a determining factor in 1981–82 policy choices. The Socialists were in the driver's seat.

The history of the Left's failure can be divided into three phases—the first year (through July 1982), when the stabilization plan and price controls were announced; from this point until March 1983, to the *rigueur* plan; and, finally, from March 1983 until the PCF left the government in the summer of 1984.[25] Here we will merge the first two phases, since the second was but a transition that marked the last efforts to save the Left's original policies while a transition to liberalism was being prepared behind the scenes.[26]

For the eighteen months after 1981, despite—or, rather, during—a wage and price freeze, the Left pushed Fordist logic to its limits. Wages, above all social wages, went up, there was a deliberate budget deficit, new civil servants were hired, the minimum wage was boosted by fifteen percent, and household consumption of industrial products went up ten percent. Despite this flurry of "conjunctural" activity, industrial production continued to stagnate and rising unemployment was only momentarily stabilized.

What caused the failure? First of all, there was France's weak competitiveness, including real "holes" in the productive apparatus inherited from earlier eras, holes that had been aggravated by blind faith in a strong franc monetary policy. Three devaluations against the Deutschmark did not resolve the problems. Among other things, the effects of rising wage costs combined with the consequences of reducing the work week led to the erosion of firms' net profit margins. Further, the maintenance of very high interest rates—imposed by the international context and the need to defend the franc—reduced net firm savings practically to zero.

The celebrated reduction in working time—one hour less per week, a fifth week of paid vacations, retirement at sixty—did not break with the existing paradigm. Indeed, these reductions could easily be fit into the spirit of the 1968 Grenelle agreements. Things would have been quite different had the government moved directly to a thirty-five–hour week without compensation for the lost hours. Then one might have been able to talk about "society's choice," where solidarity had been placed ahead of other things, "being" over "having." But this didn't happen. There was other very real, but strictly Fordist, social progress such as new and very strict regulations on "precarious" work and the legalization of 130,000 clandestine immigrants. Here it was a question of reestablishing the generality of Fordist norms of wage regulation. In contrast, there was a real failure in the direction of the "parasitic middle classes," the traditional gangrene of French Fordism. Jacques Delors, the minister of finance, proposed to make all income earners responsible for welfare-state payments, but a surprisingly strong opposition forced him to beat a hasty retreat. At the same time he also abandoned any tax reforms beyond the very small wealth tax. One consequence was that nonwage incomes continued to expand.

Thus, to revert to our central categories, the Left's first period brought few innovations either in the mode of regulation or in that of the accumulation regime . . . except, perhaps, that the accumulation regime no longer worked, but we already knew that, or at least the elites ought to have known it. In the area of industrial relations and the technological paradigm, things were more complicated. First of all, the Auroux Laws strengthened classical Fordist trade-union prerogatives by making annual wage negotiations obligatory and by increasing the information and training available for union delegates. But in organizing "direct expression" for workers, they also created openings for new employer strategies—and, why not, worker strategies as well—in the area of work relations at firm and industrial levels. But possibilities for challenging the Taylorist industrial paradigm were definitively lost as a result of a series of revolts in the name of "dignity" that came from semiskilled workers, usually immigrants, in the auto industry from 1981 to 1983. The government was quite unable to seize the occasion to launch new programs reforming work organization programs analogous to the famous "productivity missions" of the Marshall Plan years. Instead, it resorted to blaming the "Shiites" for sabotaging France's exporting efforts.

The Left was well aware of France's industrial backwardness. Its nationalizations, carried out with determination, and the Investment Bank, which was abandoned, were designed to overcome it. Its ministers of industry—the most ambitious being Jean-Pierre Chevènement, who dreamed of a French version of the Japanese MITI—set out in these directions in purely developmentalist ways, playing with an industrial erector set to redistribute the activities of nationalized firms, injecting massive amounts of capital (thirty billion francs per year), and drafting multiple "sectoral plans." The principle justification for nationalizations was unquestionably to legitimate a transfer of taxpayers' money to programs for bolstering "national industry" rather than into bosses' pockets. Technocratic methods for managing nationalized firms were not changed at all.

The principal doctrinal contribution of the Left in this area was the *filières* policy—usually contrasted to the earlier "niche" strategy—designed to reconstruct a productive apparatus that would be fully integrated from raw materials through finished products. It is now possible to point to moderate successes in electronics and chemicals. But more often there were failures, particularly in producing industrial goods. Why? First of all, there were quantitative reasons: the state simply could not do everything, even though it wanted to—develop the electronics *filière*, carry out a hyperambitious nuclear power program, and maintain, against all odds, a number of declining sectors (steel, coal mines, shipyards). But the most important reason lay in an underestimation of problems in labor relations and industrial organization. Jean-Pierre Chevènement's speech to the Journées de l'Industrie in 1982 mentioned only in the vaguest and most ideological ways what had already become practice in Italian or Japanese industry and what university experts—even on the Left—thought about "interfirm partnerships," "endogenous local development," or the "remobilization of working-class savoir faire." The core of the preoccupations of the minister and his colleagues could be summarized, in contrast, exclusively in terms of financing and automating to build *filières*.

This particular discourse was contradictory, if only in its profound misunderstanding of time. High civil servants acted as if expanding research and development spending would create a microprocessor industry to equip a robotics industry that would then equip the rest of the French productive apparatus. This was a noble project, but the creation of such a *filière* would take a decade—if enough money could be found—during which industry in general might well collapse. Beginning industrial modernization at the point of final production, in contrast, implied massive importations of sophisticated production equipment . . . an approach that would run counter to the doctrine of "reconquering the domestic market"!

In any event, in eighteen brief months the Left's "industrial policy" could not break through the bottleneck of external constraints, especially after the government's Keynesian policies created a huge commercial deficit that placed it on a collision course with these very same constraints. French Fordism was lost, in specifically economic terms. Beyond the economic dimension, however, all the problems created by the wobbly hegemonic bloc inherited from Gaullism now came to the fore. The unions, brought up in an oppositional culture, were quite unable to propose any schemes for reconstructing conditions of social compromise. And all of France's various "corporatisms," particularly those involving the peasants and the middle classes, turned into oppositional forces armed with the resources to confront any threatening reforms with massive street mobilization. Finally, after fifteen years, the libertarian youth of 1968 had converted to an ideology of liberal refusal of state regulation.

3. Mauroy II and Fabius:
The Rise of Social Liberalism

The third devaluation in March 1983 marked the surrender of Left Keynesianism. In the face of a huge trade deficit, the choices were simple: either "war social democracy," involving protectionism, competitive devaluations, and crisis with Europe, or the maintenance of free trade, deflation, and the abandonment of the Left's Fordist social ambitions of full employment and rising purchasing power. Opposed by the PCF and half the Parti Socialiste (PS) but supported by the Right, all the press including that of the Left, and even the formerly radical Confédération Française Démocratique du Travail (CFDT), the president chose the second route.

This surprising choice demonstrated the discredit into which the Fordist paradigm had fallen. On a more superficial level, memories of the conservative protectionism à la Meline in the Third Republic could easily be stirred up, from which it was easy to conclude that protectionism inevitably blocked modernization. Then there were arguments that invoked the spectre of Stalinism and the idea that limiting consumer freedom in the name of the collective interest would lead France down the primrose path to totalitarianism. In response to both of these bad dreams, the international market was presented as the regulator par excellence for installing a new model of development. Deeper down, however, PS leaders had convinced themselves that there really was a "supply-side crisis." It was thus necessary to invest, to reestablish profitability, and "therefore" to squeeze down popular standards of living, with "external pressure" available to serve as a scapegoat for the austerity that would follow.

At the same time an entirely new accumulation regime was emerging around exporting as both engine and source for financing accumulation. This new regime would no longer imply growth in the internal market; indeed, such growth might well weaken the competitiveness necessary for success. Nor did it imply growth in employment, at least in key multiplier sectors. Elites might hope, at best, that the unproductive spending of higher social classes, helped by foreign tourists—attracted to France, perhaps, by the new EuroDisneyworld in Marne-la-Vallée—would trickle down to poorer groups. This vision stood in strong contrast to Fordism, of course, in which upper social classes profited from the consumer mentality of lower groups. As for the industrial paradigm, everyone continued to announce the importation of automation, of electronification. But it was not until the Dalle Report in 1985 that any official condemnation of the "scars of Taylorism" was heard. And it was the modernist employers that seized the initiative to mobilize worker initiatives and savoir-faire, according to procedures that it designed all by itself.

The new "productivist-liberal" paradigm sketched out here, with its focus on free trade and its consequences of a dualized society and "trickle-down" spillovers from rich to poor, closely resembled the "hourglass" model of society advocated by American Reaganites.[27] This model was, of course, impossible for the PS to accept. Thus the history of the Left's "third period" involved progressive acceptance of the need to abandon Fordism—*rigueur* ceased being an interlude—and to move spontaneously towards a liberal-productivist approach, and also, at the same time, a story of embryonic attempts to try out different approaches.

The *rigueur* politics inaugurated in the spring of 1983 sought to bring France's trade accounts into balance, slow down inflation, and reestablish firm profits at the cost of declining household purchasing power. Success in each of these areas was real, if incomplete. Purchasing power declined by 1.4 percent in two years, the trade deficit was reduced to an annual level of twenty billion francs and was covered, in 1984, by a surplus in services (tourism, insurance, "other" incomes), with similar results in 1985. Total French indebtedness thus stopped growing. At the same time, the declining purchasing power of wage-earners, combined with growing productivity gains, raised profits as a percent of total value added up to the level of the "benign" crisis years of the mid-1970s. Finally, inflation dropped much closer to the European average.

These positive results were intimately connected to a recovery of international growth fed by the American trade deficit. Firms lost market share at home because of the perpetual overevaluation of the franc, among other things, a situation that repeated Socialist devaluations did not change. Markets that firms could no longer find in France had to be found elsewhere. The results did not compensate for the decline in household consumption of industrial products (down 5.6 percent). Thus French growth was among the lowest of all industrial societies, 2 percent over two years. Unemployment rose by 500,000 in consequence. Moreover, in February 1984 several unions accepted important rollbacks in unemployment compensation coverage.

The new governmental team installed in July 1984 around Prime Minister Laurent Fabius (who had succeeded Jean-Pierre Chevènement at the Ministry of Industry in 1983) and Pierre Bérégovoy at the Ministry of Finance did not change these policy directions, excepting a very prudent lowering of interest rates (with little effect on firms, given the lack of investment opportunities in these grim times despite restored profit levels). Nevertheless, the 1985 tax cuts slightly stimulated demand in the months before the 1986 elections. In such circumstances Fabius's appeal for a *rassemblement pour la modernisation* could hardly have had much effect. Investment did begin to grow again at the end of 1984, but not enough to compensate for job loss in those declining sectors that the state would henceforth stop subsidizing—steel, coal mining, shipbuilding—or that were undergoing intensive restructuring, like the automobile industry.

The state was not inactive through all this, however. During his tenure as industry minister Fabius had managed to allocate to himself an Industrial Modernization Fund independent of the Finance Ministry. Edith Cresson, his successor, benefited from this. Ninety percent of this Fund went to import high technology! This was a complete break with the *filière* policy; still, finally, modernization began. "Liberal interventionism" of this kind was not incompatible with liberal-productivism, including its American variant[28]: a doctrine of the "state as industrial shield" was succeeding that of "state as social protector."[29]

Modes of regulation did not necessarily evolve in a parallel liberal sense. To be sure, recourse to the "secondary labor market" (part-time, temporary work, etc.) became again permissible. But even if Labor Minister Michel Delebarre was unable to re-launch the reduction of work time, he did promote several important initiatives like Intermediary Enterprises, TUCs, and *Contrats de Formation-Reconversion*. The minister's purpose here was to substitute socially useful activities and retraining programs for the unemployment dole. Beginning in 1985 these policies had a real effect in keeping unemployment statistics down. But the level of political and union debate around these potentially interesting innovations was mediocre.

More generally, the idea of a "productive" use of the welfare state's money was pushed aside by the liberal vogue of the moment, which, in the social realm, took on the label of "flexibility." In December 1984, several unions, including the CFDT, went as far as negotiating serious rollbacks in social legislation with the *patronat,* getting little or nothing in return. Opposition from the base stopped the accord from being ratified. Finally, through symbolic rewards and research subsidies the state encouraged initiatives from firms seeking to innovate by introducing collective working-class incentives in production. But, as we have already noted, these initiatives—few in any event—came largely from the employers and thus provoked trade-union suspicions.

In this half-tone portrait of governmental activities combining liberal resignation with innovative, if timid, counterefforts, it is important not to overlook what was going on in the regions and localities, which had been given much more autonomy by the Defferre Law of 1982. Thus in some places one began to see new forms of territorial partnerships among firms, local governments, universities, and unions. Savoie and a number of other peripheral "countries" stood out in promoting such consensualist "local development."[30]

Despite these few innovations—the remains of interventionism and vague concern to improve industrial relations and inter-industrial organization—the Socialists' "third period" was marked essentially by managerial pragmatism and ideological emptiness. Liberal mythology, the cult of "everyone for himself" and its popular corollaries, racism and fear about personal security, rushed into the void.[31] It was these things more than economic failure—few people believed any longer that the state could do very much economically—that the "neo-Liberals," that is to say Fordists of the Right from the 1970s after their conversion experience, were able to manipulate in the elections of March 16, 1986.

4. Chirac II: Dogmatic Liberalism

The crushing victory of the Right coalition—a majority in the National Assembly without any for help from the thirty-one "ultra" National Front deputies—opened the door completely for the full application of "liberalism" by born-again Prime Minister Jacques Chirac. François Mitterrand, the sitting president, had rights of appeal to various constitutional jurisdictions against governmental initiatives but could delay things only a few days. As Chirac's all-powerful economics minister, Edouard Balladur, announced to the 1986 Davos Seminar, the government could legislate anything it wanted in the economic realm. But what did it really want?

In fact, the only authentically "liberal" quality that the Center-Right coalition shared was hostility toward legalizing the working-class victories of the preceding century. Even Philippe Séguin, considered a "Social Gaullist," could announce to the National Assembly in December 1986, during its forced march to laws on the "flexibility" of wage relationships (which unions had rejected a year earlier and which legalized night work for women, among other things), that "it is really a question of whether March 16th really happened or not." To the new majority, entrepreneurial freedom began where the rights of wage-earners ended. From this point of view what was important was won in December 1986—the privatization laws (which included a public television network), an extension in legal work hours at employer discretion, the development of a segment of young, legally underprotected, and underpaid wage-earners in the private labor market sector (through Stages d'Initiation à la Vie Professionnelle—SIVP), elimination of administrative pre-authorization for economically justified firings, and so on.

From a regulation point of view, this was indeed a retreat toward classical liberal conceptions. It reiterated almost word for word nineteenth-century anti-statist and right-wing notions like those of Leroy-Beaulieu, who, in praising private enterprises, claimed that "given their flexibility, capacities for rapid change, and the ever larger place they permit to responsibility, self-interest, innovation, competition, [they] are preferable to the state." The reappearance of this type of argument gave pause to those who knew about the Third Republic. And the similarities did not end here. "Entrepreneurial liberalism" was narrowly connected to a wave of measures favoring all those who owned something, including rentiers and *épargnants,* with laws to help real-estate owners, to reestablish the right to own gold anonymously, to abrogate the wealth tax, and to remove the highest tax brackets. Those repatriating capital that they had illegally exported earlier were amnestied.

Here there is an important contrast between Left governments before March 1986 and the Right after 1986. The liberalism of the Fabius government sought to help the firm as a *producer* of wealth and employment. The Right's liberalism was more the reestablishment of a *droit de jouissance* detached from the social utility of wealth. The Right's talk of "economic regeneration" could thus be reduced to a litany of "forever less . . . taxation, regulation, government stimulation. . . ." The *De la Genière* group's report on the competitiveness of French firms could be summarized in these terms, and there was nothing in it about the international debate, nourished by Japanese and Italian successes, on how to exit the crisis successfully, or about negotiated participation of workers, inter-enterprise partnerships, and state-corporation collaboration in the definition of industrial strategies and in financing research and training.

In the realm of practice, Alain Devaquet, the minister of research, canceled the year's recruitment into Centre National de la Recherche Scientifique (CNRS) in June 1986. Of the fifteen billion francs of budget savings decided upon in the spring of the same year, half involved research. The university budget was cut, and the *rentrée* of all 1986 brought the first decline of student matriculation in recent history. Alain Madelin even bragged about cutting back the budget of the Ministry of Industry. Among other things, the *Fonds Industriel de Modernisation* was eliminated and the *Agence pour la Valorisation de la Recherche* and the *Agence pour la Maîtrise de l'Energie* were essentially destroyed. At a moment when the big economic powers were squaring off for an industrial war pushed forward by technological revolution, France, already seriously behind, announced unilateral disarmament.

In general, the liberal-productivist paradigm was fully adopted—beginning from a relatively advanced level of social democracy—both from the regulation point of view and from that of the logic of the accumulation regime, with even a dose of dogmatism (the renunciation of "liberal interventionism") added in. Under such conditions, even the "social innovations" of the earlier period, themselves full of ambiguities (TUCS, Reconversion leaves, SIVPs) changed their meaning. Turned toward shoring up the private *patronat,* they accelerated and further institutionalized a dualized labor market.

A final word about privatizations. As we have seen, French nationalizations had served primarily to justify the direct injection of public money into a "techno-structure." In accounting terms, reversing nationalizations created an influx of private savings into the public treasury. Privatizations, in turn, directly reestablished large "auto-controlled" financial technostructures around traditional axes like Suez and Paribas, to which one could add a new pole around the *Société Générale-CGE.* To be sure, "popular capitalism" allowed some mobility of household savings from passbooks into the *bourse,* as long as the international situation and a glut of stock issues did not cause market collapse. Privatization did not translate into change in the ways firms were run, however. The small stockowners of the CGE—seventy-five percent of capital, in fact—had no representation on the Board of Directors.

What can be said about the results? It would be dishonest to judge things too quickly—especially since what happened in the second half of 1986 was the responsibility of the Fabius government. Whether from demagoguery or self-delusion, the Right had promised that the growth of profits, pumped up by a declining dollar and declining oil prices, would be enough to turn the *possédants* into entrepreneurs. Such promises overlooked both macroeconomic laws and the faintheartedness of French capitalism. In an ever more competitive domestic and world economy, profitable investment opportunities were growing ever rarer. The share of national income that was thus shifted toward profits—the 1973 level was reached—was itself diverted toward speculative games (purchasing privatized firms, for example). France's productive apparatus, propped up by Socialist interventionism, began to decline once again. Industrial investment slowed from 9.5 percent in 1985 to 3.5 percent in 1986, then 8 percent in 1987. Despite two further devaluations, trade accounts were not balanced in 1986, even with ninety billion francs in oil savings, and they turned strongly and regularly negative in 1987. Above all, trade surpluses in manufactured goods rapidly disappeared. Having dropped by fifty billion francs in 1986 relative to the previous year, it became negative (−8 billion francs) in 1987, particularly in electrome-chanical industrial sectors. The elimination of state aid to industry, including the dismembering of research, did not help, any more than did the new freedom to fire experienced workers and replace them by SIVPs paid one-quarter their wages (even though this did keep youth unemployment lower, at the expense of increased unemployment for their elders). To be honest, the politics of "Chirac 1986" do not in themselves explain such a rapid collapse. In fact, the collapse of oil prices automatically brought with it the collapse of exports to OPEC countries. . . . But wasn't it "Chirac 1974" who inaugurated the strategy of big contracts with oil-exporting countries?

At some point during April 1987 public opinion polls placed the Left, for the first time—ever?—ahead of the Right on questions about relative capabilities for running the economy. The deficit of the French welfare state had become so obvious that Philippe Séguin called the Etats-Généraux de la Sécurité Sociale for the fall of 1987. And in June 1987 a debate about "French decline" exploded. Chirac responded, in July, by promising to refloat research budgets. It was very late. The structures of French international trade had begun to resemble those of an underdeveloped country. And this under the leadership of a "Gaullist" thirty years after General de Gaulle's return to power. The electoral results of spring 1988 had become inevitable.

By Way of Conclusion

French economic history after 1962—and, in fact, ever since 1945—has in-volved a forced-march modernization led, first of all, by a peculiar variety of Bonapartism, which almost reached its legitimate conclusion in social democracy. The internal obstacles to success—the famous *société bloquée,* which necessitated proliferating corporatistic concessions and relegation of the wage-earner social base of Fordism to an impatient opposition—ought to have given way as a result of modernization itself. It is significant that the electoral propensities of women, faithfully on the side of an archaic Right at the beginning, have become Socialist. But the magnitude of the imbalance in France's developmentalist but "wobbly" hegemonic bloc, plus France's place at the bottom of the ladder of the European accumulation regime, lay the groundwork for the catastrophe that would come with the crisis of Fordism. Neither the Left Common Program nor dogmatic liberalism had brought satisfactory remedies. Instead, all one heard were paeans to technological modernization and Europe.

In this vacuum of values, this desert of citizenship paradigms, what had earlier been cast out could return. Political groups on all sides bore responsibility for the rise of xenophobia and hysteria about law and order promoted by the National Front. The PCF, after the 1977–78 breakdown of the Common Program, tried to re-moralize its disoriented social base by encouraging rejection of immigrants. The Right won the 1983 municipal elections by playing on the theme of insecurity and immigration. The PS reworked its propaganda after 1984 around the theme of *La France qui gagne*.

What is the France we see today? If a country can no longer define itself in terms of a project of life in society, then it will collapse. In many quarters today France equals the French, those who have French blood. There as well the state exists to protect the good French against those who are impure, those infected by AIDS, immigrants, industrial restructuring, and European unification. In the race to the center, toward consensus around a complete absence of positive projects, the political establishment has abandoned the victims of crisis to the sirens of hatred and irrationality.

Translated from the French by George Ross.

Notes

1. I have been trying to expand these ideas beyond economics over the past few years. For the basic texts of the regulation school see Michel Aglietta, *Régulation des crises du capitalisme* (Paris: Calmann-Lévy, 1976), translated as *A Theory of Capitalist Regulation* (London: New Left Books, 1979); Robert Boyer and Jacques Mistral, *Accumulation, inflation, crises* (Paris: PUF, 1983); Alain Lipietz, *Crise et inflation: pourquoi?* (Paris: Maspero, 1977); and Alain Lipietz, *Mirages and Miracles* (London: Verso, 1987). I have presented regulation school principles didactically in "Reflections on a Tale," *Studies in Political Economy* 26 (1988) and have discussed their origins in Jane Jenson and Alain Lipietz "Rebel Sons: The Regulation School," *French Politics and Society* 5 (Fall, 1987). My book *L'Audace ou l'enlisement* (Paris: Maspero, 1984) implicitly uses the methods of the present essay, which are more explicitly discussed in Alain Lipietz, "The Conditions for Creating an Alternative Movement in France," *Rethinking Marxism* 1 (Fall 1988), where the concept of societal paradigm is reviewed. In its actual form, it constitutes a common elaboration with Jane Jenson who, after having introduced congruent notions concerning political representation (for example, "Gender and Reproduction: Or Babies and the State," *Studies in Political Economy* 20 [Summer, 1986]), applied the same methodology in her study of the recent history of Canada, " 'Different' but not 'Exceptional': Canada's Permeable Fordism," *Canadian Review of Sociology and Anthropology* 26 (Winter 1989).

2. We should note that in all of these forms of production the domestic labor of women in invisible, unrepresented, and not even "economic."

3. Such places are not occupied by simply defined "social classes" derived from economic circumstances. Two social blocs that combine the same classes can be very different, both because of different systems of material compromises and because of varying systems of collective representation inside the bloc. One might use the analogy of "isomers," chemical molecules composed of the same atoms, but bound together in different ways. This is why we will talk of "groups" in what follows, using, in a distant way, the reading of Gramsci proposed by Nicos Poulantzas in *Pouvoir politique et classes sociales* (Paris: Maspero, 1968).

4. Habitus is here used in the sense of Pierre Bourdieu in *Questions de Sociologie* (Paris: Minuit, 1980), meaning a disposition of socially constructed individuals willing both to "play the game" and also to help it evolve within a mode of regulation.

5. See Jenson, "Gender and Reproduction," for a discussion of this point.

6. The term "paradigm," which I borrow from grammar as Thomas Kuhn did in the interests of epistemology, helps to capture simultaneously, two different concepts at the same time. A paradigm can have infinite variations—like a color, say, between red and purple—but still have clear boundaries. A societal paradigm is defined by its common principles, which are susceptible to a number of variations and rearrangements. This is why it can be seen as conflictual, or why each paradigm has a specific Left-Right polarization. Here see Alain Lipietz, "The Conditions for Creating an Alternative Movement."

7. This "regulatory" concept of the state gets its credibility from Marx and Engels (with Weber's later help), despite the fact that it is covered up in Marxism, as a result of the Leninist tradition, by an instrumentalist concept (where the state "becomes a tool of the dominating classes to control subordinate classes"). See Lipietz, "The Conditions for Creating an Alternative Movement."

8. Robert Delorme and Charles André call this the "état interne." Delorme and André are quite close to the regulation school. Here I borrow the terms "internal/external state" and "circumscribed/inserted state" from them. See Robert Delorme and Charles André, *L'Etat et l'économie* (Paris: Editions du Seuil, 1983), and Robert Delorme, "A New View of Economic Theory of the State: A Case Study of France," *Journal of Economic Issues* 18 (September 1984).

9. What follows is often based on more concrete analyses from the theoretical tradition evidenced by such theorists as Delorme and André, *L'Etat et L'économie,* Patrick Fridenson and André Strauss, eds., *Le Capitalisme français: Blocages et dynamismes d'une croissance* (Paris: Fayard, 1987); André Gauron, *Histoire économique et sociale de la Ve République,* 2 vols. (Paris: La Découverte, 1983, 1988); and Lipietz, *L'Audace ou l'enlisement.*

10. See Richard Kuisel, *Capitalism and the State in Modern France* (Cambridge: Cambridge University Press, 1981).

11. The *réaliste poétique* films of the interwar period—those of Carné and Renoir, for example—perfectly illustrate this societal paradigm.

12. There was also a strong anarcho-syndicalist tradition in both the PCF and the Confédération Générale du Travail (CGT), a tradition proud of its "professionalism" and its technical savoir-faire.

13. The passionate dialogue between the Communist historian Jean Bouvier and the *grand commis* François Bloch-Laîné (in *La France Restaurée* [Paris: Fayard, 1986]) illustrates this convergence particularly well. In response to the Communist who believes that the hopes of the Resistance were betrayed and talks about a need for "restoration," the *grand commis* patiently explains that there was nothing in these hopes that, as far as possible, had not been achieved prior to 1973.

14. It was Jean Lecanuet, MRP leader, who gave the most important *discours de censure* against the developmentalist government of Mendès-France in 1954.

15. For example, one can point to collective agreements and "social progress," the spread of paid vacations, regulations on work time, a minimum wage indexed to the cost of living and later to national productivity, growing representation by trade unions, agreements on job training programs, and so on.

16. See Hugues Bertrand, "Le Régime central d'accumulation de l'après-guerre et sa crise," *Critiques de l'Economie Politique* 7–8 (April 1979).

17. See Alain Lipietz, *Le Capital et son espace* (Paris: Maspero, 1983).

18. This is the terminology of Michel Aglietta and Anton Brender in *Métamorphoses de la société salariale* (Paris: Calmann-Lévy, 1984). Its major problem is, however, its considerable overestimation of France's approximation of a salarial society.

19. Luc Boltanski, *The Making of a Class: Cadres in French Society* (Cambridge: Cambridge University Press/Editions de la Maison des Science de l'Homme, 1987).

20. This is obvious from a comparison with similar groups in northern Europe, West Germany in particular.

21. Watch out! For the French who remain uncontaminated by the *franglais* of political science, the word corporatism does not mean an oligolistic agreement between social groups with particular representative status brokered by the state. It means, in contrast, the combination of different social groups in a unique professional organization, opposed to other professionals, to which the state delegates internal regulatory responsibilities. Fordist regulation is thus *not* corporatist regulation of the Perón-Vargas type. See Alain Lipietz, "Aspects séculaires et conjoncturels de l'intervention économique de l'Etat," *Couverture Orange* (Paris: CEPREMAP, 1986).

22. Social promotion through the teaching profession—which the familial trajectory of Georges Pompidou illustrated perfectly—was indeed one of the central mechanisms of the hegemonic bloc of the Third Republic.

23. For a detailed analysis of the double crisis of Fordism—that of its specific paradigm and that stemming from its internationalization—see Andrew Glyn et al., "The Rise and Fall of the Golden Age: An Historical Analysis of Post-War Capitalism in the Developed Market Economic," in Steven Marglin, ed., *The Golden Age of Capitalism: Lessons for the 1990s* (Oxford: Oxford University Press, 1990), and Alain Lipietz, *Mirages and Miracles* (London: Verso, 1986).

24. For a more detailed and nuanced analysis of the policies of the Barre, Mauroy, Fabius, and Chirac governments see Alain Lipietz, "An Alternative Design for the Twenty-First Century," *Couverture Orange* (Paris: CEPREMAP, 1987), no. 8738; idem, *L'Audace ou l'enlisement;* and idem, *Choisir l'Audace* (Paris: La Découverte, 1989).

25. We will exclude ideological, political, and other aspects, even when they have important economic consequences, especially those bearing on the question of the "middle classes."

26. A political periodization would place the low point of the legislature in June 1984, with the European Elections, huge demonstrations for private schools, the subsequent "Allendization" of François Mitterrand, and then breakout from the state of siege when Fabius became prime minister and the Communists left.

27. See Alain Lipietz, *Choisir l'audace*.

28. See Bertrand Bellon, *L'Interventionisme libérale: La Politique économique de l'administration fédérale américaine* (Paris: Editions du Seuil-Economica, 1986).

29. See here Alain Minc, *L'Après-crise est commencée* (Paris: Gallimard, 1982).

30. Claude Courlet et al., *Etudes sur les politiques industrielles locales dans le cadre de la promotion des PME,* mimeo (Grenoble: Report IREP/CNEPP, 1987).

31. See Lipietz, *Choisir l'audace*.

2

The Institutions of the Fifth Republic

Stanley Hoffmann

I will not attempt to describe in detail the evolution of the public institutions set up in 1958. My purpose is to show in what ways they differ from those in France's past, the main difficulties and tensions that their functioning has revealed, and the effects they may have had on the French polity.

I. The System

The Constitution of 1958 (especially as revised in 1962, when de Gaulle decided with the approval of the French that the president would be elected by universal suffrage) constitutes a major break with the French representative tradition. Under the earlier system—in the Fourth as well as the Third Republic—the sovereignty of the people (including its constituent power) was delegated to the people's representatives. French parliamentarism was singular in that (a) Parliament had the decisive role in the institutional system: the executive not only emanated from it (as it does in all cabinet systems) but had very few means of control over it, and (b) the nature of the French party system made stable coalitions unlikely and thus weakened the executive even more. In accordance with the Rousseauistic construction of democratic government, which centered it on the general will, there was no judicial control of the legislator's acts. The people's role was limited to the selection of the representatives. In the absence of a two-party system, or of a sharp division between "ins" and "outs," the choice of the head of government resulted from the "games, poisons, and delights" of parties and parliamentary factions, not from the expression of the people's will.

The Constitution that General de Gaulle had outlined in Bayeux in 1946 and that Michel Debré put together in 1958 was aimed at changing all that. Two issues will be addressed here. First, after more than thirty years, how wide is the gap between the intentions of the drafters and the reality? Second, how flexible has the system been?

The original intention was crystal clear. De Gaulle had founded the Rassemblement pour la France (RPF) in 1947 in order to achieve a constitutional break with the past and with the Fourth Republic while remaining within the democratic tradition. His main concern, which sprang from his experiences in the 1930s and even more from the trauma of 1940, was to make effective government possible, whether or not there was a stable parliamentary majority. Both de Gaulle and Debré were skeptical about the ability of the French to produce a two-party system (de Gaulle's perhaps apocryphal remark about France's hundreds of cheeses is apt), especially at a time when the Communist Party was still a very important force. But they wanted to rescue the executive from impotence, in an era of crises (Algeria) and at a time when France needed major economic and social transformations. They were clever enough to enlist in their constitutional revolution the disgruntled ex-premiers of the Fourth Republic, who had been the victims of France's brand of parliamentarism.

The fascinating thing about the Constitution of 1958 was that it could receive two very different "readings." Both had the same purpose and result (the transfer of effective power to the executive), but each had its own model. De Gaulle's reading was simple: this transfer had to lead to the preponderance of the president, the "nation's man" (especially after the 1962 reform). Whether or not he shared some of these powers with the prime minister, he was the one who could dissolve the National Assembly, call for a referendum, and resort to exceptional measures in an emergency. For a while, as was his wont, de Gaulle confused matters by calling the president's function "arbitral," but what he meant was clearly not arbitration but rather supreme decision. There was, behind this conception, a daring blend of three models. The one most of his opponents saw and denounced was Bonapartism—the confiscation of power by a charismatic figure through plebiscites that both paid homage to and manipulated the principle of popular sovereignty. But de Gaulle's conception of the president's role and functions was also—as he made clear in a famous press conference in 1964—monarchical: the president, source of all power, could be compared to the Sovereigns of the Old Regime, the "Kings who had made France" and whom de Gaulle's parents had revered. The only differences were the need for popular anointment, and the third component: the parliamentary one—the (limited) role of the legislature, and the existence of a cabinet that was to be responsible to the National Assembly as in the recent past. Shrewdly, de Gaulle preserved this component both because he knew that many Frenchmen were attached to it and would see in its maintenance a guarantee against Bonapartism pure and simple (or monarchy) and because he understood that through the very mechanism of cabinet responsibility the president might in fact exert far greater power than in a pure presidential system *à l'américaine,* where Congress, which cannot be dissolved, has the ability to paralyze the executive.

What made of the parliamentary component a boost rather than a handicap for the president was the arsenal of limitations on Parliament that Debré had written into the Constitution. He, unlike de Gaulle, had his eyes on London. He wanted to achieve a parliamentary system comparable to England's (or to that of the

Federal Republic of Germany), i.e., one in which the legislative branch did not dominate, even though the French party system was unlikely to produce stable majorities. What he thus tried to erect was a "rationalized parliamentarism," in which stability would be obtained through constitutional barriers, so that the legislature would lose many of its previous powers—over its agenda, for instance, but also over the scope of legislation, and above all over the fate of cabinets— and could be easily "contained" by the executive (with the help of a Constitutional Council intended to be able to strike down the expected attempts by deputies and senators to transgress the limits set up by the new Constitution). But in Debré's view the beneficiary of these reforms was supposed to be the cabinet and its prime minister—as in England or in Bonn. The strong president was needed because, in the absence of a clear majority in legislative elections, it was important that the choice of the prime minister be put in hands others than those of squabbling politicians, and in case "rationalized parliamentarism" did not work (which is why, unlike the power to call a referendum, the president can dissolve the National Assembly without the consent of the prime minister).

The two "readings" of the Constitution turned out to be alternatives; they are not mutually exclusive. It all depends on the configuration of forces in the Assembly—paradoxically enough, since it was precisely that state of affairs whose significance de Gaulle had wanted to reduce! As long as there is a solid parliamentary majority, for whatever reasons (see below) it is, again paradoxi- cally, de Gaulle's reading that prevails: the preponderance of the president, aimed at remedying parliamentary division, actually rests on the existence of such a majority, as long as it is one that supports the president. When this is the case, the prime minister is, in a sense, the president's chief of staff, the intermediary between him and the majority, and this explains why every president has cam- paigned so hard for the election of a National Assembly that his partisans would control, and why Mitterrand dissolved the National Assembly twice, in 1981 and 1988, in order to obtain a properly supportive one. When there is a majority in the Assembly, but one opposed to the president, Debré's "rationalized parlia- mentarism" comes into its own, but in circumstances in which the president, far from being a kind of emergency backup of the prime minister, is his rival. During those periods in which there is a plurality but no absolute majority, in the National Assembly, for the president (or for the prime minister chosen by him), or when his majority is itself divided, as it was during Giscard d'Estaing's *septennat* following Chirac's angry resignation, the presidency remains the superior office, but the prime minister gains some independence since it is thanks to his skill that the opposition can be kept at bay; and the president's preponderance rests in large part on his ability to replace at will the prime minister he has chosen.

Thus it can be said in the constitutional system of the Fifth Republic, two very different ways of determining the "general will" are in a state of latent tension. There is the Gaullian way: the popularly elected president is the person who legitimately expresses it; and there is the old parliamentary way," in which it is the legislative branch that, just as legitimately, is in charge of formulating it. The president's interest and strategy are to make sure that the latter will be subordinated to the former, by having the National Assembly controlled by a *"majorité présidentielle,"* formed around his person and his program. The cabinet and the prime minister are in an uncomfortable position, insofar as they are the hyphen between the two legitimacies—except when it is the second one that clearly prevails over the president's (as in the case when the opposition becomes the majority in the newly elected Assembly, i.e., the situation of 1986); at that moment, the reform of the parliamentary component by Debré ultimately benefits the prime minister rather than the legislature.

All of this points to the importance of the electoral system. De Gaulle, instructed by the experience of 1945 and the case of the Fourth Republic, rejected proportional representation and settled for a return to the two-ballot, single-member district system of the Third Republic. It had never succeeded in creating a satisfactory party system, and had often been accused of resulting in utter confusion: too many parties and factions, deputies and senators who behaved like little sovereigns in their fiefdoms, no majorities, etc. . . . But a *scrutin de liste majoritaire* would have perpetuated the grip of the party over its deputies, which de Gaulle and Debré, unhappy with French parties, wanted to break, and Debré's favorite system—the one-ballot single-member district system—was deemed too dangerous, as it might have made the Communists the overwhelmingly dominant opposition party. The surprise was that the old electoral system of the Third Republic succeeded, repeatedly—as late as 1988—in producing either an absolute majority for the president's party, or a majority for a coalition supporting him, or a reasonably comfortable plurality for him. The reason is that one cannot assess the effects of an electoral law in a vacuum; it has to be judged in the context of the constitutional system. In the Fifth Republic, the very centrality of the president and of the presidential election has created a *dynamique présidentielle* that was absent, of course, in the Third and Fourth Republics; in 1986, it was opposition to the president that created a *dynamique majoritaire* against him. Indeed, even though Mitterrand and the Socialist National Assembly that had been elected in 1981 had restored proportional representation in order to prevent such a *dynamique* from pitting the new Assembly against the president, this reform only resulted in reducing the size of the opposition, but not in preventing its victory. The combination of the electoral system—which induces, between the two ballots, ententes among several of the candidates who have run in the first one—with the presidential election has produced the *bipolarisation* that eluded the Third Republic, even though the second ballot contests often set the Left up against the Right. However, in those days, after the House was elected, it usually became clear that these opportunistic coalitions would not last, and indeed the typical centrist party, the Radicals, often had deputies elected in each "camp."

To be sure, *bipolarisation* has not meant a reduction of the field of parties to either two or three. Today, Debré's preferred electoral system might produce such a result, for it would most probably wipe out almost completely the representation of the Communists, confirm the quasi-total exclusion of the National Front from the National Assembly that the present electoral law produced in 1988, and oblige the "moderate" Right to form a single party. But one could argue that such a change would actually increase the influence, on the Left as well as on the Right, of the more extreme group—the Communists and the Front National—which would ask for a price in exchange for supporting the single Socialist or Conservative candidate; and if no such price is paid and more than two candidates confront one another as a result, a system in which, on the day of the single ballot, the candidate who has a mere plurality gets elected would still lead to several parties in Parliament. The roots of France's multiparty system are too deep to be wiped out even by the combination of presidential election and electoral law set up by the Fifth Republic.

So far, the new regime has met the expectations of its founders by transferring power from the legislative to the executive. Although the number of significant parties has only been reduced from the Fourth Republic's six (Communists, Socialists, Radicals, Mouvement Républicain Populaîre (MRP), Conservatives, Gaullists) to five, the *dynamique présidentielle* has been an important factor in (a) the gradual shrinking of the Communist party; (b) the creation of a highly organized Gaullist and neo-Gaullist party, in a sector of the electorate that had, in the past, resisted such organization; and (c) the renovation of the Socialist Party in the 1970s, without which its conquest of power would have been unlikely.

When the Constitution was adopted, and even more so after its tumultuous reform in 1962, many commentators criticized it as being tailor-made for General de Gaulle, but unlikely to survive him without major changes. This has turned out to be false. It has, in fact, accommodated a variety of *"cas de figure"*:

(a) It has, of course, functioned particularly smoothly (and to the president's advantage) when there was a safe "majority bloc," all the way from the president to the National Assembly: this was the case from the legislative election of 1962 to that of 1967 (Gaullist party majority), and from that of 1968 to 1974 (Gaullists from 1968 to 1973, Gaullists plus allies in 1973–74). Between 1974 and 1976, the president and the largest parliamentary group (the Gaullists) were no longer on the same wavelength, but thanks to his choice of a Gaullist prime minister who was (still) devoted to him, the president of the Republic managed to preserve his position reasonably well.

(b) The system has functioned less smoothly when the parliamentary majority supporting the president was very narrow (1967–68, when the Executive decided to resort to *ordonnances* rather than to the ordinary legislative process for several reforms), and also in the period 1976–81, when the tensions between the Rassemblement pour la République (RPR) and the supporters of Giscard, who later formed the Union pour la Démocrâtie Française (UDF), led the prime minister to resort repeatedly to the notorious Article 49, Paragraph 3, which allows the cabinet to force the adoption of a bill by staking its life on it—which obliges the opposition either to yield or to call for a vote of no confidence.

(c) The Constitution has functioned even with a heterogeneous majority (1959–

62), during the exceptional crisis circumstances of the Algerian War, when the representatives were only too happy to let de Gaulle play Hercules.

(d) The Constitution has also functioned even with no absolute majority for either side, a situation that has obliged the prime minister since 1988 to make sure that he will get the support or the benevolent abstention of a number of members of the opposition—a task made easier by the split of the latter (Communists versus the Right), the sympathy of several Centrists, and of course Article 49, Paragraph 3.

(e) The Constitution has weathered one test many people had anxiously awaited: the *alternance* of 1981, when after twenty-three years of Gaullist or conservative rule, the Union of the Left came to power—with a president, Mitterrand, and parties that had denounced de Gaulle's Republic as a "permanent coup d'état". But Mitterrand soon stated that he found the institutions "suitable," although they were dangerous (because of excessive concentration of power in the executive) before him and might become dangerous again after him!

(f) The most difficult test of all has been that of 1986. Sooner or later the concordance between the presidency and the majority in the National Assembly— between the two legitimacies described above—was likely to end. Given the French lack of any tradition of compromises among political foes, many had feared that this split would lead to a kind of constitutional war. It did not—only to guerrilla warfare, especially in the first months. *Cohabitation* never became cooperation, but it was reasonably close to peaceful coexistence.[1] Mitterrand cleverly understood that it was to his advantage to leave domestic affairs to the Cabinet (the prime minister could claim that this was not only his mandate but his right under Article 20 of the Constitution), to entrust the government to the very leader of the opposition, and to concentrate on his role as "guardian of the Constitution" (which allowed him to chide his rivals for their tendency to bypass Parliament), as well as on his functions in diplomacy and defense. The insistence of the prime minister on exerting his own powers fully in these two areas showed that *cohabitation* was not an easy formula (since the Constitution provides for an intricate overlap between the powers of the president of the Republic and those of the prime minister), nor was it a situation that could last forever. But since everyone had an eye on the next and decisive round—the presidential election of 1988—it was bearable for two years.

There is one *"cas de figure"* that hasn't happened yet, but might arise some day: if neither "pole" has a majority, and if the one that is ahead cannot count on a regular and sufficient *appoint* provided by other representatives, a genuine centrist coalition would become necessary. In the legislature of 1988, the president's distaste for such a solution—in the absence of necessity—has coincided with the preference of many Socialist deputies for a de facto coalition, whenever possible, with the small Communist contingent. A centrist coalition would probably be more a temporary interruption than an end of the logic of *bipolarisation,* for it would be either an alliance between Socialists and a centrist fragment of the conservative bloc drifting away from the grip of men like Giscard and Chirac, or a shaky "grand coalition" of (insufficiently) victorious Conservatives plus Socialists.

In sum: it is the very incongruity of the Constitution, its hybrid nature, which has given it flexibility. As in the United States, Britain, and the Federal Republic of Germany, it has provided France with a strong executive, in a democratic context; and if France does not have the equivalent of the German and Italian Christian Democratic parties, or of the Japanese Liberal Democratic Party (LDP) it has, in the past thirty-odd years, produced a kind of *alternance* from a relatively dominant Gaullist to a relatively dominant Socialist party.

II. Issues

It may be useful to analyze more specifically some of the major institutions and the problems they have raised.

First, how has the transfer of power to the executive worked? The key problem is the functioning of the "couple" constituted by the president of the Republic and by the prime minister. As I have indicated above, the scope of the prime minister's political role has varied, depending on the *"cas de figure."* But even when presidential predominance has been obvious, the prime minister has always had more leeway than the public thought, for two reasons. Even when the prime minister could count on a solid majority in the National Assembly, he had to make sure that the bills presented by the government would be well-received and -supported, and that the dominant party would be satisfied; thus, his relations with the leadership of the party and with the head of its parliamentary group have always mattered. The president has never wanted to appear as merely the man of one party—de Gaulle did not want to repeat the experience of the RPF; Mitterrand, even in 1981–84, wanted to be the head of the Left (and after 1988, of the *majorité présidentielle*) and not simply of the Socialists. Thus, the management, coaxing, or coercion of the key party has been the prime minister's delicate problem.

Moreover, although the Elysée is the ultimate center of power (except in *cohabitation,* when there is a real tug of war), Matignon is the daily center of administration. The staff of the Elysée, unlike that of the White House, is small; it allows the president to supervise the prime minister's activities and to monitor those of the ministers, but the center of daily initiative, preparation of bills and regulations, and enforcement, is at Matignon. When the president and the prime minister were enemies, Mitterrand discovered that his sources of information dried up, and his capacity to monitor events—even in some highly sensitive matters, such as New Caledonia—vanished.

Nevertheless, the position of prime minister remains uncomfortable. De Gaulle had excluded the possibility of any "diarchy" at the top of the state, but this blunt proclamation of presidential superiority did not dispose of the relations between the two heads of the executive. Between a president who, de Gaulle *dixit*, was to concentrate on essentials and on long-term directions, and a prime minister in charge of *contingences,* there can be no easy coexistence. The crisis of 1968 served as a brutal demonstration. Without the prime minister, who controls the bureaucracy and decides on daily tactics, the president of the Republic is like a huge Beaudelairian albatross, incapable of flying because his wings are too big; but without the full support of the president of the Republic, the prime minister's liberty of maneuver is seriously handicapped. In an emergency (which is not a *contingence*), the power to act decisively can fall between the two stools—with each blaming the other for fiascoes. Even without such a crisis, it is a ticklish relationship at best. For the prime minister knows that he can always be dismissed (as Chaban-Delmas was even after having received a parliamentary vote of confidence), and the president of the Republic knows that the prime minister, having had to learn to master the bureaucracy and to handle the parliamentary majority, is likely to develop presidential ambitions of his own: the dependent is a rival.

To be sure, the complicity that exists among "products of *the grandes écoles,*" *énarques* and *polytechniciens,* who populate the cells of power both at the Elysée and at Matignon, can often ease cooperation. But there have been moments when the loyalty of each of the two staffs was to its current boss, not to their common training ground, and when the war of the advisers worsened the strained relations of the masters. Even though one man is above the other (insofar as the prime minister cannot get rid of the president of the Republic, as Chirac found out in 1986–88), in daily life each one is at the mercy of the other. For the president of the Republic, it is useful to have a prime minister on whom impopularity can settle—but if the prime minister becomes too heartily disliked, the president of the Republic (except, of course, during "cohabitation") will ultimately bear the brunt of some of that impopularity. And as for the prime minister, he knows (also except for *cohabitation*) that he is easily disposable, and must appear both inspired and respectful.

Is this the best of all possible situations? The French president, unlike an American one, can, indeed, concentrate on key issues, and on broad directions, and leave the management of the cabinet to the prime minister. But presidents (except for the inimitable de Gaulle) also like to place their own men (or women) in key positions, and especially if they have been prime ministers or ministers before, to be involved in some daily issues or intrigues—and this is a source of collisions with the prime minister. Also, the president may have a grand design his prime minister does not share (for instance, de Gaulle's dream of participation, which Pompidou dismissed, or Giscard's desire for changes in mores, which Chirac, in 1974–76, did not endorse): in which case he will be frustrated, and faced with the choice between sticking to his obstructionist prime minister or replacing him, which is always a nuisance and a commotion. As for the prime minister, if he has a design of his own, the president of the Republic risks seeing this as a crime of *lèse majesté* (for example, Chaban's plan for a *nouvelle société*), and if he does his best to be low-key and pragmatic, he may both displease the president, who feels uncovered, and produce a kind of vacuum of leadership, if the president of the Republic happens to appear short of inspiration also (cf. the situation since 1988). And of course, as we have seen, *cohabitation* means overt or covert sniping and struggling for power.

All of this explains why there have been proposals for abolishing the duality and moving toward a pure presidential system. There are those who find that the duration of the mandate of the president of the Republic—seven years—is too long, especially as he can run for reelection. Limiting him to two terms of five years each would perhaps resolve one problem—the excessive length of two mandates of seven years—but it would also reduce the superiority of the president of the Republic over the prime minister, and thus risk aggravating the tension between them. As of 1990 the president of the Republic remains the linchpin of the system: what made *cohabitation* both so tense and so bearable was the fact that the prime minister's eye was on the next presidential election: Chirac's real goal was not the restoration of the supremacy of the prime minister but the conquest of the presidency. But much of political life is consumed by the divagations of the unstable balance between "God" and his top saint, between "God's" desire to have a top saint both docile and capable of relieving him of unwelcome burdens, and the top saint's ambition to be his own man and to become God.

Second, what has been the fate of Parliament in the Fifth Republic? There has been a tendency among commentators to lament its impotence; and it is of course true that by comparison with the Assemblies of the two earlier Republics, its role appears minimal. On the one hand, however, parliamentary "sovereignty" has not fared well anywhere in an age when and in societies where decision making concerns itself above all with economic management, a subject that bureaucrats and businessmen are more capable of handling than are legislators. On the other hand, cabinet systems with stable majorities have everywhere produced a transfer of effective power to the executive. The U.S. Congress is an exception from both viewpoints: the separation of powers gives it an independence that results from the very sparseness of the arsenal at the disposal of the president, except when he is a charismatic leader at the beginning of his mandate (or in wartime) and his party controls both Houses; as for economic management, it is assuredly not the main function of the U.S. Federal Government.

The impression of impotence, or excessive docility, was largely created by the behavior of Parliaments between 1959 and 1967 (but remember its sudden revolt in the fall of 1962, when de Gaulle announced his referendum on constitutional change, and the National Assembly overthrew Pompidou). This timidity resulted first from the "Roman dictatorship" situation of the Algerian war and, after the Gaullist triumph in November 1962, from the fact that the Gaullist party really had no policy other than supporting de Gaulle and his prime minister. Parliament was more restive in 1967–68. Between 1968 and 1972 the Gaullist parliamentarians reflected the latent conflicts between Pompidou and Chaban-Delmas, who was sometimes more popular among non-Gaullists than in his own party. The Socialists, when they controlled the Assembly, were unlike the Gaullists insofar as they had strong views of their own, and Prime Minister Mauroy had to heed them and to prepare his legislative program with their participation—and even so, they sometimes went against his wishes or those of Mitterrand (cf. the vote of amnesty for *Algérie française* crimes). A recent study shows that there has been a "rehabilitation" of Parliament[2] in terms of the number of questions asked, of the length of debates, of the number of amendments offered and accepted, and also of the number of texts endorsed, explicitly or implicitly, by a majority larger than the Socialist parliamentary group in the 1988 Assembly.

The current reform proposals, aimed at establishing a pure presidential system, have as their objective not so much the elimination of the executive diarchy as the emancipation of Parliament from the grip of the Executive: the model is the U.S. Congress, the nostalgia is for the Fourth or Third Republic. To be sure, the chief executive, elected by the people, would remain powerful—but much less so, if the president of the Republic should lose the power of dissolution. And the danger of a deadlock between the executive and Parliament would be serious.

Indeed, at present, one might argue that the main obstacle to the "rehabilitation" of Parliament is not the Constitution—at least if one compares France with Britain and the Federal Republic of Germany—but the European Single Act of 1985, which gives to the Council of the European Economic Community (EEC) the power to adopt rules and directives that are either self-executory or leave to national parliaments only the power of adaptation and enforcement. But this is another story. . . .

Third, much has been written about the rise of the Constitutional Council, especially since the reform of 1974, which allowed sixty parliamentarians to refer a bill to the Council in order to obtain a decision about its conformity to the Constitution. From being a body whose function was the protection of the executive's new powers from parliamentary infringements, it has become a body to which the minority can refer bills prepared by the Cabinet and adopted, at its request, by the majority that supports it. The increased importance of the Council, which has struck down a number of important bills—or portions of bills—especially between 1981 and 1988, has meant that the institutional system is even more of a hybrid than before, since the Council represents a graft of a fourth—this time, a non-French—tradition onto the Bonapartist, the monarchical, and the parliamentary ones that coexist in the Constitution. This fourth tradition is the American one of judicial review, which used to evoke in France the ghost of "government by judges" and was deemed incompatible with the Rousseauistic dogma of the sovereignty of the popular will (the heir of the Absolute Monarchy's conception of the King's sovereignty, and the origin of the notion of parliamentary sovereignty). Insofar as the three French traditions were not liberal (Rousseau's conception and its parliamentary derivative being democratic or radical rather than liberal), the idea of a judicial review aimed not only at establishing the supremacy of the fundamental law over ordinary ones, but also that of general principles found in past Bills of Rights or . . . proclaimed by the Constitutional Council (such as pluralism) is a major liberal victory. It is amplified by the recent decisions of the Conseil d'Etat, which state that French laws must be in conformity with the EEC's directives and with international law: "general will," expressed by the legislator—or rather, often, by the executive in the form of a bill submitted to and voted by Parliament—must respect limits that it has not always had to consider.

To be sure, there are sharp restrictions to this "power of the judges," too. Unless Parliament adopts the current constitutional reform proposal of President Mitterrand that would allow citizens, during a trial, to raise the issue of a bill's constitutionality, the Constitutional Council can only decide on laws *before* their promulgation; nor can it deal with executive decisions that affect the relations between branches (such as, say, de Gaulle's decision of 1962 to use a referendum for constitutional reform). Nevertheless, the rise of the Council constitutes another break with the practices of France's past parliamentary regimes.

III. A Balance Sheet

What have been the main contributions of the constitutional system to the French political community? The most obvious has been governmental stability, after almost a century of weak cabinets and presidents with minimal powers. It is true that the Third and Fourth Republics accomplished a great deal—the school system of the Third, economic modernization and the completion of social security under the Fourth, for instance. But sometimes the rules had to be suspended so that the nation could go on being governed, as in World War One and through the *décrets-lois* of the 1930s, and sometimes the achievements were either produced despite "the system" or marred by the "corporatist," parochial, or financially irresponsible interventions of Parliament, as in the process of economic transformation between 1947 and 1958. Governmental stability is not a sufficient, but is certainly a necessary, condition of sound financial management.

Moreover, the election of the president of the Republic by the people has led to contests among candidates who, whatever their flaws, were on the whole neither mediocre nor unprepared. The fact that so many *énarques* have chosen political careers—in the executive or in Parliament—has often been interpreted as a revenge of a somewhat bureaucratic authoritarianism over "politics as a vocation" or over representatives of "civil society": a sort of revenge of the State over the People. But one could also see it as a recognition, by influential bureaucrats, of the legitimacy and authority of the constitutional system, and of its capacity to attract men and women with genuine expertise in public affairs.

Another contribution is, in part at least, the result of the Constitution's flexibility and of governmental stability. It is the appearance of areas of consensus. The most significant is the broad consensus on the Constitution itself: it has been tinkered with, but the passions it evoked in 1958 are dead, and its general design is now very widely accepted. De Gaulle has succeeded, posthumously, in his attempt at synthesizing previously incompatible traditions; in this respect, it is he who brought to an end the divisions created by the French Revolution. Despite the turbulence of 1984, the consensus around *la question scolaire,* i.e., the acceptance not only of private schools but of public subsidies for them, which began with the Debré law of 1959, has held firm; consensus around the combination of economic modernization (partly through the opening to Europe) and social protection began under the Fourth Republic, but more negatively and more grudgingly than in the Fifth, when it became de Gaulle's ambitious program. The convergence of Left and Right on economic policy has lasted since 1984, through three very different *"cas de figure."* It is impossible to prove that none of this would have happened if French parliamentarism had survived the cataclysmic crisis of 1958; but it is difficult to believe that a system that led each party to "cultivate its difference" (because of proportional representation) and led cabinets to immobility (because of coalitions) would have been equally effective. The same can be said about foreign and defense policy: until the sudden end of Europe's division and the reunification of Germany, which will force the French to reconsider their role in the world, French diplomacy and strategy have remained, for the most part, within the limits and perspectives de Gaulle drew. Again, one might argue whether this is really an effect of the Constitution, but both the concentration of power on national security in the presidency and the fact that the Socialists, in order to come to power, had to "reconvert" their own foreign policy preferences, are part of the explanation.

What about the system's drawbacks? I have already discussed the debit side of the dual executive. The main criticism hurled at the Constitution has been its insufficiently democratic character. There are different angles to this. One charge is that the people's role is limited, as in the past, to elections—the choice of representatives and of the president. The Constitution introduced the possibility of referendums, and de Gaulle resorted to them many times, especially in order to help resolve the Algerian issue. But after the low participation of the public in the Pompidou referendum of 1972 on Europe, Giscard never called for one again. Mitterrand's complicated attempt at enlarging the scope of referendums in order to call for one on the school issue, in 1984, was a maneuver of extrication rather than a democratic move, and failed. The only referendum since 1972 has been the one on New Caledonia, in 1988, and again public participation was reduced. Clearly, the referendum is a double-edged sword: the public, when called, does not always come (especially when a major party decides to boycott), and the executive has to be careful not to tie the president's fate to a project on which he is not certain to win. . . . Nevertheless, in comparison with the earlier Republics, the presidential election, which is the center of political life, provides the public with an added opportunity, to which it has become deeply attached.

The charge about insufficient democracy also points to the effects of the electoral system. Except during the brief return to proportional representation, this system has led to the underrepresentation of the extremes, and particularly of the extreme Right. This is true—but in a sense, one might argue, this was its very purpose. There is a trade-off between equity in representation and efficiency in government, and the Constitution of 1958 deliberately chose the latter. In the case of the far Left, social change, intellectual evolutions, the rigidity and clumsiness of the Communists' leadership, and Mitterrand's clever strategy resulted in the decline of the Party. It is far from clear whether the attempt by the Rocard government to reach a consensus with the moderate Right on immigration policy will either succeed—for it is an issue that the Right can hope to exploit—or succeed in depriving Le Pen's Front of its power. In a sense, the Fifth Republic has thrown away the option, so often used before, of reducing an extremist group to impotence by coopting it into the parliamentary "game" and (temporary) cabinet coalitions—except in the case of the Communists trapped in the Union of the Left from 1981 to 1984. Another effect of the electoral system has been the overrepresentation of the "dominant" party: neither the Gaullist nor the Socialist party ever had a majority in the country, yet their control of the Assembly has sometimes tempted them to make highly partisan moves that have backfired because of public opposition: in education especially (1967–68, 1984, 1986).

The main charge concerns the combined effects of the reduced role of Parliament, governmental stability, and *énarchie*. It indicts the heavily administrative and technocratic flavor of the regime behind the constitutional facade. The centralized French state built by the Old Regime and rebuilt by Napoleon had, in the days of the Third Republic, one saving grace: its limited scope, and, in the Third and Fourth, two compensations: a weak executive and parliamentary control. These are gone, and ever since 1945 the scope of the state has been enormously enlarged. To be sure, so goes the argument, the "system" is more stable than the poor Fourth Republic, but at what costs! The top civil servants have "colonized" politics, and as a result the bureaucracy has been heavily politicized. Moreover, parties that realize that the real locus of power is the executive and not Parliament tend to be more militant and ideological than either a cabinet devoted to management or a public that is increasingly skeptical about *projets de société;* thus, the "system" is said to contribute to the disconnection between the political class and the electorate (the presidential candidates who win are often—Giscard in 1974, Mitterrand in 1988—those who sense the public's mood and appear cool and practical). Also, the top-heavy character and bureaucratic flavor of the regime have not yet been compensated for by the post-1981 efforts at decentralization, which have benefited local notables rather than popular participation and have added new layers of bureaucratic regulation. Finally, these features of the regime have often led to a loss of the capacity to hear the rumblings of discontent in the public; these then turn into storms: this was the story of the huge student and worker surge of 1968, and that of several strike epidemics.

Much of this indictment is fair, although all the returns on decentralization are not in, and no institutional system can ever save either a government or a majority from partisanship, clumsiness, or errors. It is in the state that the style of authority described almost thirty years ago by Crozier can still be found, and there is no doubt that it has been strengthened there by the dramatic shift from the Fourth to the Fifth Republic. Having chosen to push the parties away from the daily exercise of power, by transferring its locus from the Place du Palais Bourbon to Matignon and the Elysée, de Gaulle has thereby enlarged the sphere of the *grands corps'* influence and—involuntarily, this time—contributed to their immersion in partisan politics.

On the subject of democracy, a final question can be asked. By keeping parties at bay—except as a necessary basis of support for cabinets—and (through the failure of the referendum of April 1969) failing to find a public role for the representatives of interest groups, hasn't the institutional system of the Fifth Republic contributed to (I certainly do not mean caused) the lack of *encadrement* of a society in which associational life remains poor, and which exhibits frequent signs of anomie? Parties have fewer members than in many other democracies, and only a limited grip on society (the Parti Socialiste could never rival the British Labour Party or the German SPD, and the French Communist Party has ceased being a *contre-société*). The French Jacobin model derived from Rousseau, which looks at the French polity as a relationship between state and citizens but makes no room for *corps intermédiaires* and groups, has survived all the changes in society, and been reenforced rather than superseded by the innovations of 1958–62: perhaps despite all criticisms and complaints, it actually corresponds to the archetype of public life in French minds. Pluralism belongs to the private realm, but in the public one it is the couple citizen/state that prevails—recent discussions on integration as the "formula" for dealing with immigrants have shown the lasting power of this archetype. Behind the distinction between *société civile* and *pouvoirs publics,* there is the old notion of the superiority of the general interest, defined by the state, over the particular interests, and, in each person, of the citizen over the private human being. This may be a peculiar conception of democracy rather than an undemocratic one (it surely is not liberal democracy *à l'américaine*), especially as it sees the state both as a unifying force and as a force for social fairness. But it keeps groups and organizations in a limbo that is a collective cause of weakness in an advanced industrial society.

Notes

1. See my essay "Mitterrand vs. France," *New York Review of Books,* September 8, 1984.

2. Guy Carcassonne, "Réhabiliter le Parlement," *Pouvoirs* 49, 37–46.

3

Toward a Centrist Democracy?
The Fate of the French Right

Martin A. Schain

Among the changes in French politics during the past thirty years, none has been as dramatic as the changes in the party system. The key to the stability of the regime during the Fifth Republic can be found in the party system: by redefining and altering the content of political discourse, political parties created support for the institutions of the Fifth Republic; by negotiating agreements among themselves, the parties constrained real electoral choices in a way that stabilized the electoral and policy arenas; and by attracting loyal and stable electoral followings, the party system established an important nexus between the state and society. Indeed, the Fifth Republic became what the Fourth Republic never was—something close to a regime dominated by political parties. In most ways, the parties (rather than the constitution) have given the regime its present character, and this happened in spite of an electoral system that could have favored localism and party weakness. Indeed, much of the constitution of the Fifth Republic is predicated on the assumption that strong, consolidated parties were not in France's future. As Michel Debré argued in 1959:

> Ah! if we had the possibility to make a clear and constant majority spring up tomorrow . . . it would not be necessary to impose order and stability by cutting the ties between the parties and the government. . . . But . . . no one has the right in France, at the present time, to issue a check against a future that we know too well will be marked for a long time yet by political divisions—that is, by majorities menaced too readily by collapse and which must be forced to be wise. Because, in France, governmental stability cannot result initially from the electoral law, it must result, at least in part, from constitutional regulation.[1]

Although a great deal of attention has been given to "The Long March of the French Left," and the consolidation of the parties of the Left during the 1970s, the evolution and consolidation of the parties of the Right is perhaps more crucial for understanding both the constraints on the Left and the emergence of the key

I should like to thank James Hollifield for his helpful comments on an earlier version of this essay.

policy patterns of "the New France." The consolidation of the Right made possible a series of stable governments from 1962–81, supported in the National Assembly by a "presidential" majority. It reflected the emergence, the interests, and the political victory of a new middle class, and supported the progressive transformation of the civil service into a technocratic ruling class.[2]

Moreover, the consolidation of the Right in the early 1960s gradually changed the understood constraints of the party system, imposed considerable pressure upon the Left to reorganize and rebuild its strength, and provided the Left with a negative mobilizing force:

> The method by which the General gained power in 1958, with the appeal to the extreme putschist right and the classic right to set French society in order, as well as the forms through which power was exercised by General De Gaulle and then by his successors, strongly personalized, even personal, explains in part this opposition.[3]

The success of the Left in the 1970s, on the other hand, placed pressure on the parties of the Right to move further and faster toward party consolidation. Between 1974 and 1978, the political space between the "majority" and the "opposition" was eliminated, and the French party system was dominated by two coalitions of parties, each held uneasily together by the opposition of the other.

These uneasy coalitions were at the heart of the governmental stability of the Fifth Republic. Each provided somewhat different elements to the stability of the regime. The emerging coalition of the Right provided elements that the Right had rarely had in France: more or less coherent elites, growing discipline within the parliamentary majority, and a stable electoral following. The developing coalition of the Left also provided key elements that had not been characteristic of the left: a loyal and coherent opposition, committed to policy rather than to regime alternatives. Thus, by 1981 the party system had gained a large degree of control over political access to all levels of government, dominated the political agenda, and provided the link between the two top officials of the double executive, the president and the prime minister.[4]

In this way, the process of party polarization and consolidation both accentuated political divisions in France and built a bridge of regime stability. The most profound challenges to that stability had come from society during the 1960s (peasants in 1962, miners in 1963, small shopkeepers in 1969–70, and, of course, workers and students in 1968), challenges that also threatened party consolidation on both the Right and the Left. By 1981, however, these social forces, and most of the groups that spoke for them, had been integrated into the party system.

In retrospect, the years between the legislative elections of 1978 and the municipal elections of 1983 were a watershed both for individual parties and for the party system in general. During these years the constraints of the party system were changing. Voter volatility was increasing, partisan identification appeared to be declining, and the established parties (those that Jean-Marie Le Pen has called "the gang of four") were losing their monopoly over the political agenda.

These changing constraints affected all of the established political parties, but their impact on the parties of the Right was profound. In the end, the presidential campaign of 1988, which began with a lack of clear issues and a contest of personalities, posed some important choices to society. The choices were neither the old choices of regime, which had been resolved in 1789, nor the more recent choices between capitalism and socialism, choices favored and then abandoned by the established parties, but choices posed by the "dissident" candidate, Le Pen, which involved the acceptance or rejection of the ethnic diversity that was evident in France of the 1980s.

Thus, our analysis of the evolution of the Right during the past thirty years must be linked to the evolution of the party system, and the relationship of the party system to French society. We will first examine the long consolidation of the coalition of the Right, and then analyze the forces that have undermined its effectiveness. Finally, we will look at the question of emerging centrism in France, and how it is related to the evolution of the coalition of the Right.

The New Party System: Hegemonic Gaullism

1. The Reorganization of the Right: The Electorate

The classic problem for parties of the Right during the Third and Fourth Republics had always been elite fragmentation and poor organization of its mass electoral following.[5] Thus, it appeared as if the consolidation of the Right during the first decade of the Fifth Republic around an increasingly dominant, "catch-all" Gaullist party (Union pour la Nouvelle République [UNR], then Union des Démocrates pour la République [UDR]) finally meant that the right had become more "normal" in European terms, and that the problem of the Right had been overcome.[6]

The numerous parties of the Center-Right were in many ways in deeper trouble than those of the Left during the first years of the Fifth Republic. They were poorly organized, in general disarray, and unable to resist the growing electoral and organizational incursions of the resurgent Gaullist movement. They had allied with the Left to oppose the referendum on the presidency in October 1962 only to suffer an embarrassing defeat at the hands of the electorate. Jean Charlot has developed an impressive case for understanding the emerging Gaullist party as a catchall or "voter-oriented" party, which in the 1960s drew support from a wide range of social groups as well as from those voters who had voted for the Left during the Fourth Republic.[7] Nevertheless, by most measures, the Gaullist surge in the 1960s was largely at the expense of the established parties of the Right, rather than the Left.

The UNR, in 1958, attracted 4.1 million votes, two hundred thousand fewer votes than the Rassemblement pour la France (RPF) had attracted in 1951, and four hundred thousand fewer votes than the moderates had attracted in 1958. Forty-five percent of these votes came from people without party commitments (a tribute to the degree to which party commitment had declined), while most of the remaining votes came from voters who identified with other parties of the Center-Right. Only seven percent of the UNR vote consisted of transfers from voters who identified with either the Socialists or the Communists.[8] In subsequent elections, the number of votes for the Gaullists increased dramatically, but once again at the expense of other parties of the Right, rather than the Left. By 1967, the Gaullists had more than doubled their 1958 vote, to 8.5 million, but the support for other parties of the Right had declined from 6.6 million to 2.8 million.

The consolidation of the Gaullist Right during the first decade of the Fifth Republic touched the sources of strength of the Left only modestly. More than ninety percent of the seats that the Gaullist parties won in these elections were from other Right parties (mostly the Moderates); only seven of the 116 victories were at the expense of the Communists or the Socialists (see below).

Nevertheless, the Gaullists were successful in attracting a significant popular following that otherwise might have gone to the established Left. By 1967, the Gaullists were attracting a proportion of the blue-collar working-class vote that was almost as high as that of the Communists, and far higher than that of the Socialists. Among white-collar workers, the Gaullist vote was higher than that of any other political party (see Table 3.1).

In fact, overall, a very high proportion of French voters changed their votes in the early years of the Fifth Republic, and voter volatility generally worked to the benefit of the parties of the Right, particularly the Gaullists. François Goguel estimated that between 2.7 and 3 million voters moved to the right during this period, about 14 percent of the voting electorate. On the basis of other surveys, the movement may have been even higher. Institut Français d'Opinion Publique (IFOP) estimated that 41 percent of the electorate changed their votes between the 1956 and 1958 legislative elections, 30 percent to the Right, and 10 percent to the Left, with a net benefit of a 20 percent increase for the Right. The largest overall shifts occurred among small shopkeepers, farmers, and blue-collar

Table 3.1   Support for the Communists, Socialists, and Gaullists among
Blue-Collar and White-Collar Workers in France, 1962–78
(% of blue-collar/% white-collar workers responding)

	1962	1967	1973	1978
Communists	26/10	31/18	33/17	36/18
Socialists	26/24	18/22	27/29	31/33
Gaullists	17/27	30/35	22/23	14/19

Sources: Sondages, 1963, no. 2, 64; 1967, no. 3, 55; 1973, no. 1, 21; 1978, no. 1, 22.

workers.[9] There was clearly some shift back to the Left by 1967, but, for the first time since the end of World War II, the Right represented the majority of the electorate.

Duncan Macrae, in his important study of electoral politics during the Fourth Republic, demonstrated that for stable political parties the loyalty of voters was strong and durable. In effect, what this meant was that the stable parties of the Left commanded relatively stable followings from election to election, while voters who supported the more factionalized and transient parties of the Center-Right tended to shift their votes more frequently, first to the Gaullists in 1951, and then to the Poujadistes in 1956.[10]

Gaullists were the most unstable voters during the Fourth Republic. Perhaps the most important change in the party system in the first decade of the Fifth Republic was the stabilization of the Gaullist electorate. In contrast to the Fourth Republic, the most unstable voters during the Fifth were those who had voted for the parties of the Right, parties that had been most stable prior to 1958.

2. Elite Realignment

The result of this electoral movement within the Right can be seen in the redistribution of seats on the right-wing benches of the National Assembly. Many of these new Gaullist votes soundly defeated candidates from other (mostly Right) parties, but a significant proportion represented continuing support for local notables who had switched during the elections of 1962 and 1967 (see Table 3.2). All in all, fifty sitting deputies converted to Gaullism during the first decade of the Fifth Republic. Such conversions were a good measure of the essential localism of much of the Right and the ability of local notables to move their personal strongholds from party to party. They were also an indication of the elite consolidation that was being organized under the Gaullist umbrella at the expense of other parties of the Right.

This consolidation was facilitated by a vast generational turnover of deputies between 1958 and 1962. More than seventy-five percent of the deputies in the new assembly of 1958 had never sat in the assembly before, and by 1962 this percentage had increased to almost eighty percent. The turnover was more important on the less organized Right—among the Gaullists above all—than on the better-organized Left.[11] On the other hand, most of these deputies were not political novices. Almost half of them were departmental councilors, and three-quarters held some local elected office at the time of their election to the assembly in 1958 and 1962.[12] Thus the electoral shift, combined with the effects of the new electoral system, had brought large numbers of local officeholders from small-town France into the ranks of the Right in 1958, and into the Gaullist party by 1962.

Given the strong local bases of the new contingent of deputies sitting under

Table 3.2   Seats Won by the Gaullist Party Either Outright or by Conversion
of a Deputy of Another Party of the Right

	November 1962		March 1967		
	Wins	Converts	Wins	Converts	Total
At the Expense of					
Moderates	39	10	2	15	66
MRP	15	3	8	3	29
Miscellaneous right-wing	—	1	—	—	1
Radicals	4	3	3	3	13
Socialists	2	—	3	—	5
Communists	—	—	2	—	2
Total	60	17	18	21	116

Source: Jean Charlot, *The Gaullist Phenomenon* (New York: Praeger, 1971), p. 76.

the Gaullist banner, it is remarkable—in retrospect—that Gaullism did not become the new radicalism, and that Gaullist leaders in the National Assembly were able to mold these new deputies into a coherent parliamentary majority. Macridis and Brown were understandably wrong when they wrote in 1963 (with the 1951 RPF experience in mind, no doubt):

> The UNR's program and existence are a function of one man's immense popularity and power. The party itself has little in the way of organization, membership, or autonomy. The party of the Fifth Republic, like the regime itself, is not likely to survive De Gaulle's departure from power. . . . It should not be forgotten that many times before in France a legislature elected with one majority ended its career a few years later with a completely different alignment. This includes the first legislature of the Fifth Republic![13]

What Macridis and Brown could not predict was the rapid increase of support for the new institutions, particularly the presidency, among mass publics, an increase that rapidly transcended the personal appeal of Charles de Gaulle. Indeed, the coalition of the Right—"the majority"—was defined and held together by this institutional support. The crisis of 1962 split the largest party of the non-Gaullist right, the Centre National des Indépendants et Paysans (CNIP, the Independents), but put to rest the regime question for the leaders of the majority, which now included the RI (Independent Republicans) led by Giscard d'Estaing. During the 1960s, support for the institutions of the Fifth Republic, together with Gaullist orthodoxies on French foreign policy, became the hub of the organizing discourse of the French Right. At the same time, the opposition, particularly the Left opposition, became identified with opposition to this increasingly popular discourse.

Even as the personal mystique of the General waned after the end of the Algerian War, support for his institutions remained strong, and even increased.[14]

By 1965, seventy-two percent of those polled agreed that the general had established "a regime of personal power in France." Only 18 of the 35 percent that
acknowledged voting for him felt that he had not, and then voted for him in the
first round of the presidential elections that year. The remaining 17 percent came
from the ranks of those who had agreed with the accusation of personal power.[15]
Nevertheless, the same year, almost eighty percent of those surveyed supported
the popularly elected presidency.[16]

3. The Emergence of Party through Leadership

During the first decade of the Fifth Republic, regime support was molded by
party leadership and socialization rather than by consensus of either the electorate
or the deputies. Although political parties were changing their names, fragmenting
and reorganizing with some frequency during this period, voter tendency to orient
themselves in terms of political parties and (especially) in terms of "Left" and
"Right" increased considerably.[17] This was particularly important for the parties
of the Right. Although evaluations of the level of commitment vary considerably
from study to study, the trend is consistent.[18] There was a steady growth in the
percentage of voters reporting that they "identified with" or "felt close to" a
political party.[19] Cameron, as well as Inglehart and Hochstein, report the largest
growth of party commitment during the 1960s among previously uncommitted
voters who increasingly identified with the Gaullist and government parties.
Converse and Pierce demonstrate that by 1967 the largest single group of party
identifiers was those who identified with the Gaullist UNR.[20]

Party discipline also increased. One clear indication of the sea change that took
place among the parties of the Right was the rapid development of parliamentary
voting cohesion among both of the parties associated with the presidential majority
(see Table 3.3). In terms of parliamentary discipline, the parties of the Right
were behaving very much like the more disciplined opposition parties of the Left.
This change is even more interesting if we consider that during most of this

Table 3.3   Indices of Cohesion for Voting in the National Assembly, 1958–73

	1958–62	1962–67	1967–68	1968–73
Communists	99.8	99.8	99.7	99.8
Socialists	97.6	99.6	99.8	99.4
Radicals	63.0	91.7	99.8	94.7
Centrists	73.5	79.5	89.2	76.2
Independent Republicans	60.9	82.9	94.7	86.3
Gaullists	84.2	96.1	96.5	88.9

Source: Frank L. Wilson, "The Revitalization of French Parties," *Comparative Political Studies*
1 (April, 1979).

period, the Gaullists and the RI had only weak national organizational structures, and most of their deputies still had strong local roots reinforced by a long tradition of localism.

A second indication of the growing importance of party discipline was the increased influence of the central party leadership over the nomination process for the National Assembly. For the parties of the Right, this was a slow but cumulative process that had begun in the mid-1960s.[21] The Gaullists directly challenged the tradition of relying on local notables. As Frank Lee Wilson states:

> Instead, the Gaullists have developed a strong central party organization which exercises fairly tight control over the nomination process for the National Assembly elections. In some cases, Gaullist leaders have imposed candidates against Gaullist incumbents deemed incapable or unreliable. When the dissident Gaullist maintains his candidacy in such cases, the voters have nearly always supported the national leadership by rejecting the dissident and voting for the official Gaullist candidate.[22]

The importance of party endorsement had become clear by 1967. Converse and Pierce found that among the candidates for the National Assembly that year, almost ninety percent of the candidates who got more than five percent of the vote in the first round had major party support. Moreover, by 1967 the generational turnover was over. Three-quarters of the incumbent candidates were re-elected, and fewer than ten percent of candidates with no parliamentary experience managed to win.[23]

An indication of the growing importance of party leadership was the commitment of the Gaullists and the RI to the presidential system of the Fifth Republic. Compared with voter attitudes, Table 3.4 indicates the much weaker support for the presidential system among the deputies of all of the major parties both in 1968 and 1973. By 1973, only twenty percent of the deputies were "presidentialists," while forty-one percent supported a more parliamentary system.[24] There

Table 3.4 Percentage of Deputies Supporting Different Constitutional Positions: 1968 and 1973

Party	Presidentialist		Parliamentarian		Accommodator	
	1968	1973	1968	1973	1968	1973
Gaullist	53	46	2	4	44	50
RI	36	25	9	0	54	75
Centrist	17	20	0	0	83	80
Socialist	0	0	43	90	57	10
Communist	0	0	80	91	20	9
Total	38	20	13	41	49	38

Source: Robert J. Jackson, Michael M. Atkinson, and Kenneth D. Hart, "Constitutional Conflict in France: Deputies' Attitudes Toward Executive-Legislative Relations," *Comparative Politics* 4 (July 1977): 408.

had been some weakening of support for the system, even among the Gaullist deputies, after the resignation of President de Gaulle. Table 3.5 shows the hardening of the opposition to the presidential system among the Communists and Socialists, now unified by the Common Program. By 1973, more than half the Gaullists, eighty percent of the Centrists (now part of the presidential majority), seventy-five percent of the RI, and all of the Left opposition were in favor of some alternative to the existing presidential system.

Nevertheless, there were significant differences among the various parties, differences related to their integration within the presidential majority. Presidentialist responses were strongest among the Gaullists, were then weaker for the RI and weakest for the Centrists (committed to the majority for the first time in 1973). Among the parties of the right, the Centrist opposition (*Réformateurs*) had the weakest commitment to the presidential system. By 1973, the newly reorganized Socialist deputies joined the Communists as the strongest supporters of the parliamentary alternative. None of this is surprising, of course, but it does reflect the *relative* importance of party socialization in developing support for the presidential system. Jackson, Atkinson, and Hart found that the role of party socialization of their members proved to be the best (but not the only) variable explaining attitudes toward constitutional change across two parliaments.

Still, given the generally weak support among deputies, it is surprising that the system survived the crisis of May 1968 intact. The party structures of the majority Right clearly constrained the behavior of their deputies, and the divisions among and within the parties of the Right were never translated into a weakening of the presidential system. Thus, party organization and discipline among the parties of the Right strengthened the relatively weak commitment of the deputies to the constitutional arrangements.

The Changing Equilibrium:
The Right without de Gaulle

During the first decade of the Fifth Republic, the foundations that were constructed by the parties of the Right were sufficiently strong to enable the majority

Table 3.5   The Attitudes of Voters to the Roles of President and Parliament, 1967 (percent)

	Maintain or reinforce role of the president		Reinforce role of Parliament	
	Yes	No	Yes	No
Majority	77	13	29	52
Centrist	53	39	49	37
Left	37	51	57	26

Source: IFOP archives, reported by Jean Charlot, *The Gaullist Phenomenon* (New York: Praeger, 1971), p. 57.

coalition to traverse the post-de Gaulle transition of 1969–74. In the 1973 legislative elections the parties of the majority lost ground to the Left, but the cohesion of the Right was maintained, and even strengthened, first by the formal incorporation of Centrist candidates (Centre Democratie et Progrès, CDP) into the parliamentary majority, and second by an agreement on a system of "primaries" in the first round. The *Réformateurs,* dominated by the Radicals headed by Jean-Jacques Servan-Schreiber, were now the only party of the Right that remained outside of the majority. In addition, the majority (the URP) was able to agree on a core program—a pale imitation of the Common Program for Government of the Left—that reflected essential Gaullist orientations in foreign policy, combined with some proposals for reform in social policy and education.

On the other hand, the social and geographic bases of the Gaullists had changed in such a way that the parties of the Right were competing for similar voters in more of the same areas of the country. The Gaullist party of de Gaulle had strong support in the northeast of France and significant electoral strength among blue- and white-collar workers. The Gaullist party of Pompidou had lost electoral support in the northeast and had lost a quarter of its blue- and white-collar support. In 1973, the Gaullist strength was in conservative France and among the more traditional conservative voters.[25]

The key political test for the unity of the Right came during the 1974 presidential election, when the elites of the Gaullists parted. The fact that Chaban-Delmas, the official Gaullist candidate, received only 14.6 percent of the popular vote in the first round was an index of the problems of cohesion that the UDR was confronting at the time. The popularity of the party was closely linked to the problems of the government, whose popularity had waned in 1972–73, and then had sunk further after the 1973 legislative elections, during the first oil crisis in 1973–74.[26]

When Georges Pompidou died on April 2, 1973, Jacques Chaban-Delmas immediately announced his candidacy for the presidency. His candidacy was quickly supported by the leadership of the UDR, but party unity, painfully constructed during the previous decade, began to crumble.[27] Among the UDR deputies, and above all among local officeholders of the party, there was considerable sentiment for a candidate who could unite all the parties of the majority. This sentiment was given concrete reality, first by the brief (one-day) effort of Pierre Messmer to present himself as a unity-candidate, and finally by the organization of a UDR faction of ministers and deputies around Jacques Chirac ("The Appeal of the 43" on April 13), which effectively opposed the party choice.

Valéry Giscard-d'Estaing had announced his candidacy on April 8, presenting himself as the one candidate who could unify the diverse factions of the Right. By the end of the third week of April the polls indicated that in fact large numbers of UDR voters were prepared to abandon Chaban-Delmas in favor of Giscard-d'Estaing.[28] Thus the presidential election of 1974 reflected the divisions within the UDR and demonstrated the limits of support for an official candidate of the party, even a former prime minister. Clearly, the linchpin of the majority could have fragmented after the electoral debacle of May, 1974. However, the impact of the election was to shift the balance of forces within the UNR, and between the UNR and the other parties of the majority.

Although weakened by the divisions that had emerged during the electoral campaign, the Party (now called the Rassemblement pour la République [RPR]) was reconstructed and rebuilt by Jacques Chirac. As prime minister (from 1974–76), he wrested control of the party secretariat and forced the party "barons" into the background. He gained the support of party militants and within a year had secured his position as party leader. After he resigned as prime minister in August 1976, he consolidated his control over the newly named party through a change in statutes, adopted in December 1976.

The party was never able to regain the electoral losses to the Center that it suffered in 1974, and, in this sense, it lost its domination of the Right. On the other hand, it more than doubled its membership between 1973 and 1978 to 620,000 members, and strengthened its organizational structure throughout the country, thus resisting a drift of militants toward the centrist parties.[29]

During the years after the presidential election, Giscard-d'Estaing attempted, and failed, to construct a broader center party within the larger presidential majority. In 1974 there seemed to be a real prospect of a breakup of the RPR, and the various centrist groups coalesced around his presidency.[30] What did emerge were shifting coalitions of parliamentary groups—in fact shifting coalitions of notables without any real party coherence—between 1974 and the legislative elections of 1978. In fact, this was a more constrained version of the politics of the *marais* that was the continuing heritage of the Right. Giscard-d'Estaing's effort largely failed, in part because of Chirac's success in rebuilding the RPR, and also because of the limits imposed by the Union of the Left. The final result of the president's efforts was the electoral arrangement of the Union pour la Démocratie Française (UDF) in January 1978.

The UDF was more than the usual coalition of centrist parties, since the federation was able to agree on a group of four hundred candidates for the 1978 legislative elections, which represented a considerable strengthening of factional parties of the center. Since both the UDF and the RPR conservative electorates had become essentially similar during the 1970s, the electoral competition between the two parties was intense and strongly personal.[31] Thus, among the parties of the Right, the elections of 1978 were a confrontation of notables rather than of parties, a complex of local elections dominated by personalities who benefited from either incumbency or a position of local power, or from both. Although more than half of the UDF deputies elected in 1978 were new to the assembly, more than three-quarters of them held local office at the time they ran.[32] Nevertheless, in retrospect, within the Right, within the Left, and between Left and Right, 1978 marked a high point of party-defined competition in France.

However, in order to understand the transformation of the French Right during the 1980s, it is important to emphasize not only the development of a party system within the Right, but the nature of that system. The RPR had been created and constructed as a party of power, with a structure oriented to the needs of its leader—first to de Gaulle and Pompidou, and then to Chirac. It had been portrayed by Jean Charlot as "a voter-oriented and dominant party" in 1971. By 1978, it was still voter-oriented, but no longer dominant. In addition, its voter-orientation had changed considerably during the 1970s, and it could no longer be seen as a "catchall" party, one with significant support throughout the electorate. Like its rival, the UDF, the portrait of its electorate was classically conservative, and its membership was best established in Catholic and conservative France.[33] The RPR was organizationally strong, but it was losing many of its voters to the UDF.

The UDF, on the other hand, was organizationally weak. Its membership strength was based in the Parti Républicain (PR) (formerly the RI), but it was more characteristically a classic cadre party of local office holders and deputies, with little to bind it together except competition with the RPR and opposition to the Left. Through leadership and elite agreement, the two parties of the Right had consolidated virtually every faction of the Right and, by organizing the electorate of the Right, had eliminated the "flash party" phenomenon of the Fourth Republic.

Thus, the new party system of the Right was indeed different from the classic Right of the Third and Fourth Republics in terms of its parliamentary behavior and discipline. It was also organizationally stronger than the factions of the Right that had preceded it. In relationship to the larger party system, the fluid center *marais* that shifted between Left and Right at different levels of government had disappeared from French parliamentary politics. Nevertheless, the UDF, the electorally ascendant party of the Right, was less organized, and both parties were dependent on the ability of strong leaders for their organizational stability and for the way they attracted voters. By 1978, the RPR had lost its essential calling as "the guardian of the new institutions [that] has to rely on the electors alone for its survival for the preservation of its institutional accomplishments and its pursuit of French grandeur."[34] It was now part of a coalition dominated by a non-Gaullist prime minister. Many of the values of Gaullism dominated the coalition, but, at the same time, the Gaullists had largely lost their specific identification. In 1985, when voters who classified themselves as "Gaulliste" by persuasion were asked whom they should support, fewer than half chose Jacques Chirac (forty-seven percent); thirty-seven percent chose Raymond Barre.[35]

Indeed, identification had become a more general problem for the parties of the Right and for those who supported them. By the second decade of the Fifth Republic, what Jane Jenson calls in this volume the "organizing discourse of Gaullism" no longer provided a powerful mobilizing force of unity for the Right. This problem was accentuated after 1981, when the Left no longer contested the Gaullist regime. As long as the Gaullist discourse served to define the Right, the coherence that it provided could mask the importance of a second phenomenon, the decline of Catholicism, historically the cultural basis for the political Right in France. Although church attendance has continued to be the best predictor of voting for the Right in France, by most measures regular attendance had declined to less than ten percent of the adult population in the 1980s (half that of the 1960s).[36] On the one hand, the coalition of the Right in power endured these changes reasonably well. What Emmanuel Todd has called "the secular right," parties of the Right with no direct connection to traditional Catholicism, dominated the coalition of the Right by the 1980s, and were electing deputies outside of the traditional Catholic areas of the country.[37] On the other hand, the lack of an organizing discourse, compounded by a shrinking cultural base, posed some serious problems for the stability of the coalition of the Right after the victory of the Left in 1981.

The Challenge of the 1980s:
The Right without Gaullism

1. Electoral Volatility

The electorate of the 1980s had been organized and molded by the developing party system of the first two decades of the Fifth Republic. However, in retrospect, it is now clear that just at the point when the party system was most consolidated, the electorate had begun to change and to challenge the stability of the Right. In general, while interest in politics and willingness to engage in political activity had remained as strong as ever, it appeared that disillusionment with those in politics was growing, and general attachments to established political parties by the French electorate had been diminishing since the late 1970s.[38]

Even before 1981, only a small minority (twenty-two percent) of the French people surveyed expressed confidence "in political parties in general," and this support did not increase even during the honeymoon period of the government of the Left.[39] When asked about specific parties in 1983, respondents expressed considerable more confidence than they had in the more general survey. However, they expressed a poorer opinion of the opposition parties of the right than of the Socialists, despite the defeat in local elections of the Socialist-led government eight months before the survey, and despite the generally low confidence in the policies of the government of the Left expressed during this same period. In fact, for only two of the parties did a "good opinion" outweigh a "poor opinion"—the Socialists and the RPR—with the positive gap slightly wider for the Socialists.[40]

If positive support for all established parties has diminished, negative rejection of all of the major parties has grown. Rejection (respondents stating that there is a party that they would never vote for under any circumstances) generally increased during the Fifth Republic as the electorate became increasingly polarized, particularly among the electorate of the Right rejecting the resurgent parties of the Left.[41]

However, rejection of parties of the Right remained relatively modest in the 1960s. What has changed is the tendency toward increased rejection after 1979 of parties of both the Right and the Left (See Table 3.6). The policy failures of the Left certainly increased hostility toward the Socialists, and the increased hostility towards the Communists probably goes back to the elections of 1978. Nevertheless, it is striking that the established parties of the Right have not become more attractive as hostility toward the Left has grown.

These patterns of diminishing support and increasing hostility appear to have been translated into declining voter loyalty during the post-1981 period. There has been a growing support for a smaller, rather than a larger, role for political parties in the political process. As Jean Charlot documents, in the 1960s the weight of opinion was in favor of parties, rather than individual politicians, playing a more important role. By 1979, this trend had been reversed, and by 1983 there was a strong trend of support for a diminished party role. This trend was most pronounced among the supporters of the Right, whose attachment to political parties had always been weaker than that of supporters of the Left.[42]

Partisan identification has also declined. In a series of surveys conducted by *Eurobarometre* between 1977 and 1981, French respondents claiming to be "very close" or "fairly close" to a political party declined from a high of 29 percent in 1978 to 17 percent in 1984; those claiming to have "no ties to any party" rose from a low of 29 percent in 1978 to 42 percent in 1984. The same pattern is evident in other European democracies during this period, but the French trend is more accentuated (see Figure 3.1).

However, diminishing commitments to political parties in France has not resulted in diminishing interest in, or commitment to, politics and political participation. Politicization, in the sense of interest in politics, willingness to join political parties, attend meetings, and join street demonstrations organized by a political party, increased after 1978, particularly among women.[43] Therefore, by the early 1980s, an increasingly large number of voters in France were less committed to particular political parties, but were still committed to politics and were available for political mobilization.

In these circumstances, it is hardly surprising that voter volatility (roughly the percentage of voters who move from one party to another) in France rapidly accelerated after 1978, following a long period of decline during the earlier part

Table 3.6   Percentage of Voters Rejecting Parties of the Right and the Left: 1979–81

Year	PCF	PS	UDF	RPR
1979	46	11	18	25
1984	58	18	22	26
1985	63	20	20	27

Sources: Gérard Le Gall, "Radiographie de l'image du P.C.F.," *Révue Politique et Parliamentaire,* January–February 1985.

Figure 3.1   Party Involvement [% "Close to party / % "No Ties"]

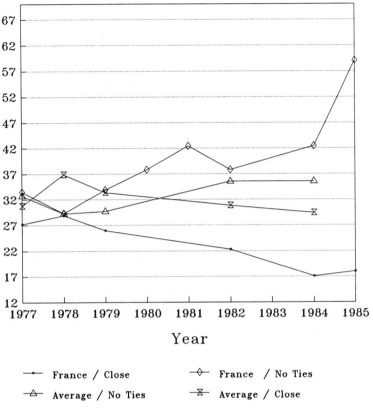

Year

- France / Close   France / No Ties
- Average / No Ties   Average / Close

Source: Eurobarometre 8, 10–12, 17, 21
Sofres, 1987, p. 162
"Average" includes France, W. Germany, the UK, Belgium, Holland and Denmark.

of the Fifth Republic (see Table 3.7). Between 1981 and 1984 only 40 percent of the electorate voted consistently for a (any) party of the Right or the Left (another 9.6 percent consistently abstained), compared with 59 percent between 1973 and 1978. However, this voter instability was only of marginal benefit for the established parties of the Right, since only 10 percent of the "unstable" voters shifted their support from Left to Right between 1981 and 1984. Most of the rest simply abstained.[45]

Granted, the elections for the European Parliament in 1984 generally provoked little enthusiasm in France (or in other European countries). However, given the high level of political interest, as well as the widely perceived impression of the 1984 election as a domestic poll, the level of abstention should probably be interpreted as a rebuke to the Right as well as to the Left.

In fact, this impression is supported by the inability of the established parties

Table 3.7   The Volatility of the French Party System, 1948–1986

1948–59	1960–69	1970–78	1979–86
21.8	11.9	7.8	12.5

Source: recalculated and updated from Mogen Pedersen, "Changing Patters of Electoral Volatility in European Party Systems, 1948–1977: Explorations in Explanation," in Hans Daalder and Peter Mair, ed., *West European Party Systems* (Beverly Hills, Calif.: Sage Publications, 1983), p. 39.

of the Right to increase significantly their electoral support among registered voters in any recent election (see Table 3.8). It is also supported by the tendency among voters who were alienated by the policies of the government of the Left (who did not abstain) to shift their vote to Le Pen rather than to one of the established parties of the Right.

A survey in May 1984 indicated that among those voters who supported Mitterrand in the second round of the presidential election of 1981, and intended to vote for the Right in the European elections the following month, about 500,000 (over one-third) planned to vote for the list headed by Le Pen rather than for the Veil list.[46] In 1986, an exit poll indicated that almost 600,000 of the 2.7 million National Front voters had supported Mitterrand in 1981.[47] And, in the first round of the presidential elections of 1988, about 500,000 voters who had supported the Left in 1986 (eighty percent of them Socialist) transferred their votes to Le Pen.[48] Thus, if we presume only a minimal movement back to previous parties or to the established Right, about a million voters who transferred from Left to Right between 1981 and 1986 moved to the National Front. This represents about a third of the Left-Right transfers in 1986, and about half of these transfers in 1988.

2. The New Framework of Competition:
The National Front and the Divided Right

Within the Right, voter volatility established a new framework of competition. Until the 1980s, the dynamics of competition within the Right were established by the electoral and organizational challenge to the hegemony of the Gaullists, in their various manifestations, by the non-Gaullist parties of the Center-Right. The Union of the Left precluded a centrist alternative, and the need to maintain a presidential majority of the Right in the National Assembly defined the framework within which the parties of the Right could maneuver. For the non-Gaullist parties of the Right, the dynamics of competition required increased unity.

After 1981, the framework and dynamics of competition were gradually altered by the challenge of the National Front. The National Front has provided both a means of protest against all of the established political parties, as well as a

Table 3.8   Major Party Support among Registered Voters in Elections before and after 1981 (% of registered voters for each party)

I. *Elections to the European Parliament*

	1979	1984
PCF	13	6
PS	15	11
UDF	17	
	} 27	} 23
RPR	10	
Abstention	39	43

II. *Cantonal Elections*

	1979	1985	1982	1988
PCF	14	8	11	6
PS	18	17	21	16
UDF	13	12	12	
	} 21	} 23	} 24	} 21
RPR	8	11	12	
Abstention	35	36	32	51

III. *Legislative Elections*
(first round)

	1973	1978	1981	1986	1988
PCF	17	17	11	7	7
PS	15	20	26	24	24
UDF	13	20	15		12
	} 42	} 39	} 30	} 32	} 24
RPR	29	19	15		12
Abstention	19	17	29	22	34

IV. *Presidential Elections*
(first round)

	1981	1988
PCF	12	5
PS	21	27
UDF	23	13
	} 37	} 29
RPR	14	16

Results reported by the Ministry of the Interior: *Le Monde, Les élections législatives du mars, 1986* (Paris: Suppl. aux dossiers et documents du Monde, 1986), p. 68; *Le Monde,* March 12, 1985, p. 6; *Le Monde,* April 26, 1988, p. 1; *Le Monde, Les élections législatives de juin, 1988* (Paris: Supp. aux dossiers et documents du Monde, 1988), p. 30; *Le Monde,* September 27, 1988, p. 2.

positive pole of attraction by its position on immigration and law and order.[49] The movement away from party commitment, in general, has vastly increased the political opportunities for a party like the National Front to mobilize voters (particularly those of the Right) who are most concerned about immigration and security.

The presence of North African immigrants in France has been a social issue of some importance for the past twenty years, and for most of that time the National Front has been attempting to mobilize voters around this issue. However, it was only when declining commitment to other parties ("the gang of four," as Le Pen calls them) liberated large numbers of voters from their previous party attachments that the National Front was able to attract a significant percentage of voters.

By attracting almost ten percent of the vote in 1984, the National Front was able to transform a social issue, about which there was considerable concern, into a political issue, about which political parties and political leaders have been forced to take policy positions, and around which political debate has been organized. Before 1988, no more than ten percent of the electorate had voted for the National Front. However, the acceptance of the "ideas" of the party has been considerably higher.

In May 1984, SOFRES found that 18 percent of those surveyed (and 21 percent of those who responded) "felt a lot or some sympathy for Jean-Marie Le Pen." Among those with a party preference, sympathizers increased to 37 percent of the supporters of the RPR, 24 percent of those of UDF, and 9 percent each of the supporters of the Socialists and the Communists. These sympathizers constituted a reservoir of legitimacy for the National Front. Even higher percentages agreed with Le Pen's position on immigrants, law and order (*sécurité*), and "the struggle against Communism."[50]

General agreement with the ideas of J.-M. Le Pen diminished somewhat after 1984 (from 26 percent in 1984 to 18 percent in 1987, to 16 percent in 1988), but acceptance of specific positions remained high. Almost a third of the respondents to a SOFRES survey in the spring of 1987 declared their agreement with the immigration and security issues raised by the leader of the National Front. This diminished to about twenty-five percent at the end of 1988, but approval of Le Pen's positions on these important issues seemed to define the political space in which the National Front could continue to harvest electoral support.[51]

The dynamics of political competition, accentuated by the uncertainties that have been created by voter volatility, has enabled the National Front to impose much of its agenda on its competitors among the parties of the Right. The established parties of the Right have wrestled with several alternative strategies for dealing with the FN since 1983: (a) attempt to ignore the National Front and its issues and hope that in isolation (encouraged by a return to single-member districts for the National Assembly) the party would just disappear; (b) oppose with conviction the policies of the National front, and thus appeal to voters on the left of center (and cede perhaps ten percent of the vote to the National Front); or (c) embrace the issues of the National Front and undermine its ability to mobilize voters who have deserted the established Right. Different parties (and personalities) within the Right have pursued each of these strategies, and, at different times, the same parties and leaders have attempted to shift from one strategy to another. As a result, immigration and security are among the principal issues around which political competition has been organized within the Right.

Estimates of the impact of the change in the electoral law from proportional representation to single-member constituencies were that the National Front would not be able to win more than two seats in the next legislative elections. However, with a presidential election in 1988, with a National Front parliamentary group from 1986–88 important for the maintenance of the governing majority, and with the National Front holding the balance of power in five of the new regional governments elected in 1986, it was somewhat premature to write off the party as a national political force.[52] Indeed, Le Pen's early declaration of his presidential candidacy in the spring of 1987 magnified the political impact of the policy positions of the National Front.

Le Pen has been particularly adept at defining the issues to which other parties and political leaders have felt compelled to react. What had become a familiar pattern emerged once again in the spring of 1987, after the announcement of the Le Pen candidacy.[53] On May 6, 1987, the leader of the National Front was interviewed on a widely viewed television talk show, *l'Heure de Vérité,* and repeated a number of well-known National Front positions, the most prominent of which dealt with various aspects of the immigration problem.[54] He vowed to deal with immigration by organizing the "return [*sic*]" of 400,000 unemployed immigrants, to deny immigrants any right to claim benefits from the French welfare and social security system, and to reserve jobs for French people first. He implied a link between immigrants and the growing problem of AIDS, urged widespread testing, and elaborated an analysis of the nature of the disease that appeared to go well beyond accepted medical opinion. He also pledged to cooperate with other candidates of the Right in the second round of the presidential elections.[55]

As in the past, the interview was regarded as a challenge by other leaders of the right, and Le Pen's remarks set the political agenda for a debate that endured most of the summer. Once again, the focus on immigration, and now AIDS, accentuated differences within the Right both with regard to strategy (how to deal with the Le Pen challenge) and with regard to policy. In the context of the presidential campaign, however, the debate was more intense than it had been before.

On the one side (then) Minister of the Interior Pasqua called for a recommitment against illegal immigration and (then) Prime Minister Chirac revived the consideration of the revision of the naturalization code that had been placed on hold at the time of the student demonstrations at the end of 1986. Pasqua had urged the RPR to take a strong stand on immigration before the National Front had made its electoral gains, and Chirac appeared to be using the proposed legislation as a way of underlining the solutions that the government had to the problems raised by Le Pen.[56]

On the other side were the "liberal" leaders of the UDF, as well as some important politicians from the RPR. François Léotard, minister of culture and communications and leader of the Parti Républicain, rapidly distanced himself from the "firmer" positions of Pasqua and Chirac. He first opposed permitting Le Pen to take the lead in defining issues for the majority, while acknowledging that it was possible for the National Front to prevent a victory of the Right in the presidential elections in 1988. He then publicly hinted that he might run for the presidency himself, only to back down when the prime minister suggested that he resign from his ministry if he intended to be a candidate. Nevertheless, Léotard continued to maintain his distance from the *durs* within the government with regard to issues of immigration and the National Front.[57]

Far stronger positions, however, were taken by one of Léotard's Parti Républicain colleagues, Claude Malhuret, and by Michel Noir of the RPR. Malhuret, (then) Secretary of State for the Rights of Man, had consistently opposed the tougher actions of the Ministry of the Interior with regard to immigration, and had warned against the acceptance of the "brutal solutions" proffered by the National Front. Michel Noir, minister of foreign trade, clearly stated the dilemma of the Right by challenging the government on moral grounds. "The responsibility of a politician is not only to win elections," he argued. "It is also to make sure that our society does not forget the values on which it was built. For that, I am of the conviction that we must be able to bypass partisan interests and even accept losing elections."[58]

The political dilemma was accentuated once again, a month later, by the local elections in Grasse, made necessary by a split in the Right-majority coalition, provoked in part by the local coalition with the National Front. Indeed, with the FN attracting more than twenty percent of the vote in Grasse, the Right probably could not have maintained their majority without the support or neutrality of the FN. When the mayor, who headed the list of the Right supported by a majority of the outgoing council members, insisted on maintaining six National Front councilors on his list, the national parties of the established Right refrained from strongly supporting his list in the election. Instead (with the exception of the Radical party) they encouraged voters not to permit the Left to win because of this split. The mayor's list was victorious in the second round, with fifty-six percent of the vote, and the National Front councilors once again took their place on the city council.

A month earlier, the national secretary of the RPR, Jacques Toubon had vowed—in response to the remarks by Le Pen on *l'Heure de Vérité*—that the RPR would not participate at any level in a coalition with the National Front.[59] However, confronted with the possibility of an electoral loss in Grasse, Toubon urged support for the coalition list.[60] François Léotard condemned elected officials "who give the extreme Right a certificate of respectability," and "letters of credit" to men whose proposals "are not responsible." He argued that the coalition in Grasse was "a grave error," but failed to note that members of the political bureau of his own party (Jean-Claude Gaudin and Jacques Blanc) had in fact formed alliances with the National Front at the regional level.[61]

The strongest position was taken by the national bureau of the Radical Party, which voted to exclude the mayor of Grasse for defying the national policy of the party. The national secretary of the party, André Rossinot, made it clear that the intention of the party was "not to cut off from the national community 10–12 percent of the electorate," but to challenge the policies of the "hard core of the National Front, which exploits with a certain demagoguery the anxieties of Frenchmen." Nevertheless, even here the dilemma of the Right was revealed by the opposition of the honorary president of the Radical Party, Edgar Faure, to this exclusion, and by the support that the mayor received from regional Radical politicians.[62]

While for some politicians of the Right opposition to the National Front and its policies was a matter of principle, for most an ambiguity was determined by practical considerations of electoral competition and coalition building. Jean Lecanuet (who has supported coalitions with the National Front) and Claude Malhuret (who has opposed such coalitions) agreed on one thing: that the role of the National Front in the French party system resembles a mirror image of that of the Communist Party (Parti Communiste Française, PCF) for the Left. For twenty years, the PCF, by frightening centrist electors, prevented the Socialists from attaining power. For Lecanuet, the error was not to recognize the success of the Mitterrand strategy, and thus not to accept the support of the National Front. "We call it national discipline," he argued.[63] For Malhuret, such an alliance would drive the centrist electors to the Left: "The liberal right, if it does not understand that it must not form an alliance with [the FN], will commit the same error [as the Socialists] that would lead down the same road. . . . If the majority remains silent, it will not win back its electors."[64]

However, if the relationship between the PS and the PCF is to be used as a model, it certainly is not clear that the Union de la Gauche did not work to the benefit of the PS, particularly in electoral terms. In the process, the policy positions of the PS shifted sharply to the left in the 1970s. If Lecanuet was correct (and his position was close to that of Chirac and especially Pasqua at the time), then the policy positions of the National Front on immigration would be coopted by the mainstream parties of the Right, and Malhuret and Noir were fighting a losing cause. In the cauldron of electoral competition, the temptation of moving toward the policies of the National Front seems to be difficult to resist.

The emotions evoked by the National Front have also challenged the unity of the Right, both within parties and among them. On the electoral level, the RPR and the UDF have worked reasonably well together since 1981, both in opposition and in government. They agreed on a common list for the European elections in 1984 and on common lists in two-thirds of the departments for the legislative elections in 1986, and cooperated in maximizing their chances in the second round of the 1988 legislative elections under the banner of the Union des Républicains de Centre (URC). However, the strong electoral challenge of Jean-Marie Le Pen, with over fourteen percent of the vote in the presidential elections of 1988, had an impact on all of the parties of the Right and resulted in a severe division between the RPR and the UDF, as well as a divisions among the leaders of both parties.

The leadership of the RPR rapidly made overtures to the National Front voters as well as to the party. Prime Minister Chirac announced on television that he "had heard" the fifteen percent of the electorate that had supported Le Pen; Minister of the Interior Pasqua, noting that "the National Front supports the same values as the majority," made available to the FN the Tuilerie Gardens for their annual May 1 celebration of *la fête Jeanne d'Arc*.[65]

The divisions within the UDF were particularly important between the Centre des Démocrates Sociaux (CDS), many of whose leaders were aroused by the support for Le Pen, and "La bande de Léo" (Léotard) within the Parti Républicain (PR), who were more inclined to draw closer to the RPR during this time of crisis. The Le Pen vote seemed to shatter the hold of the liberals on the Parti Républicain. Even before the second round of the presidential election, CDS leaders were privately discussing a parliamentary alliance with the Socialists and/ or the disintegration of the UDF.[66]

The decline of the National Front vote to its 1986 level (9.7 percent) in the first round of the June legislative elections considerably eased the pressure on the URC parties. Nevertheless, they felt compelled to "permit" local parties to make "arrangements" with the National Front to maximize their chances of victory. This was particularly important in the Marseilles region, where the URC negoti- ated eight (of the nine) arrangements for the maintenance of National Front candidates as the official candidates of the Right coalition. Only one of the National Front candidates won in the second round (Mme. Yann Piat in the Var), but the National Front candidates that remained increased their electoral support by almost fourteen percent.[67]

The electoral stagnation of the Right, however, provoked a leadership crisis that was accentuated by Mitterrand's flirtation with *ouverture* and the creation of a Left-Center coalition. Within the RPR, a leadership struggle emerged between reformers—led by Philippe Séguin—committed to drawing a clear line between the RPR and the National Front, as well as to internal party reform, and more hard-line party leaders, led by Bernard Pons and the new general secretary of the party named by Chirac, Alain Juppé. In the election for leader of the parliamentary group, Pons won by one vote. As a result, the party officially recognized the existence of a reformist current.[68]

Within the UDF the division was more severe. Tempted by the long-term possibility of the emergence of a Left-Center majority, as well as by the softness of other leaders of the UDF towards the National Front (the UDF in the Bouches du Rhône had taken the lead in negotiating electoral agreements), the Barrist CDS withdrew from the UDF parliamentary group, and formed its own group, now called the UDC (Union du Centre), with a third of the UDF deputies. The UDC has continued to emphasize its links with the UDF. It opposed the Rocard government's plan to modify the *loi Pasqua* on immigration as a "maneuver," along with the other parties of the opposition, and cooperated with the UDF in organizing electoral lists for the 1989 local elections. On the other hand, it has played an important role in sustaining the Rocard government. The 1989 budget, for example, was approved with the abstention of the PCF and the UDC, and the opposition of the RPR and UDF.[69]

3. Sociological Division and the Search for Ideological Coherence

The division of the Right in 1988 was conditioned by the emergence of three separable electorates. In contrast to the decade of the 1970s, when the electorates of the RPR and the UDF were sociologically similar, and marginally divided by some policy positions, the electorates of the three Rights in 1988 were distinct both sociologically and, in some important ways, politically. Sociologically, the Chirac electorate most resembles that of the traditional right. He attracted disproportionate numbers of older voters, farmers, professionals who work for themselves, and top executives. Barre attracted comparatively younger voters, a larger proportion of teachers, and white-collar workers. Finally, Le Pen brought to the Right a large percentage of small shopkeepers, but also a working-class electorate of blue-collar and white-collar workers, as well as a large percentage of service people.

Politically, Chirac voters tended to have the strongest identification with the Right, while Barre and Le Pen voters tended to have more mixed commitments. Chirac voters were more likely to vote for "personality" rather than for ideas or a party; Barre voters were more inclined to vote for ideas; and three-quarters of Le Pen voters claimed to be voting for ideas rather than for personality. Three issues clearly separated supporters for the three candidates: attitudes toward the death penalty, attitudes toward a multiracial society, and attitudes toward an agreement between Chirac and Le Pen. The death penalty was supported most strongly by Le Pen supporters, followed by Chirac supporters, and then by Barre voters. Support for a Chirac-Le Pen agreement followed the same order, support for a multiracial society followed the reverse order.[70]

The differences among the parties of the post-Gaullist right, finally, have also been conditioned by changing patterns of ideological commitment. On one hand, the RPR commitment to the old *étatist* Gaullism appears to be quite dead, and

the ideological slippage conducted by Jacques Chirac for the past seven years has almost totally erased the opposition between the liberal Right and the Gaullist Right. In 1987, we are far from the Gaullist anathemas against atlanticism. . . . It also takes a long memory to remember the Gaullist references to the state and to the ardent obligation to the plan.[71]

Thus, there has been—more or less—an ideological convergence of the two established parties of the Right around neoliberalism.

However, among the militants of the RPR, there has been a strong attraction to the program of the National Front. This attraction was indicated by a survey of delegates at the RPR national congress in 1984. The survey found that the delegates (from local sections) perceived themselves to be considerably to the Right of the party as a whole, and were much further to the Right than the delegates at the RPR Congress in 1978. It was the youngest and the most recently recruited militants who perceived themselves to be the furthest to the Right.

The most important finding for our study was that there had been a sharp increase in the positive acceptability of the National Front among these delegates. Indeed, twenty-five percent felt more positively about the National Front than about two of the principal parties in the UDF (CDS and PR).[72] Here, too, the strongest support for the National Front was among those militants recruited into the party since 1978 and among those with local, rather than national, responsibilities. Thus, in important ways, the gap that opened up between the two established parties of the right after the 1988 elections has been coming for some time, and has been stimulated by the rise of the National Front.

Centrism and the French Right

There are certainly good reasons to conclude that French politics have been moving toward the center. Opposition to the regime is no longer important in French political life either on the Right or on the Left; ideological alternatives for society and the economy—choices of society, "rupture"—are no longer being proposed by French political parties of either the Left or the Right; and public opinion clearly no longer favors either the statist proposals offered by the Union of the Left in 1981 or the radical privatization offered by the Right in 1986.[73] These changes indicate a certain level of agreement in French political life (support for the institutions of the regime, the basic lines of the welfare state, and a somewhat altered mixed economy), but also an exhaustion of important political alternatives among political elites.

In the short run, centrism also seems to mean that France will be governed by parties that will cross the Left-Right division, a move facilitated by the ideological convergence that has taken place and by the fragmentation taking place among the parties of the UDF. It appears that a somewhat different form of the *marais* is reappearing with the sponsorship of the Elysée.

However, a case can also be made that France is moving toward a redefinition of Left and Right, and that this centrist period is a stage of that redefinition. In fact, what seems to have happened during the past decade is that the Left can no longer be defined in terms of choices of society and the Right has lost its mission as the defender of the regime. The Socialist Left has become the party of government, more acceptable in that role, ironically, than it has ever been before. In a survey published in 1987, respondents indicated that what pleased them most about the Socialist party was that it spoke to all French people without difference, and that the Socialists were as capable as or more capable than any other party in every policy area proposed by the survey. Thus, in many ways the Right has abandoned to the Left two of the key attributes of the center: the image of stability and that of flexibility.[74]

The Right, without a hegemonic party, and without a strong mission, has been defined most clearly by the challenge of the social issues identified by the National Front. Thus, on the basis of these issues, the RPR has been drawn further to the right by its leaders and militants, and by the response of a diminished electorate, while the various elements of the UDF have been forced to redefine themselves in terms of these new social issues. Nevertheless, both the RPR and the UDF have been thrown into considerable disarray by this evolution. Although the institutional orientation and even many of the market ideas of the liberal center have been taken over by the Socialist governments, the politicians of the center have pushed more and more to the Right. The Gaullist glue is gone, and liberalism has proven to be a weak organizing dialogue with which to build unity in opposition.

Therefore, below the level of regime agreement, a volatile electorate has fueled sharpening disagreements among the elites of the Right on the future of French society, disagreements that are separating the RPR from the parties of the center and fragmenting the parties of the center. Centrism will not necessarily mean diminished conflict, and it may very well mean an increase in political instability, as electoral volatility undermines the stability of parliamentary majorities.

Notes

1. Debré's remarks are cited by William G. Andrews, *Presidential Government in Gaullist France* (Albany: State University of New York Press, 1982), p. 157. Chapter 6 is particularly good in demonstrating the irrelevance of much of the constitutional baggage for the control of parliament, given the emergence of a cohesive parliamentary majority.

2. See Philip G. Cerny, "The Political Balance," in Philip G. Cerny and Martin A. Schain, eds., *French Politics and Public Policy* (New York: St. Martin's Press, 1980), pp. 1–25.

3. Frédéric Bon and Jean-Paul Cheylan, *La France Qui Vote* (Paris: Hachette, 1988), pp. 206–8. The authors emphasize this style of an increasingly consolidated Right as an essential aspect in the movement of voters toward the Left.

4. See Cerny, "The New Rules of the Game in France," in Cerny and Schain, eds., *French Politics and Public Policy,* pp. 26–47.

5. Maurice Duverger, *Political Parties* (New York: W. W. Norton, 1955), chap. 12.

6. This is the general argument in Chapter 3 of Jean Charlot's book, *The Gaullist Phenomenon* (New York: Praeger, 1971). Charlot's notion of a "voter-directed party" seems to be generally the same as the concept of a "catchall party" outlined by Otto Kirchheimer in his "The Transformation

of Western European Party Systems" in Joseph Lapalombara and Myron Weiner, eds., *Political Parties and Political Development* (Princeton, N.J.: Princeton University Press, 1966), pp. 177–200.

7. Jean Charlot, *The Gaullist Phenomenon*, chap. 3.

8. *Sondages*.

9. *Sondages*, no. 4 (1960): 18–19 and 26–27.

10. Duncan Macrae, Jr., *Parliament, Parties and Society in France, 1946–1958* (New York: St. Martin's Press, 1967), pp. 232–43.

11. Roy C. Macridis and Bernard E. Brown analyze the turnover for 1958 in *The De Gaulle Republic* (Homewood, Illinois: Dorsey Press, 1960), pp. 276–78.

12. This is elaborated by Roy Pierce in *French Politics and Political Institutions* (New York: Harper and Row, 1968).

13. Macridis and Brown, *The De Gaulle Republic*, p. 86.

14. See Charlot, *The Gaullist Phenomenon*, pp. 52–58.

15. *Sondages*, no. 4 (1965).

16. Charlot, *The Gaullist Phenomenon*, p. 56.

17. Connverse and Pierce, using the results of their panel surveys of 1967–69, and comparing them with Converse and Dupeux's 1958 survey, found a considerable increase in Left and Right identification, but only a small increase of identification with specific political parties. See Philip E. Converse and Roy Pierce, *Political Representation in France* (Cambridge, Mass.: Belknap Press, 1986), p. 77.

18. For a review of this literature, see Annick Percheron and Kent Jennings, "Political Continuities in French Families," *Comparative Politics* 13 (July 1981), and Frank L. Wilson, "The French Party System since 1981," *Contemporary French Civilization*, (Fall–Winter 1983–84).

19. For a summary of estimates of party identification since 1958, see Jean Charlot, "Exposé introductif: l'évolution de l'image des partis politiques en France." Paper presented at the Congress of the International Political Science Association, Paris, July 1985. See also Peter Mair, "Party Politics in Contemporary Europe: A Challenge to Party?" *West European Politics* 7 (October 1984): 179.

20. See David Cameron, "Stability and Change in Patterns of French Partisanship," *Public Opinion Quarterly* 36 (1972): 19–30; Ronald Inglehart and Avram Hochstein, "Alignment and Dealignment of the Electorate in France and the United States," *Comparative Political Studies* 5 (1972): 359; Converse and Pierce, *Political Representation in France*, chap. 3, n. 7. Among the youngest age cohorts, however, the parties of the Left opposition also made sizable gains. Converse and Pierce are highly critical of the articles cited here by Hochstein and Inglehart, and by Cameron. They note that the (1968) IFOP survey, from which both articles draw much of their data, is essentially biased toward inflating party identification when compared with the Converse and Dupeux results of 1958. As proof, they cite their own survey of 1968, which shows much lower levels of party identification and only a modest increase over 1958. See Converse and Pierce, chap. 3, pp. 928–29, no. 7. Nevertheless, the high level of identification with the UNR is also supported by the Converse and Pierce results. Converse and Pierce, *Political Representation in France*, pp. 80–81.

21. See Charlot, *The Gaullist Phenomenon*, chap. 5.

22. Frank L. Wilson, "The Revitalization of French Parties," *Comparative Political Studies* 1 (April 1979): 90.

23. Converse and Pierce, *Political Representation in France*, pp. 186–87.

24. Robert J. Jackson, Michael M. Atkinson, and Kenneth D. Hart, "Constitutional Conflict in

France: Deputies' Attitudes toward Executive-Legislative Relations," *Comparative Politics* 9 (July 1977): 408.

25. See Bon and Cheylan, *La France Qui Vote*, pp. 212–17.

26. See Linden and Weill, *Le Choix d'un deputé* (Paris: Editions de Minuit, 1974).

27. The following account is derived from *L'Election présidentielle de mai 1974* (Paris: Dossiers et Documents du Monde, 1974), pp. 30–97.

28. See the articles by Alain Duhamel, and Linden and Weill, in *Le Monde*, May 5–6 and May 22, 1974.

29. See Kay Lawson, "The Impact of Party Reform on Party Systems: The Case of the RPR in France," *Comparative Politics* 13 (July 1981): 401–21.

30. See Noel-Jean Bergeroux's article, "L'U.D.F. à la recherche du parti du président," in *Les Elections législatives de mars 1978* (Paris: Dossiers et Documents du Monde, 1978), pp. 7–10.

31. Both parties attracted a disproportionate (and similar) percentage of older voters, and smaller (and similar) proportions of blue-collar and white-collar workers. On the other hand, the parties had different concentrations of geographic strength: the RPR was relatively stronger in the inner Paris region, the UDF in the outer region; the UDF was far stronger in the southeast and the Mediterranean area; the UDF tended to be stronger in smaller towns, the RPR in middle-sized cities. On issues, the RPR tended to be more conservative than its chief rival within the UDF, the PR (the former RI), and, in general, RPR voters tended to be more interested in politics. See *Sondages*, no. 1, 1978; and Guy Claise, "Voyage à travers les électorats," in Frédéric Bon et al., eds. *Le Dossier de legislatives 1978* (Paris: le Matin, 1978), pp. 34–35.

32. This is the thesis developed by Jérôme Jaffré in "L'Affrontement des notables de droite," in Bon et al., eds, *Le Dossier de legislatives 1978*, p. 12. For the breakdown of local officeholders, see Alain Guédé and Gilles Fabre-Rosane, "Portrait robot du député," *Le Matin*, November 19, 1978.

33. See Colette Ysmal, "Les Adherents des partis," in *Les Forces Politiques et les élections de mars 1973* (Paris: Dossiers et Documents du Monde, 1973), p. 7.

34. Charlot, *The Gaullist Phenomenon*, p. 66.

35. SOFRES, *L'Etat de l'opinion: clés pour 1987* (Paris: Seuil, 1987), p. 126.

36. The survey literature on the decline of church attendance is summarized by Nona Mayer in "Pas de chrysanthèmes pour les variables sociologiques," in Elisabeth Dupoirier and Gérard Grunberg, eds., *Mars 1986: la drôle de défaite de la gauche* (Paris: PUF, 1987), p. 152.

37. Emmanuel Todd, *La Nouvelle France* (Paris: Editions du Seuil, 1988), p. 265.

38. SOFRES, *Opinion Publique, 1985* (Paris: Gallimard, 1985), pp. 19 and 26.

39. Jean Charlot, "Exposé introductif."

40. See the survey done by SOFRES for *Figaro Magazine*, November 1983, p. 36.

41. Bruce Campbell, "On the Prospects of Polarization in the French Electorate," *Comparative Politics* 8 (January 1976): 282–87.

42. See the survey done by SOFRES for *Figaro Magazine*, November 1983, pp. 3–4 and 36.

43. SOFRES, *Opinion Publique, 1985*, pp. 28–29 and 195.

44. For the full definition of electoral volatility, see Mogen Pedersen, "Changing Patterns of Electoral Volatility in European Party Systems, 1948–1977: Explorations in Explanation," in Hans Daalder and Peter Mair, ed., *West European Party Systems* (Beverly Hills, Calif.: Sage Publications, 1983), pp. 31–34.

45. Recalculated from tables in Gérard Grunberg, "L'Instabilité du comportement électoral," paper

presented to the Congress of the International Political Science Association, Paris, July 1985, pp. 21 and 24.

46. Recalculated from results presented by Jerôme Jaffré, *Le Monde,* June 6, 1984.

47. The exit poll is cited by John Frears, "France: the 'Cohabitation' Election of 16th March 1986," p. 27, presented at the annual meeting of the British Political Studies Association, Nottingham, April 9, 1986.

48. *Libération,* April 27, 1988, p. 12.

49. See Martin Schain, "The National Front in France and the Construction of Political Legitimacy," *West European Politics* 2 (April 1987).

50. SOFRES, "L'Image de Jean-Marie Le Pen et de l'extrême droite à l'approche des élections Européenes," May 1984, pp. 4–6, and SOFRES, *Opinion Publique, 1985,* p. 178.

51. See *Le Monde,* October 17, 1985; the summary of the SOFRES survey in *Le Monde,* May 6, 1987; and the 1988 SOFRES survey in *Le Monde,* January 6, 1989.

52. See the reports on the new constituencies for the National Assembly in *Le Monde,* August 26, 1986, and September 4, 1986.

53. This pattern was analyzed in greater depth in Schain, "The National Front."

54. See Jean-Marie Le Pen, *Les Français d'abord* (Paris: Editions Carrère, 1984).

55. See the report in *Le Monde,* May 8, 1987.

56. See *Le Monde,* May 13, 1987.

57. See *Le Monde,* June 9 and July 25, 1987.

58. For Léotard's remarks, see *Le Monde,* July 25, 1987, and for Noir's statement, see *Le Monde,* May 15, 1987.

59. *Le Monde,* May 12, 1987.

60. *Figaro,* July 13, 1987.

61. See *Le Monde,* July 25, 1987, and *La France des régions* (Paris: Dossiers et documents du Monde, 1986), pp. 44 and 63.

62. *Figaro,* July 16, 1987.

63. *Le Monde,* May 15, 1987.

64. *Le Monde,* July 10, 1987.

65. See *Libération,* April 27, 1988, p. 8, and *Le Monde,* May 2, 1988, p. 16.

66. See "Les Secrets du 3e tour," in *L'Express,* May 13, 1988.

67. See Pascal Perrineau, "Front National: La drôle de défaite," in Philippe Habert and Colette Ysmal, *Elections législatives, 1988* (Paris: Figaro/Etudes Politiques, 1988), pp. 30–31.

68. *Le Monde,* June 28, 1988.

69. See *Le Monde,* October 23/24, 1988, January 4, 1989, and February 17, 1989.

70. See Gérard Grunberg, Pierre Giacometti, Florence Haegel, and Béatrice Roy, "Trois candidats, trois droites, trois électorats," in *Le Monde,* April 27, 1988, p. 12.

71. Roland Cayrol and Pascal Perrineau, "La Défaite du politique," in Roland Cayrol and Pascal Perrineau, ed., *Le Guide du pourvoir* (Paris: Editions Jean-François Doumic, 1988), p. 14.

72. See *Enquête auprès des délégués aux assises nationales du RPR* (Grenoble: Institut d'études politiques de Grenoble, 1986), pp. 138–151, Table 5, p. 140, and Figure 8, p. 150. My thanks to Georges Lavau for pointing out these findings to me.

73. See Cayrol and Perrineau, "La Défaite du Politique," pp. 44–51.

74. *Libération,* April 2, 1987, pp. 2–5.

4

The French Left:
A Tale of Three Beginnings

Jane Jenson

There are several ways to tell any tale. Beginning at the beginning means
starting with two referenda in 1962 that had profound effects on the subsequent
evolution of the French Left. The referendum to approve the Evian Agreements
finally closed a conflictual chapter of French political life that had contributed to
the Left's division after 1945. Then a controversial constitutional referendum
inaugurated direct elections for president of the Republic, and a piece of institutional machinery opened the way for greater collaboration between the Socialists
and the Communists. Both referenda contributed to the eventual victory of the
Socialist Party's presidential candidate in 1981 and 1988. Beginning the story
in 1962 leads toward an institutionally driven story of electoral laws and the
presidentialism that united and rebalanced the forces of the Left.

Beginning from the end, from the perspective of 1990, the story of the French
Left might be told as the tale of the march of the Parti Communiste Français
(PCF) through—and out of—the electoral institutions of France. Such a chronicle
reflects the character of the most recent decade and helps account for the electoral
successes of the Parti Socialiste (PS) to 1981, its policy shift while in office, its
defeat in the 1986 legislative elections, and the victories of 1988. The competitive
game within which the Left partners played, which ordered their strategic calculations, has run down. No longer can the PCF claim to be a contender for power
within the Left, no longer must the PS look to its left to protect itself, and no
longer does the competition between the PCF and PS anchor the French Left in
a space that is more radical than Northern European social democracy. This
starting point for the story encourages a strategic explanation of events: of the
inexorable effects of choices made at crucial points, of strategic errors and failures
to adapt.

Between these two end points there is, of course, also the middle. Halfway
between 1962 and 1990 there was the economic crisis. France's economy experienced a fundamental restructuring of relations between companies and workers
as well as major alterations in its place in the global economy. With draconian
changes in their economic and social environment altering all that had become
familiar over several decades, Left parties faced a new world. New cleavages

85

divided the electorate and reshuffled the patterns of support for parties. The crisis made redundant the long-standing economic program of the United Left, and controversy over future policy direction splintered it definitively. Beginning the story in the middle produces a tale of socioeconomic changes driving the Left to rethink policy proclivities, compelling it to discover new programs.

Depending on the starting point, then, the story of the French Left in the last decades can be an institutional, a strategic, or a sociological one. Any one of these versions might be—and has been—told as if it were complete, yet none alone can adequately capture the history of this Left. There was no inevitable march towards the 1990s. Neither the electoral institutions nor the economic crisis ordained a PS in power but racked by divisions over social questions, immigration, education, and economic strategy. Choices were made but under constraint. Strategic vision and/or failure cannot, however, account completely for these outcomes. In telling the tale, all three analyses must be woven together to produce the tapestry of the French Left's recent history, which has seen both the best of times and the worst of times, sometimes all at the same time.

Whereas elsewhere in Europe the social relations of Fordism were stabilized in the postwar years, in France consensus remained fragile and underdeveloped until well into the Fifth Republic. The Fordism that existed in France until the mid-1960s was characterized by contested state interventions and by authoritarian and conflictual wage relations. Political forces constantly interfered with the smooth functioning of economic institutions. Restrictions on commerce, old-fashioned institutions of credit, uneasy labor relations, high inflation, and an unusually large balance of payments deficit all marked French specificities. Divisions on the partisan Left as well as one of the more uncooperative business classes in any advanced capitalist society gave a peculiarly *entre-deux-guerres* cast to the first postwar decades.

The adjustments that all countries had to make to Fordism were politically more difficult and somewhat longer coming in France. As it adjusted within Fordism, the French Left updated its representations of politics and itself, simultaneously making major contributions to the institutionalization of a societal paradigm that allowed France to move out of the 1960s riding on the economic growth created by Gaullist modernization. The result was ironic. Given the timing of the events, French Left politics reached the late 1940s in the late 1960s, just in time to experience the economic crisis that signaled the decline of postwar economic and social arrangements.

This irony had its effects. All political actors, but especially the newly united Left, were deeply invested in promoting and sustaining their versions of Fordist wage relations and politics. Their carefully constructed worldviews, systems of representation, definitions of interests, organizations, and, therefore, competitive positions, depended on these versions.[1] Thus, they clung to these outlooks as the world changed around them, despite indications that something else might serve the needs of France better, and despite evidence that their positions did not represent the interests of new categories of workers and social movements. Their very visions of themselves, as well as the balance of political forces among them, prevented them from abandoning a model of development that, if it might have been appropriate for the 1950s, was disastrous as the 1980s approached. The strategic conflict engendered by a bipolar party system thus had the effect of holding back political responses to the crisis of Fordism. Only the loosening of ideological and organizational imperatives after 1983 allowed the French Left to move beyond its old visions and into the uncertain future.

In order to understand how such a disparity could develop between economic pressures developing both domestically and in the international economy and the political limits of responses to such pressures, it is necessary to examine the ways in which actors, political parties in particular, developed representations used by themselves and others to make sense of and define the social relations of which they were a part.

Politics involves, among other things, actors' efforts to carve out a constituency for themselves by mobilizing support for a preferred formulation of their own collective identity (and often that of their protagonists) and for the enumeration of their interests, which follow from that collective identity. This definition of politics depends upon a particular understanding of representation. One type of representation involves the actor's *representation of self* to others, via a collective identity. A second type, familiar from the language of liberal democracy, is the organized *representation of interests*. These two senses of representation are closely linked. Both involve the *power* to give meaning to social relations and thereby to represent and dispute over "interests." Resolution of basic definitional questions about the identity of the central protagonists places broad limits on the definition of interests of actors and also makes such definitions historical rather than "objective."

Understanding representation in this double sense underlines the centrality of the politics of struggles over meaning—the power to label social relations. Politics is conflict about collective identities—about who has a right to make claims—as much as it is conflict among groups and organizations over disputed claims about who gets what, when, and how. The terrain on which actors struggle over representation is the *universe of political discourse,* a space in which identities are socially constructed.[2] Because actors with a variety of collective identities coexist in the universe of political discourse, their practices and meaning systems jostle each other for attention and legitimacy.

One of the miracles of social life is that, despite the contradictions at the heart of social relations, there are moments when systems of social relations crystallize and take on stabilized form, stalling contradictions for a time.[3] These systems form a *model of development* that, as the particular achievement of each national society, is a combination of institutionalized social relations that reproduce themselves over time, indicating that they are *in regulation.*[4] This does not occur magically. Explanations for continuity must pay attention to the ways in which actors constitute social relations through the meanings they give them as well as through their practices. These representations are, of course, limited. Nevertheless, patterns that in the eyes of observers constitute quite similar structures can be represented by actors in diverse, albeit coherent and meaningful, fashions. Analysis must thus provide ways to conduct concrete investigations of historically developed sets of practices and meanings that provide the actual mechanisms of regulation. Making a loose distinction between the social relations of production and others, we can label these regulatory mechanisms the *mode of regulation* and the *societal paradigm*.[5]

Stabilization of a regime of accumulation depends upon its being institutionalized as norms, habits, and laws in a mode of regulation that guarantees that its agents conform more or less to the schema of reproduction in their day-to-day behavior and in their struggles within contradictory social relations. When a set of practices, and the meanings that accompany them, succeed in stabilizing a regime of accumulation, we can say that a mode of regulation exists. A societal paradigm is, similarly, a shared set of interconnected norms, habits, and laws that make sense of the many social relations beyond the realm of production. Every societal paradigm contains a view of human nature, a definition of basic and proper forms of social relations among equals and among those in hierarchical relationships, and specification of relations among institutions as well as a stipulation of the role of such institutions.

The constitution of a stable, or hegemonic, mode of regulation and societal paradigm, within which only some collective identities are represented, is the product of politics in its broadest sense. We can catalogue any number of institutions—ranging from political parties, trade unions, and other social movements to the various apparatuses of the state, churches, corporations, and scientific establishments—as the multiple sites of its constitution. Nevertheless, competing meanings for the same power relation may continue to exist in the universe of political discourse, perpetuated by the practices of actors excluded from the societal compromise and whose influence is marginal. The marginality exists because, once constituted, the effect of an hegemonic societal compromise is like a shadow cast back onto the universe of political discourse, leaving in darkness and invisibility any identities excluded from its terms and blurring into invisibility power relations whose meanings can not be seized.

The "Twaining" of the French Left:
Reports of Its Death Are Much Exaggerated

As the second legislative elections of the Fifth Republic approached in 1962, few observers of French politics would have, or could have, predicted the trajectory of the Left toward electoral victory in 1981. Moreover, at that time few would have anticipated that the non-Communist Left could have given rise to the

PS, or that the major duel in the 1970s would be between a PCF attempting to rid itself of the remnants of Stalinism and a PS newly constituted with one of the most radical democratic socialist programs in Western Europe. Nor would they have predicted the deep freeze of the New Left, which lasted for two decades until the thaw of the 1980s.

In 1962 the Left as a whole seemed to have lost its way. In the 1958 election the Left's total vote had been only 43.4%, a drop of 9% from the last election of the Fourth Republic, only two years earlier; in 1962 it climbed back only to 44.2%. Observers of elections disputed over how to interpret this, indicating that even if Fordist-style social relations had been developing in France throughout the postwar period, the representations of collective identities and interests that might contribute to a stable mode or regulation and societal paradigm were still under construction.[6] A major aspect of confusion involved the meaning to be placed on the exhaustion of the largest actor of the non-Communist Left, the Section Française de l'Internationale Ouvrièrier (SFIO). Muddled in its representation of self—forever speaking of Marxism and its revolutionary identity, yet profoundly moderate in practice—and implicated in the crisis that destroyed the Fourth Republic, the SFIO contributed conflicting terms to the societal paradigm. Moreover, the party itself appeared to lack options.[7] After 1958 it entered, perforce, into "constructive opposition," while suffering the indignity of continuing scission from its left—into the Parti Socialiste Unifié (PSU). After 1962 the SFIO's opposition to Gaullism hardened, but its prospects did not improve.

There was a second dispute over the idea of *dépolitisation*. This concept—which everyone admitted was extremely poorly defined and, in fact, often labeled something else—emerged with the change in Republics.[8] It provided an umbrella under which one could discuss a number of items, from the crisis of citizenship through the decline of parties, ideologies, and the proletariat. At this moment of social change and political adjustment, theorists reached into, and even beyond, their theoretical baggage to make sense of the declining support for the Left and the coalescence of the Center-Right around de Gaulle. These issues occupied the non-Communist Left, the New Left in particular, as the PSU emerged as the more radical and "modernizing" wing of that movement. Growing recognition of the effects of more than a decade of economic growth led many people to rethink their categories. There was talk of the "Americanization of the working class," the end of ideology, the out-of-date character of class struggle, the need to rethink socialism, the importance of industrial democracy, etc., etc. Along with such hypotheses about the effects of social change there was often an argument that political parties had lost legitimacy, that electoral participation was in consequence threatened, and that other political formations—particularly unions and/or clubs—were taking over the aggregation functions of traditional parties.

The importance of this wide-ranging and poorly defined concept of *dépolitisation* resides less in the resolution of such arguments than in the evidence they provide of controversies, within the universe of political discourse, over how to analyze the early years of the Fifth Republic and represent the conflicts that it embodied. Rethinking categories without falling into the embrace of American-style pluralism was the task New Left thinkers set for themselves. In carrying out their mandate, however, they had to come to terms with the political formation that sat dinosaur-like in the middle of the route to a new Left politics—the PCF.

A third uncertainty in political discourse came from the PCF. Despite having abandoned their strategy of militant autonomy in the mid-1950s in favor of united frontism, the Communists had as yet made few concessions to the new times. Economic thinking still derived from Maurice Thorez's theses on pauperization, which instructed French workers that the experience of postwar boom was simply illusory. Thorez asserted that the future promised only a process of relative and absolute pauperization, a position the PCF held into the 1960s.[9] Attention to social concerns was equally perverse. For example, in the mid-1950s the PCF also confirmed its opposition to the liberalization of access to birth control, vilifying the family-planning movement, which had emerged as an important site for consideration of the new social circumstances of postwar France.[10] The PCF remained aloof from the movement, calling it an imperialist plot perpetrated against the workers, equivalent in evil to the atomic bomb.[11]

Exodus from the PCF after 1956 consisted, then, of those opposed to the reactions of the French Communists to the events of Hungary and the Twentieth Congress of the Communist Party of the Soviet Union, and those angered by the position on birth control. It was, of course, the weight of Hungary and Thorez's refusal to acknowledge Khrushchev's secret speech about the "crimes of Stalin" that led directly to the events of the early 1960s, when student groups, under the influence of the quite different responses of Italian Communists to these events, attempted to change the party. At our starting point—1962—the PCF had just lived through the purges of the Affaire Servin-Casanova and Maurice Thorez remained firmly in control of a party that was still resolutely attached to strategic visions and analyses more appropriate to the Third than to the Fifth Republic. Not surprisingly, numerous commentators pointed to the "historic decline" of the PCF in the election of 1958 as well as the departure of its intellectuals. The Communists' efforts to unite the Left seemed destined only to divide it further and thereby to contribute to the continued victory of the Gaullists. The situation led Maurice Duverger to conclude, just as the Fifth Republic took form, that "le problème est sans solution, à court terme."[12]

Of course, we now know that Duverger was only partially correct. The Left did quickly agree to unite in order to fight elections. More slowly it came to an agreement on policy that culminated in Union de la Gauche around the Common Program in 1972. It could do so in part because the PCF modified its strategy and because the Socialists reconstructed their party. But, nonetheless, it did take a long time to dislodge the Right. Until 1974, the Left's support stagnated in Legislative elections at about forty-five percent. Moreover, even more distressing for its prospects, it was not attracting new support among young voters or among the social categories swollen by economic modernization. As a result, it was not growing geographically beyond the traditional Communist, Socialist, or Radical bastions.[13]

An additional element of representational confusion in these years came from Gaullism's successful appeal to workers and peasants. This meant that the reflection of class relations in electoral behavior was muted. Between 1958 and 1967, the Left lost support among those who identified themselves as working class, while on objective measures of class the Left's support among manual occupations remained stable (at fifty-one percent) while the Right's increased substantially.[14]

Until the late 1960s, then, France looked as if social change and modernizing Gaullism were threatening the traditional Left parties, the ones that de Gaulle liked to call the "parties of yesterday." Class boundaries blurred before the appeal of the great *rassembleur;* attitudes toward de Gaulle himself emerged as the best predictors of voting support.[15] In the legislative elections of 1967, the combined score of the Left was exactly the same as in 1958, while in 1968 it fell again, reaching forty-one percent. Political observers continued to write of *dépolitisation* as well as unstable voting behavior and unpredictable political institutions. They also wrote of an aging Left, one that lived more in 1900 than 1965.[16] Therefore, although polarization into a "majority" and "opposition" had occurred, the future of the opposition remained in some doubt. There would obviously be no long straight road toward the Left in power.

Yet we now know that Gaullism did not remain triumphant, that the Left did recoup its support, that class discourse and class cleavages returned to French politics, that two blocs replaced the centrism of the Fourth Republic, and that the PCF was not quite destined for the dustbin of history. Beneath the appearances of these years, therefore, we must search for the patterns of change that help to account for the events of the 1960s and beyond.

France's Fordism:
Thirty-Three Years from 1936 to 1947

A part of the reason that the Left could be discounted as a political force in the early 1960s was its failure to make much theoretical or strategical sense of the intense economic and political changes of the postwar years. It was less well-placed than it should have been to provide a critical interpretation of the effects of France's Fordism, which arrived very quickly after the war. From an agrarian, protected, empire-oriented, insular, and quaintly nineteenth-century society in the 1940s, France rapidly urbanized, bought automobiles and other consumer durables at a great rate, and shifted over to the mass-production industry from which all these goods came.[17] Missing in this process, and thus contributing to both real and feared instabilities, was a well-developed consensus or social compromise around the Fordist project.

By the mid-1960s, however, the situation had begun to change and a paradigmatic discourse shared by most participants in French politics was emerging, which itself was a crucial ingredient of the French boom of these years. This shared representation of identities and interests marked the stabilization of the Fordist mode of regulation. But, even more important, it reflected the crystallization of mutual readings of political conflict, constituting a societal paradigm for French Fordism. Changes on the Left meant that its parties made crucial contributions to the terms of this discourse. Moreover, the specific form of the societal paradigm set quite precise limits on the range of political responses available to the Left when economic crisis arrived in the 1970s.

The early years of French Fordism were characterized by deep disagreements over the institutionalization of postwar social relations. The modernization of French capitalism, which the economic growth and mass-production/mass-consumption economy reflected, derived to a large extent from the initiatives of technocrats who took over top state positions at the Liberation and put forward statist scenarios for change.[18] The initial construction depended on a social bloc involving a political alliance of modernizing capital and the popular social forces that supported the Conseil National de la Résistance. The discrediting of traditional capitalists by wartime collaboration provided a space for several years of rapid reform and institutional change, with the support of organized labor and the PCF. But this coalition collapsed in two stages, as first the Gaullists abandoned it and then, in 1947, when the PCF was forced into a political ghetto.[19] From that position the PCF and the Confédération Générale du Trâvail (CGT) sniped at the new institutions and radically increased their workplace militancy.[20]

After 1947, economic and political power rebalanced in favor of capital.[21] An important consequence of this changed balance of forces was that the state-led modernization that continued took place *without* organized labor and often at the expense of workers' wages, rights, benefits, and ability to act collectively.[22] Because capitalists refused to give up prerogatives on the shop floor, state institutions became an important mediating influence when the unregulated class war of some workplaces threatened to spread. State-guaranteed rights—paid vacations, social security, a minimum wage—characterized French Fordism. The discourse accompanying this asserted that the reforms were put into place by agreements among the "social partners," whose visceral hostility to each other required a referee.[23]

Throughout the 1950s the conservative tendencies of much of French capital and the ghettoized militancy of the Communists meant that modernization would be state-led. While technocrats could deploy the power of the state, their efforts were nonetheless threatened by the workings of a centrist politics with two disaffected wings. The political instability of the Fourth Republic encouraged modernizing technocrats to bypass the legislature and other forums of public discussion and explication. This approach followed logically from the fact that no social consensus existed capable of generating strong support for the new institutions. France's Fordism was being built, but the social and political relations that sustained it remained shaky. Fears of instability abounded. In addition, the absence of paradigmatic consensus meant that some quite peculiar twists of logic accompanied its construction.

Keynesianism was married to France's long-standing statism to produce a state-centric Fordism. However, it was not until after 1958 that Keynesianism really began to have its anticipated consequences.[24] Much of French capital in the 1950s resisted by building safeguards around traditional practices that then became greater or lesser hindrances to modernization. Although their numbers were declining, peasants—often allied with *la boutique*—retained enough political power to protect their own interests. The PCF, which represented many of the workers most implicated in new wage relations, was politically isolated. It thus all too frequently insisted on encumbering CGT union issues with Communist partisan ones, as well as opposing any cooperation with management.[25] The SFIO remained mired in Marxist talk and collaborationist practice, while the Confédération Française des Travailleurs Chrétiens (CFTC) tried to secularize. The absence of discursive agreement about how to represent, and thereby make popular sense of, postwar novelties became clearer when the modernizers "went public" in the Mendès-France experiment, were defeated, and quickly retreated.[26] Even more disruptive, of course, were the colonial wars. The deadlock over Algeria necessitated a "guns-or-butter policy" that exacerbated ongoing inflation and led governments to manipulate the minimum wage, with income inequality increasing even more.[27]

In the Fifth Republic, then, a complicated and conflict-ridden universe of political discourse persisted. There was little agreement over basic interests and how they "ought" to be represented. The traditional Right, imbued with paternalism, refused to tolerate workers' demands and granted a legitimate identity only to citizens who accumulated capital and property. The Center and modernizing industrial capital, in alliance with state bureaucrats, talked of technocracy, planning, and the need to transcend the divisive effects of "politics." Class conflict, they thought, would be smoothed over as economic boom put a *deux chevaux* and a refrigerator within the reach of everyone. This position was given a huge boost after 1958 by de Gaulle's profound interest in building French economic and military autonomy, which required a thoroughly modern industrial plant. According to Gaullist rhetoric, everyone in France had an interest in economic growth because it contributed to *grandeur*. Nationalism and traditional Catholic-corporatist values supported de Gaulle's position.[28]

The 1960s also saw a remarkable rebirth of left-wing social and political analysis. In less than a decade everyday leftist assumptions about the nature of society and its collective actors modernized away from notions formed in the 1930s. The new theories turned on several questions. The first was a great debate over the place of the "new middle classes."[29] Embedded in that debate was another over which class would lead the movement toward socialism. Competing analyses from the PCF, Mallet, Gorz, Touraine, Poulantzas, and, later, those in the PS promoting a *front de classe* addressed these questions, *from within a common Marxist vocabulary*. The strength of the PCF—both popularly and in intellectual circles—gave it power over Left intellectual discourse.[30] Left-leaning intellectuals could disagree profoundly with the PCF in these years, but they had to do so from within a terrain of discussion shaped by it.[31] The overall result was an efflorescence of analyses focused on class.

The PCF itself was revising its positions at the same time. First it adopted more conventional interpretations of electoral democracy.[32] In its commitment to democracy, the party thus expressed a new willingness to abandon power, if defeated in elections, and to play by a set of coalitional rules more acceptable to its Left allies. Both changes involved movement away from hard-line Leninist views of politics. The social logic behind this strategy, contained in new analyses of "state monopoly capitalism," claimed that the French people were starved for democracy by the institutions and politics of a Fifth Republic that represented the interests of the "monopoly caste."[33] The vast majority of the French population would eventually be squeezed by the contradictions of this economic system. Potential opposition was therefore immense. Finally, the Communists rethought their class-analytical categories, focusing on the intermediary strata as very likely allies of the working class. The theory of state monopoly capitalism and its class categories provided the PCF with a theoretical base for opposition to Gaullism (the monopoly caste in power) and Fifth Republic institutions (the strengthening of the executive at the expense of the legislature) as well as for the search for a common program with the non-Communist Left. This new Communist vision stressed the possibility of a large electoral coalition led by the working class, a coalition that could take the first steps on the road to socialism.

The PCF's long-term strategy, united frontism, meant that the basic changes it envisaged would flow from Left partisan alliances. As a result, its immediate interest was to generate Left electoral support against the Gaullists. As the SFIO grew increasingly disenchanted with de Gaulle, and as the non-Communist Left radicalized, even the most tentative gestures attenuating Communist isolation were effusively welcomed by the PCF. It was here that the institutional logic of the Fifth Republic gave a big push toward uniting the Left. In 1962, just a few days before the legislative election, the PCF and the SFIO agreed to stand down in favor of whichever of their candidates was leading after the first round, a successful and historic first move toward the further unification of the Left that provides the centerpiece of this story. Moreover, as the PCF re-dedicated itself to elections, alliances, and reformism it generated new discursive and practical reactions to French Fordism, reactions that contributed to building a consensual understanding about how to respond to the social relations institutionalized in these years.[34]

In the first years of the Fifth Republic, the SFIO remained entrenched in its own Third Republic visions of France, and Fordist social relations were simply a source of confusion. The urbanization of rural and small-town France, the huge expansion of the salariat, and the reorganization of the labor process in mass production were all phenomena whose meanings were not immediately obvious to the Socialists. The task of reflecting on such matters thus fell to other parts of the Left, including the Parti Socialiste Unifié (PSU) and an efflorescence of political clubs, groups, and intellectuals' debating forums. Here the goal, more or less explicitly announced as such, was to wrench the French non-Communist Left away from its prewar notions toward a better understanding of the social relations of postwar boom.

The official class map of the renascent Socialists eventually came from these wide-ranging debates. In its most explicit formulation, the *front de classe,* it preceded from class-analytical premises that, rather than privileging the industrial working class, focused on a broader *salariat exploité.*[35] This new form of address to French wage-earners replaced the SFIO's outdated Third Republic-style Marxism and provided theoretical justification for a broad alliance strategy. Moreover, it directly challenged the PCF's insistence that only the Communists could provide real leadership for the Left because only they were anchored in the vanguard class. The Socialists refused to grant any class the status of vanguard.[36]

Important as the updating of class maps and *marxisant* talk was, however, the non-Communist Left could not have realized its goal if it had not simultaneously developed a sensible mobilizing strategy for the new conditions. The construction of this strategy involved a good deal of learning, beginning in the run-up to the 1965 presidential election. Two quite different options were originally being offered.[37] Gaston Defferre, first into the lists, proposed a *grande fédération* of progressive forces, reaching rightward to the christian democratic Mouvement Républicain Populaire (MRP) and ignoring the PCF (while hoping, of course, to get some second-round support from Communist voters), so as to transcend the politics of parties by appealing to the club "men" and *forces vives* critical of old-style party politics and to groups that had never supported the Left, like the progressive *patronat.* The initiative collapsed in 1965 when the MRP refused to join Defferre's federation. But the breakdown of negotiations was only the final nail in the coffin of the centrist strategy for the non-Communist Left. The effort collapsed under pressure from the Communists in municipal elections, from parts of the SFIO that refused the centrist discourse of an alliance with the MRP and from the reappearance of the Catholic school question.[38]

When the Defferre initiative crumbled, a *stratégie de rechange* was waiting in the candidacy of François Mitterrand, who had already formulated the position that would serve him until 1981. Mitterrand embraced the Left-leaning option, accepting PCF support while seeking to undermine Communist voting strength through careful tending of his Left credentials. He thus embarked on the organizational reconstruction of the non-Communist Left, initially formulated in the Fédération de la Gauche Démocrate et Socialiste (FGDS). Many of the groups and individuals originally supporting Defferre's *grande fédération* also backed the FGDS, but Mitterrand's originality was to exclude the MRP and to be willing to engage in dialogue with the Communists.[39] To Mitterrand the numbers were clear: electoral alliances were essential for the FGDS, and the most important alliance partner, with its solid hold over twenty percent of the vote, was the PCF. The SFIO had already begun working with the PCF in 1962, but the notion that this relationship might become more permanent—as the PCF clearly announced it wished it to be—was not highly popular, even within the SFIO, let alone throughout the larger non-Communist Left. The 1965 election, in which Mitterrand, backed by the PCF, got a third of the votes on the first round and forty-five percent on the second, was another important lesson.

One more event was necessary to solidify the Left coalition-in-becoming. In the midst of the 1968 events Mitterrand, without consulting the leaders either of the FGDS or the PCF, announced that he was willing to lead the Left in taking up its "responsibilities" for transition after the defeat of de Gaulle, which he argued was imminent. He proposed a wide-ranging coalitional government, including personalities of the Center as well as Communists. For the FGDS, and especially for the SFIO, this initiative looked like a coup d'état. The FGDS broke up over it. The lack of a negotiated program ran contrary to the PCF's agenda for united frontism, and Mitterrand's suggestion that Mendès-France might be prime minister reeked not only of Fourth Republic centrism but also of the much more recent Charléty incident.[40] Mitterrand's "presidentialist" initiative thus completely backfired, opening the way for the disaster of Defferre's candidacy in 1969.

By running Jacques Duclos in the first round of the 1969 election, the PCF drove its lesson further home. No matter how much it wanted an alliance, it would not lie down and play dead. United-front politics would follow the PCF's scenario or would not happen at all. Meanwhile, painful internal reflections after May–June 1968 and Czechoslovakia led the PCF to an even stronger commitment to party pluralism, negotiated programs, and internal democratization. Its united-frontist wooing thus became harder to resist. The dramatic lesson the non-Communist Left had to take from 1969 helped. Defferre barely did better than the PSU and Trotskyist candidates. Together, votes for the non-Communist Left plummeted while the PCF's held, creating a runoff pitting two right-wing candidates against each other. A leftist coalition would have to be constructed anew, with the PCF in a position of strength despite the anger on the Left over its behavior in the May Events. The political forces that eventually became the PS thus drew the conclusion that, for the immediate future, only a left-leaning alliance with the PCF was likely to work.[41]

The outcomes of these complex processes had important implications for the whole Left's representation of Fordist social relations. First, forces bearing discourses of class and class conflict gained a purchase within the Left, one that became difficult to dislodge. In other countries, the upsurge of social movements in the late 1960s was often interpreted as a challenge to universalizing, class-based discourses and traditional Left identities. In France, in contrast, such social movements—the legacies of 1968—were quickly absorbed back into party politics, and the new issues they raised became part of Left-Right debate. Thus, space for autonomous politics not oriented around classes was limited.[42] Next, the Left never questioned the importance of elections in social change. The Socialists' new strategy reaffirmed traditional SFIO electionalism, isolating voices for thoroughgoing *autogestion*. Third, the state was reconsecrated as the privileged instrument for making change while the Left endorsed state-led economic development. Neither electoralism nor statism were new, of course. However, they would henceforth be anchored in a political strategy that, because of the new left-leaning coalitional logic, stressed the redistributive as well as growth-producing aspects of economic programs. The Socialists, under pressure from the PCF, became better Keynesians.

Thus, by the early 1970s the French Left was, for the first time since 1947, speaking to the same situation as the Center and the Right. This became one of the sources of stability of the Fifth Republic. The PCF's abandonment of an economics that did not explain the postwar boom and its replacement with one that could—while simultaneously criticizing its politics—meant Communists could speak in the same conversations as the Gaullist modernizers. Likewise, the non-Communist Left's various critiques and modifications of traditional class and economic theory moved it onto similar terrain. All political forces, Right and Left, now shared the basic outline of a paradigmatic discourse even if they disagreed on many of its details.[43] Moreover, restructured political institutions and patterns of conflict brought into being a societal paradigm capable of resolving many of the uncertainties and disjunctions that had bedeviled postwar politics. All major political actors (with the exception of the traditional Right) agreed that postwar modernization was remaking French society, that improved relations between workers and managers were a crucial element in its continued success, that the state had a role to play in stabilizing the system, and, therefore, that technocrats were important economic and political actors.[44]

Left and Right shared two essential elements in their representations of interests. The first was that the primary division of French society was class. Earlier religious conflicts had finally been calmed; indeed, the political manifestation of religious differences in a separate political party had ended. Moreover, the declining numbers of peasants meant that the cleavages of an industrial society finally became dominant. Thus, new attention turned to industrial workers and, as the insistent discussion of the "new middle classes" reflected, to the expanding tertiary sector. Even the Right, especially after 1968, paid increasing attention to the class relations of Fordist France and to proposals for ameliorating them.[45] Thus, a growing commitment to Keynesianism led both the Right and the Left to interpret the protocol of Grenelle in 1968 and their effects as a success for macroeconomic policy.[46] Second, the consolidation of the Fordist paradigm made electoral mobilization crucial to the projects of all actors. Success in elections became the measure of social power and winning elections the passport to the future for both the Right and the Left.[47]

Fordism in Crisis: The Great Refusal

As of the late 1960s the Communists had demonstrated that they still had considerable resources, both within the union movement and in the electorate. Powerful as it was after 1968, however, the PCF was not in a position to benefit immediately from the political energy of the *soixante-huitards*.[48] Its insistence on the most top-down and controlled forms of mobilization as well as its pressure on the CGT to make union actions conform to its electoral calendar meant that it had little to say about democratization and *autogestion*. Its united-front strategy remained exclusively an affair of parties. Top-level agreements were the goal, and it was profoundly uncomfortable with any sort of mobilizational spontaneity. Moreover, its continuing workerism could only put off students and social movement activists who considered their own revolutionary credentials to be at least as great as those of the industrial workers.[49] Old-fashioned elements in the PCF strategy in the early 1970s thus left plenty of political space for anyone willing to occupy it. This is exactly what François Mitterrand and the new Parti Socialiste (PS) set out to do.

The PS was a contradictory body from its beginning in 1971. To avoid confronting profound doctrinal and organizational divisions, the PS simply enshrined debate in its constitution and made a virtue of its confusions. Vigorous debate among *tendances* became the staff of life in a party held together by Mitterrand's presidential possibilities and long-standing vision that a place existed for a PS from which it would undercut the PCF. Traditional social democracy, with the strongest organizational ties to the working class of any *tendances,* united the remnants of the SFIO and proposed a commitment to statism either through nationalizations or through more straightforward macroeconomic manipulations.[50] It also sought greater "democratization" by breaking the *tutelle* relationship between prefects and elected local governments. The "republicans"—Mitterrand's current emerging from the Convention des Institutions Républicaines (CIR) of the 1960s—had strong positions on institutional safeguards and individual rights, but were rather moderate in their economics. Mendès-France's state-led neo-Radicalism remained their inspiration. Largely because of internal PS politics, the CIR also committed itself to a program of economic reform couched in a language of *socialisme du possible*. The third important current was CERES (the Centre d'Etudes, de Recherche et d'Education Socialistes), which was an important connecting link to the PCF because it shared an enthusiasm for economic policies quite close to those of the Communists—nationalizations, planning, state-directed transformation, expanded social spending—and because it solidly supported the Union de la Gauche.

After the founding of the PS in 1971 these three major *tendances* allied to promote the signature of the Common Program of 1972, an alliance based on a coherent strategy. First was the idea—based on a vision of social alliances—that a PS that was less threatening and more democratic than the PCF would attract middle-class groups, both old and new, by offering solidaristic social and economic policies, republican values, and a healthy economy. A PS pledged to such a Common Program would also undermine Communist electoral support by establishing new Left credentials for itself. This matter of "Left credentials" was particularly important. One lesson taken from a review of Left voting in the 1960s was that it depended greatly on "ideological" factors.[51] Class position and other social characteristics were less important in producing a vote for the Left than was self-identification with the "Left." A second element of the strategy involved playing on the "presidential effect." Here the hypothesis was that if only one candidate for the Left ran in presidential elections—and that would have to be the Socialist candidate—substantial spillover benefits would flow to the PS. The 1972 Common Program followed from this. Currents within the PS were willing—either for opportunistic reasons of "talking on the Left" or because they believed it—to accept much of what the PCF had long been proposing, which in turn was a slightly watered-down reiteration of Resistance-Liberation ideas. Thus there was to be full employment, an expanded and refined welfare state, higher wages and benefits, more nationalizations, "democratic management" at firmlevel and democratic planning nationally, greater rights for unions and workers, and institutional reforms to create more space for local democracy.

This program, an ideal left-wing platform for Fordism, was signed at almost exactly the same moment that economic crisis arrived with a vengeance. Nevertheless, given the delicately balanced programmatic and organizational construction that the Left had worked so hard to create, plus the favorable political responses that it received, few on the Left moved to abandon the Common Program, even over the long haul toward 1981. Among other things, the electoral consequences would have been dramatic. Nevertheless, as the crisis intensified in the later 1970s, the Left was not completely unaware of the inappropriateness of its proposals. Conflicts and dispute about such matters remained, however, in internal debate, and never changed the public face of electoral efforts.

The extent of the electoralist pressure is visible in the way that Michel Rocard and the ex-PSU experienced life within the PS. When they decided to split from the PSU and enter the Socialist Party in 1974, they constituted the fourth major *tendance* of the PS. They brought an enthusiasm for technocratic solutions coupled with *autogestionnaire* discourse. Amalgamated from a number of political traditions—disgruntled Fourth Republic Socialists, Left Catholics, ex-*soixantehuitards*—the Rocardians tested the limits of traditional Marxist, social-democratic and liberal analyses by rethinking capitalism, changes in class structure, planning, third worldism, etc. In all of this they were profoundly anti-Communist and unenthusiastic about Left Unity. Bringing the Rocardians into his majority allowed Mitterrand to divest himself of CERES, whose leftism became a problem as power approached. Mitterrand nonetheless refused to deviate from the essentials of his strategy, coopting the *autogestionnaires* without giving anything to them in terms of program. Then, as the effects of economic crisis became clearer in the late 1970s, the Rocardians began to point to international restructuring and domestic decline, insisting that the Common Program was not a document for its time. All this meant a decade-long debate within the Socialist Party, *and* a continuation of united frontism.[52]

The 1973 legislative elections brought the united Left back from its 1968 low; it won 46% of the vote. Then the 1974 presidential election, pitting Mitterrand against Giscard d'Estaing, gave the Socialist candidate 49.3% on the second ballot. The smell of victory was in the air, precisely, it seemed, because of the success of the Mitterrandiste strategy. The Socialists were making inroads among both middle-class and working-class voters. And, as Mitterrand and other astute observers well knew, the PCF was in turmoil.

Throughout the mid-1970s the PCF seemed to be moving simultaneously in several directions, which stemmed from deep divisions within the party over strategy, between predilections for united-front politics and militant autonomy. Communists advocating the former were more electoralist, willing to seek cross-class compromises in a serious way and open to discussion of internal party reform. Those proposing the latter sought a *pur et dur* PCF, stressing workerism, union militancy, and pulling back from reformism if it cut into the party's ability to mobilize workers. A third pro-Soviet position also existed, which could enter into alliance with either of the major two.

These currents had coexisted within the party for decades. From the early 1960s the united frontists had prevailed, but in large part only because of a tacit bargain with the others. As long as the PCF was the largest party on the Left and could call the shots, those in favor of militant autonomy were willing to accept agreements with the PS around tough programs. Thus, as long as Union de la Gauche increased the overall strength of the Left by simultaneously improving the PCF's position *within* the Left, all currents could back it. However, once united frontism began to threaten the predominance of the PCF among workers and when the *rapport de force* within the Left began to benefit the PS, the militant autonomy faction withdrew support, as in 1974. After Mitterrand's strong showing in the presidential election, a series of by-elections demonstrated that the PS was beginning to eat into Communist voting support.

Recognition of this unleashed a furious battle within the PCF. The united frontists pressed for even more modernization of Communist doctrine. Public opinion polls showed the PCF at its highest level of popular legitimacy ever. It followed, therefore, that more democratization inside the party, more emphasis on civil liberties, and greater acceptance of electoralist reformism might consolidate PCF support, especially among the crucial new middle strata. A rapid series of doctrinal changes, culminating in the Twenty-Second Congress in 1976—the highpoint of French Eurocommunism—took place. At the same time, the militant-autonomy current targeted the Socialists as likely traitors to Left ideas and programs and sought a new Communist declaration of independence *within alliance*.

This combination of strategies, founded on a complicated internal compromise in which the pro-Soviet elements often weighed in on the side of militant auton-omy, gave the outside world a picture of a more erratic PCF. Internal conflicts culminated in the 1977 decision to break off, in effect, the agreement with the PS. The 1977 municipal elections—at which the Union de la Gauche won a majority for the first time since 1958—made it absolutely clear that PCF zigzags had not halted the Socialists. As a result, the unstable internal coalition came apart, and the PCF leadership moved from united frontism to a strategy of militant autonomy. Deciding never again to allow a Socialist to stand alone as candidate for president, it also set out to rebuild PCF identity from the bottom up. There was new talk of *autogestion à la mode du PCF*, embedded in a strategy of step-by-step struggles towards socialism, involving a move away from exclusive attention to electioneering toward a more participatory and mobilizational politics. The shift in strategy was difficult to implement, however. Years of united frontism had created a rank and file that believed in alliances with the PS and that was angry and confused by the shift, even more so when, between the two rounds of the 1978 legislative elections, the PCF called for its voters to stand down as usual for the PS. The PCF erupted in internal crisis, and militants left in droves.[53]

Despite the antics of the PCF, Mitterrand and the Socialists refused to alter their strategy. Presenting themselves as *unitaire pour deux,* they stood by the Common Program to increase their electoral support and popularity in the run-up to 1981. Mitterrand's refusal to move away from the programmatic content of united frontism was not hard to understand. The strategy was working well. The Communists were losing support to the Socialists, the Left credentials of the PS had been reestablished, Communist voters preferred Mitterrand to any Right candidate, and the decline of the PCF was bringing more middle-class support into the PS fold. If he could hold on, if the economic crisis continued to work its effects, French voters would rally to the Left's presidential candidate.

Mitterrand did not have an easy time. Struggles continued inside the Socialist Party. After 1978, Michel Rocard's supporters attempted to advance him as the more "modern" candidate, to replace an "archaic" Mitterrand, who was a loser to boot. Mitterrand beat back this challenge by turning again to his Left, bringing CERES back into the majority after excluding the Rocardians. The result was that very few differences in basic substance existed among the Programme Commun of 1972, the Projet Socialiste of 1980, which CERES had a major hand in writing, and Mitterrand's 1981 Manifeste de Créteil.

As a result of the limitation imposed by strategy, Mitterrand came to the presidency in 1981 (and the Socialist Party quickly followed him) with deep commitments to radical Keynesianism, which were honored during the first year in office. The left-wing government extended republican liberties and rights, enacted governmental decentralization, expanded employment-creation programs, raised the minimum wage, increased social spending, nationalized banks and large companies, and granted workers new rights in the workplace. The economic policy aspects of these programs were not only traditionally Keynesian, but also solidaristic, with the greatest effort directed to the poorest parts of French society.

The Left government's policies after 1981 nonetheless foundered on an unfavorable international situation. Preexisting industrial weaknesses, Mitterrand's initial reluctance to devalue the franc, and the effects of the deflation in the United States combined to turn redistributive demand stimulation policies into ballooning inflation, a flood of import, and huge international trade difficulties. The government's initial response was to impose a stringent austerity—"rigor" in its words— program after June 1982. It devalued the franc, halted reforms, scaled back growth ambitions to near zero, implemented a set of measures (including temporary wage and price policies) to de-index wages from inflation, and increased taxes. Initially, considerable effort was made to prevent these austerity measures from undermining the government's commitment to redistributing income toward the poor. Middle-income earners, blue-collar and white-collar workers, bore the brunt of this. But these efforts to backpedal did not solve the problems either.

This analysis has not said much up until now about economic crisis. The reason for the silence is neither that such a crisis did not exist in France nor that the French Left did not consider the economy to be in difficulty. Rather, the analysis of the crisis by the United Left and its proposals for surmounting it were all rooted in the paradigmatic discourse of French Fordism. Responding to crisis was thought to require full employment policies and increased state spending, coupled with further *dirigiste* programs to shape investment. In other words, the French Left treated the economic problems of the 1970s as a crisis *within* the system rather than one *of* the system.[54]

Why? The stabilization of French Fordism came in the 1960s. In these terms we can interpret it as one of the legacies of 1968. Mobilizations prior to 1968 were in part driven by experiences of worker opposition to companies' responses to the first signs of declining productivity. The intensification of the labor process, de-skilling, and resort to less militant categories of workers were all patronal strategies to keep up profits. Worker opposition continued in the late 1960s and early years of the next decade. One measure of the strength of the newly stabilized mode of regulation was that such opposition could be reabsorbed by unions and parties as wage demands and efforts to extract greater workplace power for unions. One of the particularities of French Fordism in the 1950s had been an extremely unequal income distribution and an appalling lack of formal union power. The 1968 protocol of Grenelle, which brought a big wage settlement and some reform of labor relations, somewhat redressed the balance. Despite the

Chaban-Delors efforts under Pompidou to "social-democratize" labor relations, worker militancy remained high, however, encouraged in part by the political gains of the Left.[55] France was beginning to experience the consequences of "labor inclusion," which countries that were more social-democratic had faced for a time. Once the economy turned down, there was little space to recall what had been obtained by workers through their militancy in 1968 and in their individual workplaces.

As the tide of Left support advanced through 1977, the Right governments were reluctant to back off quickly from their own versions of statist Keynesianism.[56] Jacques Chirac extended state responsibility for labor market redesign and further protected against unemployment. Government economists interpreted the first oil shock with Keynesian eyes and acted accordingly.[57] But Keynesian solutions no longer had the anticipated effects. At the same time industrial investment virtually ceased after 1974. The absence of serious deflationary policies plus administrative control over employment levels meant that French capital did not restructure. Thus, at the very moment when businesses elsewhere were reassessing postwar strategies, recasting international perspectives, seeking ways to introduce new electronic technologies, and discovering the need for new "flexibility" to increase productivity, French companies were locked into an economic and political compromise that was very difficult to change. France began to de-industrialize, without re-gearing for a newly cutthroat international market. The result was the beginning of decline. The Right-Center government could not ignore the restructuring of global crisis, but for electoral reasons the steps it took could be only tentative.[58] Despite a strategy primarily designed to master political problems rather than economic necessities, Giscard and Barre nonetheless lost politically. With rising unemployment, higher inflation, and Barre's threats of austerity, the plausibility of the Left's appeal rose.

As a result of all this, not only did the Left win the 1981 election with an economic program designed in 1944, but it inherited an immense mess. Responses to crisis had been postponed precisely because the political relations of the societal paradigm had remained relatively intact. In the PS, the forces critical of the Common Program had gotten tied up in and diverted by Rocard's challenge to Mitterrand after 1978. What might have been a debate about strategic direction became a competition over the presidential nomination. In both the PCF and the CGT the forces arguing in the late 1970s that the world had changed and new approaches were needed were drummed out—in effect, purged.[59]

As of 1981, then, the universe of political discourse within which the French Left operated was still ordered by the major elements of the Fordist societal paradigm, although the economy was no longer operating according to Fordist principles. The run-up to the 1981 election and the inability of the French state to work with capital to restructure shows the impact of this legacy. A late stabilization, combined with an exceedingly close balance of electoral forces, had kept the political compromise in place but ineffectual. The French "learning curve" had been much more extended than elsewhere, bringing immense costs for the economy and society.

After 1983: Back to the Future

In 1982–83, the Socialist government undertook a dramatic policy change. Deflation measures, then austerity measures, had proven inadequate to stabilize France's international trade position and reduce its comparatively high inflation level. Spring 1983 brought the final act. The forces inside the governing coalition—the Communists, CERES, and certain important ministers and advisers to the president—that advocated some uncoupling of the French from the international economy to allow a voluntaristic industrial strategy using nationalized industries and relying on the domestic market, lost out to a combination of account-balancers, centrist economic managers, and "modernizers." Retreating from a model that promised significant changes in France's domestic social compromise in favor of labor and the poor, the Socialists accepted the constraints of the international market. From later 1983 until the Left lost its parliamentary majority in March 1986, policy and political rhetoric embraced "modernization." A neoliberal language of entrepreneurship, risk-taking, and profit-seeking dislodged notions of social equity and justice.[60]

If the measure is the content of policies and their representational terms, it might seem as if the story had come full circle, with the end now like the beginning. We are, as Hollywood says, "Back to the Future." The Left discourse, which political competition eventually made into the dominant representations in the terms of class and economistic identities of the mode of regulation and societal paradigm, was not the only one available. In 1962 the universe of political discourse had also abounded with discussions of the end of ideology, the irrelevance of class conflict and class politics, the decline of political parties, and the changing French voter. By the late 1980s these themes again had a central place on the menu of popular and academic discourse. In 1962 the PCF still remained isolated from other Left forces. In 1990 the PCF was back in its ghetto as a result of the stridency of its old-fashioned workerism. What it said mattered to no one since it no longer had the resources to impose its will. In 1962 the non-Communist Left was in disarray. In the late 1980s the Parti Socialiste was suspiciously absent from the scene. Mitterrand's 1988 electoral victory was in part assured by his distance from his erstwhile *camarades,* being the candidate of *la France* more than of any party. The smaller Left factions disagreed over which, if any, political formations to rally behind. Old Left Trotskyist or new-look ex-Communists competed with the new New Left in the *Verts* ("Greens") for the allegiance of disaffected ex-Communists and ex-Socialists.

After years of decline of intellectual Marxism and collapse of the class discourse, any discussion of social classes tended to be treated as quaintly archaic, hardly to be taken seriously. What was to be taken seriously, however, were the technocrats. Just as they had emerged from their offices once de Gaulle had legitimized modernization after 1958, technocrats of leftish credentials came out once again to steer the country over the shoals of post-Fordism. And, finally, the psephologists announced that the voters had become postmodern, uninterested in the traditional Left messages of social transformation and more interested in "issue voting" and non-"ideological" politics *à l'américain*.[61] The French party system had returned, in other words, to the fragmentation and instability that the first twenty-five years of the Fifth Republic had overcome. What happened after 1983? and, of course, since nothing falls from the sky, what happened to make these last years happen?

Back to a Paradigm:
Is There a Post-Fordist Future?

After the 1986 election, many observers were willing to announce the death of the Left, following any number of paths to that conclusion. For some, the Left was dying because the PCF was at 9.7%, and no Left without the PCF was conceivable. For others, the Left was dead because the PS government had turned from social democracy toward a new form of technocratic Colbertism and had less concern for the social effects and more for the investment effects of state actions. For yet others, the Left was dying in 1986 because it had been on its deathbed for years. For these observers, the electoral statistics and public opinion polls were particularly important, leading them to the conclusion that France was experiencing "homogenization" and was "tired of ideology."[62]

This last proposition was, to a large extent, based on a flawed argument. In observing that the correlation between social characteristics and vote was weakening over time (hence homogenization), they concluded that issue voting or retrospective voting were undermining the relationship between social structure and politics. Its replacement would be voting based on conjunctural factors, corresponding to the individualist liberalism that was supposedly becoming the dominant ideology.[63]

A first difficulty with this argument is that it confuses correlation and causation. This is more than a technical quibble. The correlation/causation problem arises less in the interpretation of the contemporary situation than in the comparison with the past. The underlying assumption was that somewhere in the golden past the social location of individuals had caused their vote and, therefore, what was new was the breakdown of this structural relationship. Obviously, the thrust of the argument made in this paper is that social structure cannot cause political behavior; there is an intervening factor, which has been called the societal paradigm here. As part of the constitution of the paradigm, social forces give meaning to the worlds they inhabit and—depending on these representations—

mobilize the population along quite particular lines of social cleavage and in specific kinds of political practice. In this process collective identities come into being and groups of "interests" emerge. Therefore, the ideology or values of the electorate tend to follow the actions of political actors more than being autonomously created.

Left politicians had in the past understood the importance of creating their electorates. The experience of the 1970s had been a lesson that talking Left *and* acting Left, according to the terms of the Fordist paradigm, produced great electoral support. Yet, after 1981, the continued use of such a discourse and such practices was extremely costly because it did not correspond well to the lived experiences of economic restructuring. Because the Left's electorate had been encouraged to think the world of 1981 would respond to the same state actions as had the world of 1945, it was totally unprepared for the altered reality. Having made no adjustments in its program and the representations of reality embedded within it because of the political benefits that accrued from not doing so, the Left in government was destined to sow little but discontent and confusion among its constituency. One consequence of such disappointment with the failure of this program and the gap between promise and reality was electoral defeat in 1986.

The postwar societal paradigm imploded in a very short period of time in France. The balance of political forces—capital, organized labor, political parties, and the state—that had sustained it quickly gave up their Keynesian and social-democratized discourses. In consequence, the universe of political discourse became cacophonous as social forces competed over the power to give meaning to the conditions of the future.

Some very loud voices were raised for a "return" to liberalism, new "flexibility" in labor relations and contracts, and a family-based individualism that has not been this popular since well before 1945.[64] This was the preferred solution of much of business, and it was supported by the rightward-moving Gaullists. Yet it is not a position that can sustain a set of stabilized social relations. Just as the last point of high liberalism in France—the mid-nineteenth century—was a time of social crisis and instability, the implementation of this version of neo-liberalism for the 1990s would also quite likely be accompanied by such problems. There-fore, other social forces, appalled by, or at least nervous about, the potential costs of pure neoliberalism sought ways to modify, humanize, or tame it.

The Socialists sought a new meaning system that would both be politically practical and make sense of the new conditions. In its search, the PS swung away from its use of the terms of the Fordist mode of regulation and societal paradigm with a vengeance, as it realized that the balance of political forces had changed dramatically. The Communists had lost their ability to mobilize the shrinking working class. The new middle class was vacillating among partisan alternatives, including, by 1989, support for the *Verts*. Unions were no longer able to mobilize effectively against the restructuring efforts of capital, and French capital, as a result, was becoming more international and more dependent on social "flexibility." The task that the Socialist government assumed after 1983 was to create a version of neoliberalism that could respond to the economic situation of global restructuring and domestic problems of accumulation, state spending, unemployment, and international competitiveness. The Socialists began to develop new representations of social relations, in part by delegitimizing old collective identities. In doing this they reached "back to the future" for a vision of social relations that had been relegated to the shadow world of the universe of political discourse by the success of the late-blooming consensus at the end of the 1960s. France's New Left had contained legions of Left Catholics, anti-statist *autogestionnaires,* and technocratic optimists as well as radical democrats. In the 1970s, when the Rocardians moved into the PS (where they were outgunned in most of debates until after 1983), the movement was weakened, but it never died. The New Left, now dressed in its *deuxième gauche* clothing, emerged inside the government to direct the Socialists' turn to the center.[65]

The *deuxième gauche's* roots in Left Catholicism, in Protestant notions of "charity," and in radical republican social analysis provide it with a discourse of "solidarity." Solidarity can be coupled with a macroeconomic analysis emphasizing new forms of state-business relations, changes in labor-market policy, and an acceptance of business-defined needs for restructuring. This discourse is different from that of the Left rooted in the Second or Third Internationals, although it is not totally incompatible with them, as the recurrent alliances of Left Catholicism, social democracy, and united-frontist Communism have demonstrated. The difference is that there is no insistence on *equality* in solidaristic discourse. Thus a discourse of solidarity is compatible with a two-tier labor force (as long as the worst effects of marginal work are eliminated), with notions of gender "difference" (as long as difference is honored), with socially differentiating institutions like schools (as long as the elites that issue from them become technocrats with good hearts), and with a generally more fragmented society.

Formation of a new societal paradigm around variations on neoliberalism would beget the unfortunate problem of founding a consensus that accepts rather than challenges socially constructed hierarchies. Charity has never been adequate to overcome social inequality precisely because it does not empower people. Moreover, the discourse of solidarity does not have an adequate response to the neofascism of the Front National. Without a discourse of equality in difference, the Left will not be able to challenge those on the Right who want to eliminate all difference in the name of a false equality of "Frenchness." The challenge facing the French Left is, then, to turn from the social relations of Fordism toward the future, without abandoning the fundamental principles that make it "the Left."

Notes

1. The analysis presented here emphasizes only the Left, since that is my assigned task. However, the implication of the analytic categories used is that not only the Left but also the Right came to this

modernization in similar ways. I will refer at times to the experience of the non-Left when it is essential to the story, but this experience is not systematically presented.

2. Jane Jenson, "Gender and Reproduction: Or, Babies and the State," *Studies in Political Economy* 20 (Summer, 1986).

3. Much of the rest of this theoretical section has been developed in dialogue and therefore in collaboration with Alain Lipietz. For his use of some of these concepts see his paper in this volume. For further elaboration see Jane Jenson, " 'Different' but not 'exceptional': Canada's Permeable Fordism," *Canadian Review of Sociology and Anthropology* 26 (Winter 1989), and idem, "Paradigms and Political Discourse: Protective Legislation in France and the United States Before 1914," *Canadian Journal of Political Science* 22 (June, 1989).

4. Lipietz's paper in this volume develops the argument about the structures of economic and political power. This paper deals only with their manifestations in the world of lived experience.

5. The term "paradigm" derives from linguistics, where a paradigm links different forms of the same root, thereby ordering difference and demonstrating connections across forms that might not otherwise appear linked. The best-known use of the concept in social science is by T. S. Kuhn, who suggests that paradigms are historical constructs whose selection from a range of possible paradigms is based on struggle for allegiances. Paradigms illuminate the world until the contradictions that they can no longer absorb permit other scientists to imagine an alternative and gain support for that vision.

6. Lipietz in this volume describes the process by which the regime of accumulation and social bloc were constituted in postwar France.

7. Maurice Duverger, *La Vème République* (Paris: PUF, 1960), p. 212.

8. The survey of meanings of *dépolitisation* is from the overview article by Jean Touchard. After exploring the problem in detail, the Fondation Nationale des Sciences Politiques could shed little more light than when it began, in part because the participants in the colloquim admitted from the start that the term had more everyday political resonance than "scientific" rigor. See the introduction by Vedel and Touchard in Georges Vedel, *La Dépolitisation: Mythe ou réalité?* (Paris: FNSP, Cahier 120, 1962).

9. There is obviously more to be said about these theses. It is important to remember that the postwar boom in France was constructed in voluntary collusion between senior civil servants and managers of big business, as Shonfield has informed us. Therefore, that experience, coupled with the discourse of modernism promoted by Mendès-France in the mid-1950s ought to have given pause to anyone on the Left. The interests of workers were never at the forefront of concern, nor was any attention to France's abysmal record on income redistribution a central element of economic planning. Nevertheless, average per capita income nearly tripled between 1946 and 1962, increasing from $511 to $1,358 in constant dollars. See Mark Kesselman and Joel Krieger, *European Politics in Transition* (Lexington, Mass.: D. C. Heath, 1987), p. 157. France's "Fordism without the workers" did not bring pauperization, even if did not bring new power for workers. Thus, Thorez's lack of nuance in promoting his theses did little more than provoke a huge debate within the Left (see *La Revue Socialiste* in the late 1950s), while saddling the PCF with a thoroughly inappropriate set of economic doctrines for the times.

10. Jane Jenson, "Changing Discourse, Changing Agenda: Political Rights and Reproductive Policies in France," in Carole Mueller and Mary Katzenstein, eds., *The Women's Movement of the United States and Western Europe: Consciousness, Political Opportunity and Public Policy* (Philadelphia: Temple University Press, 1987), p. 79ff.

11. Once again the situation was complicated. The 1950s were a time in which the interests of imperialism and the international family-planning movement did move together. Many commentators expressed concern about the real effects of indiscriminate promotion of birth control in the Third World. Yet the PCF seems to have confused that critique with another position—the opposition in

postwar USSR to birth control—and combined the two in a rigid way that was, again, inappropriate for France.

12. Duverger, *La Ve République*, pp. 218–19.

13. Collette Ysmal, *Le Comportement électoral des français* (Paris: La Découverte, 1986), p. 11.

14. Philip Converse and Roy Pierce, *Political Representation in France* (Cambridge, Mass.: Belknap Press of Harvard University Press, 1986), Tables 5–2 and 5–3, pp. 155–56.

15. Converse and Pierce, *Political Representation in France*, p. 14.

16. François Goguel, *Chroniques électorales: La Cinquième République du général de Gaulle* (Paris: FNSP, 1983), chap. 6.

17. For statistical details of this economic change, see George Ross and Jane Jenson, "The Tragedy of the French Left," *New Left Review* 171 (September–October 1988): 15–16.

18. Pascal Petit, "Problems of the State in Dealing With the System of Wage/Labour Relations: The Case of France," in Robert Boyer, ed., *The Search for Labour Market Flexibility: The European Economies in Transition* (Oxford: Clarendon Press, 1988), p. 121.

19. The PCF's departure from government in 1947 came over its withdrawal of support for the government's wage and price policies. The wildcat strike at Renault Billancourt forced first the CGT and then the PCF to choose between workers opposed to the wage-squeezing effects of the "battle for production" or support for the government. In other words, the PCF had reached the limits of reformism. Further acceptance of the low-wage policies would impose huge organizational costs. "If a line was to be drawn beyond which the PCF would not go in its United Frontist moderation, it had to be drawn here. Beyond all the compromises and maneuvers of the postwar years, the PCF knew it would either be 'the party of the working class' or nothing at all." George Ross, *Workers and Communists in France: From Popular Front to Eurocommunism* (Berkeley, Calif.: University of California Press, 1982), p. 47.

20. Politically isolated by the SFIO's participation in third-force alliances, the PCF pressed the CGT to politicize union activity around foreign policy and general antigovernmental actions. This pressure on the union confederation led to a series of difficult strikes and problems for the CGT until at least the mid-1950s. See Ross, *Workers and Communists in France*, chap. 3.

21. Jean-Pierre Rioux, *La France de la Quatrième République* (Paris: Editions du Seuil, 1980), chap. 5.

22. In the short run, the initial growth after the Liberation did not bring an increase in the purchasing power of salaries. In the spring of 1947, salaries were still one-third less than in 1938. Over the 1950s as a whole, despite the introduction of SMIC, the inequalities in distribution of income grew. Jean-Charles Asselain, *Histoire économique de la France*, vol. 2 (Paris: Editions du Seuil, 1984), pp. 116 and 122.

23. This pattern of statist guarantees of negotiations between warring social partners differs substantially from both the more corporatist pattern of social democracy and the collective-bargaining pattern of North America. On the role of the French state, see Petit, "Problems of the State," and Robert Delorme and Christiane André, *L'Etat et l'économie* (Paris: Editions du Seuil, 1983).

24. It took more than a decade to rebuild and modernize industry, to find and establish an adequate mechanism for wage and price determination, to expand the social transfer system, to adapt money creation to less public financing of investment, and to get foreign trade and financial flows into better equilibrium. Robert Boyer, *The Influence of Keynes on French Economic Policy: Past and Present* (Paris: CEPREMAP, Série Orange, vol. 8404, 1984), p. 19.

25. Ross, *Workers and Communists in France*, chaps. 3 and 4.

26. For some details of this moment see Rioux, *La France de la Quatrième République*, chap. 2.

27. Asselain, *Histoire économique de la France,* p. 122.

28. Ross and Jenson, "The Tragedy of the French Left," pp. 16–17.

29. George Ross recounts these debates in great detail. See "Marxism and the new Middle Classes: French Critiques," *Theory and Society* 5 (1978), and "Destroyed by the Dialectic: Politics, the Decline of Marxism, and the New Middle Strata in France," *Theory and Society* 16 (1987). The summary in the following paragraphs is based on these two analyses.

30. Ross, "Destroyed by the Dialectic," pp. 58–59.

31. For example, opposition to the pauperization theses of Thorez provided one spur to debate about new class relations. Indeed, it was as a detailed refutation of these theses that the non-Communist Left's economic analysis took form.

32. For further details of this period in PCF history, see Jane Jenson and George Ross, "The Uncharted Waters of De-Stalinization: The Uneven Evolution of the Parti Communiste Français," *Politics and Society* 9 (1980): 270ff.

33. The analyses of state monopoly capitalism were developed in these years to replace Thorez's pauperization theses.

34. This change is most clearly visible in the altered behavior of the CGT. Gradually over the 1960s, the PCF allowed the CGT to act more as a union, by not insisting that the confederation carry a heavy foreign policy and isolationist agenda. The CGT was then freer to begin to search for unity-in-action possibilities and to bargain more effectively. The CGT still remained an important element of the PCF's arsenal, but the politics the party wanted from the CGT had changed toward support for its united frontism and electorally based reformism. Ross, *Workers and Communists in France,* chap. 6.

35. For the Socialists, "the underlying logic of the argument was that advancing capitalism created a 'broad, change-oriented social collectivity far transcending the narrowly defined working class of older [read "PCF"] Marxism.' " Ross, "Destroyed by the Dialectic," p. 13.

36. Obviously, within the debates on the non-Communist Left there were several suggestions of possible replacement vanguards, coming from Mallet and Touraine in particular. The *front de classe* had the advantage for the PS of not forcing any choice on that divisive question.

37. The description that follows is based on the detailed discussion of Defferre's campaign in Frank L. Wilson, *The French Democratic Left, 1963–1969: Towards a Modern Party System* (Stanford, Calif.: Stanford University Press, 1971), chap. 5.

38. Deferre presented this strategy as his way of modernizing the party system. Thus, for some observers, this was "the defeat of the *modernes* by the *anciens.*" Wilson, *The French Democratic Left,* p. 132. It can also be seen, however, as the next-to-last gasp of Fourth Republic politics.

39. For a thorough discussion of this moment in French political engineering, see Wilson, *The French Democratic Left,* chaps. 6 and 7.

40. The threat of revived third "forcism" that this initiative carried had so frightened the PCF as to make the leadership radically alter its position in the Grenelle negotiations. See Ross, *Workers and Communists in France,* pp. 201–3.

41. Polarization was given a great push by the simplification of electoral competition that followed from the 1967 agreement among the PCF, FGDS, and PSU to stand down for each others' candidates in the second round. There were usually only two Left candidates in any riding—a Communist and a *Fédé* or a PSU one. In the second round, almost everywhere, there was only one. See Goguel, *Chroniques électorales,* chap. 7.

42. On the experience of the French women's movement with the parties, see Jane Jenson, "The French Communist Party and Feminism," in Ralph Miliband and John Saville, eds., *The Socialist Register, 1980* (London: Merlin, 1980), and Jane Jenson, "Ce n'est pas un hasard: The Varieties of

French Feminism," in Jolyon Howorth and George Ross, eds., *Contemporary France: An Interdisciplinary Review* (London: Frances Pinter, 1989). On the reabsorption of trade-union militancy, see the articles by Ross and Mouriaux in Mark Kesselman and Guy Groux, eds., *The French Workers' Movement* (London: Allen and Unwin, 1984).

43. Boyer, *The Influence of Keynes on French Economic Policy*, pp. 21–22, describes the shared discourse of the Right and the Left, comparing Valéry Giscard-d'Estaing's economic analysis to the Left's, as well as the developing strength of Keynesianism within the universities in the 1960s.

44. The growing consensus on certain basic economic strategies also appeared in public opinion polling, when views on the state's role in the economy, postwar nationalizations, and state subsidies to church schools all revealed less of a distinction between Left and Right. See Wilson, *The French Democratic Left*, pp. 56–58.

45. One Gaullist experiment involved the discussion of the *nouvelle société* proposals that Jacques Delors attempted to manage after 1968. See Ross, *Workers and Communists in France*, pp. 216ff.

46. Boyer, *The Influence of Keynes on French Economic Policy*, pp. 22–23.

47. Obviously, not all actors had the same normative position on the desirability or the future of this design, but they did agree that it described France at the end of the 1960s. Nevertheless, the Gaullists, despite their *nouvelle société* initiatives, were not about to incorporate the labor movement or its political representatives into decision making. Grenelle had forced a massive settlement, but it had also taken a massive mobilization and a threat to the life of the regime to do so. Therefore, while Right and Left both had new understandings of the place of the industrial working class in French society, there was sufficient dispute between the two to give the Left plenty of mobilizational space for a different, more labor-inclusive kind of Fordism.

48. The PCF's response to the student-led mobilization in 1968 not only were particularly unfortunate, but also indicated that the PCF had not figured out its class maps sufficiently to understand a political outburst by the "intermediary strata." Instead, it resorted to its famous "dismissal tactics," which might have succeeded in earlier periods when intellectuals felt guilty for not being workers, but which did not work in 1968.

49. This is *not* to imply that *soixante-huitards* were not, in the majority quite workerist. Because of the paradigmatic discourse which had emerged in the mid-1960s, in fact the French New Left was one of the most workerist around, a characteristic that had both benefits and costs. One benefit was that the social movements, like feminism, were not cut off from the organized working class. One cost was that it was hard to get beyond considerations of class politics. On the costs and benefits for feminism, see Jenson, "Ce n'est pas un hasard."

50. The description of the currents within the PS is from George Ross and Jane Jenson, "Crisis and France's 'Third Way,' " *Studies in Political Economy* 11 (Summer, 1983): 76–78.

51. Converse and Pierce, *Political Representation in France;* Ysmal, *Le Comportement électoral des français*, chap. 3.

52. These debates were ongoing, but they were particularly intense just before 1981, when CERESian statism and nationalization for industrial policy squared off against Rocardian decentralizers in a changing global economy. Colbertist Jacobinism came under severe attack from *autogestionnaires*. While the debate was productive of much academic and political creativity, it was more or less beside the point, as the Mitterrandistes steered single-mindedly toward the presidential election with the PCF in tow.

53. For participant-observers' views of this experience within the PCF see Jane Jenson and George Ross, *The View From Inside: A French Communist Cell in Crisis* (Berkeley, Calif.: University of California Press, 1985).

54. There are several reasons for this response. The first and most obvious is that in the early 1970s a period of learning was required before the full dimensions of the crisis could become visible.

Not only the Left but also the government of the Right acted as if it faced a crisis within Fordism. See Pascal Petit, "Problems of the State," pp. 36–37 and 41ff.

55. The unions, and especially the CGT, had a great deal of difficulty making sense of these new forms of militancy. Pressures from companies to increase rates of productivity gave rise to considerable industrial conflict, especially after 1970 among new industrial workers and semiskilled factory operatives rebelling against speedups and other deteriorating working conditions. The CFDT was more prepared to accept and try to lead the "hypermilitant" actions that often broke out, while the CGT, overdetermined by ties to the PCF's own agenda, tried to keep to its long-term agenda of steady mobilization, especially in the Days of Action. The interunion conflict was severe in these years, but gradually the two confederations moved closer together, in the direction of the CGT's preferred strategy. See Ross, *Workers and Communists in France,* chap. 9.

56. This was the case, despite the more classical than Keynesian content of the Sixth Plan for 1971–75—which identified problems in trade and argued that wages and productivity were negatively related.

57. Boyer, *The Influence of Keynes on French Economic Policy,* 25ff; Pascal Petit, "La Fin des politiques de plein-emploi," *Les Temps Modernes* 501 (April 1988).

58. Ross and Jenson, "The Tragedy of the French Left," pp. 34ff.

59. On the effects within the PCF of this internal conflict, and the strengthening of forces of reaction, see Jenson and Ross, *The View From Inside,* Conclusion. On the sad story of the CGT's "proposition-force unionism," see Ross, *Workers and Communists in France,* Conclusion.

60. Ross and Jenson, "The Tragedy of the French Left," pp. 8–9 and 40ff.

61. Of course, it was hard within this perspective to explain why increasing numbers of these postmodern voters were not voting for the freewheeling and pluralist Center but for the neofascist Le Pen. The hypothesis was advanced nonetheless.

62. On homogenization see, inter alia, Alain Lancelot and Marie-Thérèse Lancelot, "The Evolution of the French Electorate 1981–86," in George Ross, Stanley Hoffman, and Sylvia Malzacher, eds., *The Mitterrand Experiment* (New York: Oxford University Press, 1987). On the exhaustion of ideology see the article by Perrineau and Schweisguth in Elisabeth Dupoirier and Gérard Grunberg, eds., *Mars 1986: La Drôle de defaite de la gauche* (Paris: FNSP, 1986).

63. Lancelot and Lancelot, "The Evolution of the French Electorate, 1981–86," p. 98.

64. Petit, "Problems of the State," p. 133.

65. At the same time, more radical elements reappeared in civil society, attired in the colours of the *Verts.* See Jane Jenson, "From *Baba Cool* to a *Vote Utile:* The Trajectory of the French *Verts,*" *French Politics and Society* 7 (Fall 1989).

5

Immigration and Modernization

James F. Hollifield

> The newly-born infant, upon first opening his eyes, must gaze upon the
> fatherland, and until his dying day should behold nothing else. Your true
> *republican* is a man who imbibed love of the fatherland, which is to say love of
> the laws and of liberty, with his mother's milk. That love makes up his entire
> existence: he has eyes only for the fatherland, lives only for his fatherland; the
> moment he is alone, he is a mere cipher; the moment he has no fatherland, he
> is no more; if not dead, he is worse off than if he were dead.
> —Rousseau, *The Government of Poland*

In *The Government of Poland* Rousseau paints a nationalist, republican picture
of citizenship. Throughout his work, he makes a forceful argument for instilling
in the individual a sense of republican virtue, civic duty, and commitment to the
ideals of liberty and equality.[1] Since the Revolution, this ideology of citizenship
has served as a political counterweight to the regional and ethnic diversity of
France.[2] Jacobinism has been a powerful ideal for the assimilation and political
socialization of ethnic minorities within, and foreigners from without.[3]

In addition to imposing a republican order on an essentially traditional (nonin-
dustrial) society, one of the most important problems of political development
during the Third Republic was how to incorporate ethnically distinct groups. The
most significant event in this regard was the Dreyfus Affair, which led to a
reaffirmation of Jacobin ideals of citizenship and equality before the law, regardless of ethnic identity.[4] At the time of the Dreyfus Affair, immigration began to
play an important role in the social and economic life of France. Just as they
were to do after the Second World War, immigrants helped to meet the demand
for labor created by relatively late but rapid industrialization and the weakness
(or in some areas the absence) of a French working class. In sectors such as coal
and steel, immigrants from Belgium, Italy, and Poland formed the backbone of
the labor force.[5] During the first decades of the Third Republic, the state was not
centrally involved in controlling immigration, as firms, starved for labor, took
the lead in recruiting workers from neighboring countries where there was an

excess labor supply, especially Italy. In most cases, these new immigrant workers were rather quickly assimilated, with schools, trade unions, and the new Communist Party taking the lead in the socialization process.

Political opposition to immigration was not long in coming. In the heated political climate of the 1920s, foreigners were viewed with suspicion. Reactions from the Right were especially severe, as immigrants were denounced as a source of labor unrest and Communist agitation. The state took the first tentative steps in the 1920s to regulate immigration, largely in response to political pressures.[6] The onset of the Great Depression in the 1930s and stagnation of the economy resolved the immigrant "problem," at least temporarily. But the stage was set, both politically and economically, for a *reprise de l'immigration* following the Second World War. Firms were well aware of the contribution that immigrant labor could make to productivity. More importantly, the state was refurbished with powerful instruments for intervening in the economy and was prepared to use immigrants in order to avoid labor shortages.[7]

Economic modernization was the watchword of the Fourth Republic, and remained a dominant theme during the first decade of the Fifth. Immigration was essential to the strategies of economic development in the 1950s and 1960s. The objective of the state was to "manage" the market for foreign labor in order to assure continued economic growth. Communists and trade unionists were the most vocal opponents of immigration during the heady years of the *trente glorieuses,* because immigration seemed to undercut the market position of French workers.[8] But a larger crisis of assimilation and participation was just around the corner, as the number of non-European and non-Catholic immigrants began to rise in the 1960s in the wake of decolonization. By the mid 1970s, a "new" Jacobin influence began to manifest itself on the Left and the Right, as the state struggled to master, not only the *phenomenon* of immigration, but the *issue* as well.

The history of immigration is a *window* through which we can view the workings of the political system and the philosophical assumptions embedded within it. The way in which (democratic) states deal with the presence of foreigners can tell us a great deal about the relationship between state, society, and economy. The French political system has struggled with the issues of immigration and citizenship because of contradictions in the Jacobin tradition, which demands that the individual conform to certain ideals of civil/political behavior. In effect, a national, republican identity must take precedence over other aspects of individual identity—ethnic, religious, and linguistic.[9]

An important aspect of the Jacobin tradition is the predominance of a centralized state and reliance on administrative power to resolve intractable political-economic problems.[10] What might otherwise be called *étatisme* has played an extraordinarily important role in the political economy of immigration in postwar France. The tension during the Fifth Republic between Jacobinism and the representative, parliamentary tradition of earlier republics is crucial to understanding the way in which the political system has dealt with the issue of immigration. Attempts to use immigration for largely economic purposes, as "guestworkers," have been frustrated by parliamentary and legal constraints on the power of the administrative/Jacobin State.

If the Jacobin tradition is such an important feature of political and economic development, what bearing does it have upon the way in which aliens are treated in France? Is it possible to discern elements of this tradition in the policy-making process? Before addressing these questions, we must understand the crucial role that immigration has played in the economy, and the gradual transformation of immigrants from "factors of production" to objects of political controversy.

Immigration and Modernization in the Fourth Republic: *Des "français" pour la France*

France has a long and varied history of immigration, which dates roughly from the middle of the last century. Unlike other European states, France never became a major country of emigration. Transoceanic migrations of French nationals were limited both in scope and duration. Major exoduses are associated with the persecution and expulsion of Protestants and with the development of the French Empire.[11] Yet by 1876 there were more than 800,000 foreigners in France. Increases in the levels of immigration, particularly during the Second Empire, clearly were related to the declining population and the beginnings of industrial development. The rural exodus that provided labor for English and German industrialization in the eighteenth and nineteenth centuries did not begin in France until the twentieth century, due in part to the strength of traditional society and the persistence of small-scale agriculture. Thus, French capitalism was forced to invent a working class by adapting to the unwillingness of rural workers to leave their farms and, more important, by importing labor from abroad.[12]

From the beginning of the twentieth century until the Second World War, the percentage of foreigners in the total population steadily increased, reaching a high of 6.6 percent in 1931, before falling back again to 4.1 percent during the turbulent decades of the 1930s and 1940s. Italians and Belgians, together with the Spanish, Poles, and Germans, were the largest groups entering between 1921 and 1931 (see Table 5.1). As early as 1916, the state tried to assert control over immigration by requiring all foreigners over the age of fifteen to obtain a residency permit (*carte de séjour*). But employers took an active role in recruiting immigrant workers, with the formation in 1924 of the Société Générale d'Immigration (SGI). The SGI was a private organization set up for the purpose of helping firms locate sources of foreign labor.[13] Not until the late 1920s and 1930s did the state take concrete steps to control immigration. Regulatory measures initially were a

Table 5.1   Evolution of the Foreign Population in France, 1921–1982
(census data)*

Year	1921	1931	1954	1975	1982
Total population	38,797,540	41,228,466	42,781,370	52,599,430	54,273,200
Total foreign population	1,532,024	2,714,697	1,765,298	3,442,415	3,680,100
% of foreigners in the total population	3.9	6.6	4.1	6.5	6.8
European nationalities (including USSR)	1,435,976	2,457,649	1,431,219	2,102,685	1,760,000
Germans	75,625	71,729	53,760	42,955	43,840
Belgians	348,986	253,694	106,828	55,945	50,200
Spaniards	254,980	351,864	288,923	497,480	321,440
Italians	450,960	808,038	507,602	462,940	333,740
Poles	45,766	507,811	269,269	93,655	64,820
Portuguese	10,788	48,963	20,085	758,925	764,860
Yugoslavs	4,032	31,873	17,159	70,280	64,420
African Nationalities	37,666	105,059	229,505	1,192,300	1,573,820
Algerians			211,675[a]	710,690	795,920
Moroccans	36,277	82,568	10,734	260,025	431,120
Tunisians			4,800[b]	139,735	189,400
French West Africans		16,401		70,320	138,080
American Nationalities	22,402	32,120	49,129	41,560	50,900
Asian Nationalities (not including USSR)	28,972	86,063	40,687	104,465	293,780
Turks	5,040	36,119	5,273	50,860	123,540

(a) French Muslim Algerians.

(b) Individuals from within the French Empire (l'Union française) are counted as French, except French Muslim Algerians who were counted as foreign during this period.

*Sources: J. Costa-Lascoux, De l'immigré au citoyen (Paris: Documentation Française, 1989), p. 19; INSEE; Ministère des Affaires Sociales et de la Solidarité Nationale.

response to political pressure, but they found their ultimate justification in the deteriorating economic conditions of the Great Depression.[14]

With Liberation and the end of the Second World War, the dominant trade unions, including the Confédération Générale du Travail (CGT) and the Confédération Française des Travailleurs Chrétiens (CFTC), argued forcefully for the creation of a "neutral" state agency for controlling immigration. They made the same demands unsuccessfully in the 1920s, when the SGI had a virtual monopoly over the recruitment of foreign workers. The hope was that French workers' interests would be served better by public rather than by private control of immigration. The unions wanted to limit the number of foreign workers employed in industry and, wherever possible, to avoid competition between French and foreign workers. The state was under pressure to regulate immigration in such a way as to avoid damaging the interests of labor and capital. Yet it was another group whose council the authorities would follow from the beginning of the postwar period—the *populationnistes* were a group of academics and politicians associated with the old pronatalist Alliance Nationale pour l'Accroissement de la Population Française, which had been very active during the Third Republic in publicizing the dangers of a declining population and in promoting measures to increase birth rates.[15]

In the wake of economic devastation caused by the War, two prominent members of the pronatalist group, Robert Debré, a physician and father of a future prime minister, and Alfred Sauvy, an economist and demographer, argued forcefully that one of the central problems facing liberated France was to find workers to supplement a weakened population and to rebuild the country. Immigration, they argued, was the answer to France's perennial demographic problem of low birth rates and a declining population:

> Au lendemain de la guerre actuelle, la France aura un besoin vital d'immigrants. Pour relever les ruines, pour reprendre le travail agricole et industriel, il faudra ajouter à l'effort des Français celui d'une main-d'oeuvre étrangère certainement nombreuse. Les objections du public ("l'étranger vient manger notre pain et prendre notre place"), les plaintes des ouvriers ("l'étranger fait baisser les salaires"), les alarmes des bourgeois ("l'étranger vient prêcher chez nous le désordre et l'émeute"), les craintes des édiles ("les étrangers remplissent nos hopitaux"), les clichés des journalistes ("l'étranger que nous recevons, rebut de l'Europe, abaisse la moralité publique") ne peseront pas lourd devant l'impérieux appel de l'économie nationale. On doit retenir de ce concert quelques notes justes (souci d'éviter la baisse des salaires, nécessité d'une selection attentive), mais on peut rejeter tout ce qui n'est que généralisation injustifée.[16]

The first order of business, however, was to reestablish the legitimacy of the state, following the debacles of defeat, occupation and Vichy.[17] Although the disruptions of politics and society caused by the War provoked a crisis of legitimacy, they also created the conditions for "modernization" of the economy, which had for so long lagged behind other industrial powers of Europe.[18] This was the era of industrial planning on a national scale. With the creation of a National Planning Commission (hereafter CGP) and the adoption of the first five-year plan (the Monnet Plan), the state took an active role in shaping the economic future of the country. Little was to be left to the uncertainties of the marketplace. The drive to "rationalize" capital and labor markets was as much the result of fear of political disruptions that might be caused by the demise of the traditional and farming sectors as of fear that industrial development could not succeed, and economic independence could not be achieved without the intervention of the State.[19]

The selective allocation of capital to cooperative firms was not the only weapon in the planners' arsenal. The planners recognized that achieving economies of scale in industrial production would require new sources of *labor* as well as capital. There was a well-founded fear that new industries could not attract enough labor from the agricultural sector to sustain high rates of growth.[20] Thus, steps were taken by the state at a very early stage in the postwar period to recruit foreign workers and place them in those sectors where they would be most needed. To this end, a new agency, the National Office of Immigration (hereafter ONI), was created to regulate the influx of immigrant workers. By appealing to foreign labor, it was hoped that severe occupational and geographical dislocation of workers, particularly in traditional sectors such as farming, could be avoided, while, at the same time, the additional labor would help to prevent labor shortages that might lead to increased wages and lower investments. In many respects, the economy was repeating the pattern of development of earlier periods of industrialization, with one major difference—the state was leading the effort to recruit foreign labor and modernize the economy, rather than following the lead of businessmen.

Thus immigration was a key component of state-led strategies for economic modernization during the Fourth Republic. Foreign workers came to be seen as "factors of production" and tools for managing population and the labor market. By creating the ONI, the Provisional Government under de Gaulle hoped to establish a state monopoly over the recruitment and placement of foreign workers. The ONI was put under the control (*tutelle*) of the Ministry of Labor, and the agency was given a distinctly "corporatist" character. A twenty-four–member administrative council was established to oversee the activities of the ONI. The council included representatives from the major trade unions and employer groups, as well as from the various ministries concerned with immigration matters—namely, the Ministries of Labor and Population, both of which competed for control of the ONI. This arrangement was in keeping with the corporatist ambitions of the Provisional Government—ambitions that can be attributed to the desire to achieve consensus as quickly as possible and get on with the task of rebuilding the economy.[21]

Two groups dominated immigration policy-making at this early stage. First were the *populationnistes,* who controlled the Ministry of Population. Led by Alfred Sauvy and the *pronataliste* politician, Robert Debré, the *populationnistes* were prime movers in setting an intellectual agenda for immigration.[22] Trade unions were the other group that was initially successful in influencing immigration policy. The CGT went so far as to push for restrictions on immigration that would screen (Italian) workers according to their partisan affiliations in the home country. To this end, there was cooperation between the CGT and its Italian counterpart (the CGIL). Such screening was opposed by the other major trade union, the CFTC, which saw screening as a blatant attempt by the Communists to use immigration for partisan purposes.[23]

Undoubtedly, the loser in the immigration policy-making process during the period of the Tripartite Government was the employer. Employers lost the considerable influence they had enjoyed during the interwar period.[24] As in other policy areas, the administrative state enjoyed great leeway in setting policy goals. Thus, from the beginning of the postwar period, immigration policy was controlled by policy-makers with specific objectives in mind; and employers were denied unrestricted access to cheap foreign labor. At the urging of the *populationnistes,* the decision was made to push for a permanent immigration of Southern European Catholics, primarily Italians, who would be culturally and ethnically compatible with the French population. A major problem with this strategy was that the French state (and employers) had to compete with the Swiss and, eventually, with the Germans for excess Italian labor.[25]

The selective nature of immigration policy and the opposition of trade unions to opening the labor market to foreign workers helped to keep immigration down in the early years of the Fourth Republic (see Table 5.2). Another factor that contributed to low levels of immigration was the still uncertain economic climate. Employers were reluctant to expand their workforce, and there is evidence that they viewed domestic labor supplies as adequate for anticipated increases in aggregate demand.[26] In the area of employment, as in the area of investment, the state was doing everything possible to convince employers of the virtues of expanding production. In the Monnet Plan, the CGP estimated that the economy would require approximately 430,000 new immigrants in 1946–47 alone.[27] At the time, many experts saw these figures as wildly exaggerated. Yet the planners were convinced that if their ambitious goals of modernization were to be realized, a large influx of foreign labor would be necessary. The problem for the planners was to convince employers to think big, in terms of investment *and* in terms of employment. The reticence of employers to go along with the planners' designs for the economy is well documented.[28] We can see from Table 5.2 that the rate of entry of permanent immigrant workers did not begin to increase substantially

Table 5.2   Immigration in France, 1946–87*

	1946–55	1956–67	1968–73	1974–80	1981–87
Permanent workers	325.2	1205.9	801.3	192.9	195.1
	(32.5)[a]	(109.6)	(133.6)	(27.6)	(27.9)
	(48.94)[b]	(44.06)	(39.16)	(13.77)	(17.42)
Seasonal workers	247.6	1126.9	821.9	857.3	664.2
	(24.8)	(102.4)	(137.0)	(122.5)	(94.9)
	(37.26)	(41.17)	(40.16)	(61.18)	(59.30)
Family members	91.7	404.2	423.2	351.0	260.6
	(9.2)	(36.7)	(70.5)	(50.1)	(37.2)
	(13.80)	(14.77)	(20.68)	(25.05)	(23.27)
Total	664.4	2737.1	2046.5	1401.2	1120.0
	(66.4)	(248.8)	(341.1)	(200.2)	(160.0)
	(100.0)	(100.0)	(100.0)	(100.0)	(100.0)

*Figures are in thousands.

Numbers in parentheses are [a]the average annual rate of immigration and [b]the percentage of total immigration for each type of immigration for a given period.

Source: Office des Migrations Internationales (OMI).

until 1956. But, thanks to the efforts of the state, immigration was soon to play a crucial role in the economic boom, which has come to be known as the *trente glorieuses*.

Despite efforts at long-term economic planning, the economy was plagued with stop-and-go fluctuations in demand that led to inflationary pressures. The first sustained period of growth in the postwar period did not begin until 1953. The expansion of industrial production that followed and the increased confidence of employers in the new *dirigisme* were reflected in the labor market. Demand for labor soared during the period from 1953 to 1957, and, as the planners had predicted, immigrant labor became one of the most important productive factors in a rapidly expanding economy.[29] The domestic supply of labor was quickly exhausted and the policies of recruitment put in place by the tripartite planners must have seemed prophetic to many employers. The principal users of foreign labor in the early years of the Fourth Republic were mining, manufacturing, principally steel but also chemical and glass industries, and construction (*Bâtiment et Travaux Publics*).[30]

It would be wrong, however, to attribute too much foresight to the planners. Marshall Plan aid and the intensification of the conflict in Indochina played an important part in industrial development. Likewise, the departure of the Communists from government cleared the way for closer cooperation between the state and employers. By 1953 the confidence of businessmen in the planning process was increasing, as employers chose to accept the commitment of the Monnet planners to a relatively free market, and to ignore the socialist implications of *dirigisme*. In the area of immigration policy, employers' influence increased with the departure of the Communist minister of labor, Ambroise Croizat, in 1947; and firms began to recruit foreign workers more directly in the sending countries, thus bypassing the ONI and normal institutional channels for hiring foreigners.[31]

Immigration soared at the end of the Fourth Republic, surpassing 120,000 in 1956, a floor that would not be broken again until 1987. The *taux de régularisation* (legalization rate), which is a measure of immigration not initially controlled by ONI, jumped in 1956–57 from twenty to the fifty-percent range, as the state progressively lost control of immigration in the early years of the Fifth Republic. The geographical and occupational mobility of French workers also increased during this period.[32] These changes in the labor market were indicative of the rapid industrial expansion that began in the mid-1950s. Although immigration of permanent workers controlled by the ONI remained relatively low, if we count Algerian immigration (which was not controlled by ONI), net immigration more than doubled during the first decade of the Fourth Republic (see Tables 5.2 and 5.3).[33] Until the granting of independence in 1962, Algeria was considered to be part of metropolitan France, and, as such, Algerian workers and their families were allowed to move freely into and out of France.[34]

Despite increases in immigration and the central role of the state in helping to

Table 5.3   Algerian Immigration, 1946–73*

Workers	1946–55	1956–67	1968–73
Men over sixteen	1130.3	1489.5	1842.5
	(99.28)	(87.35)	(85.43)
Women and children	8.2	215.8	311.1
	(0.72)	(12.65)	(14.57)
Total	1138.4	1705.3	2135.6
	(100.0)	(100.0)	(100.0)

*Figures are in thousands.
Numbers in parentheses are the percentage of total immigration for each group.
Sources: Tapinos, L'Immigration étrangère en France, page 130 and Ministère de l'Intérieur.

recruit foreign workers, there was no political reaction to the growing foreign presence, such as was seen in the 1920s. Nonetheless, as public opinion surveys showed, the public remained skeptical of the benefits of immigrant labor, and there was a general sense of opposition to immigration.[35] Georges Tapinos attributes these negative attitudes to three factors: a Malthusian fear of unemployment that might result from immigration; a xenophobic reaction (la France aux français); and a general ignorance of the economic benefits of immigration.[36] Another important historical factor must be taken into account in explaining negative public attitudes: the heightened tension caused by the colonial wars in Vietnam and Algeria, and the beginning of the end of the French Empire. By the same token, the public's preoccupation with the violent process of decolonization also helps to explain why there were so few recorded outbursts of racial violence or demonstrations against immigration during this period.[37] The full impact of decolonization on the politics of immigration would not be felt until the end of the Algerian conflict and the granting of independence to the various colonies of North and West Africa.

The important point to retain from looking at immigration during the period from 1946 to 1962 is that the administrative elite, acting first under the authority of the provisional Tripartite Government and subsequently under various governments of the Fourth Republic, took the lead in formulating and implementing a recruitment policy. The policies of this period set the parameters for the use (and abuse) of foreign labor during the 1960s and 1970s. Employers became dependent on immigrant labor, eventually taking almost complete control of the recruitment process in the 1960s, whereas trade unions (and the Communist Party) came to oppose immigration because of the competition that foreign workers represented, and because of the problems of caring for and housing immigrants in crowded, working-class urban areas. Despite the impending political crisis of 1968 and the economic crises of the 1970s, which focused attention on immigrants as scapegoats for the problems of industrial development, the populationnistes succeeded in bolstering the population and helping the economy overcome a potentially severe labor shortage. In the 1960s, however, the supply of highly assimilable Southern European Catholics began to exhaust itself (with the notable exception of Portugal), and non-European, largely Muslim, immigrants would take their place.

Immigration and the *Trente Glorieuses:*
The Gaullist Years

The rise to power of the Gaullists in 1958 with nationalist and Jacobin designs for the economy and a commitment to turn France into a military-industrial power reinforced the interventionist role of the state. Several events, however, made the necessity of intervening in the labor market less pressing. The settlement of the Algerian conflict and the decolonization of North Africa brought an influx not only of white colonists but of nonwhite Frenchmen and Africans seeking employment in a rapidly expanding economy. The period of decolonization from 1958 to 1962 was the beginning of a massive and largely uncontrolled immigration. Average annual immigration jumped from 66,400 in the period from 1946 to 1955, to 248,800 in the period 1956 to 1967 (see Table 5.2). At the same time, the *taux de régularisation* went from the 40–50- to the 70–80-percent range. In effect, immigration flows were exploding, while the control of the state over the migratory process was decreasing.

The return to power of de Gaulle was not entirely unexpected. From 1956 to 1958 the crisis in Algeria intensified, resulting in the demise of the parliamentary system of the Fourth Republic and the creation of the Fifth Republic with its bias in favor of the executive. De Gaulle waited in the wings for some time, and the insurrection in Algiers in May 1958 provided the occasion for his return. Despite the political crises of 1956–58, economic stabilization had already begun. The policy-makers of the Fourth Republic succeeded in creating a favorable climate for growth. Monetary stability was restored in 1958, and the confidence of investors was on the rise.[38] Thus, if the political situation inherited by the Gaullists was chaotic, the economy was nonetheless in fairly good shape. The Gaullists brought a distinctive pro-big business philosophy to government. This did not mean that there was less economic planning, but rather that there was a much higher degree of cooperation between business and government in the making of economic policy.[39]

In the area of immigration and labor-market policy, employers were given much greater freedom to recruit, hire, and fire foreign as well as French workers. There was a decline in the political power of labor, confirmed by the fact that Left political parties as well as trade unions suffered with the creation of the Fifth Republic. The reform of the electoral system, from proportional representation to a dual-ballot system with single-member districts, drastically reduced representation of the Parti Communiste Française (PCF) in the new Parliament. At the

ONI, the input of trade unions was restricted, while employers were given a freer hand to recruit workers directly abroad.[40] The new system of administering migration was in fact similar to the system that existed during the interwar period, when employers through the SGI were allowed to recruit abroad. The major difference is that the ONI retained a measure of administrative control over legalization (*régularisation*).

While employers' power in the labor market increased in the early 1960s, the position of workers was deteriorating. The decline was accentuated by the rapid increase in uncontrolled immigration. Employers succeeded in boosting the overall supply of workers, while putting pressure on real wages.[41] The political risks of this strategy were not apparent until 1968, when the May events, together with a general strike, led the government to intervene in the market on behalf of workers.

During the first decade of the Fifth Republic, the power of the administrative state was consolidated in the hands of the executive, making the government more powerful in a formal-legal sense, but also more vulnerable and more partisan.[42] Despite these institutional reforms, the major instruments for intervening in the economy were still operative. Planning remained a central feature of economic policy-making. The Third Plan (1958–61) called for continued recruitment of foreign labor and estimated the levels of foreign manpower needs to be on the order of 175,000 for the period covered by the plan. If we count Algerian immigration during this period (see Table 5.3), immigration met and surpassed levels forecast by the plan.[43] Nonetheless, immigration was not high on the agenda of the first Gaullist governments. The Interministerial Committee on Immigration did not meet from the end of the Fourth Republic until 1965. Only the Left, particularly the CGT and the PCF, sought to focus attention on the issue of immigration. Yet there were noticeable signs of splits within the leadership, which was trying to walk an ideological tightrope by arguing for international proletarian solidarity in the face of growing opposition to immigration among the rank and file.[44]

The rise in immigration during the 1960s can be attributed to the process of decolonization and to the rapid growth of the economy, which kept the demand for labor high. But what had begun as an effort by the state to secure an adequate supply of labor in the 1950s was rapidly becoming an open process whereby employers had virtually unlimited access to new supplies of immigrant labor. Despite the fact that the recruitment responsibilities of the ONI were extended through a variety of treaties concluded in 1963 with Morocco, Tunisia, and Portugal, and in 1965 Yugoslavia and Turkey, employers continued to usurp powers of recruitment. Private recruitment was easier in sending countries that still had a special relationship with France, particularly Algeria and various countries of the franc zone of West Africa (Senegal, Ivory Coast, Togo). Algerians were required only to pass a medical examination after 1963, whereas the West Africans were not subject to control. Residency and work permits, which were required for all other nationalities, were not required for the Algerians and the West Africans.[45]

In 1965 the Interministerial Committee on Immigration was convened to study the problem of the private recruitment of foreign labor and to recommend ways of dealing with what came to be called "immigration from within." The Committee decided that the government should take a more active role in setting levels of immigration, and that the ONI should be reorganized and given a new mandate. However, the belief was still widespread, as late as 1966, that industry was in danger of running out of labor. J. M. Jeanneney, then minister of social affairs, was quoted as saying that "clandestine immigration itself is not useless, because if we stick to a strict application of international regulations and agreements, we will perhaps be short of labor."[46] Partly as a result of this preoccupation with the possibility of labor shortages, the Fifth Plan estimated that the economy would require 325,000 foreign workers for the period 1966–70.[47] Because the plan also predicted considerable unemployment for the same period, trade unions saw immigration policy as a blatant attempt on the part of the state and employers to suppress wages by maintaining an "industrial reserve army." Both the CFDT and the CGT denounced employment of foreigners as a mechanism for exploiting the working class.[48]

As a means of legitimizing new immigration, the administrative reorganization of the ONI again brought trade unions back into the decision-making process. However, this did not silence the criticism of the policy-making process by the leaders of the trade-union movement. Their attacks on the use of foreign labor by employers followed the argument that foreign workers were a more attractive source of labor because, unlike French workers, they were not covered by expensive and cumbersome social-welfare protections. Thus, it was much easier to exploit foreign workers, to pay them lower wages, to avoid social security and other payments, and to use foreign workers to divide and weaken the working class itself.[49] The trade unions argued that by abandoning Italian labor, which was now covered by the Rome Treaties, in favor of a vulnerable and more tractable supply of African workers, employers were able to circumvent regulations designed to protect all workers.

Among the effects of the growing hostility of workers toward immigration was an upsurge in feelings of racism and xenophobia among the general public.[50] By the end of the "Gaullist decade" there was a public perception that immigration was contributing to a rapid deterioration in urban living standards and conditions. Many immigrant workers were living in urban enclaves in the worst housing conditions, thus making the "immigrant problem" look much worse than it actually was. Immigrants came to be viewed as different and/or inferior because of poor housing conditions and a lack of education, and even though the national leadership of trade unions and left-wing political parties sought to promote harmony between French and foreign workers, the situation of race and ethnic relations in the 1970s began to worsen, and to spill over into the political arena.[51]

The state was not oblivious to the situation. One indication of the awareness of social problems associated with large-scale immigration was the creation in 1966 of a Ministry of Social Affairs, which included a Department of Population and Migration (DPM). The DPM was given the responsibility of taking care of immigrants at each stage of the migratory process, from recruitment and placement to naturalization and assimilation. The creation of the DPM marked the beginning of a new effort by the government to regain control of the migratory process.[52]

The minor recession of 1966–67 brought a slowdown in hiring, but the rate of immigration continued to climb. Shortly thereafter, the upheaval of 1968 changed the nature of the labor market and altered the relationship between state and economy. The events of May 1968 increased regulation of the labor market through the Grenelle Agreements, and at the same time brought to power a more probusiness faction of the Gaullist party. The Pompidou government put a new emphasis on the role of the market in determining patterns of growth and industrialization. The plan as an instrument of intervention in the economy was weakened, and the recommendations of the CGP became pro forma. The net effect of the events of 1968 was paradoxically to increase both the power of labor and capital, while reducing the interventionist capacity of the state.

Undoubtedly, immigration played a central role in the economic growth of the *trente glorieuses;* and the state, largely through the process of economic planning, was able to mobilize a much-needed supply of foreign labor. However, by the late 1960s the composition of immigrant flows was changing rapidly from European to largely North African nationalities, and the government was struggling to regain control of the migratory process, which had been taken over by employers. As the economy began to slow and the prospects of unemployment loomed, a political reaction against immigration was building. Not surprisingly, the first in a series of backlashes against immigration came from the Left. What had been a tremendous economic advantage in the 1950s and 1960s was becoming a political liability for which the Jacobin state, and the parties of government, especially the Gaullists, would be held responsible in the eyes of public opinion. The turbulent years of the 1970s began with debates over immigration, but it would be another decade before the issue would break through into party politics and disrupt the entire political system.

Neo-Gaullists and the Uncertain Role of the State

In 1968, the State paid the price for an unrestrained economic growth that had damaged the interests of traditional classes, while postponing a more equitable distribution of wealth that would favor workers and consumers. The events of May 1968 marked the end of Gaullist Jacobinism, which had used the power of the administrative state to solve the political conflicts associated with economic modernization. The compromises that had been worked out in the decade since 1958 favored business. Unrestrained access to foreign labor was but one example of the probusiness philosophy of the period, which was justified in terms of national grandeur. The student strike was an opportunity for workers to regain a measure of influence in the political process, despite the fact that the parties of the Left remained incapable of winning elections. As most observers of the events of 1968 have pointed out, however, the workers had few revolutionary designs and little sympathy with the radical leaders of the student movement.[53] The trade unions wanted a share of the profits from the economy that they had helped to build. The upheaval ended with the Grenelle Agreements, negotiated by Prime Minister Pompidou, who had convinced employers to accede to some of the demands of the trade unions. The issue of immigration was not a part of these negotiations. In some respects, immigration would become the Achilles's heel of the workers' movement, because employers were able for a time to use foreign labor to circumvent some aspects of new labor market regulations imposed by the Grenelle Agreement.[54]

The economy rebounded quickly from the political uncertainty of 1968. The demand for labor soared in 1969–70, as the new Pompidou government placed a greater emphasis on full employment and manpower policy in general.[55] All indications are that the neo-Gaullist *pompidoliens* were determined not to repeat the "mistakes" of their predecessors in the area of immigration policy. Economic policy relied more on market forces to solve the problems of resource allocation, while the state set about to minimize the sociopolitical costs of renewed growth. Centralized planning was no longer an objective but rather a tool for the private sector. Earlier Gaullist governments had struck an agreement with business, but there was little doubt that the state was the senior partner in the alliance. With Pompidou the situation was reversed, with government doing everything politically possible to foster the growth of a free market. The result was that traditional interests were undercut and industry became more concentrated than ever.[56]

The free-market orientation of the Pompidou administration initially gave employers greater access to foreign labor, as levels of immigration climbed from an average annual rate of 248,800 during the period 1956–67 to a rate of 341,100 for the period 1968–73 (see Table 5.2). Yet, at the same time, the administrative state was trying to reassert control over the migratory process through the ONI, which was struggling to fulfill its primary mission of recruitment and placement of foreign workers. The *taux de régularisation* dropped from 80 percent to 50–60 percent range, while the rise in immigration of permanent workers was accompanied by substantial increases in family and seasonal immigration (see Table 5.2). Family immigration was concentrated among those nationalities who had immigrated in the previous decade, primarily Italian, Spanish, and Portuguese. The new immigrant *workers,* however, were coming from North and West Africa, Yugoslavia, Turkey, and Portugal (the latter continued to be a major supplier of foreign labor). Algerian immigration also increased markedly during the period from 1968 to 1973 (see Tables 5.1 and 5.3). Looking at these numbers, many policy-makers and students of immigration came to the conclusion that foreign workers were a permanent and necessary feature of advanced capitalist society.[57] Indeed, conditions for immigration and the use of foreign labor were never more favorable than in the early 1970s, as both demand for labor and government policies seemed to encourage the recruitment and hiring of foreign workers.

Nevertheless, as the political economy reached the end of the *trente glorieuses,* the focus of the debate over immigration shifted from economic and demographic issues to the sociological and political problems of assimilation. The hope of the *populationnistes* for a permanent immigration of Southern European Catholic workers and their families had been realized. The older Italian and Spanish migrations of the 1950s and early 1960s gave way first to Portuguese immigration and eventually to large-scale immigration from Africa. The distinguishing feature of this new immigration was its cultural distinctiveness: it was composed predominantly of Muslims from North Africa (see Table 5.4). From the 1970s through the 1980s, the political system struggled to cope with the presence of millions of ethnically and religiously distinct individuals. A new *Jacobin* and nationalist debate over French identity and the meaning of citizenship was starting to take shape.

Table 5.4   Immigration of Workers and Family Members by Nationality*

Nationality	1946–55	1956–67	1968–73	1974–81	1982–87
Italians	27,838	36,813	9,359	4,529	1,367
	66.8	*27.4*	*4.6*	*5.1*	*2.5*
Spaniards	1,490	49,785	24,240	2,714	804
	3.6	*37.1*	*11.9*	*3.1*	*1.5*
Portuguese	424	26,359	91,413	17,082	4,991
	1.0	*19.6*	*44.8*	*19.3*	*9.3*
Moroccans	600	7,994	27,383	19,576	12,288
	1.4	*6.0*	*13.4*	*22.1*	*22.8*
Tunisians	—	2,418	15,852	5,912	5,314
	—	*1.8*	*7.8*	*6.7*	*9.9*
Turks	—	279	8,505	10,157	5,528
	—	*0.2*	*4.2*	*11.5*	*10.3*
Yugoslavs	29	3,125	11,208	1,820	693
	0.1	*2.3*	*5.5*	*2.1*	*1.3*
Others	11,302	7,407	16,131	26,624	22,841
	27.1	*5.5*	*7.9*	*30.1*	*42.4*
Total	41,683	134,179	204,090	88,414	53,825
	100.0	*100.0*	*100.0*	*100.0*	*100.0*

*Figures are annual averages. The second row of numbers represents the percentage of total immigration for each nationality for a given period.

Source: Office des Migrations Internationales.

The role of the administrative state was increasingly ambiguous. Even though the plan continued to calculate inputs, such as the number of foreign workers, that would be needed to fulfill growth targets, the planners became more cautious in their estimates. The Sixth Plan, which covered the period 1971–75, predicted a net annual immigration of 75,000, compared with 130,000 for the period of the Fifth Plan.[58] These estimates were easily surpassed by actual levels of immigration, which is further evidence of the increasing irrelevance of the planning process, except as a device for forecasting growth and providing information and support for industry.

The principal instrument for controlling immigration remained the Office National d'Immigration. Yet from its creation after the war ONI was given a hopeless task. It was charged with the responsibility of making the supply of foreign workers correspond to demand, within the limits of immigration law and policy. Given the availability of foreign labor and the reticence of employers to avail themselves of the services of the ONI, it is not surprising that business continued to circumvent the official channels of recruitment. Right up until the "cutoff" of immigration in 1974, employers continued to undermine policy measures designed to control their access to foreign labor. The "normal" procedure was to hire workers first, then seek legalization *régularisation*.[59]

In 1967 the Ministry of Social Affairs took steps to limit noncontractual immigration. A large number of exceptions to the new rules, however, made a crackdown on unofficial immigration ineffective. The Portuguese and those foreign workers in all categories of skilled labor that could not be filled with French workers were exempt. New sanctions against employers of undocumented workers were adopted in 1968; it is difficult, however, to measure the effect of these sanctions, which required employers to reimburse the state for any payments made to foreign workers who had not passed the medical exam administered by ONI. The *taux de régularisation* declined in 1968; it would therefore seem that the sanctions had some effect. However, we should keep in mind that even though employers' control over the migratory process decreased, levels of immigration increased dramatically (see Table 5.2).

The rapid rise in immigration in the early 1970s provoked a change in policy. The *circulaire Fontanet* (basically an administrative memorandum, named for its author and having the power of an executive order) was disseminated through a bulletin of the Ministry of Social Affairs early in 1972.[60] This *circulaire* and others that followed sought to eliminate all forms of noncontractual immigration. The stated purpose of these measures was to prevent the exploitation of foreign workers and reestablish public control of the migratory process.[61] One of the most controversial aspects of the new regulations was the attempt to link residency permits to work permits. In this respect, the French authorities were following the example of the West Germans, who always had insisted on the linkage of residency and work permits.[62] This brought an outcry from trade-union leaders and immigrant associations, for by threatening to fire a foreign worker an employer could effectively jeopardize the right of the worker to remain in the country.

Employers were concerned with the effects of the new regulations on their ability to recruit and hire foreign workers at a time when the demand for labor was high.[63] The *circulaire Fontanet* created a complex bureaucratic procedure for the recruitment and placement of foreign workers, including long delays between actual recruitment and starting work. The employer was charged with the responsibility of finding housing for the new immigrant—all in all, a bureaucratic nightmare. The Ministry of Labor was bombarded by criticism from employers' associations, particularly those representing sectors such as construction (Fédération Nationale du Bâtiment—FNB) that relied heavily on foreign labor.[64] The result of these appeals was to convince the Ministry of Labor to issue a new *circulaire* that would liberalize the procedure for *régularisation*. At the same time, the CFDT brought the question of the legality of these new regulations to the Conseil d'Etat, which declared them illegal in 1975.[65] The uncertainty surrounding the legalization procedure is reflected by fluctuations in the *taux de régularisation,* which dropped from 63 percent in 1971 to 49 percent in 1972 before jumping back up to 60 percent in 1973.

The state was actively pursuing other ways to influence levels of immigration, particularly by controlling it at the source, that is, in the sending country. This could be done only with the cooperation of the government of the sending countries. In 1971 the French and Portuguese governments signed a protocol that gave French authorities greater control over what had been a quasi clandestine flow of workers. In exchange, the French government agreed to raise levels of Portuguese immigration, thus granting Portugal "most favored nation" status as a supplier of labor for the French market. Similar agreements were signed with Algeria, in an attempt to gain control of the flow of Algerian workers and their families into France. In 1969–70, Algerians in France were required to obtain a single permit that would give them the right to live and work in France. These agreements slowed the rate of increase of the Algerian population in France (see Tables 5.1 and 5.3). However, they became moot in September 1973, when the Algerian government unilaterally suspended all emigration to France because of hostile reactions in France against Algerian workers. Attempts were made to extend control over West African immigration, which was quite small in comparison with other nationalities (see Tables 5.1 and 5.4). In 1970–71 all workers from the countries of the franc zone were required to obtain work permits. But immigration of West Africans continued in the form of false tourism.[66]

Overall, the Pompidou years were marked by a high degree of inconsistency in immigration policy, as various attempts were made to increase public control over the migratory process—with mixed results. One of the reasons for the ineffectiveness of immigration policy was the Pompidou government's approach to economic management, which was decidedly liberal in comparison with the Jacobin philosophy of earlier Gaullists. Employers reacted to this new liberalism by recruiting and hiring record numbers of foreign workers, making it more difficult to use foreign labor as an instrument for regulating labor supply. Administrative attempts to reassert control over the migratory process in the early 1970s were met with resistance from almost every sector of society, including trade unions (which distrusted the government), immigrant associations seeking to protect the rights of foreigners, and employers, who wanted to maintain access to cheap foreign labor.

Efforts to stem the rising tide of immigration clearly were linked to the general unpopularity of Third World immigration. Uncontrolled migration was blamed for a host of social problems, as immigrant enclaves turned into urban slums in many cities. Although public control over the migratory process was greater than before, the problem of assimilating a growing foreign population was more severe. Public sentiment was running heavily in favor of suspending immigration.[67] During this period, 1972–74, the first rumblings of a nationalist reaction against immigration were evident.[68] Amid the rising controversy, the government attempted to seize the bull by the horns with the various *circulaires* (Fontanet, Marcellin, and Gorse). But, these new regulations only added to administrative confusion, while intensifying political conflicts over the issues of immigration and unemployment. Employers, particularly in the construction and agricultural sectors, were skeptical of attempts to regulate immigration, since foreign workers were seen as an essential source of labor. Trade unions wanted the government to reassert control, but not at the expense of isolating and alienating the already large foreign workforce in France. The onset of the worldwide economic recession that followed the oil shock of 1973 set the stage for a protracted political battle over immigration, which was destined to become one of the most important partisan issues of the 1980s.[69] In 1973–74 the economic crisis was compounded by a political crisis with the death of Georges Pompidou and the eventual election of Giscard-d'Estaing as president of the Republic. This brief period of political uncertainty succeeded in delaying by several months administrative efforts to cut off immigration, which already had begun in other countries of Western Europe, notably in the Federal Republic of Germany.[70]

Immigration, Economic Crisis, and Strategies for Adjustment: The Etatiste *Reflex*

By the end of the *trente glorieuses,* and with the fading memories of 1968, France looked more like its industrial partners. It had built a mass-based, consumer society and a stable democratic regime. The task of "modernization" appeared to be complete. Giscardian "liberalism" held out the promise of a *société décrispée,* which was to be the beginning of the fulfillment of the Radicals' dream of a liberal political order based on *laissez-faire* economics.[71] But, the new "liberalism" was tempered immediately by the oil crisis of 1973–74 and the global recession that followed. The role of immigrants, which was changing in step with the political economy, was uncertain. Immigrant workers had served their economic purpose, and it was politically expedient to stop immigration, especially from the Third World.

After the energy crisis, which struck a severe but not fatal blow to Giscard's economic policies, there was increasing unease in this country accustomed to prosperity and relative full employment. Among the first casualties of the economic crisis were foreign workers. A halt in further immigration was decreed in July 1974. This was one of the initial responses of the government to the increase in unemployment. In an effort to avoid a complete collapse in the older nationalized industries, such as steel and shipbuilding, Giscard also was compelled to intervene massively in the public sector. The intervention was costly, and it contradicted the liberal ambitions of the Giscardians, but it was seen as necessary in order to avoid even larger increases in unemployment. Politically, such intervention placated the Gaullists who still favored some type of industrial planning, and it diffused the criticism from the Left that the government was doing little to ease the pains of industrial adjustment. During this period the ban on hiring foreign workers was lifted for certain industries, that, it was argued, could not survive without access to cheap labor. The mining and construction industries are perhaps the most prominent examples. Agriculture also was allowed to continue to use seasonal labor for harvesting crops—*la vendange* could not proceed without foreign "assistance."[72]

Despite the evidence of an *étatiste* reflex, for the first time in the postwar period a government was elected that was committed to dismantling the more overtly interventionist features of the Jacobin state.[73] Still, however, the new economic and political liberalism did not extend to foreigners. Only months after taking office, a series of *circulaires* were adopted by the Council of Ministers of the Chirac government that sought to suspend further immigration.[74] These "drastic" measures were not unexpected, since most other labor-importing countries in Western Europe already had adopted similar positions. The policy was generally accepted as necessary, given the unpopularity of high levels of immigration, the social costs of uncontrolled migration, and rising unemployment. Public opinion was favorable, and the major trade unions offered little resistance. But while trade unions were pleased to see the government finally taking steps to control immigration, employers were divided. The official position of the Conseil National du Patronat Français (CNPF) was in favor of increased public control, yet many member organizations of the CNPF, such as the FNB worried that they would lose a vital source of cheap labor.[75] Industries that were heavily dependent on unskilled (foreign) labor, such as mining and construction, complained bitterly about the restrictions. Eventually, exemptions were granted, but on the whole the policies of suspension were maintained throughout the Giscardian era.[76]

This did not mean that all forms of immigration were stopped. The secretary of state for immigrant workers, Paul Dijoud, accepted immigrant workers as a structural component of labor supply.[77] Policies were set in motion that would assist in the assimilation of immigrants.[78] However, the new policies were quickly overwhelmed by the waves of family, seasonal, and clandestine immigration that resulted from the policy of suspension.[79] Nonetheless, immigration of permanent workers dropped sharply from 64,461 in 1974 to 25,591 in 1975 and 17,380 by 1980. This drop is even more significant if we take into account the fact that the immigration of workers from the European Community as a percentage of total worker migration was much higher after 1974, as employers began to turn to more regulated and more expensive sources of foreign labor. Yet according to the statistics of the ONI total immigration in 1976 was 205,800 compared to 264,282 in 1974, which was not the dramatic decrease that had been hoped for (see also Table 5.2).

The difference can be accounted for by increases in family and seasonal immigration, which picked up just as worker immigration declined (see Table 5.2), thus lending weight to the argument that foreign labor had become a structural component of labor supply (i.e., a necessary pool of surplus labor that could be more easily hired and fired in times of crisis).[80] In effect, family and seasonal immigration replaced "permanent workers" as the principal source of foreign labor (see Table 5.2). From 1978 to 1980, the number of family members admitted to the labor market by the Ministry of Labor surpassed the total number of family members admitted to residency through the ONI. The discrepancy between family immigration statistics of the ONI and admissions to the labor market, as recorded by the Ministry of Labor, can be attributed to the use of kinship rules to gain access to the labor market. Spanish, Portuguese, Moroccans, and Tunisians made up the bulk of this new flow of immigrants (see Table 5.4). Hence, the new immigration policies were not successful in controlling immigration—in the words of one Ministry official, "On ferme la porte et on ouvre la fênetre."

After the suspension of immigration, the position of employers on the use of foreign labor was not clear. The leadership of the CNPF argued that immigration should stop. Some employers, however, were not so willing to give up an important source of unskilled labor, and they intervened in the policy-making process to plead their case with the new secretary of state for immigrant workers, Paul Dijoud. The construction industry, represented by the FNB, was the most vociferous in its objections to the new policy.[81] A sectoral study of the impact of restrictions on employment of foreigners in the construction industry concluded that such restrictions would impose great hardships and severely limit the capacity of the industry to adapt to new economic realities. The same study conducted a survey of executives in the construction industry, which revealed that employers did not expect the suspension to last.[82]

The effects of employers' lobbying appear to have been limited, at least as far as a formal change in policy is concerned. The secretary allowed some exemptions to the restrictions on recruitment and hiring of foreign workers. But these exemptions were limited and circumscribed by a variety of administrative requirements that made it difficult for most employers to escape the new controls.[83] When a request for hiring a foreign worker was made by an employer to the DPM (Direction de la Population et des Migrations), it was often made through an intermediary, such as the employer's union or a member of Parliament. Presumably, a request made in this way would carry more weight than if the employer went directly to the Ministry. In her study of employers' attitudes toward immigration, Marie-Claude Hénneresse found that over ninety percent of the requests for exemptions submitted to the DPM by employers in 1974–75 were approved. These exemptions, however, account for only fourteen percent of total worker immigration controlled by the ONI.[84] It seems unlikely, therefore, that there was any overt collusion between employers and the state to keep immigration high.

Some sectors, however, appear to have received more favorable treatment by the government than others. Mining, which was in full decline, accounts for more than forty percent of all exemptions in 1974–75, while the small-business sector, i.e., those employers represented by the Confederation Générale des Petites et Moyennes Entreprises (CGPME), were denied access to foreign labor by the DPM. In this respect, the government was pursuing a strategy for economic development that dated from the Fourth Republic, namely, favoring big over small business. It is therefore not surprising that small businesses in the service and construction sectors were the most likely to use some form of extralegal immigrant labor.[85]

Trade unions and Left political parties, particularly the CGT and the PCF, were critical of the selective and ad hoc allocation of foreign labor, which was seen as an underhanded way for the government to deal with problems of industrial adjustment. The relationship between trade unions and immigrant workers was more complex after the suspension of immigration. The main reason for difficulties was that immigration and the employment of foreigners were now highly politicized and emotionally charged issues. Many workers were convinced that immigration was a principal cause of unemployment. The leadership of the unions promoted this view, while at the same time speaking out for greater working-class solidarity in the wake of the economic crisis.

On the shop floor, immigrants were suspicious of attempts to organize them, and their decision to join or not to join a union usually depended on what services the union could offer rather than on ideological affinities. Throughout the 1970s the CGT and the PCF were more involved than the Socialists in immigrant issues, for two simple reasons: immigrant labor was more highly concentrated in the old industrial sectors, such as steel and automobiles, where the CGT was strongest, and immigrants were housed near the factories in Communist neighborhoods. With the beginning of industrial "restructuring" at the end of the decade, the CGT made an effort to enlist immigrants in the fight to save jobs in declining sectors. This strategy was an explicit recognition of the important role of foreign workers in the labor market, and of the necessity of preventing the state and employers from "using" immigrants to diffuse opposition to closing unproductive firms.[86]

Immigrant workers had other reasons to distrust the CGT and the PCF. On a number of occasions, there were outbursts of racial violence in working-class neighborhoods, especially in the so-called red belt around Paris. Government housing policies for immigrants led to greater and greater concentrations of foreign workers in dormitories in largely Communist towns, such as Bobigny and Ivry-sur-Seine. These immigrant enclaves not only led to increased ethnic conflict, they also strained the social infrastructure set up to house and educate foreign workers. Scenes of a Communist mayor directing a bulldozer to block the entrance of an immigrant dormitory and other incidents cast a shadow over relations between immigrants and the Left.[87]

The government's motives for attempting to stop immigration were closely related to the changed context of growth after the oil shock. Independent of public opinion and interest-group pressures, Giscard's government decided that the social costs of immigration were too high, especially given the fact that domestic labor supplies appeared to be more than adequate for future growth. The decision to suspend immigration, however, failed to take into account the structural role of foreign labor in the labor market. Because of the large increase in the wage rate brought on by the Grenelle Agreements, employers in some sectors had come to rely on immigrant workers to cut production costs. Efforts were made in these sectors to retain foreigners wherever possible. Before the suspension, the turnover rate among foreign workers was much higher.[88] Likewise, those firms that were heavily dependent on foreign labor (particularly in the construction and service sectors) turned to immigrant family members in order to replace foreign workers who had returned home or had been expelled. Both clandestine and seasonal migration helped to maintain the structural role of foreign labor in the labor market.[89] There is also evidence that seasonal workers were moving out of the agricultural sector and into the small-business sector.[90]

The entry of second-generation immigrant children into the school system and the SONACOTRA rent strikes of 1975 brought the problem of immigration closer to home for many. The public became increasingly conscious of the social costs of immigration, and public opinion brought greater pressure to bear on the government to maintain the official policy of suspension and to devise policies for dealing with assimilation of the existing foreign population.[91] The initial response of the government was to a commission a study by the Economic and Social Council (CES).[92] The report made several recommendations, the most important of which concerned the need to eliminate uncontrolled immigration.[93] To accomplish this, the government needed to adopt more radical measures for controlling the market for foreign labor. The simple suspension of legal immigration of permanent workers had proven to be insufficient. As a result, stricter measures were taken in an attempt to limit family immigration and repatriate as many immigrants as possible. Financial incentives were offered to immigrants if they would return to their countries of origin. This "return" policy was modestly successful, with 54,631 immigrants actually receiving some aid in their effort to repatriate over the period 1977–81. In total, 86,019 immigrants and family members benefited from this aid over the same period.[94]

None of these measures was sufficient to stop immigration. Any hopes of using immigrants as guest workers to manage the labor market and solve problems of unemployment were dashed by the failure of repatriation policies in the late 1970s. The same experience was repeated in the Federal Republic of Germany, which tried to prevent family immigration and induce foreign workers to return "home" through various incentives. Such heavy-handed administrative attempts to control immigration in Western Europe set the tone for debates over immigration in the 1980s, contributing to the politicization of the issue and setting the stage for the rise of extreme nationalist movements, such as the Front National (FN) in France, and the Republikaner in West Germany.

Immigration and Citizenship:
La France aux français and the Jacobin Reflex

For most of the postwar period, immigration was looked upon and analyzed in the context of economic and demographic change. The role of foreign labor in the process of economic modernization and the contribution of immigration to demographic growth, were stressed.[95] In the 1970s immigration became the subject of *political* debate, as the contribution of immigrants to economic growth began to recede into collective memory. The way in which the *political* problem of immigration was posed is particularly revealing of the political culture. The issue came to be defined in the *Jacobin* terms of citizenship and identity, rather than in demographic or economic terms. Suddenly some of the oldest themes of French political development came to the fore. The Jacobin model of the "republican synthesis" was seemingly threatened by the presence of a large Muslim population, which was reluctant to abandon the religious and cultural dimensions of its identity in favor of a truly "French" identity. This political crisis in turn led to a reopening of the issue of church-state relations, which had been so difficult to resolve during the nineteenth century.

How could immigration have shifted so abruptly from being a problem of labor markets and employment to one of citizenship, nationality, and political participation? If we step back to take a comparative and historical view of immigration and ethnicity, we see that every society that has experienced large-scale immigration has been forced to come to terms with the settlement of a new, ethnically and culturally distinct population. In most cases, coming to terms with immigration has entailed similar "crises" of national identity, citizenship, and political participation, but the way in which these crises have been resolved is dependent on political culture and the political system. In the classical case of the United States, successive ways of immigration were absorbed, in the first instance through a stringent (Anglo-Saxon) assimilationist ideology—the famous melting pot—and in the second instance through a federal political system sufficiently decentralized to allow immigrants to find an institutional niche in which to pursue their interests, historically at the local, municipal level, through the "good" offices of the party boss and the party machine.[96] In the American case, it was not immigration per se that would lead to a crisis of political development and citizenship, but the second-class status of African Americans, which provoked a Civil Rights "revolution" in the 1950s and 1960s, leading eventually to a much broader definition of citizenship and a gradual moving away from the assimilationist ideology of the melting pot and toward a new cultural pluralism. The "pluralist" settlement of citizenship issues in the United States has been reinforced by the political system, and especially by the courts, which play a central role in guaranteeing the rights of individuals, be they citizens or foreigners.[97]

While not of equal magnitude, either in terms of numbers or the crisis that it has provoked, the settlement in France of a culturally and ethnically distinct minority (the *maghrébins*) raises many of the same questions as the existence of distinct, ethnic minorities in the United States. In both cases, political parties have been on the front line in determining whether integration will be a relatively smooth process or one fraught with conflict and violence. One can trace the beginning of the political crisis over immigration and citizenship in France to the SONACOTRA rent strikes of 1975–76, which demonstrated clearly that institutions that succeeded in integrating and assimilating foreigners in France during earlier periods would not be so successful with the Muslim, African groups.[98] One of the most important institutions in this regard (along with the schools) was the PCF , which was able to rally earlier waves of immigrants to the causes of the working class. This was the case with Italian, Belgian, and Polish workers during the interwar period and, to a lesser extent, with European immigrant groups in the postwar period.[99] But part of the condition of this integration was that immigrants should abandon much of their traditional identity in favor of a new proletarian, national, and Jacobin identity.[100]

Although the PCF was having problems in its relationship with the immigrant population, particularly in cities and towns controlled by Communist mayors, other political parties were not faring much better, with the notable exception of the Parti Socialiste (PS). The coming to power of the Left and the election of François Mitterrand in 1981 marked an important turning point in the politics of immigration. The first Socialist government of Pierre Mauroy moved quickly to carry out many of the campaign promises of the Left, which included a general liberalization of politics, particularly in the areas of civil rights (abolition of the death penalty, stopping arbitrary search and seizure, and *contrôle d'identité* by the police). The new spirit of political (if not economic) liberalism extended to foreign residents, at least insofar as the rights of association and political participation were concerned. In addition to giving official sanction to immigrant associations (heretofore restricted by the state), the Mauroy government, under the direction of President Mitterrand, went so far as to propose giving the right to vote in local elections to all foreigners who had resided in the country for five years. This proposal was not welcomed by the parties of the Right (Rassemble-

ment pour la République [RPR] and Union pour la Démocratie Française [UDF])
nor for that matter by the Communists, who were participants in the first Socialist
government.

The package of measures proposed by the Mauroy government included a
conditional amnesty for illegal aliens that was enacted and carried out in 1981–
82. The amnesty was designed to improve the living conditions of immigrants
and to rally the new North African constituency (le vote beur) to the Socialist
cause. Thus, problems of assimilation and socialization were to be solved through
a combination of measures that would solve the "immigrant problem." These
measures were accompanied by stricter control of immigration, ending once and
for all the old policies of managing labor supplies and the labor market through
the use of foreign labor. Yet while the average annual rate of immigration dropped
from 200,200 during the period 1974–80 to 160,000 for the period 1981–87 (see
Table 5.2), it remained relatively high, and the foreign population reached a
historical high in 1982 of 6.8 percent of the total population, slightly higher than
in 1931 (see Table 5.1).

Immigration continued in the 1980s, but not as a result of any new recruitment
policy or a relaxation on the part of authorities. Like other Western democracies,
France has experienced an upsurge in refugee immigration. As measured by the
Office Française de Protection de Réfugiés et Apatrides (OFPRA), the number
of asylum seekers in France has moved from 22,471 in 1982 to 26,196 in 1986.
True to its Jacobin tradition, France is an important country of asylum, welcoming
refugees from countries throughout the world. In the 1980s, substantial numbers
of refugees have arrived from Asia, Africa, and the Middle East. Beginning in
1985, the majority of these asylum seekers came to France as tourists before
requesting refugee status, a pattern that is familiar in other asylum countries,
particularly the United States, Canada, and the Federal Republic of Germany. In
the last two decades of the twentieth century, refugee immigration is becoming
the preferred mode of immigration. Unlike the United States, France has not
reduced its refugee policy to a debate over political versus economic immigration,
in part because of the refusal to link refugee policy to foreign policy. France does
not discriminate so overtly as the United States against refugees from non-
Communist states, which again is part of the Jacobin tradition of equality before
the law and welcoming of foreigners as potential "citizens."[101]

With the stated desire of the Socialists in the early 1980s to assimilate the
foreign population while stopping future immigration, statistics have taken on
added political significance. A partisan debate raged throughout the 1980s over
the counting of foreigners and the accuracy of immigration statistics.[102] In the
wake of the amnesty, which was only moderately successful, and with the easing
of police controls and the upsurge in Middle Eastern terrorism during the 1980s,
the stage was set for a political reaction against immigration and the policies of
the Socialist government.[103] The dimensions of this reaction, which would take
the form of a political movement (the Front National), were largely unanticipated.

As the assimilationist policies of the Socialists began to take effect, in the period from 1981 to 1983, the economic situation in France deteriorated rapidly. Unemployment in particular was rising among both the French and foreign populations. Immigrants were hit hard by the economic recession of the early 1980s. They accounted for over ten percent of all job seekers during this period, according to the labor-market statistics of the National Employment Agency (ANPE). The combination of economic insecurity, created by rising unemployment, with the perception of a larger immigrant population is cited as an important factor in the breakthrough of the FN in the municipal elections of 1983 and the European elections of 1984.[104] Yet the level of political activity surrounding immigration was rising steadily from 1981 to 1983, culminating in rallies by pro-immigrant, antiracist and human-rights groups, such as SOS-racisme, whose leader, Harlem Désir, was to become the most prominent immigrant activist of the decade. In December 1983 François Mitterrand addressed a rally of North Africans—*Marche des Beurs*—at which he announced further liberalization measures, including the creation of a single identity card for foreigners, to be valid for ten years.

Just as the Socialists' economic policy was to take a 180 degree turn in 1983 away from *dirigisme,* nationalizations, and neo-Keynesian stimuli and toward more liberal policies of deregulation and economic restructuring, so too Socialist immigration policies became more restrictive. Several conditions were attached to the new ten-year residency permit, restricting it to only a small minority of foreigners. In addition, left-wing Jacobin traditions of *laïcité* and the whole range of church-state issues began to cause problems between the PS and its *beur* constituency. The opening of channels of political participation for immigrants facilitated the revival of Islam in the North African community, particularly among second-generation Algerians, a minority of whom were spurred on by the new militancy of Islamic movements in the Middle East.[105]

The reaction to the new militancy of Muslims was not limited to an assimilationist, Jacobin reflex, even though the Jacobin argument became increasingly prevalent among intellectuals of both the Left and the Right.[106] The entire debate over immigration in France shifted radically to the Right with the rise of the FN under the leadership of Jean-Marie Le Pen, who made no efforts to disguise his anti-immigrant positions, which often were confounded with a more sinister and anti-Semitic nationalism. The rallying cry of the FN, from the municipal elections of 1983 to the presidential and legislative elections of 1988, was "La France aux français!" This clarion call met with considerable electoral success (Le Pen has consistently garnered around ten percent of the vote in various elections since 1984.) and forced all political parties to redefine their position on immigration. The brief shift to proportional representation for the legislative elections in 1986 allowed the FN to win thirty-three seats in the National Assembly and to form its own parliamentary group, thus driving a wedge into the heart of the Right, which continues to struggle both with the FN and with the issue of immigration.

The neo-Gaullist RPR, under the leadership of Jacques Chirac, and the centrist UDF, under the leadership of Raymond Barre, Giscard-d'Estaing, and others, clearly longed for the day when immigration was an issue of population decline and labor supply rather than one of citizenship and national identity. Nonetheless, from the European elections of 1984 to the present, the RPR has been forced to take a stand on the issues of immigration, citizenship, and nationality in order to avoid further erosion of its right-wing nationalist constituency, particularly in the south of France where alliances have been struck between local RPR and FN candidates. The most important attempt by the Right to deal with the immigration issue in the 1980s came in 1986, when the Chirac government convened a *Commission des Sages* to study and debate possible revision of citizenship law (Code de la Nationalité), which is based on the dual principles of *jus soli* (place of birth) and *jus sanguinis* (kinship), and which allows considerable freedom for resident aliens to choose citizenship. In effect, persons born in France of foreign parents can choose citizenship when they achieve majority, at the age of eighteen; and naturalizsation procedures in France are quite liberal.[107]

The Chirac government also proposed legislation to reform citizenship law and to give greater authority to prefectoral administrations (i.e., local police) to expel illegal aliens. These measures were designed to curb immigration, restrict access to citizenship, and cut down on naturalizations, which were *not* dramatically higher in the 1980s than in the 1970s.[108] Despite the spate of political, administrative, and intellectual activity around the issues of immigration and citizenship, no real changes were made in the law. The *Commission des Sages* simply reaffirmed the liberal traditions of French jurisprudence in the area of immigration and naturalization, and bills for further restricting immigration and naturalization, proposed by the Chirac government, were withdrawn. Nonetheless, there was a clear distinction between the positions of the Right and those of the Left on the issue of immigration in the 1980s. Socialist policies had a liberalizing effect on immigration (via the amnesty of 1981–82) and on assimilation and political participation (via new rules governing associations), which picked up markedly in the 1980s. The Right is constrained by pressure from the FN, which compels the RPR and UDF to take a tough stance with respect to future immigration and immigrant political activities. What continues to unite both the Left and the Right, however, is a fundamentally Jacobin attitude towards questions of citizenship and national identity.

No event better symbolizes the continuing importance of the Jacobin tradition in French politics in the 1980s than the controversy surrounding three Muslim girls in the *collège* Gabriel-Havez in Creil, north of Paris, who chose to wear traditional Islamic headscarves (*foulards*) into the classroom. They were expelled from the school for their refusal to remove the offending scarves, ironically by a school principal from the West Indies. In the fall of 1989, in the midst of the revolutions that were sweeping Eastern Europe, the *affaire des foulards* transfixed public opinion and the intelligentsia. Should the young women be allowed to express their cultural identity through such an overt display of religiousity in the *école laïque?* The initial position of the Socialist government, headed by Michel Rocard, was to allow the women to wear their scarves so long as they did not proselytize. In the meantime, the whole issue was referred to the Conseil d'Etat, which sided with the Rocard government, ruling that schools (and by extension the state) cannot discriminate against individuals based on their religious preferences, and that it is legal for students to wear religious symbols in the classroom, so long as these symbols do not interfere with the religious freedom of others. The whole episode took on great symbolic importance, as intellectuals and politicians rallied in defense of the Jacobin model of assimilation and the *école laïque*.[109] The editor of *Libération,* Serge July, summarized the event in the following way:

> Derrière le foulard corainique, la question de l'immigration, et derrière l'immigration le débat sur l'intégration, et derrière l'intégration la question de la laïcité. De toute évidence deux conceptions de la laïcité s'affrontent dans cette affaire. Autrement dit, c'est quoi la laïcité, cette vénérable vielle dame française? Sans remonter aux affrontements jacobins et girondins, on retrouve néanmoins des éléments de confrontation traditionnels. Pour simplifier: le laminage de l'assimilation pure et simple d'un côté, la promotion des ghettos à l'anglaise de l'autre au nom d'une exaltation du droit à la différence.[110]

The *affaire des foulards,* like the issue of immigration itself, divided political parties and the public roughly along three lines: liberal or pluralist, Jacobin, and nationalist. It is too early to tell whether the politics of immigration and ethnicity in France will evolve along the lines of cultural pluralism, as would seem to be the case in the United States in the postwar period, or whether the political system and political parties will revert to a more philosophical Jacobin tradition.[111]

While the 1980s in France saw an opening of the avenues of political participation for immigrants, they also have seen the birth of an ultranationalist and xenophobic political movement (the Front National) and a Jacobin reaction against the assertiveness of Muslim immigrants. Although immigration is no longer debated in economic or demographic terms, the stagnation of the population and the potential for economic growth in the 1990s, spurred on by the continuing process of European integration, could combine to create a new demand for immigrant labor. The dynamic populations of Africa stand poised once again to provide manpower, not only for France, but for Europe as a whole.

It is unclear what effect the creation of a single European market for capital (and labor) will have on immigration and citizenship in the member states of the EEC. Scholars and politicians have turned their attention to the impact of the Single Europe Act on the political economy of Western Europe. Certainly, one of the thorniest issues in this process of integration will be immigration, and how to control the movement of foreigners within the Community. The French government was engaged in negotiations in 1989 with four other European countries (West Germany, Belgium, Holland, and Luxembourg) to create a border-free zone. The so-called Schengen initiative promised to eliminate border controls within these five states by 1990 and hopes to create a border-free Europe by 1992. Not surprisingly, the Schengen initiative was put on hold by the events in Eastern Europe, particularly the disintegration of the German Democratic Republic and other formerly Communist regimes, which threatens to increase the flow of political and economic refugees from East to West.

Both at the level of domestic and international politics, immigration will be one of the most controversial issues in Europe in the 1990s. Certainly, immigration has helped to transform French society and modernize the economy in the postwar period, and the issue of immigration has disrupted French politics over the past decade and a half. If the economies of Western Europe begin to grow at a high rate after the implementation of the Single Act in 1993 and the expected demographic push from Africa materializes, immigration is likely to preoccupy politicians in France and throughout Europe into the next century, and we may see some of the debates of the 1950s and 1960s played out again, hopefully in a liberal political and economic climate.

Conclusion:
Immigration and the End of Jacobinism?

The practical effect of immigration in postwar France was to provide an important source of labor and human capital for economic modernization. The planners of the Fourth and Fifth Republic understood the need for immigration. Yet the effects of immigration on France go well beyond the confines of economics and demography. Immigration exposed the strengths and weaknesses of France's political culture and political system.

The struggle to deal with culturally and ethnically distinct groups taxed the ability of political parties to mobilize support and aggregate interests. Nowhere is this clearer than with the French Communist Party, which successfully integrated earlier waves of European immigrants in the 1920s and 1930s but ultimately failed to adapt to the demands of a new Muslim underclass in the 1970s and 1980s, a group that sought cultural recognition as much as class solidarity. Likewise, the institutions of the Jacobin state were slow to adjust to the realities of a permanent, settler migration in the 1970s and 1980s. Heavy-handed administrative efforts to cut off immigration in 1974 resulted in a number of unintended consequences, which increased the foreign population and contributed to the insecurity and instability of immigrants. Ultimately, immigration turned the state against itself, as the most paradoxical of administrative organs—the Conseil d'Etat—annulled the executive orders to stop immigration in the mid 1970s. Again in 1989, the Conseil d'Etat intervened, this time on the side of the liberal policies of the Rocard government, to permit Muslim school children to wear traditional Islamic dress.

Immigration has disrupted French politics by provoking a renaissance of the extreme nationalist Right, which had lain dormant since the demise of the Vichy regime. The carefully crafted political alliances of the Gaullist era were torn apart, first by the victory of the left in 1981 and subsequently by the emergence of the Front National. The party system proved incapable of handling the issue of immigration within the context of "normal" party politics, and the shift to proportional representation in 1985–86 gave the anti-immigrant Front National a foothold in the parliament. It is unlikely that we have seen the end of the Le Pen phenomenon, or of immigration.

Despite these political developments, Jacobin political culture shows signs of adapting to the realities of social and cultural pluralism. The liberalizing influence of Socialist policies in the 1980s, together with the political assertiveness of immigrants, has created the conditions for ethnic/minority politics in a society that traditionally refused *le droit à la différence*. We have seen signs of the growing weight of the *vote beur,* which could play a crucial role in politics, as the French electoral system moves closer to American-style presidential primaries. Having helped France to overcome "Malthusian" problems of social and economic development during the Fourth Republic, immigrants may contribute to breaking the political stalemate *(immobilisme)* of the Fifth Republic.

Notes

1. Cf. various passages from J-J. Rousseau, *A Discourse on Political Economy* (New York: Dutton, Everyman's Library, 1973), pp. 173ff.

2. Fernand Braudel emphasizes the diversity of society in *L'Identité de la France* (Paris: Flammarion: 1986), pp. 27ff.

3. On the Jacobin concept of citizenship and its importance in French political development, see the concluding essay of this book. Cf. also Lucien Jaume, *Le discours jacobin et al démocratie* (Paris: Fayard, 1988). Although he does not discuss the Jacobin tradition as it relates to immigration, much of Gérard Noiriel's analysis of the history of immigration is driven by a concern for the role of the state in defining who is and is not foreign, and how foreigners should be assimilated. See G. Noiriel, *Le creuset français: histoire de l'immigration XIXe–XXe siècles* (Paris: Seuil, 1988).

4. Michael Marrus, *Politics of Assimilation: A Study of the French Jewish Community at the Time of the Dreyfus Affair* (Oxford: Clarendon Press, 1971), Dominique Schnapper, *Juifs et israélites* (Paris: Gillimard, 1980), and idem, "Le juif errant," in Yves Lequin, ed., *La mosaïque France: Histoire des étrangers et de l'immigration* (Paris: Larousse, 1988), pp. 373–83.

5. Again, see Noiriel, *Le creuset,* passim, and idem, *Ouvriers dans la société française, XIVe–XXe siècles* (Paris: Seuil, 1986), idem, *Longwy, immigrés et prolétaires, 1880–1980* (Paris: PUF, 1984). Cf. infra, Table 1.

6. See Ralph Schor, *L'Opinion française et les étrangers, 1919–1939* (Paris: Publication de la Sorbonne, 1985).

7. The National Planning Commission (Conseil Général du Plan, CGP) was set up to oversee the reconstruction and modernization of the economy in the 1950s. See Stephen S. Cohen, *Modern Capitalist Planning: The French Model* (Berkeley, Calif.: University of California Press, 1977).

Likewise, a new agency, the Office National d'Immigration (ONI), was established to recruit foreign workers and place them with firms.

8. Léon Gani, *Syndicats et traveilleurs immigrés* (Paris: Editions Sociales, 1972); and André Vieuguet, *Français et immigrés, le combat du P.C.F.* (Paris: Editions Sociales, 1975).

9. This push for ideological conformity is not, of course, unique to France, which has encountered difficulties of late with the ethnic and cultural diversity of society. The American "state" historically has demanded of immigrants a high degree of cultural and linguistic conformity, which is the ideal of the melting pot. Yet, in the postwar period, the Civil Rights revolution has contributed to a new cultural pluralism, which is the dominant feature of contemporary American political culture. Cf. Thomas Archdeacon, *Becoming American: An Ethnic History* (New York: The Free Press, 1983), and James Hollifield "Migrants ou citoyens: la politique de l'immigration en France et aux Etats-Unis," *Revue Européenne des Migrations Internationales* 5 (Spring 1990).

10. Cf. Michel Crozier, *Le phénomène bureaucratique* (Paris: Editions du Seuil, 1963); Pierre Birnbaum, *Les sommets de l'Etat* (Paris: Editions du Seuil, 1977); and Pierre Grémion, "Crispation et déclin du jacobinisme," in Henri Mendras, ed., *La sagesse et le désordre* (Paris: Gallimard, 1980), pp. 330–38.

11. See H. Bunle, *Mouvements migratoires entre la France et l'étranger* (Paris: Imprimerie Nationale, 1943).

12. See Gérard Noiriel, *Ouvriers dans la société française;* and Lequin, *La mosaïque France,* especially "L'invasion pacifique," pp. 335–52.

13. For a history of immigration in France from the 1880s to the 1930s, see Gary S. Cross, *Immigrant Workers in Industrial France* (Philadelphia: Temple University Press, 1983), especially pp. 214ff. See also Georges Mauco, *Les étrangers en France* (Paris: Colin, 1932); and Pierre Milza, ed., *Les Italiens en France de 1914 à 1940* (Rome: Ecole française de Rome, 1981).

14. For an account of the politics of immigration during the interwar period, see Schor, *L'Opinion française et les étrangers.* On the history of immigration policy during the interwar period, see J-C. Bonnet, *Les pouvoirs publics français et l'immigration dans l'entre-deux-guerres* (Lyon: Centre d'histoire économique et sociale de la région lyonnaise, 1976), especially pp. 61–185.

15. On the pronatalist movement, see Alison C. McIntosh, "The Rise of Twentieth-Century Pronatalism," *International Journal of Politics* 12 (Fall 1982): 42–57.

16. From Robert Debré and Alfred Sauvy, *Des français pour la France: Le Problème de la population* (Paris: Gallimard, 1946), p. 225. At the end of this war, France will have a vital need for immigrants. In order to rebuild and revitalize agriculture and industry, we must supplement the effort of the French with a large foreign work force. The public will object: foreigners are coming to steal our bread and take our place. Workers will complain: foreigners are forcing wages down. The middle class will be alarmed: foreigners are relying on public assistance. The press will dredge up the old clichés: the foreigners that we are taking are from the bottom of the barrel, the rejects of Europe, who will destroy public spiritedness. Yet all of these cries of alarm will count for little in the face of the needs of the national economy. We should keep in mind that some of these concerns are justified: the need to keep wages at a reasonable level and the need to select immigrants carefully. But we can reject many of these unjustified claims.

17. For a good account of political development during this period, see Herbert Luethy, *France against Herself* (New York: Praeger, 1955).

18. On the problems confronting the postwar French economy, see Charles P. Kindleberger, "The Postwar Resurgence of the French Economy," in *In Search of France,* ed. Stanley Hoffmann (Cambridge, Mass.: Harvard University Press, 1963). See also C. P. Kindleberger, *Europe's Postwar Growth: The Role of Labor Supply* (Cambridge, Mass.: Harvard University Press, 1967). Kindleberger points out in both of these works the central role played by immigration in France's postwar economy.

19. See Cohen, *Modern Capitalist Planning*, pp. 81ff., and Peter A. Hall, *Governing the Economy* (New York: Oxford University and Polity Press, 1986), pp. 137ff.

20. On manpower, immigration policy, and the planning process, see Georges Tapinos, *L'Immigration étrangère en France* (Paris: PUF, 1975), pp. 16–18; and Pierre Bauchet, *La planification française* (Paris: Editions du Seuil, 1966), p. 212. On the question of labor productivity and internal migration, see Jean-Jacques Carré et al., *French Economic Growth* (Stanford, Calif.: Stanford University Press, 1975), pp. 94ff.

21. The corporatist elements of economic planning were not simply window dressing. They were attributable in part to the legacy of Vichy and the experiences of industrial management during the Occupation. On these points, see Cohen, *Modern Capitalist Planning*, pp. 253ff.

22. For more on the *populationnistes'* position, see Alfred Sauvy, "Besoins et possibilités de l'immigration en France," *Population* 2–3 (1950): 209–434.

23. Cf. Gani, *Syndicats et travailleurs immigrés*, pp. 53–54; and Milza, *Les Italiens en France*.

24. Cf. Bonnet, *Les pouvoirs publics français et l'immigration*, pp. 89–93; and Marie-Claude Hénneresse, *Le patronat et la politique française d'immigration, 1945–1975* (Paris: Thèse, Institut d'Etudes Politiques, 1978), pp. 60–65.

25. See Sauvy, "Besoins et possibilités."

26. See Tapinos, *L'Immigration étrangère en France*, pp. 10–36; and Bruno Courault, *Contribution à la théorie de l'offre de travail: le cas de l'immigration en France, 1946–1978* (Paris: Thèse, Université de Paris I, Panthéon Sorbonne, 1980), pp. 211–13.

27. CGP, "Premier rapport de la commission de la main-d'oeuvre (octobre 1946)," in *Documents relatifs à la première session du Conseil du Plan, 16–19 mars 1946* (Paris: Imprimerie Nationale, 1946), pp. 23 and 26. See also Tapinos, *L'Immigration étrangère en France*, pp. 14–17; and the section on planning and economic growth in Carré et al., *French Economic Growth*, pp. 458ff.

28. See, for example, Bauchet, *La planification française*, pp. 287–90.

29. On the development of the labor market during this period, see Carré et al., *French Economic Growth*, 94ff.

30. See James F. Hollifield, *Immigrants, Markets and States* (Cambridge, Mass.: Harvard University Press, 1991), Chapter 7.

31. Marie-Claude Hénneresse documents the gradual movement of employers toward extralegal recruitment of foreign labor in the 1950s. See Hénneresse, *Le patronat et la politique d'immigration*, pp. 155–81.

32. See Carré et al., *French Economic Growth*, pp. 432–37.

33. Also, Tapinos, *L'Immigration étrangère en France*, pp. 34ff.

34. Nonetheless, entries and departures of Algerians were tabulated by the Ministry of the Interior (see Table 5.3). On the evolution of the legal status of Algerian workers in France, see Malek Ath-Messaoud and Alain Gillette, *L'Immigration algérienne en France* (Paris: Editions Entente, 1976), pp. 40–54. On the method of counting Algerian immigrants, see Tapinos, *L'Immigration étrangère*, Appendix 1, pp. 128–30.

35. See Alain Girard, "Le problème démographique et l'évolution du sentiment public," *Population* 5, no. 2 (1950): especially 338–40; and Alain Girard and Jean Stoetzel, *Français et immigrés: Travaux et Documents*, INED, Cahier no. 19 (Paris: PUF, 1953–54).

36. See Tapinos, *L'Immigration étrangère en France*, p. 40.

37. For a discussion of the relationship between decolonization, immigration, and ethnic conflict, see Gary P. Freeman, *Immigrant Labor and Racial Conflict in Industrial Societies: The French and British Experiences, 1945–1975* (Princeton, N.J.: Princeton University Press, 1979).

38. The economic successes of the Fourth Republic were due at least in part to the fiscal and monetary policies of the Pinay governments and to the application of the recommendations of the Rueff-Armand Commission, which restored a measure of competition to industry. These short-term policies complemented the efforts of planners to encourage investment. See Carré et al., *French Economic Growth*, pp. 388–89 and 449–50. See also Vera Lutz, *Central Planning for the Market Economy* (London: Longmans, 1969), pp. 3–5.

39. Cf. Henry Ehrmann, *Organized Business in France* (Princeton, N.J.: Princeton University Press, 1957), pp. 207–76; and Georges Lefranc, *Les organisations patronales en France* (Paris: Payot, 1976), pp. 182ff.

40. Gani, *Syndicats et travailleurs immigrés*, pp. 44–55; and Hénneresse, *Le patronat et la politique d'immigration*, pp. 124–81.

41. On total labor supply, see Carré et al., *French Economic Growth*, pp. 55–57. Wages in France remained relatively low during the 1950s and early 1960s, largely due to the fact that the French labor market was more competitive than other OECD countries. Ibid., pp. 426–30.

42. Ezra Suleiman, *Politics, Power and Bureaucracy* (Princeton, N.J.: Princeton University Press, 1974), pp. 352–71.

43. Tapinos, *L'Immigration étrangère*, p. 53. See also, Louis Chevalier, "La population étrangère en France d'après le recensement de 1962," *Population* 19, no. 3 (1964): 569–78; and the CGP, "Rapport général de la Commission de la Main-d'Oeuvre (IIIè Plan)," *Revue Française du Travail* 20 (April–June 1958): 40–73.

44. Gani, *Syndicats et travailleurs immigrés*, pp. 52–58. Vieuguet, *Français et immigrés: le combat du P.C.F.*; and Bernard Granotier, *Les travailleurs immigrés en France* (Paris: François Maspero, 1973).

45. See Stephen Adler, *International Migration and Dependence* (Westmead, England: Saxon House, 1977), especially pp. 90ff. On the legal status of various African groups in France, see M. Bonnechère, "Conditions de séjour et d'emploi en France des travailleurs africains," *Revue pratique de droit social* 392 (December 1977): 379–82. See also K. Amousson, *L'immigration noire en France depuis 1945* (Thèse, Université de Paris VIII, 1976).

46. Quoted in Gani, *Syndicats et travailleurs immigrés*, p. 68.

47. CGP, "Rapport général de la Commission de la Main-d'Oeuvre du Ve Plan," *Revue Française du Travail* 28 (January–March 1966): 90–132.

48. On the concept of an industrial reserve army and the use of foreign labor for maintaining "flexibility" in the labor market, see Stephen Castles and Godula Kosack, *Immigrant Workers and Class Structure in Western Europe* (London: Oxford University Press, 1973), pp. 57–115. See also Gani, *Syndicats et travailleurs étrangers*, pp. 68ff.

49. Cf. Gani, *Syndicats et travailleurs immigrés;* and various works of Michael Piore, especially *Birds of Passage: Migrant Labor in Industrial Societies* (Cambridge: Cambridge University Press, 1979); as well as Edna Bonacich, "The Split Labor Market: A Theory of Ethnic Antagonism" *American Journal of Sociology* 37 (1972): 1050–87.

50. Alain Girard et al., "Attitudes des français à l'égard de l'immigration étrangère: nouvelle enquête d'opinion," *Population* 29, nos. 4–5 (1974): 1015–64.

51. Cf., for example, Vieuguet, *Français et immigrés: le combat du P.C.F.*, pp. 104–45; and Granotier, *Les travailleurs immigrés en France*, pp. 238–39.

52. See Jacqueline Costa-Lascoux, *De l'immigré au citoyen*, pp. 20ff.

53. See Stanley Hoffmann, *Decline and Renewal: France since the 1930s* (New York: Viking Press, 1974), pp. 145ff.

54. Because of certain clauses in the work contract between immigrant workers and their employers, the former were in a vulnerable position. Most notably, the work contract severely limited the mobility of the immigrant worker, who was practically forbidden from changing jobs during the first year of employment in France. See Henri de Lary de Latour, "Le particulrisme du contrat de travail pour les travailleurs immigrés," *Droit Social*, no. 5 (May 1976): 63–72; and Michael Piore, "Economic Fluctuation, Job Security, and Labor-Market Duality in Italy, France and the United States," *Politics and Society* 9, no. 4 (1980): 379–407.

55. On manpower, employment, and immigration policies during the Pompidou years, see the statement by J. Fontanet in OECD, "Manpower Policy in France," *Reviews of Manpower and Social Affairs* 12 (1973): 22–28. As was the case throughout this period, the emphasis was placed upon employment equilibrium, and upon the difficulty of achieving this goal through policy manipulations of the labor market.

56. One major difference between the new and the old Gaullists is that the former under Pompidou went to great lengths to assuage the fears of the traditional sector. Pompidou created a ministry to be headed by Jean Royer, to deal with the interests of the traditional sector. See Suzanne Berger on the political representation of traditional interests, "Regime and Interest Representation: The French Middle Classes," in S. Berger, ed., *Organizing Interests in Western Europe: Pluralism, Corporatism, and the Transformation of Politics* (New York: Cambridge University Press, 1981), pp. 83–102.

57. The "structural" role of foreign labor in the growth process was the subject of numerous works on immigration, labor markets, and labor mobility in the mid-1970s. Many of these works adopted the Marxist position that immigration and the use of foreign labor were responses to the crises of capitalist production. Perhaps the best-known of these works is Castles and Kosack, *Immigrant Workers and Class Structure*, particularly pp. 374ff. Also Manuel Castells, "Immigrant Workers and Class Struggles in Advanced Capitalism: the West European Experience," *Politics and Society* 5, no. 1 (1975): 33–66, Piore, "Economic Fluctuation, Job Security, and Labor-Market Duality"; and Jean-Paul de Gaudemar, *Mobilté du travail et accumulation du capital*, pp. 49–51. Finally, for an application of the Marxist-structuralist argument to the French case, see Christian Mercier, *Les déracinés du capital* (Lyon: Presses Universitaires de Lyon, 1977).

58. See the section on immigrant labor by Vidal and Sallois in CGP, *Rapport de la Commission Emploi (Préparation du VIè Plan)*, vol. 2 (Paris: Documentation Française, 1971). Also François Eymard-Duvernay, "L'Emploi au cours du VIè Plan," *Economie et Statistique* 74 (January 1976): 40–42.

59. See Tapinos, *L'Immigration étrangère*, pp. 88–91.

60. It is important to note that the normal procedure for issuing executive decrees is through the *Journal Officiel*.

61. In 1975 the Conseil d'Etat declared this and other attempts to regulate immigration by means of administrative memoranda to be inconsistent with French jurisprudence. On the important role of the Conseil d'Etat in the politics of immigration see C. N'Guyen Van Yen, *Droit de l'immigration* (Paris: PUF, Thémis, 1986); and Patrick Weil, *L'analyse d'une politique publique: la politique française d'immigration, 1974–1988* (Paris: Thèse, IEP, 1988).

62. On this point, see Nikolaus Notter, "Le statut des travailleurs étrangers en Allemange Fédérale," *Droit Social* 4 (April 1973): 223–30.

63. Hénneresse, *Le patronat et la politique d'immigration*, p. 417.

64. Ibid., p. 419. Cf. also J. Wisniewski, "Travailleurs migrants dans le bâtiment et les travaux publics," *Hommes et Migrations*, no. 885 (June 1975): 3–19.

65. Cf. Weil, *L'analyse d'une politique publique*.

66. J. Barou, *Travailleurs africains en France* (Grenoble: PUF, Actualités Recherches, 1978),

pp. 40–55. Also M. Bonnechère, "Conditions de séjour et d'emploi en France des travailleurs africains."

67. See Alain Girard et al., "Attitudes des français à l'égard de l'immigration étrangère: nouvelle enquête d'opinion."

68. See Freeman, *Immigrant Labor and Racial Conflict*, pp. 280–83; and Mark Miller, *Foreign Workers in Western Europe: An Emerging Political Force* (New York: Praeger, 1981).

69. See Martin A. Schain, "Immigration and Change in the French Party System," *European Journal of Political Research* 16 (1988): 597–621.

70. See Tomas Hammar, ed., *European Immigration Policy: A Comparative Study* (New York: Cambridge University Press, 1985).

71. Giscard summarizes his ambitions for changing French democracy in his political testament, *Démocratie française* (Paris: Fayard, 1976).

72. For an account of the exemptions to the ban on hiring foreign workers granted to various employers, see Hénneresse, *Le patronat et la politique française d'immigration;* and Hollifield, *Immigrants, Markets and States,* Chapter 4.

73. There have been other periods in French economic history when liberal economic policies were pursued, primarily during the Third Republic before the First World War. See, for example, Richard F. Kuisel, *Capitalism and the State in Modern France* (Cambridge: Cambridge University Press, 1981), pp. 1–30. On the imminent demise of planning, see Diane Green, "The Seventh Plan— The Demise of French Planning?" *West European Politics,* no. 1 (1978): 60–76.

74. These measures were adopted at the urging of the new secretary of state for immigrant workers, Postel-Vinay. For the complete texts of the *circulaires,* see the *Journal Officiel,* July 5, 9, and 19, 1974.

75. On the position of employers vis-à-vis the suspension of immigration, cf. Bunel and Saglio, "Le C.N.P.F. et la politique d'immigration," *Economie et Humanisme* 221 (January 1975): 41–50; and Hénneresse, *Le patronat et la politique d'immigration,* pp. 414–84.

76. Three national groups retained their privileged status after the suspension. The Portuguese retained it by virtue of numerous bilateral arrangements that made Portugal a "most favored" supplier of foreign manpower, the Moroccans because of their prominent role in the mining industry, and the francophone Africans of the sub-Saharan region because of their neocolonial relationship with France. See Courault, *Contribution à la théorie de l'offre de travail,* pp. 300–301.

77. His views were outlined in a publication of the secretary of state for immigrant workers, *La nouvelle politique de l'immigration,* reprinted in the introduction to a special issue of *Droit Social* (5 [1975]).

78. For a discussion of these measures, see Costa-Lascoux, *De l'immigré au citoyen* pp. 24ff.

79. For an analysis and explanation of the unintended consequences of the administrative suspension of immigration, see J. F. Hollifield, "Immigration and the French State: Problems of Policy Implementation," *Comparative Political Studies,* 23 (April, 1990), 56–79.

80. See various works of Michael Piore cited above. Numerous official and unofficial studies of the relationship between immigration and economic growth were conducted during the period immediately following the cutoff in immigration. All were able to document the continuing importance of foreign workers in the economy. Cfr., for example, H. Bussery, "Incidence sur l'économie française d'une réduction durable de la main-d'oeuvre immigrée," *Economie et statistique,* no. 76 (March 1976): 37–46; P. Bideberry, *Le chômage des travailleurs étrangers* (Paris: Inspection Générale des Affaires Sociales, 1974). Also A. Lebon and X. Jansolin, *Rapport sur l'immigration en France en 1978* (Paris: OECD, SOPEMI, 1979), pp. 41–60.

81. See Hénneresse, *Le patronat et la politique d'immigration* pp. 485–510.

82. See Anicet Le Pors, *Immigration et développement économique et sociall* (Paris: Documentation Française, 1976), pp. 147–51.

83. See Hénneresse, *Le patronat et la politique d'immigration*, pp. 433–34.

84. Ibid., pp. 436–37.

85. Ibid., pp. 439–44.

86. See René Mouriaux and Catherine de Wenden, "Syndicalisme français et Islam," *Revue française de science politique* 37, no. 6 (December 1987): 794–819. On the structural role of foreign labor in industrial production in France, see J. Nicol, "Les incidences économiques de l'immigration," *Problèmes économiques*, no. 1583 (26 July 1978): 3–7; and D. Provent, "Le travail manuel dans la société industrielle: recherche des conditions de sa revalorisation à travers l'analyse des structures de travail et d'emploi," *Revue française des Affaires sociales*, no. 2 (April–June 1976): 85–144.

87. Cf. Miller, *Foreign Workers in Western Europe*, pp. 149–55; Tewfik Allal et al., *Situations migratoires* (Paris: Editions Galilée, 1977); and R. D. Grillo, *Ideologies and Institutions in Urban France: The Representation of Immigrants* (Cambridge: Cambridge University Press, 1985).

88. See A. Lebon and O. Villey, "L'immigration et la politique de la main-d'oeuvre," *Economie et Statistique*, no. 113 (July–August 1979): 25–80.

89. In the service sector in particular, clandestine immigration became much more prominent after 1974. For example, the number of immigrant workers flowing into service-related firms rose from 58,800 in 1973 to 92,400 in 1979. A substantial portion of the increase was due to some form of "extralegal" migration. See Jean-Pierre Garson and Yann Moulier, *Les clandestins et la régularisation de 1981–1982 en France* (Geneva: ILO, working paper, May 1982), p. 32. Cf. also Olivier Villey, "Le redéploiement actuel de la main-d'oeuvre étrangère passé le premier choc de la crise," *Travail et Emploi* 8 (April–May 1981): 47–55.

90. See Garson and Moulier, *Les clandestins et la régularisation*, pp. 43–47.

91. The public's perception of the costs of supporting a large immigrant population, as is so often the case, may have had little bearing on the reality of immigrants' contribution to the economy. A study of the costs and benefits of immigration was carried out by Anicet Le Pors—a future Communist minister in the first Mitterrand government—who concluded that the economic benefits of immigration far outweighed the social costs. See Le Pors, *Immigration et développement économique et social*, pp. 91–136.

92. On the historical role of the Economic and Social Council in the political process, see Jack Hayward, *Private Interests and Public Policy: The Experience of the French Economic and Social Council* (London: Longmans, 1966).

93. Le rapport Calvez, "La politique de l'immigration," *Avis et Rapports du Conseil Economique et Social* (23 May 1975): 349–75.

94. See Nicole Lafay and Kinh Tran, *Rapport sur l'immigration en France en 1980* (Paris: OECD, SOPEMI, 1981), p. 26. Cf. André Lebon, "Sur une politique d'aide au retour," *Economie et statistique* 193 (July–August 1979), pp. 37–46. Also Weil, *L'analyse d'une politique publique*.

95. Cf. Tapinos, *L'immigration étrangère en France*, and idem, "Une approche démographique," in Lequin, ed., *La mosaïque France*, pp. 429–46.

96. See Archdeacon, *Becoming American*.

97. In the United States the struggle over citizenship and political participation pitted liberal constitutional principles embodied in the Fourteenth Amendment (due process, equal protection, etc.) and federal authorities, especially judges, against entrenched regional (and racist) interests determined to keep "foreigners" (in this case African Americans) out of the political process. See James Hollifield, "Migrants ou Citoyens?"

98. See Miller, *Foreign Workers in Western Europe.*

99. See Gani, *Syndicats et travailleurs immigrés;* and Freeman, *Immigrant Labor and Racial Conflict in Industrial Societies.* For a discussion of the evolution of the relationship between trade unions and Muslim immigrants in the 1980s, see Mouriaux and de Wenden, "Syndicalisme français et Islam."

100. Catherine Withol de Wenden, *Les immigrés et la politique* (Paris: Presses de la F.N.S.P., 1988).

101. On the univerrsalist tradition of the French Revolution and the treatment of foreigners, see J. P. Poussou and F. Malino, "De la grande nation au Grand Empire," In Yves Lequin, ed., *La mosaïque France,* pp. 291–322.

102. Not surprisingly, this polemic has been joined by right-wing academics, some with close ties to the Front National. See P. Bourcier de Carbon and P. Chaunu, "Un génocide statistique: on recherche 1,893,000 étrangers disparus dans les ordinateurs de l'INED," *Histoire, Economie et Société* 1 (1986). For a more dispassionate account of the evolution of immigration and the foreign population in the 1980s, see the various "Chroniques de l'immigration," by Michèle Tribalat, in the January issues of *Population.*

103. Over a three-year period, from 1981 to 1984, 88,492 immigrants were admitted to permanent resident status, as a result of the amnesty. For a discussion of the effects of the amnesty and other measures on the rate of immigration and naturalization, see André Lebon, "Attribution, acquisition et perte de la nationalité française: un bilan, 1973–1986," *Revue Européenne des Migrations Internationales* 1–2 (1987): 17–34; and idem, *1986–1987: Le point sur l'immigration et la présence étrangère en France* (Paris: Documentation française, 1988).

104. Nonna Mayer and Pascal Perrineau, *Le Front National à découvert* (Paris: Presses de la FNSP, 1989).

105. See Gilles Kepel, *Les banlieues de l'islam* (Paris: Seuil, 1988). Also Riva Kastoryano, *Etre turcque en France* (Paris: L'Harmattan, 1986).

106. For a discussion of the immigrant problem from the standpoint of religion and politics, see Rémy Leveau and Dominique Schnapper, "Religion et politique: juifs et musulmans," *Revue française de science politique* 37, no. 6 (December 1987).

107. For a discussion of French citizenship law, see Brubaker, ed., *Immigration and the Politics of Citizenship,* pp. 99–128; and Costa-Lascoux, *De l'immigré au citoyen,* pp. 115ff. See also Danièle Lochak, *Etranger de quel droit?* (Paris: PUF, 1986).

108. Although French naturalization statistics are sketchy, particularly for the period prior to the 1980s when citizenship became such a big political issue, figures given by the DPM show that from 1973 through 1987 the numbers have ranged from a low of 33,616 in 1973 to a high of 60,677 in 1985, before falling back to 41,754 in 1987–hardly a dramatic increase. See Costa-Lascoux, *De l'immigré au citoyen,* p. 121; and Lebon, *Le point sur l'immigration et la présence étrangère en France,* pp. 31–38.

109. The most famous initiative in this regard was taken by a group of five intellectuals, including Alain Finkielkraut and Régis Debray, who in an open letter to the minister of education, Lionel Jospin, warned that the year of the bicentennial of the French Revolution might become the "Munich de l'école républicaine." See *Le Nouvel Observateur,* November 2–8, 1989, p. 30.

110. Serge, July, editorial, "La Ligne de Crète," in *Libération,* November 6, 1989, p. 7. . . . behind the scarf is the question of immigration, behind immigration is the debate over integration, and behind integration, the question of *laïcité.* By all accounts, two notions of *laïcité* are at issue here . . . what is *laïcité,* this venerable, old lady of French history? Without going back to the conflicts between jacobins and girondins, we can see some traditional elements of French history at work here.

To simplify, we have a strict assimilationist position on the one hand, and anglo-American ghettos promoted in the name of the 'right to be different,' on the other.

111. In interviewing a high government official charged with immigration affairs in 1986, I posed a question concerning policy toward ethnic minorities. At the very mention of the issue of ethnicity, the official, showing great consternation, stated in response to my question simply: "Monsieur, en France nous sommes tous républicains."

6

In Search of the Etat Providence

Douglas E. Ashford

The search for the *Etat providence,* the French "welfare state," may be more elusive than the search for the French political and social identity undertaken by Hoffmann and others twenty-five years ago. The first question is whether this elusiveness is the product of scholarly oversight or French neglect. It is interesting that the last search into the condition of French society and the French state had no essay on the welfare state even though the battery of social legislation from 1946 to 1948 that institutionalized the French welfare state was among the major accomplishments of the Fourth Republic. But the same omission is repeated in the comparative and descriptive studies of welfare states. Inadvertently perhaps, the welfare state is often treated as a Protestant monopoly and, most often, as intellectually inspired by the Nordic welfare state.[1] To be sure, in 1960 the visible product of the French welfare state was not impressive, especially to social scientists most concerned with measuring performance. But the same could be said of the more celebrated Swedish welfare state of the 1960s.

Both the theory and the methods of studying welfare states weighed against serious study of the French welfare state. If being a welfare state presupposes energetic efforts to alleviate social inequities and to respond to social needs, it is probably correct to say that until the 1960s France was not a leader. The interesting question, however, is that in the short space of a decade France became a big spender in the quantitative international league. In 1974 the *budget social* exceeded the *budget national.*[2] This is, of course, not the first time that the preconceptions of social science misdirected attentions, but it does raise peculiarly difficult issues of assessing and comparing welfare states. First, the French were never without interest in the interdependence of society and the state. Indeed, the entire history of republicanism in the nineteenth century is compelling proof that France was self-consciously searching for a social model that would relieve the political and social strains of modern industrial life. Starting at the turn of the century, France regularly produced enormous tomes on the social condition of France.[3] If French social policies and problems could not be caught in the coarse net of contemporary social science, perhaps it is because over much of the nineteenth century the French, culminating with Durkheim, were busily engaged in producing a harmonious concept of state and society. Perhaps the French welfare state is so distinctly republican as to be unmeasurable by crude aggregations. In any event, French social policy debates date from the earliest years of republican stability in the 1880s. With the exception of the Dreyfus Affair, the social functions of the state monopolized political debate in France for the last decade of the nineteenth century.[4]

Rosanvallon notes that the phrase *l'Etat providence* was first used during the Second Empire.[5] If so, its appearance pre-dates the much acclaimed Bismarckian *Wohlfahrtsstaat* by a decade or more. Most agree that the English phrase was not in common usage until the 1930s.[6] Thus, if the meaning of the welfare state is extended to include a broad understanding of how nations dealt with the stresses and strains of modern industrial life and how they imagined an interventionist state, in the late nineteenth century France was a leader. Experts on social work, public assistance, and public health flocked to France to study the innovative Bureau d'Assistance Publique that was the social analogue for the *école libre* among turn-of-the century republicans. Social reform leaders and dignitaries of settlement-house movements from throughout the world attended the social reform seminars of the *Exposition universelle* of 1901. Le Play's major study of social reform was required reading for social reformers throughout the world, and his journal, *Réforme sociale,* was the major international journal on social reform until 1914.[7]

While it may provide little consolation to those who look upon the modern welfare state as an instant cure for social injustice, there are important reasons to examine the development of the welfare state, particularly in France, as part of an historic clash of ideas that helped redefine the nineteenth-century liberal state.[8] Without entering into methodological tangles, doing so presupposes that we can discuss the meaning of ideas independently of their consequences or, to put the point more directly, momentarily agree that ideas have consequences apart from the social and political realities of the day.[9] France is intriguing because the republican vision presupposed a rational model of social and political interaction. In this respect, the phrase *l'Etat providence* is a peculiarly inaccurate description, and this from a people generally known for their linguistic precision. Providential care suggests charitable good works, religious benevolence, and voluntary dedication to social service, all notions of social assistance and social protection that were, as we shall see, treated with suspicion by staunch republicans. It would not be an impossible generalization to say that the French invented sociology, if not *le social,*[10] in order to identify the problem of reconciling social need and social change with republican governance.[11] To an extent that exceeds the efforts of any other democratic society, the interdependence of political and social values was a conscious presupposition of French democracy.

As a footnote to French intellectual history, it is interesting to note how many nineteenth-century French political commentators thought that the most aggressive social reformer among the democracies, Britain,[12] could not serve as a model for France. Unfortunately, Tocqueville never lived to write the book he promised on British politics, but he did note briefly that British elitism made early British efforts unsuitable for France.[13] Boutmy's admiration for British parliamentary stability notwithstanding, he noted with remarkable prescience that the British failure to link wage and social policies was a fatal flaw in their social thinking.[14] Halévy was no doubt reflecting a shared French way of thinking when he wrote that the "disinterested Machiavellianism" of British social policy was inappropriate for France.[15] Thus, the first step in understanding the French welfare is to see state intervention in society as a peculiar dilemma for the French republicans. The French were never unaware of the emergent welfare state; they simply were not sure they wanted one.

Early Republican Quandaries

No doubt there was significant social and economic resistance to a more interventionist French state, but an equally important obstacle, one that receives little attention in pluralist and socialist socioeconomic explanations of the welfare state, is that intervention had to be reconciled with republican preconceptions about democracy. These ideas were rooted in prerevolutionary political thought and manifested in the *loi Le Chapelier* of 1791. The notion that any form of association outside the structure of the state menaced the unrestrained and, therefore, perfectly rational expression of the popular will was peculiarly French, although it has arisen in other forms in other countries.[16] This is why the republicans of 1848 found the *atelier* movement so disturbing. Without a juridical rationale for associational activity, the possibility of individuals voluntarily organizing themselves to provide social protection or to give social assistance to others was not only perplexing but contradictory to republican principles.

The depths of this contradiction can best be understood by noting how seriously it was treated by Emile Ollivier, a conservative republican whose juridical skills were, for the same reason, also exercised to justify stronger local government.[17] It is easily forgotten that the possibility of a "grande commune de France," later to become the Senate, was at one time considered a very progressive, if not alarming, idea to explain how local government might avoid diluting the republican purity of national government. Much the same dispute whirled around the formation of voluntary insurance companies, the *mutualités,* which remain an essential element of the French social insurance system. While it is true that voluntary insurance eventually becomes social protection for the privileged, it is also true that voluntary insurance made the lack of protection for workers more visible. In any event, Ollivier's advocacy of the mutual insurance law of 1864 was thought to be a radically republican position. Very similar intellectual acrobatics were needed to explain how voluntary associations for other forms of saving for old age might be reconciled with republican ideas.[18]

Because the language of class politics is so easily superimposed on these early historical events, it is worth noting that in more authentic liberal states, such as Britain, the reconciliation between state and voluntary assistance was even more awkward. Until the 1911 Insurance Act, which insured only a small portion of the workforce, British workers had a choice between contributing their pennies to the local Friendly Society or the punitive benevolence of the local poorhouse in order to avoid a pauper's grave. To take the more enlightened case of Sweden, a dimly understood element of Teutonic folklore, *folkhem,* was resurrected in order to calm conflicting demands for social insurance.[19] Only one country, Germany, had a national social insurance scheme in the nineteenth century, and it was imposed to arrest democratic development rather than to enhance it. France had neither the comfort of retreating into a mythical past nor the inclination to make the poor into a separate social class. Republicanism was too rational to accept the first and too politically sensitive to permit the latter.

The net result was that, amidst a host of other unsolved problems, it was left to the Third Republic to settle the question of how the French might cooperate to protect the poor and the neglected. Because the underlying assumption of this essay is that the limits of the welfare state are nothing less than the limits of the human imagination, the experience of the Third Republic is crucially important. In the socioeconomic language of welfare, it is no doubt true that the crucial first step toward state intervention in society was the *loi Roussel* of 1883 that gave medical care to schoolchildren. Children have, of course, been critically important in the early definition of welfare in many countries. Although the British Poor Amendment Act of 1834 calmly consigned poor adults to virtually subhuman conditions in poor houses,[20] even the stern evangelicalism of the early Victorians allowed that children should have an equal chance at schooling and good health. Concern for children is one reason to think of welfare states as partially realized visions of the future, but there were more explicit reasons given in late nineteenth-century, republican France.

The two branches of the French debate, economic and social, as in most democracies, might have eventually merged to form a version of social democracy. In this respect, France was a potential leader because republican ideas about associations gave the question of trade-union formation precedence over the development of social insurance. There is a vague but intriguing correspondence between the French and the Swedish experience: in each case the concerns over the organization of social democracy also took precedence over the provision of social benefits and insurance.[21] Historical parallels can easily become historicisms, but Waldeck-Rousseau's preoccupations in the mid-1880s are not at all unlike those of Wigforss in the 1920s.[22] As French minister of the interior in 1884, Waldeck-Rousseau was preoccupied with the question of how worker organizations might meet the stringent regulations imposed on voluntary associations.[23] Whatever his capitalist insensitivities, he was acutely aware that enterprises and unions were treated differently under French law. The *mutualité* rationalization would not work for the obvious republican reason that unions, unlike cooperative insurance schemes, were not in principle open to anyone. Within the odd logic of French political thinking, there was an inner contradiction between universal privileges and privileges bestowed only on workers.

Unhappily for France, perhaps, Waldeck-Rousseau's term in the ministry of the interior, which was still the guardian of republican virtue, was short-lived. But the effort to link social and labor policy continued under Waldeck-Rousseau's government of 1899, where an independent socialist, Alexandre Millerand, broke from Socialist orthodoxy in order to take office as the first Socialist minister in French history.[24] As minister of commerce he enlarged and revised the Conseil Supérieur du Travail and began to popularize the idea of using local labor councils as mediation boards. He created the Office Nationale de Statistique et de Placement, in some respects the historical precedent for INSEE, in 1900. Under his auspices, a number of moderate Socialists were brought into the government, among them André Fontaine, who became a leader in the formation of the Ministry of Labor after 1906, and Léon Mirman, later to become the first director of the public assistance boards in 1905. Under the impulse of the radical republicans, Millerand cultivated a nursery of officials sensitive to labor needs. The formation of the Ministry of Labor in 1906, more than a decade before similar progress was made in Britain, was largely the result of Millerand's concern that labor feel itself part of the French policy-making process.[25]

The second strand in the republican vision of the welfare state was the insistence on reforming the Bureaux de Bienfaisance. During the Revolution, local governments had been given responsibility for eradicating *mendicité*. As in most nineteenth-century democracies, French departments acquired responsibility for public assistance, and local agencies were formed to help the poor. Henri Monod was the republican official at the Ministry of the Interior responsible for organizing public assistance. His tireless struggle to eradicate the charitable and religious nature of the local social assistance offices is the French analogue to the equally extended struggle to remove Poor Law administration from the control of the no less fierce Protestant evangelicals in Britain.[26] Monod became the republican champion of social reform. In what may well be the first serious debate about territorial redistribution of resources, Monod argued (to the "wild applause" of the Chamber of Deputies) that richer departments had an obligation to assist poorer areas in building local insurance funds.[27] But the clash of ideas and of policy options was more intense in France than in most democracies because the Bureaux de Bienfaisance were seen as an intrusion of the Church into local social policy and, by implication if not in fact, an obstacle to the application of republican standards in the provision of public assistance.

Monod's aim was not unlike that of most contemporary welfare states, that is, to nationalize public assistance. The historical difference, of course, was that his campaign coincided with the Dreyfus Affair and the rise of radical republicanism. But the organization of the state-controlled Bureau d'Assistance Publique became a pivotal claim of the radical republicans. Within a year of the 1905 law on welfare reform, state assistance to the 644,000 persons on welfare grew to over a hundred million francs. By 1912 over one million people were receiving free hospital care, and there were pensions for over 100,000 aged people under the disputed 1908 pension law.[28] But the result may be less important than the idea. When an aristocrat objected to the 1905 law as an intolerable burden on communal and family obligations, Monod was ready with figures to show that only one in sixty French people would require assistance and that the resulting sum would be a negligible burden on local budgets.[29] Contrary to the view that French bureaucrats await the paralysis of French society, Monod was setting the pace for a parochial and rural society. While France never suffered from the depression of the late 1920s and early 1930s to the extent that Britain did, it is nonetheless worth noting that as late as 1935 Britain was still trying to displace the costs of the long-term unemployed and the poor onto local government. The result was to discredit local government and to institutionalize poverty in a way that few other European powers did.[30]

There is an unfortunate tendency to read history backward. France did not achieve the apparent victories in social reform that we associate with British social insurance of 1911 or with Bismarckian benevolence in 1880s. What is left out is, in the first instance, that British reforms were conceptually unimaginative and in most respects quite consistent with punitive social assistance as it had developed throughout Victorian times. The welfare breakthrough of Imperial Germany was skillfully designed to forestall the appeal of a rising labor movement and to cripple the Social Democratic Party. Regardless of social and economic implications, welfare reforms have political meanings that may have been clearer in the previous century than they are now, but that nonetheless helped define the course of democratic government. For the radical republicans, Catholic and charitable welfare was indistinguishable from conservative, antirepublican, and anti-Semitic efforts to undermine the French republic. If the socioeconomic product was less impressive than in other democracies, the political accomplishment was more integral to French democratic institutions than elsewhere.

In terms of generating new state capacities, redefining the political constructs under which state intervention may take place is critically important. In a relatively short period the republicans devised a new formula for associational life, the *établissement public,* under the law of 1901. Next to the fervent republicanism of the Ligue de l'Enseignement,[31] the Ligue de Prévoyance was the most important organization agitating for more liberal associational laws.[32] It is indicative of the ambiguities surrounding the concept of the French state, and consequently the French welfare state, that the idea used to give the republic juridical consistency produced political confusion. Today the *établissement public* is used to organize any imaginable organization, ranging from the Comédie Française to the Centre National de la Recherche Scientifique. It has been claimed that the French state is excessively hierarchical and inadaptive; other European democracies, however, were left with even less adaptive instruments for expanding the realm of social and economic intervention. In Britain, political and organizational rights remain at the mercy of Parliament so that the British welfare state can be as easily dismantled by the Tories as it was built by the Liberals and Labour. In Germany, the intricate legal edifice constructed to advance social policies and programs, illustrated by the agglomeration of sickness funds,[33] produced an unwieldly and unresponsive corporatist agency that makes the organization of sickness insurance virtually incomprehensible. Compared to other European states, the French republicans were relatively flexible and ingenious in developing the emergent welfare state from the not inconsiderable political constraints of the Third Republic.

Institutionalizing the French Welfare State

France is not, of course, the only country where the accomplishment of protecting democracy in World War I permitted liberals to rule foremost in the interwar period with little or no serious competition from the Left. But this was doubly the case in France because the victory over the Kaiser in 1914 left an enormous task of reconstruction in northern France.[34] To be sure, the Senate blocked major social insurance legislation, but the rapport Anotelli was no less persuasive than many social reform proposals of the interwar period.[35] There was an energetic movement within the Catholic Left to redefine the French state within a humanist tradition.[36] Very little time intervened between the bitterly divisive peace of 1918 and the frantic effort to defend France in the late 1930s.[37]

After the war, all the democracies reconstructed their welfare institutions, so it is more than a little unfair to accuse France of being a laggard among welfare states. British social insurance was, of course, organized in 1911, but it was substantially overhauled and amended by the 1935 Unemployment Act and by the exigencies of the war itself. Although Germany was soon to rebuild its insurance system within the framework of the Imperial German system, the elaborate social programs of Weimar had been suspended for a decade or more. Like the other liberated countries of Europe, the euphoria of victory and wartime promises of a more just society propelled France into constructing its first complete edifice for social insurance and social assistance. There was little resistance to the 1945 *ordonnance* establishing the new system. What is politically intriguing in the process of institutionalization is how traditional republican habits came to the surface. Indeed, the experience of building the French welfare state contradicts the notion of France as a highly centralized state with a powerful administrative hierarchy.

Alexandre Parodi, de Gaulle's minister of labor in the provisional government, arrived in France with a plan in hand and with a highly skilled and dedicated civil servant from the Conseil d'Etat, Pierre Laroque, ready to implement it. To pave the way for the system, an advisory committee of experts and union and business officials was formed to review the plan. The rapport Mottin revealed cross-cutting pressures that can be traced back to the Third Republic.[38] Catholic-Communist animosities broke out over permitting Alsace-Lorraine to retain the more liberal system put in place there by Germans in the 1880s. Suspicions between Communists and Socialists came to the surface as the Communists tried to impose an electoral system for local social security committees that would favor their factory-level organization.[39]

Both Socialists and Communists were exasperated by Catholic insistence that the Caisse des Allocations Familiales be permitted to keep its prewar status as an *établissement public* and thereby evade administrative controls planned for the other two main components, the pension fund and the health fund. Laroque's preference for a unified system under a single fund (the *caisse primaire*) was rejected.

While the administrative machinery was being assembled, the new legislation slowly made its way through the Consultative Assembly, where the rapport Buisson rehearsed many of these differences over again.[40] The *rapporteur* for the parliamentary committee, Ambroise Croizat, a Communist who was soon to become the first elected postwar minister of labor, coined the often repeated (and misquoted) description of French social security:

> We conceived social legislation as a vast palace that could contain everyone. You know what happened to our palace: a number of small and separate pavillions were substituted, some from conversions, some without roofs, some furnished and others not. We live in these small lodgings. Later we try to install every possible comfort.[41]

As proved to be the case in his ministerial role, Croizat was a skillful and adept parliamentarian. To soften the compromise over the *caisse primaire,* he suggested more flexible transfers among the three main funds. His impassioned plea for a more liberal accident compensation was not only a clear appeal to Communist interests but also a response to the historic resistance of French business to adequate compensation. His main firepower was saved for the mutual or cooperative insurance companies who wanted, and eventually obtained, the right to keep their semi-autonomous status outside the social security system.

Like the republicans of the Third Republic, the postwar parties wanted a politically responsive social security system. As *tripartisme* gradually eroded over 1946 and then virtually dissolved over 1947, the new social insurance scheme recovered its fundamentally republican qualities. First, the *régimes spéciaux* (prewar funds) reasserted the special privileges and additional government subsidies that the miners, railroad workers, civil servants, and others received. Much the same tactic would be used again by growing numbers of *cadre* and self-employed who protected their privileges within the private pension system (*régimes complémentaires*). Pursuing individual and occupational self-interest within social security systems was, of course, not invented in France nor was it invented at the advent of social insurance. But under the banner of political rights that had been established well before Laroque tried to nationalize social security, it was taken to an extreme in France. The result was that the main social insurance depository account, the *régime général,* which Laroque hoped would become a central accounting device to impose fiscal discipline on the social insurance system, never controlled more than about two-thirds of the total contributions to the social security system.[42] In a way that is quite foreign to a federally geared social security system such as that found in the United States or Germany, insistence on political rights even penetrated *within* the social security system. A distinct form of social politics developed, involving beneficiaries, officials, local interests, and politicians. The cleavages and strains of French politics were simply reproduced within the sprawling organization for social security.[43]

A second effort was to make the expansion of the French social security system an obscure and sometimes almost occult game of playing one fund or agency against another. After the electoral successes in 1946 the MRP was among the first but by no means the last to enlarge those benefits that seemed closest to their political interests. All the democratic social insurance plans were enlarged much faster than the experts had planned. In France it was the MRP that had the first chance to do so. The MRP social policy spokesman, Prigent, took his revenge for earlier efforts to curtail the family fund and to remove its special legal status by extending family benefits of workers to the disabled, the unemployed, and various socially vulnerable groups among noncontributors. In effect, Prigent was building institutional protection and political support for the favorite Catholic social fund with such obviously politically popular additional benefits as a seven-months prenatal benefit for mothers, a tripling of the birth incentive, and a reformulation of the child-benefit scheme to favor larger families. The law was passed unanimously. There soon followed legislation to extend the minimum pension (AVTS) to all the aged regardless of their contribution to the pension system. All of these debates led to major revisions of the Laroque plan.[44]

The third political struggle involved another fundamental republican aspect of the French welfare state, elections to the social fund administrative committees (*conseils d'administration*). Contrary to the notion of an omnipotent state, both unions and employers wanted the system to be organizationally distinct from the state. On the left, Edouard Vaillant, a major figure in the socialist internecine struggles at the turn of the century and according to Dommanget[45] the "grandfather" of French social security, helped establish the principle that contributors, employees and employers, should control their own retirement funds. Possessiveness is of course not limited to the bourgeoisie, and the early socialists were determined that they too should have a role in administering social funds, a notion that escaped the British and American labor movements. In any event, organizing the elections for communal, departmental, and national administrative committees was serious political business. The 1947 elections were another indicator of the breakdown of *tripartisme*. The Communists warned their eight million voters in the social security elections to guard against "patronal and confessional maneuvers." But between 1947 and 1950 the Communist vote in social security elections declined from forty-two to thirty percent, allowing non-Communist coalitions within the three main funds to distribute the patronage and influence of the administrative committees.[46] As the Left learned over the 1960s, there is nothing more deadly in French elections than to permit a three-cornered contest. With adjustment to accommodate the growing importance of the new technical and professional middle class, the *cadre*, the political stability of the social security funds has been assured.

The recent appearance of *cohabitation* and the formation of a minority socialist government under Rocard makes the importance of the internal politics of French policy-making again visible. Many of the early evaluations of the Fifth Republic thought such indulgences to be fatal distractions, but trying to change these political habits proved disastrous. The continuity between the Fourth and Fifth Republics are greater than either the Left or the Right wishes to acknowledge. One of the key figures contributing to the continuity of social policy is a deputy, Boutbien, whose report of 1955 is a remarkable prophecy of how the French social security system, barring some dramatic efforts to centralize policy-making in the 1960s, was to develop.[47] Boutbien's prophecy of the future of the French welfare state was remarkably accurate. He suggested, first, that the large surplus of the family fund be used to pay off the mounting deficits of the sickness and pension funds; second, that medical and sickness insurance be extended to the *non-salariés*, meaning the farmers, the self-employed, and the professions; and, third, that the meager old-age pensions, then only about half the minimum wage, be increased substantially. What he recommended is very close to what happened over the early years of the Fifth Republic, suggesting a continuity within French policy-making, if not French politics, that had a stabilizing effect on welfare-state institutions.[48]

Although it has now become common to associate Keynesianism and economic growth with the development of welfare states, a more politically sensitive account of welfare state transformations suggests that change is often not quite so simple. Mendès-France is associated with the arrival of Keynesian thinking in France, although he placed a high value on many neoclassical economic goals. His more interventionist mode of government was nonetheless alarmed by the social welfare deficits of the mid-1950s. The possibilities for a more imaginative reformulation of French social policy were lost over the 1960s for much the same reason as in the late 1940s. In what was clearly a frustrating experience for its left wing,[49] the Mouvement Républicain Populaire (MRP) engineered Mendès-France's downfall in hopes of taking power and thereby delaying reform of social politics. One reason for their tactical maneuver was that they feared that he might diminish their cherished social benefit for low-income families, the *allocation de salaire unique* or single-parent benefit, in order to reduce the social security deficit. Less noticed at the time, Mendès-France also drafted a law for the more efficient organization of the social security system, a law very similar to the 1960 Gaullist reforms.

In the early Gaullist years, social policy-making changed very little. Indeed, the MRP minister of labor, Bacon, remained in place until 1962. When social policy-making shifted to more clearly Gaullist designs, the ministry was put under Gilbert Grandval, a leader of a small, centrist faction. But signs of change were apparent. From 1960 to 1965 social expenditure doubled, and by 1969 it had doubled again. Another sign of change was Laroque's reentry into the Conseil d'Etat. Although his influence over social policy-making remained important, and although the next two directors of social security, Roson and Méric, were *conseillers d'Etat,* the institutionalized French welfare state, like those of Germany, Britain, and the United States at roughly the same time, was developing an autonomous political presence within government that eventually exceeded the capacities of any single *grands corps.* De Gaulle was of course neither the first nor the last conservative president to find that manipulating social spending is difficult. His economic advisor, Rueff, wanted to discontinue national subsidies to cut in half various social programs and funds, and the inflation index of the Salaire Minimum Interprofessional de Croissance (SMIC, the minimum wage), and to make drastic cuts in public salaries. If the social security system had not been running an enormous surplus of nearly fifty billion old francs by 1958, his suggestions might have seemed credible. As 1968 made unmistakable, de Gaulle and his advisors badly misjudged French attachment to their newly gained social protection. *Le Monde's* rather self-satisfied comment on October 6, 1965, that "social security has reached most of its objectives" could not have been more wrong.

In order to hasten the modernization of France, de Gaulle relied on the social security system more than his predecessors did. He increased state pensions for over four million persons at a cost of fourteen billion francs. He desperately needed both improved social services in rebuilding French cities and extended benefits to integrate the returning Algerian *colons* into French society. As became increasingly apparent in the mid-1960s, and was finally fully recognized with Chaban-Delmas's *nouvelle société,* a modern, competitive economy meant improving rather than dismantling social programs. Two key reports were commissioned. The first, by Laroque, suggested an *allocation minimum de base,* or a vaguely defined minimum income, financed from general taxation; this was, of course, totally unacceptable.[50] Prigent's review of family policies, which was never published, recommended large increases in family benefits to be paid for with an earnings-related contribution; this review obviously alarmed the *cadre,* who, no doubt correctly, anticipated that the cost would fall on their higher salaries. Contrary to the Jacobin accusations so commonly leveled against de

Gaulle, he was not particularly interested in the *étatisation* of social security or the dismantling of its semi-autonomous structure.

Explosive events such as 1968 are not necessary to see how conservative interludes may increase both the motivation and the governmental capacity for welfare state expansion. The French moved in this direction with a battery of social policy reforms in 1960. The first was to increase both the professional and administrative status of the Ministry of Labor and of social service careers by creating the Inspection Générale des Affaires Sociales (IGAS). A second major quarrel within the system was resolved by creating a separate administrative agency to manage the benefits, careers, and wage bargaining for social sector employees (UCNASS). To distinguish more clearly the interests of the social service employees from government, the minister of labor acquired the power to nominate the directors of the three main social security funds (pensions, sickness, and family) and established a separate training and evaluation agency.[51] Third, in the kind of internal political contradiction that was to become more common with Reagan and Thatcher, the Gaullists put pressure on their natural political allies, the doctors, to sign a fee agreement with the sickness insurance fund.[52] Fourth, the enormous state subsidy for agricultural social insurance and benefits was consolidated into a single budget (BAPSO), which forced French policy-makers and politicians to recognize that farmers, not workers, are the most favored welfare-state clients. Even in the 1960s farmers paid little more than a tenth of the cost of their protection at an annual charge to the state budget of about eighteen billion francs. In interviews, Laroque and the other previous directors of social security agreed that the 1960 reforms were much more important than the hotly debated 1967 reforms.

Contrary to frequent charges of Gaullist social neglect, the system of social protection and assistance rapidly expanded in the 1960s. Medical and drug charges on the sickness fund were increasing at the soaring rate of twenty percent per year. In 1966, 4.5 million families were added to the sickness insurance fund, making publicly insured medical and health care almost universal. About half a million persons per year were being added to the retirement system, and the first national unemployment insurance fund, established in 1958, was providing benefits for 100,000 persons. The national product doubled from 1957 to 1969, but social spending tripled. To be sure, the system had lost much of the attractiveness and popular support of the postwar years in part simply because of the scale and complexity of modern welfare-state machinery. A report by Friedel, commissioned in 1965 to examine the organization of the system, frankly acknowledged that, historical links to *solidarité* of the late nineteenth-century republicans notwithstanding, beneficiaries were strangers to one another and "[did] not feel the least solidarity in the world."[53] The dispersion of social programs throughout the national budget made government policy virtually unintelligible, and, as in Britain at the same time, the increased reliance on supplementary assistance to compensate for inadequate benefits was gradually undermining public confidence in the system.

The blunder of the 1967 reforms arose because the republican principles on which the system was based were momentarily forgotten. Blame is most often placed on a report by Piketty, of the Conseil National du Patronat Français (CNPF), that insisted that more systematic risk determination be superimposed on the system, and that the administration of the three social funds be compelled to operate according to more stringent efficiency standards.[54] The most intense debate arose over restructuring the administrative councils of the funds to eliminate the equal representation of contributors, unions, and employers.[55] An indication of Gaullist political insensitivity was the fact that they presented the changes in an arbitrary way. There were positive features to the reforms, including a new benefit for those unemployed for economic reasons (*indemnités de licenciement*), the creation of national employment agency (ANPE), and large increases in training programs, and these features might have created an entirely different picture of government intentions.[56] Ultimately, the fault must rest with J.-M. Jeanneny, the first minister of a consolidated Ministry of Social Affairs (later to be intermittently dispersed and reunited), who was a highly trained technocrat given political responsibilities that he either could not or preferred not to understand.

There is a curious historical similarity in the political blunders made in nearly all the welfare states in the 1960s. The American War on Poverty seemed unequal to its promise. The Swedish Social Democrats concluded a decade of divisive debate over pension reform, escaping defeat by only one vote. Britain was paralyzed by the "battle of Downing Street," as Prime Minister Wilson tried to force unwelcome reforms on the unions and nearly destroyed his own government. Explanations must of course vary from country to country, but the common thread was a failure by political leaders and postwar social policy-makers (many of whom are still in place), to understand their own success. In France, and elsewhere, two decades of expansion and assistance had made the welfare state an indispensable and integral part of social and political life. In a word, the welfare state had been successfully institutionalized. It was left for others, Chaban-Delmas and *la nouvelle société* in France, to recognize the political complexity and to exploit the political promise of the welfare state. The transformation is most visible in the attraction of many talented politicians to responsible posts in social policy ministries. Under Boulin, a widely respected and ingenious minister of health and social security, France witnessed the first serious parliamentary debate about the interlocking nature of retirement, health, and medical benefits.[57] Governmental responsibility for a major segment of personal income had become permanent, a first step toward a social democratic state. Mme. Veil had similar success in displaying the underlying realities of modern health and medical care. Social democracy, although not the Nordic version, was entering by the back door.

Rediscovering the political meaning of the French welfare state meant that it was only a matter of time before its republican foundations would also be rediscovered. It is not entirely paradoxical that this was left to the socialists of the 1980s.

Republican Welfare and Socialist Government

There are a number of reasons why the Socialists were well-suited to redefining the republican dimensions of the French welfare state. First, their early history was firmly rooted in Jaurès's support for welfare legislation at the turn of the century. As in most European countries, the Left had had few chances to govern between the wars, and so had few vested interests after World War II. But their own internal divisions and latent nationalism made it difficult for them to construct an original position in the postwar years. They should not be treated too harshly for this failure; it was common among most postwar socialist parties. Attlee made few changes in the Beveridge Plan, which had been written in 1942, and in the 1950s the Swedish Social Democrats were still confused over the contradictions between welfare-state benefits and wage solidarity. In retrospect, it was more often the Right, leaders such as Macmillan, Nixon, and Adenauer, who institutionalized the postwar welfare states and, at times, made highly original contributions. Perhaps the French socialists found it easier to uncover the republican roots of welfare because they had few vested interests in the emergence of the French welfare state.

It should also be noted that Giscard-d'Estaing's liberal reformism of the 1970s had taken most of the remaining political plums off the welfare-state tree. By 1980 France had a system of social benefits and social programs that equaled that of any of the major European states, and that in spending terms was in advance of Britain, Italy, and Germany. Giscard had made some important modifications, but there was not much more to be done with the major entitlement programs. He got more publicity than he deserved by bringing such neglected groups as priests and prostitutes into the social security system. His adept minister of health, Mme. Veil, helped make the French, and even French doctors, aware that their unbelievably indulgent system of medical care would be curtailed.

The result was that the Socialists did not initially have a very exciting social program.[58] They relied on Mme. Questiaux, herself a social security legal expert from the Conseil d'État, rather than on the more innovative social programs that were beginning to appear within local governments.[59] While certainly not lacking the compassion of a strong welfare-state advocate, Mme. Questiaux lacked the administrative skills to effect any radical restructuring of the French welfare state and, partly because of her link to the Centre d'Etudes, de Recherche et d'Education Socialistes (CERES), had limited political resources within the government to make major new departures. Now, nearly a decade later, Socialists are quicker to see that the political threat to the welfare state from the Left does not arise from reducing class politics but from asking more of the state than it can do. In any event, on taking office the Socialists made increases of about forty billion francs in entitlements. By opting for the most direct and costly forms of expansion, they sacrificed chances of experimenting with new welfare-state institutions and of fostering new forms of care and assistance. The ministry exhausted its financial grace within a government that was increasingly threatened by inflation and unemployment. Given the size of the French social budget and, compared to most countries, the sensitivities of French citizens to disarray among the social insurance funds, Questiaux's fate was sealed from the moment she announced to the press that it was up to the minister of finance to find the funds for new social spending.

While there is little doubt that hard times enabled a number of conservative governments to make painful cuts in some benefits and contributed to the widening of income differences, the 1980s are interesting for the ways in which they have forced complacent social reformers to reexamine their assumptions. It is in this perspective that the essentially republican impulses of Mitterrand's socialism, so apparent in the reorganization of local government,[60] were later transplanted in the French welfare state. The first of these was actually part of local reform. After a not entirely successful inquiry with the aim of finding programs that ministers would agree to devolve on the departments and communes, it was agreed that *aide sociale* would be given to the departments.[61] Although not precisely the equivalent of locally organized social assistance in other countries, *aide sociale* has three major components: retirement homes for low income persons (*héberge-ment*), maternal- and child-care programs, and local services for the handicapped. In 1984 52 billion francs were spent for *aide sociale*: 32 billion from the state budget and 20 billion from local budgets. Nearly 40 billion of this total was spent by local governments. Using new charges on automobile registration and 8.7 billion from the new local subsidy, the DGD (dotation globale de décentralisa-tion), the actual amount transferred to the departments was 11.6 billion francs.[62] Thus, decentralization brought an infusion of about a billion dollars in local discretionary social assistance.[63]

The second major social policy departure that had a distinctly republican background was an intensive program to revive voluntary and charitable good works. This Tocquevillian revival actually pre-dated the Socialists' victory in 1981 but received their enthusiastic endorsement. With the support of Bloch-Laîné, the tireless higher civil servant of 1960s fame, an organization to encourage new associational activity, Fondation pour la Vie Associative (FONDA), was formed in 1978. Frictions arose when the Mauroy government appointed a special advisor on *économie sociale* with the announced aim of enlarging local economic and social activities along the same lines.[64] There were at least three aspects to the new associational campaign. First, localities were to be invigorated with a new community work program (*travail d'utilité publique*); second, the historic community concerns of the mutual insurance industry, which reaches about twenty-five million French people, were to be enhanced; and, third, a concentrated program was launched to improve social-work training.[65] The distinctly socialist appeal of these activities was based on a little-noticed provision of the decentralization law permitting local governments to engage in economic activities. The hope was that these new programs would enable other localities to emulate Grenoble, the one-time socialist stronghold where Doubedout had tried to reconstruct municipal socialism. In the fiercely politically competitive world of French local politics, these new incentives and subsidies may have interesting effects. The centrist mayor of Nimes has, for example, devised a local minimum income, a truly amazing innovation in a system allegedly so repressed by the national bureaucracy.

A third important modification of the French welfare state, reducing the retirement age from sixty-five to sixty years, has less distinct republican overtones, although the Socialists have enthusiastically participated in the studies of the *troisième age* and instituted the thirty-nine-hour week. It was the Blum government of 1936 that appointed the first minister of leisure, and the reduction of work fits within a humanistic interpretation of socialism, which, incidentally, has strong intellectual roots in the development of French socialism.[66] Early retirement was also one of Mitterrand's Hundred Propositions and so carried a certain urgency for the new government. The internal dilemma for the government was how to pay for early retirement after the economic downturn of 1982 and without increasing the *prélèvement obligatoire*.[67] Somewhat in the tradition of the Swedish socialists, an agreement was worked out with private pension plans, whose members would be important beneficiaries of early retirement, to borrow four billion francs from the private pension funds (*régimes complémentaires*) to float the cost of the program until the national retirement contributions could handle the costs. The incentive for the private pension plans was that their obligation to unemployment benefits, called the *garantie de ressources* (not the main national unemployment insurance program) would diminish.[68] The expectation is that about 85,000 of 200,000 persons retiring each year in France will take advantage of early retirement. Everyone seemed to agree that the solution was both ingenious and fair.[69]

Disencumbered by overly ambitious plans to transform the welfare state into a visionary socialist program for the future, the French welfare state, like those in the other democracies, offers numerous possibilities for reaffirming and reinvigorating socialist values. The initial Socialist response was surprisingly conventional and, in economic hard times, simply unworkable. There is little reason to think a simple strategy of massively increasing entitlements will have the social and economic effects that Socialists desire. It seems the early Socialist splurge was more the product of the euphoria of electoral victory and the absence of more careful reflection than an intended strategy of simple overspending.[70] Whether socialism by stealth or a neoliberal trick, the modern welfare states are too large, both fiscally and organizationally, to tack with every partisan breeze. Once the

Socialists saw more clearly how certain features of the French welfare state might give their government credibility and support, they selected specific changes whose logic and purpose were consistent with the republican foundations of the French welfare state. These reforms enhanced local capabilities to respond to diverse social needs and encouraged localities to devise new economic programs based on socialist values while remaining within well-established republican traditions.

Conclusion

The French welfare state was not particularly visible in the early 1960s, but, then, neither were other welfare states as political objects. There was then really little to choose between a heavy-handed Parsonian fascination with the French middle class and a determinist Marxist preoccupation with the welfare state as a capitalist plot. If any reproach is due, it might be that France had always closely linked social and political thinking such that democratic stability in both the late nineteenth and twentieth centuries involved reform and *solidarité*.[71] It is interesting to recall that France did not figure very heavily in the Almond-Pye political development studies until the historians made their claim in the two final volumes of the series. Although a good descriptive study of the early years of the postwar French welfare state, Galant's study ends with 1952 and clearly adheres to a formal concept of the welfare state that preoccupied the experts from the Conseil d'Etat.[72] If the legal technicians seriously overlooked the intellectual and historical dimensions of the French welfare state, it is to the Socialists' credit that they eventually rediscovered republican virtue within it.

Embedded within each welfare state are the historical and political circumstances surrounding the early definition of how liberal states might intervene in social and economic matters. From at least the Third Republic onward these conditions were more clearly distinguishable in France than in most other versions of the welfare state. First, the capacity to exercise reason fully and to contribute to the well-being of society found a clearer definition in French revolutionary writing than in any other modern state.[73] Finding an appropriate social model for France was always a self-conscious and intentional activity as opposed, for example, to the situation in Britain, where Fabian "socialism in a bluebook" inspired neither public nor partisan interest.[74] Comte's worship of reason was based upon a "Religion of Humanity," whereas Thomas Arnold's clerisy ended up being the public school "all-rounder."[75] France was never a very enthusiastic liberal state in the economic sense of the word. Quite possibly, as Rosanvallon suggests,[76] there was a "moment" under Guizot when the French were free to enrich themselves without restraint. The radical argument concerning the *embourgeoisement* of France was always double-edged. With so many French people fighting to protect themselves, an inadvertent form of equality was always possible.

Second, there was the constant pressure within the labor movement for equal participation. Whatever the self-destructive tendencies of nineteenth-century socialism in France, internecine warfare ceased long enough for all the *tendances* to claim their right to govern both the funds presumably established for their own good and their own contributions. Moderate and radical republicans were aware of the contradiction between making political concessions to mutual funds and voluntary associations without making similar concessions to the workers and their demands for protection. The outrage over the 1967 reorganization of the social fund committees by decree may not have been as visible as the anger in the streets of Paris in 1968, but the 1967 fight had a historical foundation in the development of the French welfare state. Much the same effect is found within the American social security system, where the rhetoric of individual rights and the moral rectitude of saving made the American system virtually immune to modification.[77] The semi-autonomous structure of the French welfare state and the subsequent feuding among social funds reproduced within the social security system the same cleavages that divided employers and employees in French industry and Left and Right in the French parliament.

Last, there is the vexing question of the slow growth of benefits before the 1970s. An unexplored explanation is that there were still sufficient alternative sources of protection and support. A more persuasive one might be that welfare states do not "take off" until some form of social democracy is clearly perceived in the conjunction of social and labor needs. The historical irony is, of course, that de Gaulle's insistence on the economic and industrial modernization of France entailed enlarging the welfare state. The fact that wages lagged about ten percent behind increased productivity over the 1960s does not explain the events of 1968, but it does explain why the French welfare state expanded so rapidly in the 1970s and why by 1980 there were so few social issues left for the Socialists to mobilize around. In France, as elsewhere, the welfare state had exhausted its initial purpose. The fascinating contribution of the Mitterrand government has been to begin to restore a purpose by reexamining the republican origins of the *État providence*.

Notes

1.   A major study by Peter Flora and Arnold Heidenheiner, eds., *Development of Welfare States in Europe and America* (New Brunswick, N.J.: Transaction Books, 1981), typically limits the comparison to northern Europe but contains an interesting acknowledgment of southern European influences. See Wilensky's essay in this volume, pp. 345–82, on the difference within Germany between the north and Bavaria.

2.   François Lagrange, "Social Security in France from 1946 to 1986," in Douglas Ashford and

E. W. Kelley, eds., *Nationalizing Social Security in Europe and America* (Greenwich, Conn.: Jai Press, 1986), pp. 59–72.

3.   E. Levasseur, *Questions ouvrières et industrielles en France sous la Troisième République* (Paris: Rousseau, 1907); and H. Dérouin et al., *Traité et pratique d'assistance publique* (Paris: Sirey, 1914).

4.   François Ewald, *L'Etat providence* (Paris: Grasset, 1986); and Judith Stone, *The Search for Social Peace: Reform Legislation in France, 1890–1914* (Albany, N.Y.: State University of New York Press, 1985).

5.   Pierre Rosanvallon, *La crise de l'état providence* (Paris: Seuil, 1981), p. 141.

6.   Henry Pelling attributes the English phrase to Alfred Zimmern, Quo Vadimus, 1934. It was popularized in Archbishop Temple's Christian socialist movement of the late 1930s. See Henry Pelling, *The Labour Governments* (London: MacMillan, 1984).

7.   M. F. Le Play, *La Réforme sociale en France* (Paris: Plon, 1864).

8.   Douglas Ashford, *The Emergence of the Welfare States* (Oxford and New York: Blackwell, 1986).

9.   Quentin Skinner, "Meaning and Understanding in the History of Ideas" *History and Theory* 8 (1969): 3–53; idem, "Some Problems in the Analysis of Political Thought" *Political Theory* 2 (1974): 277–303.

10.   Jacques Donzelot, *L'Invention de social* (Paris: Fayard, 1984).

11.   William Logue, *From Philosophy to Sociology: The Evolution of French Liberalism, 1871–1914* (Dekalb, Ill.: Northern Illinois University Press, 1983); and John Scott, *Republican Ideas and the Liberal Tradition in France* (New York: Columbia University Press, 1951).

12.   The motives and results of the 1911 National Insurance Act are easily misinterpreted. Both Lloyd George and Winston Churchill had little use for academic models of the welfare state and carefully avoided getting involved with the Fabians. See Ashford, *The Emergence of the Welfare State*, pp. 59–73.

13.   Alexis de Tocqueville, "Memoir on Pauperism," with an introduction by Gertrude Himmelfarb, *Public Interest* 70 (Winter 1983): 102–20, and Seymour Drescher, *Tocqueville and Beaumont on Social Reform* (New York: Harper, 1968).

14.   Emile Boutmy, *The English People: A Study of their Political Psychology*, trans. J. E. Courtney (London: Unwin, 1904), p. 168.

15.   Quoted in W. H. Greenleaf, *The British Political Tradition: The Ideology Heritage* (London and New York: Methuen, 1983), p. 380.

16.   Indicative of the stronger grip of capitalist thinking on Britain, the comparable political debate in Britain was over the repeal in 1828 of the Combination Acts, which legalized limited liability. True to the extraordinary grip of individualism on British thinking, many leading aristocrats and industrialists felt limited liability to be an immoral evasion of personal responsibility.

17.   Vincent Wright, "Les Préfets d'Emile Ollivier," *Revue Historique* 487 (July–September 1968): 115–38, and Odilon Barrot, *De la décentralisation et de ses effects* (Paris: Didier, 1870).

18.   Emile Laurent, *Le Paupérisme et les associations de prévoyance* (Paris: Guillaumin, 1865).

19.   Seppo Hentillä, "The Origins of the *Folkhem* Ideology in Swedish Social Democracy," *Scandinavian Journal of History* 3 (1978): 323–45.

20.   Douglas Ashford, "Rhetoric and Reality in the French Welfare State," mimeo (Bielefeld: Zentrum für interdisziplinäre Forschung, 1989).

21.   The Swedish concept of *folkhem* had almost the same intellectual function as the French

concept of *solidarité*, and was applied during a very similar crisis in the development of each welfare state. See Hentillä, "The Origins of the *Folkhem* Ideology."

22.   Winton Higgens, "Ernst Wigforss: The Renewal of Social Democratic Theory and Practice," in *Political Power and Social Theory,* ed. M. Zeitlin (Greenwich, Conn.: Jai Press, 1985), pp. 207–50.

23.   Pierre Sorlin, *Waldeck-Rousseau* (Paris: Colin, 1966).

24.   Martin Derfler, *Alexandre Millerand: The Socialist Years* (The Hague: Mouton, 1977).

25.   J.-P. Tournerie, *Le Ministère du Travail: Origines et premiers développements* (Paris: Cujas, 1971).

26.   A. M. McBriar, *An Edwardian Mixed Doubles: The Bosanquets Versus the Webbs: A Study in British Social Policy, 1890–1929* (Oxford: Clarendon, 1987).

27.   *Journal Officiel: Débats Parlementaires,* session ordinaire, Paris, May 29, 1903, p. 1783.

28.   John Weiss, "Origins of the Welfare State: Poor Relief in the Third Republic," *French Historical Studies* 13 (Spring 1983): 47–78.

29.   *Journal Officiel,* May 29, 1903, pp. 1788–91.

30.   Gertrude Himmelfarb, *The Idea of Poverty: England in the Early Industrial Age* (New York: Random House, 1985).

31.   Katherine Auspitz, *The Radical Bourgeoisie: The Ligue de l'Enseignement and the Origins of the Third Republic, 1866–1885* (Cambridge: Cambridge University Press, 1982).

32.   Stone, *The Search for Social Peace.*

33.   Axel Murswieck, "Health Policy-Making," in *Policy and Politics in the Federal Republic of Germany,* ed. K. von Beyme and M. Schmidt (New York: St. Martin's Press, 1985), pp. 82–106.

34.   William Oualid and Charles Picquenard, *Salaires et tarifs, conventions et grèves: la Politique du Ministère de l'Armement et du Ministère de Travail* (Paris: Presses universitaires de France; New Haven: Yale University, 1928).

35.   Rapport Anotelli, *Journal Officiel, Débats Parlementaires,* 1930, pp. 526–29.

36.   Michel Winock, *Histoire politique de la Revue "Esprit," 1930–1950* (Paris: Seuil, 1975).

37.   For this reason the logic of Maier's impressive study of interwar diplomacy should be applied to domestic policy-making with great care. International tensions across Europe created a crisis mentality well into the 1920s, a mentality followed by the depression and Hitler. In effect, there was barely a decade for serious thinking about internal matters.

38.   Rapport Mottin, "Rapport relatif aux travaux de la commission chargée d'étudier le projet d'ordonnance relatif à l'organisation de la sécurité sociale," mimeo (Paris, July 9, 1945).

39.   Actually, the Communists reversed themselves on the principles for social security elections as the Cold War intensified. See Antoinette Catrice-Lorey, *Dynamique interne de la sécurité sociale,* 2d ed. (Paris: Economica, 1982). The importance of the elections was not simply electoral success but the voice the *conseils d'administration* would have in distributing substantial discretionary funds for social service employees in each fund.

40.   Rapport Buisson, "Rapport fait au nom de la commission de travail et des affaires sociales," *Journal Officiel,* annexes, no. 554, Assemblée Consultative Provisoire, July 24, 1945.

41.   Rapport Buisson, p. 727.

42.   Comptes de la Protection Sociale, 1984.

43.   It was not unusual, for example, to take some soaring cost, such as medical education, and distribute it among all the funds according to administrative agreement about the relative importance

of doctors to families, women, the aged, and the unemployed. In the 1970s this practice surfaced in the fight over *charges indues.*

44. Henri Galant, *Histoire politique de la sécurité sociale en France, 1945–1952* (Paris: Colin, 1955), pp. 113–15.

45. Maurice Domanget, *Vaillant: Un grand socialiste, 1840–1915* (Paris: Table Ronde, 1956), p. 161.

46. François Goguel, "Géographie des élections sociales de 1950–1951," *Revue Française de Science Politique* 3 (April 1953): 246–71.

47. Rapport Boutbien, *Journal Officiel,* 1955. It is recapitulated in "Études sur les problèmes posés par la securité sociale," *Journal Officiel,* Conseil Economique et Social, January 19, 1974, pp. 9–37; March 27, 1974, pp. 667–80; and July 3, 1974, pp. 1317–26.

48. Douglas E. Ashford, *Policy and Politics in France: Living with Uncertainty* (Philadelphia: Temple University Press, 1981).

49. Michel Winock, *Histoire politique.*

50. Alain Barjot, "L'Évolution de la sécurité sociale (juin 1960–juin 1966)," *Revue Française des Affaires Sociales* 25 (1971): 61–79.

51. Catrice-Lorey, *Dynamique interne.*

52. Monica Steffen, "Régulation politique de stratégies professionelles: Médicine liberale et émergence de Centres de Santé" (doctoral dissertation, Université des Sciences Sociales de Grenoble II, 1983).

53. Rapport Friedel, "Commission d'études des structures de la sécurité sociale," mimeo (Paris: Prime Minister's Office, 1966), p. 7.

54. Rapport Riketty, 1965, unpublished report, cited in Antoine Ferry, "La Sécurité sociale depuis les ordonnances de 1967," *Revue d'Economie Politique* 82 (October 1972): 983–97.

55. The hypocrisy of this debate should not go unnoticed. No one has ever suggested that the unions, which probably represent no more than a fifth of social security contributors, should share their monopoly with unorganized distributors. Next to the favoritism shown farmers, this is probably the least democratic feature of the French social security system.

56. Space does not permit enlarging on the quasi-social democratic designs of Jacques Delors, Chaban-Delmas's social policy advisor in the early 1970s, to use retraining and handicapped-worker programs in constructing more participatory social programs.

57. Rapport Boulin, *Pour une politique de la santé* (Paris: Ministère de la Santé Publique et de la Sécurité Sociale, La Documentation Française, 1971).

58. "Proposition loi relative à la protection sociale," *Journal Officiel,* annex no. 1856, June 25, 1980.

59. Neither Mitterrand nor Mauroy was particularly attracted to Doubedout's brand of municipal socialism. There were also exciting experiments afoot to restructure medical care around municipal clinics. See Monica Steffen, "Régulation politique."

60. Douglas Ashford, *British Dogmatism and French Pragmatism: Center-Local Relations in the Welfare State* (London and Boston: Allen and Unwin, 1982).

61. Much of the bargaining was carried on by a young Socialist deputy with special interest in social policy and poverty, J.-M. Belorgey. See the Rapport Belorgey, "Rapport de la commission des affaires sociales," *Journal Officiel,* Assemblée Nationale, session ordinaire de 1985–86, December 20, 1985.

62.   Amédée Thévent, *L'Aide sociale aujourd'hui après la décentralisation*, 6th ed. (Paris: Editions EDF, 1986), p. 278.

63.   P. Duran and J. Herault, "*Aide Sociale* and French Decentralization," in *Discretionary Politics: Intergovernmental Social Grants in Seven Countries*, ed. Douglas Ashford (Greenwich, Conn.: Jai Press, 1990).

64.   *Le Monde*, November 27, 1981.

65.   Gérard J. Martin, "Social Services, Job Creation and New Technologies" (paper delivered at the European Center for Social Welfare Training and Research, 1986); and Rapport Théry, "La place et le rôle du secteur associatif dans le développement de la politique d'action éducative, sanitaire et sociale," *Journal Officiel, Conseil Economique et Social*, 1986 session, July 29, 1986.

66.   Daniel Lindenberg and Pierre-André Meyer, *Lucien Herr: Le Socialisme et son déstin* (Paris: Calman-Lévy, 1977).

67.   The government's dilemma was that Mitterrand and Bérégovoy had agreed that the total charge on incomes or *prélèvements obligatoires* should decline by one percent a year from the mid-1980s. Borrowing funds from private insurance companies avoided including the expense as an addition to the government deficit.

68.   The *garantie de ressources* has a long history going back to the 1960s and taking form in 1980, oddly enough, from a very generous formula that Chirac urged on the government a year before the oil crisis in his fight with Giscard-d'Estaing. Essentially, those unemployed for economic reasons could get around ninety percent of their salaries, which, if an unemployed person was making no contributions, often left the unemployed better off than those with jobs.

69.   Based on interviews over the spring of 1987 with the Elysée social policy advisor, Mme. Moreau, then director of social security, M. Mercereau, and the social policy advisor to the UIMM, Mme. Séenus.

70.   C. Blum-Girardeau, *Les Tableaux de la solidarité* (Paris: Economica, 1981).

71.   John Weiss, "Origins of the Welfare State."

72.   Henri Galant, *Histoire politique*.

73.   Douglas Ashford, "Rhetoric and Reality."

74.   Peter Clark, *Liberals and Social Democrats* (Cambridge: Cambridge University Press, 1978).

75.   Christopher Kent, *Brains and Numbers: Elitism, Comtism and Democracy in Mid-Victorian Britain* (Toronto: University of Toronto Press, 1978).

76.   Pierre Rosanvallon, *La crise de l'état providence*.

77.   Martha Derthick, *The Politics of Social Security* (Washington, D.C.: The Brookings Institution, 1979).

7

Trade Unions, Unemployment, and Regulation: 1962–1989

René Mouriaux

Rereading *In Search of France*[1] after more than two decades helps one to understand the magnitude of the changes that have occurred since the end of the Algerian War. As of 1963, France's economic and social future seemed to promise continuous expansion. One index of this is that the word unemployment appears nowhere in the book. Yet unemployment and the precarious economic nature of life, at least for an important minority of the French, returned to become an ominous reality in the 1980s. In 1963, state intervention was accepted as necessary and beneficial, as *In Search of France* confirms from beginning to end. Today, the French Right is united in its commitment to create a more modest state, following the first socialist experiment of 1981–86.[2] And even the Socialist Rocard government today champions civil society against the state.

This historical turnaround is not merely rhetorical. It is based upon a profound transformation of the labor market and a change in thinking about the role of the state. It is best to avoid schematic interpretations of such comparisons between the 1960s and the Mitterrand period, however. For, despite such changes, attitudes toward trade unions are similar now to what they were a quarter-century ago. Today they elicit but tepid interest. And then Hoffmann could comment that little attention had been paid to "trade unions which continue to be generally unpopular, politically divided, and unable to adapt to social change." Today, the reversal of trends in employment, changes in the role of the state, and continuing divisions among the unions seem to lead to the same results. Yet underneath this similarity is a complex reality that bears careful examination if we are to make sense of the changing position of French trade unions.

The period 1962–89 has involved complex interactions among economic, political, and trade-union cycles. Economic changes were dramatic, for example. Prospects for economic growth, excellent throughout the 1960s, fell off sharply after 1974 and did not improve until the later 1980s, and then only slightly. Likewise, over the quarter-century the nature of government action changed both between and within presidential mandates. The split within the Confédération Francaise des Travailleurs Chrétiens, (CFTC, the Catholic union organization) leading to the Confédération Francaise Démocratique de Travail (CFDT) in 1964

173

and the dramatic rise of the Fédération de l'Education Nationale (FEN, the teachers' union) led to a shift from a quadripartite union system (Confédération Générale du Travail [CGT], Force Ouvrière [FO], CFTC, Confédération Générale des Cadres [CGC]) to one with six important actors, with the once dominant, Communist-influenced CGT progressively losing ground in favor of a relative majority of "reformist" unions (the CGT = FO, the CFDT, CFTC, FEN, plus the CGC).

It is difficult to review the shifting contours of the recent history of the French labor movement without choosing a specific angle of approach. In what follows we have chosen that of the changing relationships of labor, employers, and the state toward employment and employment policy. Our reasoning is that no issue can be more central to any labor movement than employment.

I. Defending Full Employment

The preamble to the Constitution of the Fourth Republic, which was included in that of the Fifth, announced: "Everyone has the right to work and to have a job." The modern French labor movement committed itself to this principle, especially because economic growth had historically helped to maintain the movement's strength. The opening of borders as a result of the Treaty of Rome caused some fears in the later 1950s, but the French economy survived this trial, at least in the short run. Production rose, as did the standard of living. Strains began to appear at the end of the Algerian War, however, when inflation picked up and trade balances deteriorated. Moreover, the return of peacetime conditions coincided with the reemergence of social unrest. The successful miners' strike of the winter and spring of 1963 was the first major labor action under the new Gaullist regime.[3] In the situation that followed, one of an overheated economy and rising social temperatures, the Pompidou government adopted a "stabilization plan" in September 1963. The consequences of this plan ultimately made matters even worse.

The Stabilization Plan of 1963–66

The stabilization measures produced in 1963 by Finance Minister Giscard-d'Estaing had three major objectives: to tighten the money supply, to control prices, and to reduce budget deficits. Giscard even tried to push through a law embracing the general principle of a balanced budget at this point! In consequence, the CGT and CFTC steeled themselves against an impending economic downturn. And, indeed, it was not long before employment effects were felt. In 1963 the number of job seekers declined slightly from 158,400 to 110,000 before rising again at the end of 1964. A number of key sectors, including coal and iron mining, steel, shipbuilding, and textiles, were affected by layoffs resulting from rationalization and efforts to improve productivity. Mono-industrial regions in the East, North, West, and Center were hit particularly hard.

French labor reacted in various ways to these events, even though all major unions were profoundly concerned. The CGT, like other union organizations, was quick to notice the deterioration of the labor market. In its "programs of action" adopted at the Congresses of 1963 and 1965, the most powerful French union confederation spelled out the measures—summarized in Table 7.1—that it felt would be necessary to slow the rise in unemployment. Force Ouvrière also announced its intention to protect the employment of its members, even though its proposals for doing so were much less specific than those of the CGT. It was suspicious of the nationalizations, among other things, proposed by the CGT, for example. The CFTC, and later the CFDT, proposed yet another approach, stressing the need for democratic economic planning, which had been debated at length by the union at its 1959 Congress.[4]

Confronted with unemployment and layoffs, the workers themselves began to react. A period of bitter strikes ensued, which often involved the occupation of factories and mines and considerable violence (see Table 7.2). The CGT and CFTC supported these strikes in defense of employment, at times even demanding the nationalization of threatened factories. They organized regional demonstrations in Saint-Nazare, Nantes, and Saint-Etienne, as well as marches on Paris. Local elected officials and religious authorities often participated in these mobilizations.

Spurred on by this explosion of new struggle, the CFTC began the "deconfessionalizing" self-transformation in 1964 that made it into the CFDT.[5] The CFDT, in turn, faced obdurate refusal to negotiate, despite a warlike atmosphere on

Table 7.1 **Employment Demands of the Confédération Générale du Travail (CGT), 1963 and 1965**

1963	1965
40-hour work week without salary reduction	same
end to new entrance of immigrant workers	same
creation of a real unemployment insurance scheme run by Social Security	same
extension and improvement of the December 31, 1955, agreement on unemployment (UNEDIC)	same
slower assembly-line pace	same
maintenance of employment in industry, public administration, and public services	same
development of the FPA	same
nationalization of key sectors of the economy	same
—	economic and social development plan

Compiled from the reports of the Congresses of the CGT.

Table 7.2   Number of Work Days Lost, 1963–68 (in thousands of days)

1963	1964	1965	1966	1967	1968
5,991	2,497	973	2,502	4,203	150,000

Source: Ministère de Travail.

many shopfloors, on the part of the Conseil National du Patronat Français (CNPF, the employers' peak trade association). Ambitious to make its mark, and unable to get very far in the face of what seemed like a wall of opposition, the CFDT turned toward collaboration with the CGT. At "the base" this rapprochement was perceived as ever more desirable, particularly because the various political trials and tribulation of the Algerian War experience had rekindled aspirations for unity and reinforced the belief that the effectiveness of the labor movement was dependent upon interunion cooperation and united action.

Faced with new union pressure, the Pompidou government applied itself to the tasks of constructing new defenses. The law of December 18, 1963, created a National Employment Fund designed to help workers adapt to "occupational changes resulting from technological innovation or some modification in the conditions of production."[6] And, as the Fourth Plan had projected, regional funds were made available to ease economic shocks while simultaneously promoting the regrouping of firms in order to consolidate industry into units of larger size. The merger of four shipyards in November 1964 was a good example of government efforts to restructure and revitalize the productive system in the face of working-class resistance.

Such corrective and "inciting" state measures were accompanied by industrial policy initiatives. The Bull affair, an early effort to foster a "national champion" in the computer industry that came to a head in 1964, was an indication of the government's desire to maintain a measure of national autonomy in certain economically strategic areas. The financial difficulties of the Honeywell Bull Company, due to the bad sales of the "Gamma 60" machine, opened the door for General Electric to control twenty percent of the stock. The search for a wholly French solution failed, and ultimately Americans acquired a share in the company.

The Failure of Recovery: 1966–69

When he presented his 1963 price freeze, Finance Minister Giscard d'Estaing projected that in six months the desired results would be achieved. Twenty-eight months later the freeze ended. Partly in response to this, on the day after the first direct election to the presidency of the Fifth Republic in 1965, Georges Pompidou reshaped his cabinet and on January 8, 1966, Michel Debré replaced Giscard d'Estaing. The new minister of finance and the economy elaborated a recovery program that was then adopted by the Council of Ministers on February 16, 1966.

The government's stated goal of stimulating economic activity, favoring productive investment, and promoting industrial restructuring and concentration ran up against prevailing trends. To begin with, it had to contend with changes on the labor front. The declaration of intention concerning unified action by the CGT and CFDT announced in 1965 led on January 10, 1966, to the first joint CGT-CFDT agreement, a landmark for a French unionism, which had suffered the weakening consequences of internal divisions for so long. This document presented nine general objectives, including "the guarantee of a right to employment through the creation of new industries with public funds and under public control."[7] This declaration, which was backed by wide agreement in both organizations, expressed common outrage at a rise in unemployment that rank-and-file workers found very worrisome. The 1967 CGT Congress thus spelled out a list of objectives upon which widespread CGT-CFDT agreement existed (see Table 7.3).

If general responses to a deteriorating labor market in themselves rarely caused tension between the CGT and the CFDT, issues of a tactical nature concerning industrial struggles were a different matter. From May 17, 1966, to December 13, 1967, there were an average of three "national days of action" undertaken in common annually. These *grandes messes* proved as controversial with the CFDT as they were popular with the CGT, which conceived of the strikes as a good way to superimpose the political concerns of the Parti Communiste Français (PCF) on union activity. Meanwhile, the rank and file were growing increasingly impatient. There were bitter strikes at Dassault Aviation in Bordeaux and the Rhodiaceta synthetic textile works in the Rhône-Alpes region. And there were violent demonstrations in Le Mans and Mulhouse at the end of 1967 and early 1968. Attacks by young workers on the police in Caen, Fougères, Quimper, and Redon were quite as remarkable, revealing a degree of frustration and militancy that had not been seen for many years.

The government was driven by its own industrial logic. In order to divert savings to investment and to redefine the role of the Treasury, Michel Debré reformed the banking system in March 1966. The social unrest did not escape

Table 7.3   Employment Demands of the Confédération Générale du Travail (CGT) in 1967

- 40-hour work week without salary reduction
- prohibition of layoffs without retraining
- job-development policy
- professional retraining to fit workers to jobs
- financial support for the fully or partially unemployed
- slower assembly-line pace
- nationalization of key sectors of the economy

the attention of Prime Minister Georges Pompidou, who on April 8, 1967, appointed Jacques Chirac secretary of state for employment and, on August 3 of the same year, Pompidou formally invited unions and the *patronat* to begin bargaining. This invitation was partially accepted: on February 21, 1968, an agreement on short-term unemployment was signed by the CNPF and the various unions.

This attempt to promote damage control through renewed collective bargaining fell short, even though it stands out in retrospect as an important turning point in French negotiating history, when the student-led revolt of May 1968 sparked a massive industrial explosion. The largest strike in French history brought forth a wide variety of worker demands. In addition to the hopes for worker self-management—*autogestion*—expressed in conflicts like the one occurring at Usin-or-Dunkerque, there was widespread insistence on wage increases, better working conditions, job security, and changes in systems of internal discipline within firms.[8] In the employment realm, the Grenelle protocol of May 27, 1968, was predicated on a gradual return to the forty-hour week and a commitment to substantial job reclassification and retraining programs. The reduction of the work week came about very slowly. A national *interprofessionnel* agreement on job security to hasten it was concluded on February 10, 1969.

This huge social explosion, and all of the consequences to which it led, was dangerous for the franc—devaluation was narrowly averted on November 8, 1968—and threatened a more generalized political crisis. When General de Gaulle attempted to rebuild his depleted stock of political resources through his ill-fated referendum on participation on April 27, 1969, 53.2 percent of the votes were negative, representing 41.6 percent of all registered voters. The head of state resigned, and his successor, Georges Pompidou, began a political opening toward the center that served as a cover for conservative industrialism.

The New Society: 1969–72

Jacques Chaban-Delmas was given the task of moving beyond 1968. By naming Jacques Delors as his social advisor, the new prime minister hoped to begin a reform process that, among other things, would pull the CFDT along in the wake of the "new society" (and away from the CGT). A devaluation of the franc revealed Georges Pompidou's option for an export-led economic policy. French banks stepped up their international activities, while the building of Europe took centerstage, with the setting up of an European Economic Community (EEC) budget to support the Common Agricultural Policy. On the domestic front, the government cautiously pushed regional reform forward in an area that was limited to certain state economic procedures. Bolder reforms were proposed for the nationalized sector. Indeed, the state granted so much new autonomy in the management of nationalized firms that Pierre Dubois could write about the "death

Table 7.4   Employment Demands of the Confédération Générale du Travail (CGT) in 1969 and 1972

1969	1972
40-hour work week without salary reduction	40-hour work week with full compensation
active implementation of the February 10, 1969, Accord	economic development program
no layoffs without prior retraining	no layoffs withouit some prior retraining
development policy to promote employment	implementation and improvement of accords on the necessity of employment
improvements in employment placement services	strengthened control over unions and *comités d'enterprise*
organization of further training and *recyclage*, strengthened AFPA	termination of short-term employment contracts
guaranteed financial support	fixed number of employees to avoid the hiring of temporary workers
	education and training

of the *Etat-patron*."[9] One important corollary of the loosening of state financial control was an "autonomous" wage policy for the public sector, which took the form of the famous *contrats du progrès*.

Jacques Delors's efforts were well-received by the CFDT, but they quickly ran out of steam in the face of economic problems over which Delors had no control. Inflation accelerated, as did unemployment, which by January 1972 had risen above 400,000. The CGT stuck to its original employment strategy, strongly emphasizing the need for the retraining programs that had been legislated in July 1971, programs that embodied in law the results of national collective agreement promoted according to Delors's strategy (see Table 7.4).[10]

Labor conflict in the aftermath of 1968 demonstrated a very real underlying militancy. The strikes of 1971 were particularly revealing, when actions by semiskilled workers demonstrated a growing rejection of Taylorist methods (see Table 7.5). The factory occupations and *grèves bouchons* that characterized industrial conflict in the early 1970s were put to a variety of different uses. Data available for 1971, however, show that employment issues were relatively low on the list of strikers' concerns (see Table 7.6). Skepticism about the categories used in Table 7.6 is appropriate, as Pierre Dubois, when looking at the same period, found that 33.3 percent of public-sector conflicts were indeed about larger employment issues.[11] At any rate, the conflictual atmosphere of the period led

Table 7.5   Number of Work Days Lost, 1969–73 (in thousands of days)

1969	1970	1971	1972	1973
2,200	1,700	4,400	3,800	3,914

Source: Ministère du Travail.

Table 7.6   Compared Frequency of Reasons Given to Strike, 1970

	Ministère du Travail (%)	Enquête CRESST (%)
Salaries, qualifications	59	42
Length of work	10	14
Rights, regulations	11	11
Workplace conditions	7	11
Employment	6	8
Education, promotion	1	6
Accords, agreements	3	5

Source: Claude Durand and Pierre Dubois, *La Grève* (Paris: Presses de la Fondation nationale des sciences politiques, 1975), p. 23.

the CFDT to follow Delors's strategy. The new agreement signed by the CGT and CFDT on September 15, 1970 stressed the need for a rapid and uniform reduction of the work week as well as a lowering of the retirement age.[12]

Conservative Industrialism: 1972–74

Following an attack by the *Canard Enchaîné* on the tax situation of his prime minister, on July 15, 1972, Georges Pompidou sacked a weakened Chaban-Delmas and appointed Pierre Messmer to replace him. Messmer went on to lead the majority to victory in the legislative elections of March 1973. The president gave him a vote of confidence by reappointing him. The second half of Pompidou's five-year presidency was characterized by a certain indecisiveness and a hardening of positions in social matters.[13]

Even though the ultra-left politics of *gauchisme* were in retreat, innovative strikes continued. The movement at Lip in Besançon that began on April 17, 1973, and lasted eleven months was the spectacular last hurrah for post-1968 hypermilitant strikes, a moment that ended when Charles Piaget, the Lip leader, failed to mount a credible candidacy in the presidential elections of 1974. Lip popularized the slogan, "We produce, we sell, and we pay ourselves." In the midst of a brouhaha that they were not always able to keep under control, the Lip workers of Palente tried to regain jobs that had been lost to competition.

The Sixth Plan supported the creation of large industrial groups while at the same time trying not to cut itself off from dynamic small- and middle-sized firms. However, as Yves Ullmo states in *La Planification Française,*

> the State did not hesitate to intervene in sectors that were not mentioned in the Sixth Plan and in more traditional sectors, such as steel, aeronautics, and shipbuilding. In effect, the State persisted in a strategy of selective, *coup par coup* [day to day] intervention, even though this was less prominent than it had earlier been.[14]

Pompidou, torn between a desire to control inflation and fear of rising unemployment (a factor that, the president was keenly aware, had been important in setting off the explosion of May 1968), pursued his project of industrialization in a conservative manner that masked the first signs of coming international economic crisis. At the end of 1973, in response to the oil embargo brought on by the Yom Kippur War, the president decided to launch a massive program for the construction of nuclear power plants, highlighting once again his Saint-Simonian predilections.

II. Therapy Or Inevitable Crisis?

The death of Georges Pompidou coincided with the end of the postwar boom of high growth and, in particular, with the end of the St. Simonian phase of industrial policy that Christian Stoffaes has labeled "Gaullo-Pompidolian."[15] A new and different economic horizon was slowly appearing. The new political leaders were unsure about how to respond to the economic crisis, and unemployment levels continued to rise.

The Era of Stop-and-Go Change

"Today we begin a new era of French politics." Thus spoke Valéry Giscard d'Estaing, the new president, on his accession to power on May 27, 1974, responding, he asserted, "to the huge upsurge of the French people" that had asked for this new era. Strangely enough, however, in the economic sphere the Fourcade plan of June 1974 was rather reminiscent of the 1963 stabilization plan. Prices were monitored, credit tightened, and the budget once again balanced.

The logic of such measures combined with worldwide depression to produce a rapid rise in bankruptcies and a considerable increase in unemployment. The union movement was quick to perceive that the economic situation was changing, but had a range of opinions about the seriousness of the changes. At first the CFDT judged that the CGT's assessment of the international situation was an overdramatization caused by the CGT's "catastrophist" ideology. George Séguy's union, sensitive to the rising dangers, refused to change its platform and strategy: it believed that it had reached an accurate understanding of the underlying causes of the situation. The CGT therefore updated its positions from time to time but did not undertake any fundamental revisions of them (see Table 7.7).

The government understood the danger as it watched the number of unemployed soar above 500,000, a level that Georges Pompidou had considered critical. Prime Minister Jacques Chirac wrote a public letter to request that the principal social partners begin negotiations to find new ways of dealing with the deterioration of the labor market. In consequence, an agreement was reached on October

Table 7.7   Employment Demands of the Confédération Générale du Travail
(CGT) from 1975 to 1985

1975	1978	1982	1985
increased purchasing power	same	same	end of austerity
lower retirement age	same	same	new jobs for EDF, EMF, and CMCT contracts
shorter working hours without salary reduction	same	same	
no layoffs without some prior retraining	same	same	same
implementation of agreements on the necessity of work	same	same	absent
termination of short-term employment contracts	same	same	same; transformation of the TUC
limited recourse to temporary work	same	same	same
revision of conditions relating to the introduction of immigrant labor	same	end to new immigrant labor	same
financial guarantees	same	same	same
education and training	same	same	same
	better public employment services	same	same
		creation of local employment committees	absent
		implementation of solidarity contracts	absent

14, 1974, to set up a supplementary unemployment benefit (allocation supplémentaire d'attente, ASA) that would cover ninety percent of net income for one
year. Workers laid off for structural or cyclical reasons would be eligible. Then,
on November 21, 1974, the government took further action to create official
procedures for "economic" layoffs—i.e., those necessitated by the changes in
economic circumstances. The CGT and the CFDT refused to sign the proposed
agreement on the grounds that it gave unions no voice in the process and did not
provide job placement for those laid off. In an attempt to moderate such union
opposition, the government legislated the core of its proposals in January 1975,
thus requiring employers henceforth to seek administrative permission (from the
inspecteur du travail) before any new layoffs.[16]

This "social" approach to managing unemployment proved inadequate, largely
because the government's macroeconomic policy efforts fell short. Chirac in-

jected thirty million francs into the economy. State help to small businesses in difficulty was channeled through a new Interministerial Commission for Industrial Restructuring (Comité Interministériel pour l'Aménagement des Structures Industrielles, CIASI). Loans and subsidies were also granted to stimulate investments in those areas of the country hardest hit by the crisis. Despite such measures, the results of Chirac's economic stimulation were disastrous. Inflation and unemployment worsened, as did trade and balance of payments deficits. The number of official job seekers soared from 425,000 in April 1974 to 918,000 in August 1976. Jacques Chirac had run head-on into a "stagflationary" wall. In consequence, the president decided to change his economic policy along with his prime minister.

Barriste Redeployment

On April 22, 1976, Valéry Giscard d'Estaing announced that his ambition was to place France in the "leading group of middle-sized countries in the world." His "globalizing" strategic option indicated that French capital had begun to move abroad and that big foreign corporations had made major breakthroughs in France. The head of state was in favor of cooperating with American firms, as in the case of CII-Honeywell-Bull. Raymond Barre, successor to Jacques Chirac, fully embraced this strategy.

The first Barre plan included a number of classical measures: it raised interest rates, lowered the Value Added Tax (VAT), froze prices and purchasing power, proposed measures to encourage investment, and developed a "pact" for increasing the level of youth employment. The goals were to restore balance to the nation's trade and budgetary accounts and to improve industrial competitiveness. Barre succeeded in restoring the balance of payments, but was unable to stop inflation or to reduce the budget deficit. As for unemployment, it continued to grow. In Barre's view, the process of labor-market deterioration was ineluctable, just as the previous period of full employment seemed to him to have been "artificial for the most part."[17]

The major way unions opposed the Barre plan was to organize large "days of action" protests. On October 7, 1976, the FEN joined CGT and CFDT processions. On May 24 and December 1, 1977, the national movement was reinforced by actions sparked by local and regional initiatives. "Industrial counterproposals," which had been used in the past, most notably during the Lip conflict, were very much in evidence, even if some commentators have exaggerated their importance (see Table 7.8).[18]

The breakdown of the Common Program alliance between the PS, the PCF, and Left Radicals in 1977, along with the Left's defeat in the legislative elections of March 1978, changed the parameters of the situation. In the economic and social realms two processes flowed from these changes. From this point on Raymond Barre felt freer to stress certain of the tougher sides of his policy. And,

Table 7.8   Work Days Lost Due to Strikes during the Giscard Presidency (in thousands of days)

1974	1975	1976	1977	1978	1979	1980	1981
338	3,869	5,010	3,665	2,200	3,656	1,674	1,495

Source: Ministère du Travail.

on the union side, the CFDT, after changing its analysis of the nature of the crisis—which it believed inevitable from this point—"recentered" its efforts in the hope of finding realistic new grounds for compromise.

During the second phase of his government, Barre, the "Joffre" of the French economy, sought to accelerate industrial restructuring by opting, paradoxically, for a strong franc,[19] removing industrial price controls, and allowing greater instability in employment[20] while funneling savings into industrial investment using the new "SICAV-Monory" savings account package.

One consequence of CFDT recentering was that Edmond Maire decided to move away from the CFDT's strategic alliance with the CGT. Thus, the CFDT refused to participate in the early 1979 march of Lorrain steelworkers on Paris. The CFDT's new approach involved a renewed commitment to collective negotiations, which initially led to an agreement to restructure unemployment benefits, concluded on March 17, 1979. The ASA—the supplementary unemployment benefit created in 1975—was turned into a "special benefit" and lowered from ninety to sixty-five percent of wages, with a floor equal to ninety percent of the minimum wage (SMIC). The ASSEDICs—the basic unemployment compensation programs—would henceforth cover all of the various standard benefits (the minimums, special benefits like the ASA, severance pay, payments due statutorily at the moment when benefit eligibilities had been exhausted, exceptional emergency payments, etc.). The CFDT also ratified the Second General Agreement for the steel industry, signed on July 24, 1979, which represented a considerable compromise from earlier CFDT and other union positions.[21]

Meanwhile the government had begun artificially lowering unemployment figures by changing the ways in which joblessness was statistically reported.[22] The CGT nonetheless continued its struggle to stop any layoffs that did not guarantee job placement. The CFDT, in contrast, abandoned this strategy for checking the rise in unemployment in the interests of a new line centered on reducing the length of the work week, a work-sharing proposal that was part of a broader investment strategy supported by Michel Albert, head of the Planning Commission. Negotiations to reduce the work week lasted from June 1979 to January 1980, only to end in failure. The government then charged Pierre Giraudet to produce a report that would help to bring the two sides closer together. His efforts were in vain. Given the precedents of certain local agreements, such as that struck with BSN, the big glass-agrobusiness conglomerate, the CFDT thought there was hope of resolving the unemployment problem through extensive collective bargaining, even though a majority of employers opposed the idea outright. In fact, the attachment of most employers to the status quo was reinforced by the evident decline in worker militancy, which the crisis and union divisions were producing.

Socialist "Relance" and Social-Delorism

France's millionth registered unemployed worker was counted in 1975. The two millionth was counted in February 1981, causing what *Le Monde* (November 6, 1981) labeled a "psychological shock." According to electoral specialist Alain Lancelot, among the reasons for the success of François Mitterrand were "very lively anxieties" among voters "about their jobs and their living standards."[23] The first Socialist president of the Fifth Republic was elected on the basis of a 110-point program that included complicated plans to stimulate the economy.[24]

From June 1981 to June 1982 the Mauroy government set out to stimulate the economy through measures like direct support to financially troubled firms, sectoral intervention, the creation of public sector jobs, and large increases for the lowest paid. It also undertook a series of structural reforms, most notably nationalizing the banking system and an important part of the industrial base. In addition, efforts were directed at improving the employment picture by reducing the work week, lowering the retirement age, and adopting *contrats de solidarité* in which employers and unions engaged themselves to create new jobs when older workers could be persuaded to retire early. In effect, the government was carrying out many of the provisions of the 1972 Common Program, which the CGT continued to demand (see Table 7.7), and to which were added new proposals to promote work sharing. Finally, the government undertook a wide range of other reforms in the employment area, most notably the Auroux Laws and the Defferre decentralization program.

These policies for stimulating the economy did lead to greater activity and did slow the rise in unemployment. The international context worked against them, however. The French inflation rate remained well above those of France's trading partners. The trade balance worsened, forcing a second devaluation—following that of October 1981. Finally, austerity measures were adopted in June 1982. This brought inflation down but did little to lower the trade deficit. Following the municipal elections of March 1983, a plan was put in place to increase taxes, raise prices for public services, reduce budgetary expenditures, and lower social-welfare benefits. Finally, a third devaluation further lowered the value of the franc.

The CGT interpreted this turnaround—promoted by the Socialists—as a betrayal. As it occurred, the CGT therefore tried to formulate counterproposals, to sift the positive from the negative aspects of the new policy, and to mobilize its troops when it judged the consequences of governmental action to be completely unacceptable, as in the case of the plan for restructuring the steel industry in the spring of 1984. Henri Krasucki, CGT general secretary, opted for selective opposition rather than a broadside attack on the government, "ringing the alarm" but shying away from total confrontation, even though CGT hardliners were calling for a complete break with the government. The CFDT, in contrast, demanded even more *rigueur* and proposed programs that would ask for further sacrifices to support *les exclus*. For this reason, Edmond Maire's Confederation supported the unemployment insurance program adopted on February 24, 1984. The CFDT expanded on its new theme of solidarity—which dated from December 1981—in a text of its National Confederal Committee urging CFDT members to "Adapt our unionism."[25]

After the Communists left the government (in July 1984), the CGT began to denounce socialist policies openly. The CFDT, in contrast once again, foresaw the return of the Right to power and pushed its "recentered" strategic evolution one step further to begin advocating "cold negotiating"—collective bargaining in the absence of mass mobilization and strikes. For obvious reasons, in this context of economic difficulties, political problems, and union division the number of strikes was declining year by year (see Table 7.9).

State-Sponsored Privatization (1986–88)
and Rocardian Management

March 1986. The electoral pendulum has swung back to the Right. The Chirac government proposes to implement the RPR-UDF program. In consequence, either by fiat or with parliamentary approval, steps are taken to eliminate the wealth tax, reduce taxes to benefit businesses, abolish exchange controls, remove all price controls, and reduce government spending. The government also launches an ambitious program to privatize the public sector, including the TF1 television network in the package, a program that leads to a stock-buying spree on the part of many savers lasting until the bourse crashes on October 19, 1987.

Jacques Chirac's government was aware that the situation of several industrial sectors had reached a critical point. In the shipbuilding industry, Minister of Industry Alain Madelin promoted the departure of individual workers and the establishment of new firms through tax breaks. A new collective agreement was

Table 7.9   Work Days Lost Due to Strike, 1981–88 (in thousands of days)

1981	1982	1983	1984	1985	1986	1987	1988
1,495	2,250	1,483	1,357	834	1,041	949	1,250

Source: Ministère du Travail.

signed in the steel industry on July 16, 1987. Additional subsidies were approved in March 1987 for the chemical, aeronautical, and electronic industries, as well as for the railroads and the superhighway systems. Renault began to implement a reorganization plan.

Philippe Séguin, minister of social affairs, was charged with the task of weakening labor laws while at the same time developing strategies to cope with unemployment. The principal strike of this period, by railroad workers, did not fall directly within the jurisdiction of his ministry. Hence the obstacles encountered by Séguin, who had been one of the most vocal opponents of the Auroux Laws, were primarily political. He was able to ram the elimination of administrative controls over layoffs—Chirac's 1975 reform, it will be remembered—through Parliament. When he tried to "flexibilize" work-time arrangements by decree, however, President Mitterrand refused to cooperate. When the government then transformed this decree into a legislative amendment on December 17, 1986, the Constitutional Council declared it to be unconstitutional. It was not until June 19, 1987, that a law was passed to weaken the prohibition on night-shift work by women and to allow for a more flexible disposition of working hours.[26] A new UNEDIC (unemployment compensation) agreement was finally ratified on December 30, 1987, and brought into effect in March 1988. By manipulating various menial *petits boulots* and short-term contracts, Séguin was able to stabilize the number of those looking for work, which fluctuated between 2,562,000 in December 1987 and 2,388,500 in March 1988.

The economic mess, which, with the exception of 1975, was at its worst in 1983, began to abate somewhat in 1987. The GNP grew by 2.1 percent in 1986, by 2.3 percent in 1987, and by 3.6 percent in 1988. In 1988 François Mitterrand was reelected as president of the Republic and Michel Rocard became prime minister in a more favorable economic climate, which had a good chance of lasting, as far as the economic prognosticators could tell. As Monique Foult and colleagues stated in April 1989, "In the watershed years of 1988 and 1989, business leaders are still optimistic."[27] Watershed or not, unemployment continued to rise, even if it was somewhat offset by growth in marginal kinds of jobs.[28]

The leader of the "second Left," Michel Rocard pursued a prudent general policy, constantly reminding everyone of the persistent deficit in the balance of payments and the fragility of many French firms. He did not redo the 1988 budget he had inherited from the Right, and proceeded along similar, rather classical lines in preparing his budget for 1989. In the employment area, on September 14, 1988, the Council of Ministers adopted measures designed to achieve four objectives: to encourage more hiring by lowering employers' contributions to social security, to develop a greater entrepreneurial spirit, to improve training, and to revive regional and local initiatives.[29] The spirit of the Tenth Plan—with planning in eclipse, of course, was to approach unemployment by focusing on overall macroeconomic problems, rather than trying to pursue a more voluntaristic full-employment policy. On May 17, 1989, the Council of Ministers adopted some new, quite specific measures for collective bargaining arrangements, unemployment insurance, the employment of foreigners, and the struggle against the underground labor market.

If the policies of the Rocard Government seemed timid, it was because they depended upon a pragmatic coalition of social partners. The CNPF, seeking to divide the labor movement even more than it already was divided, went a long way to elicit CFDT and CGC support for programs such as the Stages d'Initiation à la Vie Professionalle (SIVP)—a "makework" program to soak up youth unemployment at subminimum wage levels, skill training for young people just entering the labor market (March 1, 1989), and professional retooling agreements (March 10 and 19, 1989). Two important interoccupational agreements were also reached, one on September 23, 1988, dealing with technological change and one on March 21, 1989, concerning changes in the work week.[30] These agreements have helped to facilitate the "modernization" of firms.

The flexible policies of Michel Rocard were not welcomed with enthusiasm by wage-earners. Indeed, worker militancy picked up after a long lull in the 1980s. In 1988, the workers at Michelin, at SNECMA, at Saint-Nazaire, at the printing firm of Jean Didier, and at Gardannes, along with, in the fall alone, prison guards, nurses, and postal and railroad workers, all went on bitter and sometimes very disruptive strikes. The following year, prison guards, teachers, Corsican state employees, and the staff of the *météorologie nationale* all struck, while employees inside the Ministry of Finance carried on an extended movement in the first part of the year. According to the reflections of a CNPF leader in May 1988, France had once again become a country that was "predisposed to strikes."[31]

This upsurge in strike activity did not lead to a rebirth of trade unionism, however. Divisions among the unions continued, which made it difficult for workers to express their grievances, and, in consequence, they often tried to overcome this by establishing *coordinations* based on the rank and file and independent of unions altogether. Such was the case for the 1988 railroad workers' strike, as well as for numerous movements in the public sector in 1989. Today, union strategies for confronting unemployment remain highly varied, as a reading of the resolutions passed during recent Congresses of the different union confederations dramatically demonstrates.

With the replacement of André Bergeron by Marc Blondel, it appeared quite clear that the once "extremely moderate" FO was hardening its stance and that it would be less and less likely to allow the CGT to dominate all militant union activity. On the other hand, the CFDT continued to pursue a "constructive" course that could never be misinterpreted as militant or interventionist. The signing of the March 21, 1989, agreement on working time was a clear indication of its "You scratch my back, I'll scratch yours" strategy: "Now is the time to insure that specific changes in work schedules of firms be accompanied by a shortening of work time, however it is measured, and a rollback of marginal forms of employment."[32] In other words, the CFDT had begun a strategy of careful

Table 7.10   Employment Demands of the Confédération Française Démocratique du Travail (CFDT), the Confédération Générale du Travail (CGT), and the Force Ouvrière (FO) Adopted at Their Most Recent Congresses

Forty-first Congress of the CFDT, 1988
  find a new pattern of growth
  qualitative modernization of the economy
  shorter working period
  professional qualifications for all
  push the development of new forms of employment
  ensure proper arrangements for new entrants and reentrants to the job market

Forty-third Congress of the CGT, 1989
  achieve full employment
  ensure stable, skilled employment for wage-earners
  contruct an effective public employment service
  train workers
  enlarge and reorient research and innovation efforts
  reduce the work period

Sixteenth Congress of the FO, 1989
  raise the growth rate
  adopt a growth policy
  create professional training to improve skills
  suppress the Stages d'Initiation à la Vie Professionelle (SIVP) and all formulas concerning social treatment
  restore the public placement service

Source: Syndicalisme CFDT, December 15, 1988, no. 2238; *Le Peuple*, June 22, 1989, nos. 1291, 1292, and 1293; *Compte rendu XVIe Congrès confédéral Force ouvrière* (Paris: FO, 1989), p. 467.

"concession bargaining" in which it was willing to bargain away earlier union victories in exchange for new work-sharing goals (see Table 7.10).

Concluding Remarks

Although at times schematic and sketchy, this retrospective justifies concluding that there was very strong continuity in state structure in the employment area over the period 1962–90. The administrative machinery remains essentially the same, along with the determining role of the Ministry of Economy and Finance. The rue de Bercy (recently transplanted from the rue de Rivoli) is one nerve center, but it is not the exclusive center of power. Two changes are evident during this period, however. The Planning Commission has suffered a decline of influence that the coming to power of the Left has not checked.[33] Valéry Giscard d'Estaing bears special responsibility for this. Regionalization has gradually established new subnational positions of power—in consequence of decentralization reforms—allowing, among other things, the state to concede some power, including taxation, in favor of localities.

In terms of demands and tactics, trade-union strategies demonstrate considerable continuity. The greatest changes in union behavior in this period undoubtedly occurred between the periods of united action (between the CGT and CFDT from 1966 to 1980) and general division. The most important general modification of the French labor movement has involved transition from a system dominated by the CGT to a system characterized by a multiplicity of competing unions in which the CGT maintains only a simple, relative majority. The CGT has been considerably weakened, in other words. Still, it is quite evident that the unions, even though they may differ in their interpretations of the meaning of the economic changes of this period, all still tend to view the role and function of the state in the same light. The state is above all a collection of institutions, from which certain norms emanate. It regulates, and even in order to deregulate, it must regulate some more. The state is also seen as a producer, via the nationalized firms. Next, the state budget, especially on the military side, makes it a client of important sectors of the economy. Fourth, the state is an essential financial player. Finally, the state plays a central regulatory role in the social realm. The unions are attentive to any change in these five functions. They are sensitive to any disengagement of the state, but they have not been able to diagnose any profound changes in its functions.

Ideology, reflecting and supporting different economic choices, has amplified changes in state behavior. Changes in objectives may occur in reaction to external constraints or in response to changes in the political sphere. From 1962 to 1990, the elements that have changed more than anything else are French civil society and the new place of the French economy in the international market. Insofar as union strategies have remained wedded to a national strategy and a national perspective, they have run up against these changes.[34] One is tempted to conclude that the functions of the state have changed slowly and less by themselves or through any changes in the general evolution of the human spirit and more as a result of the construction of a European market and the participation of the state in the globalization of production and exchange.

In this uncertain situation, and in the absence of some credible alternative project that could serve to mobilize them, French workers are hesitant.[35] Those who have their backs against the wall struggle to defend their jobs. Others wait for better days. Working-class fatalism and resignation has, however, been less evident from 1986 to the present, as recent strikes and mobilizations show. In general, as in 1963, it is once again possible now to speak of French individualism, trade-union division, and politicization as central features of the labor environment. One cannot overlook the constitutive role that disappointment with the Socialist policies of the period 1982–86 has played in this development. Nor should one underemphasize the workers' disarray in a world that inspires little enthusiasm, but one that they do not know how to change.

Translated from the French by James Hollifield and George Ross

Notes

1. Stanley Hoffmann et al., *In Search of France* (Cambridge, Mass.: Harvard University Press, 1963). Unions are mentioned only with respect to difficulties in the interwar period, on p. 22.

2. The term is borrowed from Michel Crozier's book *Etat modeste, Etat moderne* (Paris: Fayard, 1987).

3. For a brief presentation of this strike, which lasted from March 1 to April 5, 1963, see Georges Lefranc, *Grèves d'hier et d'aujourd'hui* (Paris: Aubier-Montaigne, 1970), pp. 168–76. See also the interesting and skilled analysis by Pierre Belleville, "Les Enseignements de la grève des mineurs," *Perspectives Socialistes* 59 (April 1963), pp. 2–19. The movement was in revenge for the failure of the struggle by Decazeville. See Stanley Hoffman et al., *In Search of France*, pp. 225–27.

4. See René Bonety et al., *La C.F.D.T.* (Paris: Editions du Seuil, 1971), pp. 64–96.

5. On the CFDT see Guy Groux and René Mouriaux, *La CFDT* (Paris: Economica, 1989). For a more "engaged" and less rigorous interpretation of the same material, see Pierre Cours-Salies, *La CFDT: Un passé porteur d'avenir* (Paris: La Brèche, 1988).

6. Marie-France Mouriaux, *L'Emploi en France depuis 1945* (Paris: Colin, 1972), p. 59.

7. The text of the accord of January 10, 1966, is reproduced in Jacques Capdevielle and René Mouriaux, *Mai 68: L'Entre-deux de la modernité: Histoire de trente ans* (Paris: Presses de la F.N.S.P., 1988), pp. 141–42.

8. Antoine Prost, "Les Grèves de mai-juin 68," *l'Histoire* 110 (April 1968), pp. 34–46. Of all the industrial conflicts studied in twenty-nine enterprises by Daniel Vidal, seven started over layoffs and employment policies. See Pierre Dubois et al., *Grèves revendicatives ou grèves politiques?* (Paris: Anthropes, 1976), p. 460.

9. Pierre Dubois, *Mort de l'Etat-Patron* (Paris: Editions ouvrières, 1974).

10. Gérard Adam, Jean-Daniel Reynaud, and Jean-Maurice Verdier, *La Négociation collective en France* (Paris: Editions ouvrières, 1972), p. 17.

11. Dubois, *La Mort de l'Etat-Patron*, p. 290.

12. The complete text is reproduced in René Mouriaux, *Les Stratégies syndicales aux lendemains de mai 1968* (Paris: CEVIPOF, 1987), pp. 4–5. An English translation appears in David L. Hanley and Anne P. Kerr, eds., *May '68: Coming of Age* (London: Macmillan, 1989), pp. 119–20.

13. René Mouriaux, "Le Bilan social d'un quinquennat (15 juin 1969–2 avril 1974)," *Etudes* (June 1974): 869–77.

14. Yves Ullmo, *La Planification française* (Paris: Dunod, 1974), p. 350.

15. Christian Stoffaes, *Politique industrielle* (Paris: Cours de droit, 1984), p. 95.

16. Jean-Daniel Reynaud, *Les Syndicats, les patrons, et l'Etat* (Paris: Editions ouvrières, 1978), p. 18.

17. André Granou, *Années de rêves, années de crise (1970–1981)* (Paris: La Découverte, 1988), p. 51.

18. Jean-Pierre Huiban, "La Contre proposition industrielle comme élément de stratégie syndicale (1973–1980)," in *1968–1982: Le Mouvement ouvrier français: Crise économique et changement politique*, ed. Mark Kesselman and Guy Groux (Paris: Editions ouvrières, 1984), pp. 295–313. See also George Ross, "The Perils of Politics: French Unions and the Crisis of the 1970s," in Peter Lange, George Ross, and Maurizio Vannicelli, *Unions, Change and Crisis: French and Italian Union Strategy and the Political Economy, 1945–1980* (London: Allen and Unwin, 1982), pp. 13–93.

19.   Alain Lipietz, *L'Audace ou l'enlisement* (Paris: La Découverte, 1984), p. 60.

20.   Jeremy Richardson and Roger Henning, *Unemployment: Policy Responses of Western Democracies* (London, Sage, 1984), pp. 148–66.

21.   The social convention in Lorraine iron and steel was July 27, 1967. The first CGPS was initialed on June 3, 1977.

22.   Jean-Louis Besson, Maurice Comte, and Paul Rousset, *Compter les chômeurs* (Lyon: PUF, 1981).

23.   Daniel Boy et al., *1981: Les Elections de l'alternance* (Paris: Presses de la F.N.S.P., 1986), p. 15.

24.   Reproduced in René Mouriaux, *Syndicalisme et politique* (Paris: Editions ouvrières, 1985), pp. 170–72.

25.   Bernard Aupetit, *Classes et catégories sociales* (Roubaix: Edires, 1985), pp. 97–106. On the industrial and employment policies of the left, see Cecilia Casassus et al., *Stratégies industrielles et politiques d'emploi* (Paris: GST-CRESST, 1984), 2 vols.

26.   René Mouriaux, *La C.F.D.T. face à la flexibilité de l'emploi, 1985–1987* (Paris: CEVIPOF, 1987).

27.   Monique Fouet et al., "Dernière sortie avant l'inflation," *Observation et Diagnostique Economiques* 27 (April 1989): 38.

28.   Unemployment fell in May 1989. When corrected for seasonal fluctuations, there were 2,516,800 unemployed people, or 9.9 percent of the labor force. See *Premières Informations* 129 (June 1989). Although enrollment in the TUC and SIVP programs fell in 1988, overall unemployment continued to increase. See *Premières Informations* 108 (December 1988) and 119 (February 1989).

29.   The prime minister would have been struck by the OFCE analysis according to which France would be the country whose labor market would deteriorate the worst in the coming years. See "Plan pour l'emploi du gouvernement," *Liaisons Sociales* 8488 (September 15, 1988): 466.

30.   *Liaisons Sociales* 6148 (October 5, 1988): 2,348, and 6221 (March 29, 1989): 2,359.

31.   Jacques Capdevielle and René Mouriaux, *Approche politique de la grève en France (1966–1988)* (Paris: CEVIPOF, Cahiers no. 3, 1989), p. 5.

32.   Nicole Notat, "Le 19 septembre: un grand rendez-vous social," *CFDT-Magazine*, July–August 1989.

33.   Philippe Mioche, "Syndicats et CNPF dans le plan: l'Amorce d'un consensus," in *La Planification en Crise* (Paris: Editions CNRS, 1987), pp. 79–114.

34.   René Mouriaux, *Le Syndicalisme face à la crise* (Paris: La Découverte, 1986), pp. 110–12.

35.   Within the confines of this essay, it is not possible to analyze the project of "recomposition syndicale" (union reconstruction) that was embraced by the FEN in 1986 and that tried to reconcile the independent CFDT and FO. The January–February 1989 congress of the FO placed a wall in front of this goal. The FEN continued to hope: "Both the CGT-FO and the CFDT continue to adhere to the same International, the Confédération Internationale des Syndicats Libres (CISL); we ourselves belong to the Secretariat Professionel International de l'Enseignement (SPIE), which is also tied to CISL. If a reconciliation within the international can take place, it is surely on this social European question. We are ready to discuss where to go and when." *FEN-Hebdo* 333 (July 7, 1989).

A more combative tone appeared under the pen of Guy Le Neouannic: "French unionism is without doubt at a turning point today. It can continue quietly to die little by little, to lose members who no longer see any usefulness in it in the sense that they don't discern fundamental questions in its internal quarrels. It can also take command of itself again at the expense perhaps of leaving on the wayside those who have not yet discovered that the world moves without them and that they must no longer theorize, but build. See Guy Neouannic, "l'Heure des choix," *Enseignement Public* 58 (June 1989).

8

Educational Pluralism in the French Fifth Republic

John S. Ambler

It is not without cause that French education is frequently cited as a striking example of Jacobinism in action. To be sure, the autonomy of the Ministry of National Education has always been limited by the existence of a private sector and by intrastate conflict.[1] The fact remains that since the First Empire, and particularly since the Third Republic, Paris has prescribed curriculum, hired teachers, allocated funds, and in general presided over an educational structure that is more centralized than those found in other Western democracies. It will be the purpose of this paper to examine two assaults on Jacobinism in French education in the course of the Fifth Republic. Each has provoked massive street demonstrations that loom as key political events of the past quarter-century. The first, the institutionalization of state support for private education, represents a major defeat for the Jacobin view that pluralism is a threat to the general interest and to the Republic itself. The second, the less successful attempts at decentralization led by Edgar Faure, Alain Savary, René Monory, Alain Devaquet, and others, demonstrates the continuing strength of the ideas and interests linked to the centralized *université*. The partisans of state support for private education were more successful in part because their assault came from outside the state structure of education and hence was not subject to all of the constraints upon reformers working within that structure.

The concept of the centralized state did not originate with the French Revolution. As Tocqueville so admirably demonstrated, the Revolution only built on a structure created by the Old Regime for the purpose of weakening the nobility and enhancing the power of the king.[2] Yet it was the Jacobin dictatorship of 1793 to 1794, led by Robespierre and the Committee of Public Safety, which extended unprecedented controls over the country, tracked down and destroyed enemies, and attached its name forever to the concept of the centralized state. The Jacobin

I am indebted to the American Philosophical Society for its support of the research in Paris on which much of this paper is based. I am also grateful to Antoine Prost, who took time from his new position as an educational advisor to Prime Minister Michel Rocard to comment on an earlier draft, and to the editors of this volume, for their helpful comments.

tradition, like the faction for which it is named, rests on a pervasive republican fear of disloyalty from localities, regions, and subcultures that are not under firm central control. It takes a revisionist Rousseauian view that only the central government can protect the public good—defined to include equal rights for all citizens—against the selfish, if not treasonable, designs of "partial" societies.[3]

As applied to government administration, Jacobinism means a strictly hierarchical structure in which policy decisions and personnel assignments are made from the center, with very limited local autonomy. In French education, it has come to mean national diplomas attained through the study of nationally prescribed curricula, within a standardized structure in which teachers and students of the same level and category have the same highly specified rights and duties wherever in the country they may be. The term Jacobinism will be used here to refer to a centralized administrative structure and to the attitudes that support that structure. It should not be taken to imply that there is a generalized force toward centralization in French society. French education may not be unique, but it clearly is an extreme case of centralization in a diverse society that now includes a wide variety of patterns of authority relationships.

In education as in local government, recent assaults on Jacobinism normally have flown the banner of decentralization. And yet the Jacobin tradition is hostile not only to local autonomy, but also to nonterritorial enclaves of autonomy, such as the Catholic schools. Hence, in education at least, the antithesis to Jacobinism is best described as pluralism, here meaning autonomy, or at least partial autonomy, for major components of the educational system. As we shall see, there are not only many different degrees of autonomy, but also several distinct forms, depending upon the nature of the local authority to which power devolves.

Subsidies to Higher Education

For nearly two centuries the French Left rallied to the defense of the Republic against the perceived threat of clericalism and the Catholic schools that presumably propagated its message. Catholic universities were dissolved by the Revolution, and private Catholic schools were officially nationalized. Catholic education revived under subsequent conservative governments, particularly after the Falloux Law of 1851, which provided state subsidies to private schools and authorized religious instruction in public schools. Republican parliamentary majorities repealed both measures in the fundamental secular laws of the 1880s and 1890s. Members of certain teaching orders were periodically banned, only to be allowed later to return to their schools.[4] Subsidies were reintroduced by the Vichy Government, then repealed in 1945 on the urging of the Communist, Socialist, and Radical parties.[5] As late as the 1950s, François Goguel, one of the most astute observers of French political behavior, reported that "in the current vocabulary of many of the French provinces, the word 'Catholic' is quite naturally contrasted not with the words 'Protestant' or 'freethinker' but with the word 'republican.' "[6]

The issue of church schools contributed to the legendary instability of the Fourth Republic and frustrated attempts to build a new progressive coalition across the clerical divide between the Socialists and the Popular Republican Movement.[7] For the French Socialists, defense of public schools against Catholic education was more than a policy position; it was a traditional core value, more durable and powerful than public ownership of large industries. For some, laïcité meant total prohibition of all private education on the Jacobin grounds that only state schools could protect the general interest. Left-wing schoolmasters on the Constitutional Committee in 1945, arguing that church schools were "mental incubators" incapable of offering unprejudiced education, persuaded the Committee to omit from the constitution any guarantee of freedom of instruction.[8] The president of the secularist parents association, Jean Cornec of the FCPE, took the same view in his testimony to the Lapie Commission in 1959: "I consider that to speak of the freedom of the . . . choice of parents is to betray to a certain degree the freedom of the child."[9] For the Socialist Party (Section Française de l'Internationale Ouvrière, SFIO) as a whole, laïcité meant at the very least "public funds for public schools, private funds for private schools."

Faced with anticlericalism on the Left, Catholic education has sought support from conservative parties, which in turn have used the school issue to mobilize voters. The traditional basis for the alliance often was less religion than a common aversion to radical social change. As chairman of a commission created to strengthen Catholic education in the wake of the June Days uprising of 1848, Adolphe Thiers announced his displeasure with "socialists and communists" in the ranks of elementary teachers:

> I demand formally something beyond those detestable little lay teachers. I prefer the Brothers, although previously I had been opposed to them. I wish to render all-powerful the influence of the clergy and make it stronger than it is, for I count on it to propagate that good philosophy that knows that man is here to suffer.[10]

Although the tone of political rhetoric has changed since the era of Thiers, and although the Church is no longer as socially conservative, the mutual dependence of conservative parties and Catholic education has survived.

The political influence of the Catholic school lobby grew during the life of the Fourth Republic as a result of the political isolation of the Communist Party after 1947, the vigorous efforts of the Association of Private School Parents (Association Pour l'Ecole Libre—APEL, or UNAPEL, as its national union is called), and competition between the Gaullists (Rassemblement pour la France, RPF) and the Popular Republican Movement (Mouvement Républicain Populaire, MRP) for Catholic votes. Beginning in the late 1940s, the RPF systematically pressed the MRP on the issue of state subsidies, knowing that the MRP-Socialist coalition seriously restrained its rival's room for maneuver.[11] As the MRP moved with reluctance toward subsidies for private schools, certain of its leaders were carrying on extensive negotiations with Maurice Deixonne—a socialist deputy reputed to be a "priest eater"—Guy Mollet, and with the papacy in Rome in a futile attempt to resolve all Church-related issues and thereby eliminate this barrier between the Popular Republicans and the moderate Left.[12]

The Gaullists, the Popular Republicans, the traditional conservative groups, and even one wing of the Radicals came under strong pressure from the Catholic school lobby to support state subsidies. The 800,000-member APEL joined with ten other groups in 1948 to form the Secrétariat d'Etudes pour la Liberté de l'Enseignement. Under the vigorous leadership of Eduard Lizop, the Secrétariat inspired the creation in 1951 of the Parliamentary Association for the Freedom of Instruction (Association Parlementaire pour la Liberté de l'Education, APLE) and asked all candidates in the parliamentary elections of 1951 to pledge to join.[13] In addition to the 296 of 627 elected deputies who became formal members of APLE, there were sufficient informal supporters to give the "free school" movement a clear majority.[14] The result offers an example of the impact of the school question on coalition formation in the Fourth Republic. The first two prime ministerial candidates proposed after the 1951 election failed to form a government, largely for lack of a school policy that would satisfy both the Catholic school lobby and the Socialist Party. The third and successful candidate, René Pleven, attempted to appease the new majority with the Marie Law, which created scholarships to support secondary students in either public or private institutions. Still unsatisfied, leaders of APLE met in the offices of the Secrétariat to draft the Barangé Law, a general allowance per pupil to go into a departmental account for public school children and directly to the parents' associations of schools for those in the private sector.[15] With Pleven and his cabinet abstaining. the bill passed by a vote of 313 to 255.[16]

Barangé was only a partial solution to the increasingly serious financial problems of Catholic schools. A sharp decline in recruitment into the priesthood and the teaching orders forced the Church to hire increasing numbers of lay teachers at far greater expense. By 1959 the Barangé grants were paying only sixteen percent of the operating costs of Catholic education.[17] The 1958 elections dramatically strengthened the hand of the church school lobby, even though the school question had not been a major issue in the campaign. The election results decimated the ranks of Communist and Socialist deputies and produced a National Assembly in which 380 of 578 members eventually joined APLE.[18] Sensing its new political strength, the APEL organized mass meetings to demand enhanced state subsidies with minimal state controls. The APEL's secularist counterpart, the National Council for Secular Action (Conseil National pour l'Action Laïque, CNAL), counterattacked with a proposed bill in which the first enumerated principle called for the abolition of private schools: "Schooling is compulsory from six to eighteen years, and this compulsory instruction is given exclusively by the public service."[19]

In contrast to the Pleven Government of 1951, the first government of the Fifth Republic took the initiative in seeking a lasting solution to the *question scolaire*. Bolstered by new constitutional powers, by a large parliamentary majority and by the enormous prestige of President de Gaulle, Prime Minister Michel Debré acted much more boldly than his predecessors of the Fourth Republic would have dared. The government appointed a nonparliamentary commission to study the school question, then drafted a bill that built upon the commission's recommendations. The Debré Law, approved in December 1959 with only minor parliamentary amendments, offered private schools the new options of a "simple contract," a transitional status to expire after nine years, or a "contract of association" with the state. The first format, chosen by most Catholic elementary schools, requires the contracting school to "refer to" programs in force in the public schools and to accept the pedagogical and financial supervision of the state. In return, the state pays the salaries of teachers, who formally remain school employees. Schools preferring the "contract of association," as did most Catholic secondary schools, must meet a "recognized school need," "respect" public school programs and schedules, and relinquish to the state the formal right to appoint their teachers. In return the state agrees to pay operating expenses as well as teachers' salaries. Under both contract options the participating schools are obligated to accept pupils "without distinction of origin, opinion, or belief," and to teach them with "respect for the freedom of conscience."[20]

The passage of the Debré Law was more difficult than the final Assembly vote of 427 to 71 would suggest. Speaking for the Socialist Party in the Assembly debate, Guy Mollet pledged that when the Left returned to power it would carry through the logic of the Debré Law by nationalizing all subsidized private schools.[21] The cabinet itself was far from united over the subsidy plan. The Socialist minister of education, Robert Boulloche, resigned on the eve of the debate in the Assembly.[22] In mid-December, de Gaulle felt compelled to intervene directly in order to push through the reform, which was under attack from the Right as well as from the Left.[23] Lizop and others affiliated with the "free school" movement repeatedly criticized the government for jeopardizing the independence of Catholic schools. After the law was enacted, Lizop issued a warning: "This law is full of dangers for private education and it is with constant watchful vigilance that it must be implemented."[24] The initial reaction of the bishops to the law was so negative that Debré, fearing a boycott, wrote to them in early 1960, warning that if the Church rejected the contracts, there would be no other aid.[25]

Indeed Michel Debré's plan, like the man himself, had strong Jacobin features. He sought, unsuccessfully, to end the *querelle scolaire* and in so doing to unify the nation by closely associating public and private schools. He viewed with suspicion all special interest groups, even those like the private school lobby with which he shared some goals. Twenty-five years later, Jean-Pierre Chevènement, President Mitterrand's second minister of education, concluded that while the Debré Law had sometimes been interpreted by conservative governments as a simple subsidy, it also could be interpreted in a Jacobin manner, emphasizing the "public service" nature of subsidized private education.[26]

The institutionalization of public support for private schools continued in 1971 when, at President Pompidou's urging, Parliament approved legislation that extended indefinitely the option of the simple contract for elementary schools. In 1977 the Guermeur Law enhanced funding, loosened state controls for all contract schools, and reversed Debré by transferring the authority to name teachers from the rector, representing the minister of national education, to the school director, representing Church authorities. Benefits of private school teachers were improved and teacher training was funded. Finally, the Guermeur Law required local governments to contribute a per-pupil grant for the operating expenses of simple contract schools, a provision that led to dozens of battles between leftist municipal governments and local Catholic schools. In the course of the 1970s, the "school need" qualification for acceptance of new contract schools was interpreted broadly to include offering parents a choice between public and private, even where total facilities were already more than adequate.

When the Left came to power following the presidential and legislative elections of 1981, after more than two decades in opposition, it confronted a Catholic educational system that still enjoyed considerable autonomy, despite its heavy dependence on state funding. The powerful secularist lobby within the Socialist Party expected that this affront to socialist (and Jacobin) ideals would be ended by the rapid implementation of President François Mitterrand's campaign promise of "a great public service of National Education, unified and secular." Forty-eight percent of the Socialist Party deputies elected in 1981 were teachers or former teachers in the public schools. The major teachers union, the Federation of National Education (Fédération de l'Education Nationale, FEN) and its components, the National Union of Elementary Teachers (Syndicat National des Instituteurs, SNI) and the National Union of Secondary Teachers (Syndicat National des Enseignements de Second Degré, SNES), understood Mitterrand's pledge to mean simple integration of subsidized schools into the public system. This understanding was shared by a network of secularist associations, including the Federation of Parents' Councils (FCPE), the Ligue de l'Enseignement, and the CNAL. With the exception of the SNES, which was under the leadership of its communist faction, all had close ties to the Socialist Party.

The militant secularist camp had heard only one part of Mitterrand's campaign promise. He also pledged to "convince and not compel" in the implementation of unification. President Mitterrand and Prime Minister Pierre Mauroy chose as minister of education a moderate known for his diplomatic skills, Alain Savary, rather than the Socialist Party's leading spokesman on education, former teacher Louis Mexandeau, who was judged to be too *engagé*.

On the Catholic side, while the right wing called for total intransigence, the moderates were in control and ready to put an end to the *querelle scolaire* by reaching agreement with a government of the Left, so long as this could be done without sacrificing the religious character of their schools.[27] The threat of forced unification with public education quite naturally alarmed Catholic officials and inspired UNAPEL to demonstrate its strength by organizing a series of giant rallies. And yet the struggle over the Savary Bill already revealed what French Catholics already knew: the Catholic community encompasses social and political views ranging from Christian socialist on the Left to conservative *intégriste* on the Right. At the time of the 1981 elections, the president of the episcopal committee on school affairs was Jean Honoré, Bishop of Evreux and an outspoken modernizer who favored negotiations with the new Socialist government.[28]

In May 1981 the UNAPEL, a group often dominated in the past by strong conservatives, elected as president Pierre Daniel, a moderate who was in essential agreement with Honoré. The two men agreed that personnel changes were needed in the Secretariat of Catholic Education, which had issued a number of combative, antisocialist statements during the election campaign.[29] The secretary-general, Father Jean Chapot, was replaced by Father Paul Guiberteau. Despite misgivings by Honoré and Daniel, Nicole Fontaine, a candidate for the Union pour la Démocratie Française (UDF) in the 1979 European elections, was allowed to stay on as assistant secretary-general until she was elected to the European Parliament in 1983.

After two years of intermittent negotiation, in the course of which he won the trust and respect of representatives of Catholic education, Savary succeeded in drafting a plan that came "within two fingers" of acceptance on the Catholic side.[30] Savary's ultimate defeat is attributable largely to his inability to win over the powerful secularist lobby within his own party. When it became apparent that Savary was moving toward a compromise that would allow subsidized private education to survive, the CNAL withdrew from the negotiations and mobilized its many friends for a counterattack.

In the National Assembly the Savary Bill was submitted to a special committee headed by André Laignel, a militant *laïciste* who enjoyed the support of Pierre Joxe, president of the Socialist parliamentary group. Several amendments were added to strengthen the secularist character of the bill, including one that linked local government contributions for the maintenance expenses of private schools to the proportion of their teachers who had been integrated (*titularisés*) into the public schoolteachers' corps. Laignel then told the National Assembly, with Savary present: "We cannot imagine that your government would choose to sacrifice those for whom, as the President of the Republic, François Mitterrand, has written, '. . . the choice of secularism has been linked, since the beginning of time, with men's struggle for their freedom.' "[31] Savary objected to the amendments, warning correctly that they would destroy a delicate compromise. He was overruled by Mauroy, who, after hearing the advice of such leading

Socialist figures as Louis Mermaz, president of the National Assembly, and Lionel Jospin, first secretary of the Socialist Party, as well as that of Laignel and Joxe, feared that the use of the blocked vote to force through the government's unamended bill would split the party.[32] Mitterrand supported Mauroy until the private school demonstrations of June 24, 1984, persuaded him that the political costs were too great.

Savary was not without supporters among Socialist deputies. One of these was Didier Chouat, who had no desire to antagonize the more than a third of his constituents who sent their children to private schools.[33] Chouat attributes the crisis partly to Socialist leaders who themselves understood that majority opinion was favorable to public funding of private schools, but who continued to use the traditional mobilizing slogan of *laïcisme,* failing thereby to educate party militants. Reeducation would not have been easy, however, given the strength of traditional anticlerical beliefs and the supporting self-interest of the public school-teachers' unions. It took the massive demonstrations of June 24 to show the depth of public support for private schools.

The initial effect of the Laignel amendments was to discredit Catholic negotiators, to polarize opinion, and to throw the private-school lobby into the welcoming arms of the conservative parties. The mood of polarization was short-lived. Militant secularists could not escape the fact that subsidized private education had broad public support. They suffered a debilitating setback when Mitterrand withdrew the Savary Bill. Savary's successor, Jean-Pierre Chevènement, who was instructed by Mitterrand to "restore peace," proceeded to draft legislation that incorporated some of the less controversial financial provisions of the Savary Bill and harmonized educational funding with recent legislation on governmental decentralization.[34] A SOFRES poll in early September found that forty-seven percent of respondents in a national sample approved of Chevènement's proposal, while only seventeen percent were opposed.[35] By the time of the legislative elections of March 1986, the private school question had ceased to be an important issue.[36] In effect, the moderate Left had accepted state subsidies for private schools.

François Mitterrand's abandonment of the goal of a "unified and secular" educational system represents, not a victory of the Right in the traditional French struggle between political families, but rather a new acceptance of educational pluralism. Subsidized private education prevailed because a strong majority of French people—including a majority of those who voted for Mitterrand in 1981—approved of it. Because Catholic schools in 1984–85 enrolled ninety-five percent of all pupils in subsidized private schools, support for state subsidies is essentially support for Catholic education, and this in a period when the percentage of French adults attending mass regularly had dropped from twenty-five percent in 1965 to less than fifteen percent in 1984.[37] This apparent paradox is easily resolved. Evidence from attitude surveys demonstrates that support for subsidized private schools is not based primarily on religion. In a survey conducted in November

1984, only fifteen percent of parents of children attending Catholic schools cited religious education as one of the reasons for choosing a private school.[38] Reasons more frequently offered were the greater attention children receive (sixty-eight percent) and the quality of teachers (forty-eight percent). Religious education presumably was even less important as a reason why thirty-five percent of Socialist Party supporters declared themselves in October 1983 to be ready to sign a petition in favor of private education, or why, among those parents with children in *public* schools, sixty-four percent of those offering an opinion in June 1984 disapproved of the amended version of the Savary Bill passed by the National Assembly.[39]

Catholic schools, like the families that support them, also are becoming more secular. Bishop Jean Honoré described the transformation of Catholic education in the 1960s and 1970s as "the passage from clerical school to a lay school."[40] In 1959 the clergy still provided almost forty percent of Catholic school teachers and the overwhelming majority of school directors.[41] By 1985–86, lay teachers made up ninety-five percent of the teaching corps in Catholic elementary schools and ninety-six percent in secondary schools.[42] Laymen served as directors of eighty percent of Catholic elementary schools and seventy percent of secondary schools. The secularization trend was supported by the Debré Law, which provides that schools under contract must agree to admit pupils without regard to religious preference. Catechism continues to be a mandatory subject for most Catholic school pupils until the last three or four years of secondary school. It is taught predominantly by lay teachers to pupils who were not sent there for religious instruction. Indeed, devout Catholics both within the schools and without often complain that the restrictions of the Debré Law, coupled with competitive pressures to attract pupils and meet parental expectations, have deprived Catholic education of much of its *raison d'être*.[43]

The basis of mass support for private schools seems to rest less on religion than on a combination of idealism and self-interest. A SOFRES poll of March 1983 asked a national sample how serious it would be if "the free choice of the school where children are placed" were eliminated. Seventy-seven percent replied "very serious" and another sixteen percent replied "rather serious."[44] The option of private education is broadly perceived to be a fundamental right. Moreover, subsidized private education represents an inexpensive alternative for parents who become dissatisfied with the public schools. In a period of rapid growth in school population, the proportion of children in private schools declined slightly from 18.3 percent in 1958–59 (before the Debré Law introduced large subsidies) to 16.7 percent in 1982–83.[45] Yet approximately one-third of all French children pass through a private school at some time in their educational careers.[46] Beyond this set of parents are others who know that if the public school in their district is weak, or if it decides that their child must repeat a grade, abandon the university-preparatory course, or accept a less prestigious track toward the *baccalauréat,* their only recourse may be a private school.

It is not surprising that bourgeois families make more use of the private-school alternative than do working-class families, particularly at the secondary level in urban areas.[47] Nonetheless, in 1978–79 thirty-two percent of pupils in private elementary schools were children of manual workers, demonstrating that subsidized private education is a realistic alternative for a broad spectrum of French society.[48]

The potential private-school lobby is much broader than the current membership of the Catholic parents associations. Indeed, the *question scolaire* is no longer viewed by the public as exclusively or even predominantly an issue of religious versus secular education. As a reporter from *Le Monde* put it after the June 24, 1984, demonstrations, "The defenders of 'the public school, the school of the Republic' were stupified to discover that consumerism had invaded education."[49] The Jacobin educational fortress had been breached; its mission as protector of the Republic now appeared archaic.

The Second Assault: Decentralization

Discontent with the Jacobin model is in part the consequence of a dramatic postwar transition from elite to mass education at the secondary and higher levels. In 1950 the majority of French children entered the workforce at the legal school-leaving age of fourteen, and only 6 percent entered some form of higher education. By 1987 well over 90 percent of all fifteen-year-olds were still in school, 40 percent of the age group reached the level of the baccalauréat, 33 percent passed that examination, and well over a quarter went on to higher education.[50] Enrollments in institutions of higher education soared from less than 200,000 in 1950–51 to over a million by 1975–76.

The rigorous academic selection that traditionally eliminated most children from the university preparatory track at age eleven or twelve was tempered by the gradual introduction of a heterogeneous middle school offering a common-core curriculum. The new *collège* emerged with the creation of the Collèges d'Enseignement Secondaire (CES) in 1963 and culminated in the implementation of the Haby reforms of 1975, which prohibited ability grouping. The *école unique*, an old ideal of the Left, was imposed by governments of the Right against strong opposition from the political parties and teachers unions of the Left. Although the Haby Law was only partially implemented, it had sufficient effect to alarm middle-class parents and to upset teachers unaccustomed to mixed-ability classes.

In France as elsewhere in the Western world, the rapid increase in the number of degree holders has devalued degrees and set off a scramble for the most selective programs, particularly the math-oriented *Bac C,* the *classes préparatoires,* and the *grandes écoles*. This is a scramble that leaves most working-class children out of reach of elite careers. As Fritz Ringer has shown, an "inclusive" education system need not be "progressive" in the sense of promoting upward social mobility.[51] Mass education in France and elsewhere has failed to eliminate the powerful class bias of educational selection.[52] It has produced escalation of the degree requirements for many jobs, as well as a middle-class backlash against a presumed decline of educational standards. Criticism of education became virtually a national pastime in the 1980s. Among the critics, both on the Left and on the Right, are those who argue that it is the Jacobin model that inhibits the flexibility and local initiative necessary to make mass education work.

Elementary and Secondary Education

While Gaston Defferre in the Ministry of Interior was drafting legislation that would loosen central government controls over local and regional government, Alain Savary in the Ministry of National Education was devising ways to encourage local authorities and individual schools to accept more responsibility and take greater initiative. In this respect Savary acted within the 1978 Socialist Party plan for education, which enumerated as one of its general principles, "Expand the role of territorial governments, a step toward self-management socialism."[53] A few months after his resignation in 1984, Savary explained in an interview what he had sought to accomplish:

> An important part of my message . . . was to make a larger place than in the past for initiatives from teachers, schools, and, more generally, from society rather than from the state in the field of education. In a very hierarchical system, as National Education still is, I wished that at each level people would take more responsibility and stop waiting simply for national directives for solutions to problems which obviously can no longer be dealt with in this manner.[54]

Savary was encouraged in this direction by several of his advisors, who had roots in the self-management wing of the Socialist Party. How can one explain that Party's dual commitment to the centralization of Catholic education under state control and to the decentralization of public education? To some degree, it was a question of different currents within the Socialist Party, with the hard-line secularists generally more Jacobin than the self-management wing. The original core of the self-management school was the French Democratic Confederation of Labor (Confédération Française Démocratique du Travail, CFDT), formerly the French Confederation of *Christian* Workers. And yet most Socialist deputies probably should have seen little tension between a policy that sought to eliminate public subsidies to religious schools and another that encouraged local initiative within a secular public school system.

Savary was able to build upon local initiative programs developed by his conservative predecessors, particularly the "ten-percent *pédagogiques*" program of Joseph Fontanet in 1973, which left ten percent of the school day to be used at the discretion of each school, and the Projets d'Activités Educatives (PACTE) created by Christian Beullac in 1977–79. The new Socialist minister developed the Projets d'Action Educative (PAE), which offered state subsidies to local schools to develop programs designed to link the school with the life of the community and to adapt education to the particular needs of pupils. A distinctly new program designated Education Priority Zones (ZEPS) in areas with high dropout rates and offered subsidies to local governments and schools in these zones to develop plans for improving the performance of weak students, organizing parental support, and linking the schools with the community.

Savary sought to institutionalize cooperation among teachers, administrators, parents, and local government officials, in the hope that "opening the school to life" would help force it out of a traditional, over-intellectualized style of instruction, which he perceived to be unsuited to mass education. Yet the minister was aware that a simple shift of control over schools from the national to local governments might result in less rather than more school autonomy. He sought to inspire local initiative and cooperation by expanding the individual School Councils to include parents and local government officials, but left the presidency of these councils in the hands of the school principal.

Savary's successor, Jean-Pierre Chevènement, implemented the school council reform, yet he represented a more Jacobin strand of the Socialist tradition. While Savary had hoped to energize and modernize French education through local initiative, Chevènement favored reform from above. Savary sought consensus through continual consultation with relevant groups; Chevènement mobilized public opinion with a stream of ambitious and eminently quotable pronouncements (e.g., "the republican elite," and "eighty percent of the age group to the level of the *bac* by the year 2000"). There was a "back to basics" motif in Chevènement's policy that was not very compatible with local curricular experimentation. Chevènement perceived French education as *"une grosse machine"* that "must be commanded"; the minister's job was to mobilize public opinion in order to "get the system moving."[55] He had little confidence in reform from below.

Even while Chevènement remained minister, decentralization reemerged as a central theme in a report, commissioned by President Mitterrand in 1985, of the Collège de France. Among the report's recommendations were the following:

> Unity in and through pluralism. Education should go beyond the opposition between liberalism and statism by creating the conditions of true emulation among diversified and autonomous institutions, while protecting the most disadvantaged individuals and institutions from the scholastic segregation which could result from uncontrolled competition.[56]

Decentralization continued to find supporters on the Right as well as on the Left, as evidenced by the program of René Monory, minister of education in the

Chirac government, which was installed after the conservative victory in the legislative elections of March 1986. Portions of the Monory Plan, presented in early 1988, have a distinctly Savaresque flavor:

> The management of national education obviously is an example of management of complex systems. Just as diversity is the only answer to heterogeneity, so creativity is the only answer to complexity. But diversity and creativity cannot be managed from the center; they manage themselves from the periphery.[57]

Monory, like Savary, emphasized the autonomy of individual schools more than local government control. In the Monory Plan, however, it was the school principal more than the School Council that emerged as the key actor. Monory's successor after the 1988 elections, former Socialist Party chairman Lionel Jospin, returned to Savary's emphasis on school councils.

Over the past two decades a number of education ministers have called attention to the lack of local initiative in French education and have proposed some form of decentralization as a remedy. There have been some successes. In 1983 the Ministry called on middle schools—the *collèges*—to increase the proportion of children going on for a full secondary education by adapting teaching methods to suit heterogeneous classes. By 1987 the general inspector's office was reporting that the process of "renovation," based partially on plans devised by local teachers, was succeeding in almost half of all *collèges*.[58] Decentralization of local government also has strengthened the role of municipal, departmental, and regional officials in such educational matters as the maintenance of school buildings and the selection of the location for new schools.

Despite these successes, policy-makers are aware that the obstacles to decentralization are formidable. Teachers and their unions have typically reacted with indignation and alarm to proposals for devolution of authority. Any attempt to increase school autonomy by strengthening the authority of principals, or by including parents and local officials in policy-making councils, draws heated protest from the Fédération de l'Education Nationale (FEN) on the grounds that teachers will be exposed to arbitrary authority and subjected to excessive demands. In its abhorrence of personal authority and its preference for detailed national standards and identical treatment for each of the many classifications of teachers, the FEN is one of the best remaining examples of Michel Crozier's model of the bureaucratic society. Security in a highly impersonal and centralized system means doing exactly what the regulations require, but no more.

In a report submitted to René Monory in December 1987, the economist Jacques Lesourne noted the relevance of Crozier's model:

> This blind and anonymous administration has, over time, produced individual and collective reactions among teachers which have, in turn, reinforced the bureaucratization of the whole. In the absence of a national administration with

a human face, the teachers, faced with their hierarchy, have ceased to perceive themselves as persons and, in order to protect themselves from arbitrary actions, have sought refuge in regulations. Thus a culture has developed within national education which rests on the dual principle of absolute equality between positions for a given category and egalitarian treatment of personnel between these positions.[59]

Crozier's original argument in *The Bureaucratic Phenomenon* was essentially cultural in nature, based on the assumption of French distaste for face-to-face authority relations. Lesourne's assessment begins with centralized bureaucracies and views Crozierian behavior as a rational response to life within such a structure. Organizational structure and behavior are obviously interdependent. The increasing rarity in France of bureaucratic systems like those in education (a trend Crozier himself recognizes) suggests that centralized structure in that field breeds its own reinforcing attitudes and behavior.

Alain Savary, reflecting on his four years on the *rue de Grenelle,* offers this perceptive comment:

I think that one of the most difficult things to understand for many union organizations is the insistence with which I asked schools to draw up plans within the framework of greater autonomy. The reason is understandable: more responsible schools would impose an important transformation on the unions, for their power hierarchy reproduces state centralization very exactly.[60]

Like interest groups throughout the democratic world, the FEN concentrates its power at the point where policies are made. Not surprisingly, it struggles to prevent the displacement of policy-making to arenas where it is weak.

The FEN's opposition to decentralization is based not only on self-interest but also on belief. The FEN views itself as one of the principal guardians of *laïcité,* the guiding principle of the centralized educational structure created in the 1870s and 1880s to serve the Republic. Less than a year after the withdrawal of the Savary Bill on private schools, Antoine Prost, a noted authority on French education, author of a report to Alain Savary on the *lycées,* and a former member of the Commission Pédagogique of the Syndicat Général de l'Education Nationale (a CFDT affiliate), explained contemporary *laïcité* to an interviewer in these terms:

That which characterizes militant secularists today, in my opinion, is their attachment to centralism, their refusal to recognize a "particular character" of public schools. This is a historical, not a logical refusal, for one can very well conceive of instruction which is both secular and decentralized. But this refusal is a willing blindness, an ostrich-like policy.[61]

René Monory no doubt would agree with Savary's trusted advisor. For both Savary and Monory, the trick was to put in place, against strong opposition, a more decentralized educational system, in hopes that in a new institutional setting teachers would exercise more initiative and accept more responsibility. Savary hoped to do so by persuasion and negotiation. Monory, in the spring of 1988, was more prepared to impose reform on a defiant FEN. A year later, in March 1989, Lionel Jospin experienced the intensity of the anxiety of teachers over change when his proposals to "renovate" the curriculum and to base pay increases upon "merit" drew tens of thousands of angry teachers onto the streets of Paris. Although in the long term the pressure for decentralization may prevail, any education minister must bear in mind that the FEN has "had the skin" of at least one of his or her predecessors.[62]

Higher Education

The tensions produced by rapid expansion were greater in the universities than in secondary schools. As it was judged politically unfeasible to impose entrance requirements other than the *baccalauréat,* the government could do no more than to build to accommodate the influx. Metropolitan universities grew into gigantic, impersonal institutions in which student contacts were largely with a rapidly expanding corps of teaching assistants, who by the late 1960s were themselves anxious about career prospects and alienated from the senior faculty. It was out of this anomic university environment of swollen enrollments, devalued diplomas, bureaucratized relationships, and uncertain career prospects that the student movement emerged in the spring of 1968. The initiative came not from the prestigious *grandes écoles,* nor from the professionally oriented faculties like law, but from the faculties of humanities and social science, where students had particular reason to fear that their career aspirations would not be fulfilled.

The cooling of the May events and the subsequent Gaullist victory in the June 1968 legislative elections set the stage for one of the most dramatic reforms of French educational history. Education Minister Edgar Faure quickly drafted a *Loi d'Orientation* for higher education that broke the enormous urban universities into more manageable units and established as their guide the triple objectives of autonomy, participation, and multidisciplinarity. The solution to the anomie of an overcentralized, overbureaucratized system was to be the human-scale university governed by elected representatives of students, faculty, staff, and local governments and associations. Within national guidelines, the new universities were delegated the authority to write their own bylaws, determine instructional methods, and spend their budgets as they chose with only post hoc accountability.

The Faure Law was a striking political success. It passed through both chambers of Parliament without a negative vote, then became the basis for a gradual restoration of order in French higher education. It was less successful in achieving its announced objectives. At least three major obstacles emerged to hamper the development of autonomous, participant universities. First, the national government remained the only significant source of funding. Individual universities could propose new programs, but had to appeal to Paris for additional funding to support them. Second, student and faculty elections under a prescribed list system exacerbated a process of politicization already underway. As the more utopian veterans of '68 lost interest, and as student turnout in university elections plummeted from an initial fifty-two percent to under fifteen percent, universities in which the humanities and social sciences predominated tended to fall under the control of Communist unions. More professionally oriented universities and senior faculty in most disciplines often veered to the Right with the coming of new conservative unions.[63] For the next decade, relations between Paris and the universities—even many of those led by moderates—took on the character of a cold war. By the late 1970s, Giscard's secretary of state for the universities, Alice Saunier-Séïté, was deploying the full artillery of central controls in order to curb unwanted university autonomy. The last of the major obstacles facing the Faure reform was the tendency of faculty and students to cling tightly to rights and privileges that depend upon the maintenance of centralized authority. Government proposals to allow individual universities the right to select their own students have helped to provoke student strikes and demonstrations from 1968 through 1986.

Any entrance requirement beyond the *bac* is still perceived as an infringement on sacred rights, even though unacknowledged selection exists in many universities and formal selection has long been accepted in medicine, pharmacy, the Instituts Universitaires de Technologie (IUT), and, most strikingly, in the *grandes écoles,* which were exempted from the Faure reforms. Similar objections are raised to the proposal that diplomas should be issued by individual universities, or at least carry the name of the university the student attended. These objections are rooted in a Jacobin myth that holds that all universities, and hence all diplomas, must be considered equal. To allow open competition would undermine the value of certain diplomas and threaten the equal rights and privileges of university faculty as national civil servants. The Syndicat National de l'Enseignement Supérieur (SNE Sup) has been an impassioned defender of this centralist perspective, even when its Communist-oriented leadership was locked in battle with Saunier-Séïté. In higher education, as at lower levels, one sees the Crozierian logic at work.

The Faure Law succeeded in challenging the "mandarins" at the professional rank, but at the cost of intensifying political conflict and corporatist defense of vested interests. Michel Alliot, principal assistant to Edgar Faure in drafting the 1968 law and later president of the University of Paris VII, eventually concluded that "democracy is incompatible with innovation."[64] Confronted with student strikes and resistant university councils, Madame Saunier-Séïté seemingly agreed that the maintenance of high standards and the necessary adaptation of the universities to the needs of the marketplace could only be achieved through central controls. Her critics in the unions of the Left retorted that *Madame la Secrétaire d'Etat* was herself responsible for the failure of autonomy through her imposition of restrictive conditions for the award of national diplomas and her support of the Sauvage Law of 1980, which required universities to allocate half of all council seats to full professors.

French higher education is no exception to the general rule that preferences as to the distribution of power among institutions are closely linked to assessments of which group will have control and with what policy consequences. On both the Left and the Right, enthusiasm for decentralization depends partly on whose ox is being gored.

The SNE-Sup and the Syndicat Général d'Education Nationale (SGEN) had their revenge in the Savary Law, which was passed in late 1983. That law invokes the Faurian formula of autonomy, participation, and multidisciplinarity, then proceeds, among other provisions, to specify that each university shall elect three councils, and that full professors shall hold not less than 20 percent and not more than 22.5 percent of the seats on the administrative council. The egalitarian thrust of the reform is evident in the increase in student representation and in the provision (later struck down by the Constitutional Council) that professors should be selected for council seats by a single faculty electoral college in which junior faculty would usually predominate.

The Savary Law specifically prohibited selection on the basis of academic record or examination for admission into the first cycle of university studies. Nonetheless it raised the explosive issue of selection and provoked large student demonstrations by permitting universities to choose among candidates for the *second* cycle on the basis of academic record and competitive examinations. Savary attempted to pacify the protesters by promising that in most fields all students completing the first cycle would be eligible to continue. The National Assembly further responded to student fears with an amendment requiring that restricted entry fields be designated in advance by decree.

The restructuring of elected councils provided for in the Savary Law had been fully implemented by only fifteen of seventy-five universities when the conservative parties returned to power in March 1986.[65] Now the conservative faculty unions were poised for revenge. Less than a month after the election, Jean Foyer entered a bill in the National Assembly to replace the Savary Law. The Foyer Bill had been drafted by the Groupe pour la Renovation de l'Université Française (GERUF), in which two faculty unions were well represented: the Union Nationale Interuniversitaire (UNI) and the Fédération des Syndicats Autonomes de l'Enseignement Supérieur et de la Recherche. The new *ministre délégué* for higher education and research, Alain Devaquet, would have preferred simply to amend the Savary Law, but the winds of the new liberalism were rising rapidly in post-socialist France. The powerful partisan sentiments mobilized by Jean Foyer and his strategically placed friends persuaded Devaquet to accept abrogation of the Savary Law, but on his own terms.[66]

Devaquet soon discovered that autonomy had multiple meanings:

> Autonomy therefore! Autonomy . . . that noble word, repeated in emulation of others, endlessly harped on, masks all of the difficulties, all that one cannot, or will not, resolve. For some it represents a real concern for adaptation to the needs of society, but others see in it the legitimation of a spirit of competition manifestly designed to clear the way for the emergence of an elite.[67]

The *ministre délégué* accepted the need for increased autonomy in order to introduce greater flexibility into a complex system. He opposed both *triage* by competition and the exemption of universities from public evaluation and guidance, "as if the university were the property of academics, indeed of some among them."[68]

As presented to the National Assembly in November 1986, the Devaquet Bill essentially returned university councils (now two) to the composition provided in the Faure Law of 1968. It proposed modest increments of university autonomy with respect to tuition charges, instructional programs, and legal status. Its major innovation was to authorize each institution of higher education to select its entering students, with the stipulation that all candidates not selected would be placed by the rector in institutions with unfilled positions.

In protest against what it perceived to be the Americanization of French universities, the FEN organized 100,000 demonstrators in Paris on November 23, 1986. More important, the spectre of selection was again sufficient to mobilize hundreds of thousands of Parisian students and *lycéens* in defense of their perceived rights. The UNEF-ID, one of the two student unions that emerged from the split of the Union Nationale des Etudiants de France, organized meetings and brief strikes in October. In late November a student coordinating committee was formed and student strikes spread to fifty universities. The mobilization culminated in a demonstration of some 400,000 people on December 4, followed by violent encounters between demonstrators and police on the nights of December 4, 5, and 6, in the course of which a demonstrator was killed. On December 8, Jacques Chirac announced the withdrawal of the Devaquet Bill. Again as in 1968, 1983, and 1984, street politics forced the government to alter or abandon plans for educational reform. On all but one of these occasions, fear of tighter controls on university admission was an important motive for mobilization.

In higher education as at lower levels there have been some successful efforts at decentralization. When in 1976 the government proposed that universities consult with local industries in the preparation of new, more professionally oriented programs, the immediate result was a massive student strike that closed many universities for several months. In the long term, most universities responded to the financial incentives offered by the Ministry by proposing degree programs related to perceived economic needs. The introduction of dozens of new masters programs was an indication of a new capacity for local innovation. One of the most notable successes in local innovation has been at the University of Pau, where university officials have succeeded in expanding far more rapidly than central funding would have allowed by soliciting contributions from local government and industry for research, continuing education, and the development of new degree programs.[69] With the approval of the Ministry, university officials managed to construct new buildings by working out a financial package consisting of twenty-five percent funding from the central government and twenty-five percent each from governments at the regional, departmental, and municipal levels. An industrial park is being constructed next to the campus to facilitate cooperation between the university and local industry. Pau is an extreme case, but hardly unique. The development of university programs is no longer exclusively under the control of the Ministry of National Education. One indirect indicator of the growing interest of the private sector in higher education is the increase of privately funded hours of continuing education within universities from 7 million in 1980 to 14.7 million in 1987.[70]

In his first months as minister of education in 1988, Lionel Jospin took an important step toward decentralization by instituting four-year contracts between the Ministry and individual universities. Within the framework of established national objectives, universities will submit development plans and then be held accountable for the success in achieving them. There are two major limitations to this strategy. First, many universities (especially those characterized by "assembly regime" governance) are poorly equipped to plan and negotiate.[71] More important, without the authority to issue their own diplomas—or even to put the name of the issuing university on national diplomas—and without control over the selection of their students, universities are severely limited in their ability to establish their own identities. National diplomas and equal access of all *bacheliers* to the universities remain sacred tenets of the Jacobin creed.

Conclusion

The successful assault of Catholic schools upon educational Jacobinism is explicable in Jacobin terms. It is the traditional Jacobin belief that a besieged Republic must defend itself and the public interest by preventing its enemies from establishing local strongholds. In the 1880s, with the Catholic Church challenging the legitimacy of republican institutions, that perspective was not realistic. A century later the Republic was firmly entrenched, Catholics had rallied to its support, and the mass public in an increasingly secular and consensual society was losing interest in the rhetorical battle between defenders of "republican values" and protagonists of "free schools."

Strength of affiliation with the Church still remains a strong predictor of voters' preferences for the Left or the Right and yet the evidence does not support the view that June 1984 represents a revival of France's wars of religion. Practicing Catholics, however devoted to the defense of private-school subsidies, represent a declining minority. Critical to their success was the support they received from friends of private education whose motives had more to do with a sense of fairness and the interests of educational consumers than with religion. Support for subsidized private education extends beyond upper-income groups, even though it is the bourgeoisie that takes most advantage of private schools in urban areas. At the level of mass opinion, Michel Debré's hope of 1959 has been largely realized: the binary educational system is approved by well over two-thirds of the population.

The intensity of the battle over subsidized schools was a result of the polarization of party militants and interested groups. It was the strategic position of the secularist lobby within the Socialist Party that allowed it to upset Savary's delicate compromise. The FEN and the CNAL could count on the support of the Socialist parliamentary group to toughen the Savary Bill, thereby arousing those many Catholic conservatives who believed that negotiators for Catholic education had already betrayed their trust. The failure of the secularists "lifted the mortgage," in the terminology of the Fourth Republic, by demonstrating that a choice preferred by one group is unacceptable to the majority, leaving the government free to seek a solution with broader support.

Since 1984 France has come nearer to mutual accommodation on the church school issue than ever before in its republican history. Catholic schools are increasingly secular and are drawn by competition to respond to parental expectations. Under the leadership of Savary and Monory, the French Ministry of National Education has gradually allowed local public schools more autonomy and, through *désectorisation,* is giving parents greater choice among public as well as private schools. Strong secularists now admit that, if private schools increase inequality, they also have much to teach the public schools with respect to innovative methods and individual attention to pupils.[72] In sum, the Jacobin argument against private education, while still alive among committed secularists, is no longer persuasive to the general public, even to that portion that elected François Mitterrand in 1981.

The success of the private-school lobby is attributable in part to its ability to mobilize political support outside the structure of state education, thereby preventing the educational Jacobins from absorbing the subsidized private sector. The second assault, that of the decentralizers, confronts the more difficult task of changing the existing structure of public education. The decentralizers must overcome resistance from the whole network of interest and attitudes tied to the Jacobin structure. The FEN has repeatedly failed to block state subsidies to private schools; it has a stronger record in slowing or subverting unwanted reforms within public education.[73] Decentralizers have had little success in mobilizing the external political support necessary to overcome resistance to change. It is the "Jacobins" who have mobilized mass demonstrations in defense of the uniform rights of faculty and *bacheliers.*

Despite the inertia of *"la grosse machine,"* it would be inaccurate to describe French education in Crozierian terms as "blocked" when it has expanded dramatically to meet demand and has increased educational opportunity through the development of the new *collège,* which delays definitive academic segregation. Central government incentives have encouraged individual universities to exercise more initiative in developing degree programs, while the enhancement of the powers of local and regional governments generally has increased cooperation between educational institutions and local officials. Nonetheless there are policy areas in which the structures and ideology of centralization combine to obstruct change. University admissions policy clearly is one of these. Indeed, most proposals for decentralization of authority arouse strong opposition from officials and teachers—particularly the FEN—whose rights and privileges might be threatened.

Alain Devaquet is quite correct in noting that decentralization comes in many styles. One version is rooted in the tradition of socialist self-management, which views decentralization as a purer form of democracy. The SGEN, the CFDT affiliate, has been particularly sympathetic to educational *autogestion.* In contrast, the UNI conceives of decentralization rather as a device for allowing competition to establish an appropriate hierarchy of excellence among institutions of higher education. Yet another view, expressed by Alain Devaquet and René Monory, sees decentralization primarily as a means for improving the efficiency and responsiveness of education. This version of decentralization—or "deconcentration," as it might be called—may involve no more than delegating some additional authority to school principals who are chosen by and responsible to the Ministry of National Education. All of these versions challenge the Jacobin tradition, but to different degrees, with the Americanization of higher education representing the most serious affront.

The major candidates in the presidential election of 1988 found little to disagree about in the field of education. Decentralization, variously understood, now is widely offered as a solution to many of the failings of French education.[74] Can we conclude that the FEN is the villain and the decentralizers are on the side of efficiency, modernity, and good sense? The case for greater autonomy is strongest with respect to universities, where enhanced local control over admissions might in fact have the effect of democratizing the recruitment of elites in French society by pushing forth universities capable of challenging the near monopoly of the *grandes écoles.* It is difficult to imagine how France could in fact adopt the American model of higher education when no important alternatives to state funding are available.

In elementary and secondary education, the clearest examples of decentralized educational systems are found in the United States and the United Kingdom. It is by no means clear that these countries have found better solutions than France to the stresses of mass education, nor is it obvious that the French would prefer schools to be controlled by local governments that might be Socialist, Communist, Gaullist, or National Front depending on the area.

Education in contemporary France is an anomaly. In many respects, France today is more consensual then ever before in its republican history. Despite the flurry of support for the National Front, politics has become more centrist and less conflictual under the peaceful and largely prosperous conditions of the past quarter-century. The institutions of the Fifth Republic are popular and secure, having survived the alternation of parties in government. After a disappointing experiment with Socialism in 1981–83 and an aborted experiment with laissez-faire liberalism in 1986, the return to power of the Socialists in June 1988 aroused neither great enthusiasm on the Left nor great anxiety on the Right. Apart from the National Front and the rump Communist Party, the level of ideological conflict has declined significantly in recent decades. And yet education continues to produce impassioned debate and angry street demonstrations. The events of May 1968, which shook the Fifth Republic, began in the universities. The universities were in turmoil again in the spring of 1976, in protest against government plans for the development of new, professionally oriented degree programs. In June 1984 the massive "free school" demonstration in Paris led to the withdrawal of the Savary Bill, then to the resignation of both the minister of education and the prime minister. Again in the fall and winter of 1986, massive demonstrations against the Devaquet Bill for university decentralization led to the withdrawal of that reform and contributed to the cooling of Chirac's liberal crusade. The march of angry teachers in the streets of Paris in March 1989, this time against the Jospin reforms, demonstrated that the consensus on education that characterized the 1988 presidential campaign did not extend to teachers and students.

How can the political volatility of French education be explained? The strains of the democratization of education and the bureaucratization of mass education are problems confronted by most industrialized democracies. Why have they produced higher levels of conflict in France than elsewhere? Although a full exploration of this complex question is beyond the scope of this paper, some elements of an answer suggest themselves from the preceding case studies. The key, I would suggest, is to be found in the interaction of three factors: governmental structure, teachers and student unions, and ideas. It was the Jacobin belief that centralized government is necessary in order to root out privilege and hence to defend the equal rights of all citizens. In education, centralized administration naturally led to the emergence of Jacobin unions, centralized in mirror image of the official structure that they hoped to influence and dedicated to the defense of equal rights for their members. The centralization of decision making in education had the effect of focusing on Paris all efforts to influence policy. Educational politics inevitably were national politics. Issues that might have been settled at the local level in the United States, or at the state (*Land*) level in Germany, became national political issues in France. Unions (particularly the FEN) in turn strove to keep alive a set of Jacobin attitudes that inhibited decentralization, or indeed any changes that threatened union power or challenged the established rights of teachers.

Although unions are weaker among students than among teachers, they have profited from student attitudes that frequently support a Jacobin educational structure. Repeated student demonstrations against selection at the entry level demonstrate the power of the idea that holders of the *baccalauréat* have an inviolable right to enter the university of their choice and, if they succeed, to receive a national diploma that carries identical status, whatever the university in which studies have been conducted. The militancy of students in defense of their perceived rights is linked, no doubt, to status anxiety. Even more than in most industrialized countries, in France higher education is the once-in-a-lifetime gateway to elite careers. Those students who are excluded from the "royal road" through the highly selective *grandes écoles* fear that autonomous universities, each in control of its own admissions, might close off their only remaining opportunity for a prestigious career. Among students already enrolled in higher education, the fields of study that provide the most demonstrators normally are those in which career prospects are uncertain, that is to say the humanities and the social sciences rather than engineering or business administration. (The hostility of medical students to the Savary Law in 1983 is also explicable partially in terms of status anxiety, as a growing surplus of doctors made students particularly sensitive to any attempt to impose new barriers to the profession and to lucrative specialization within it). Jacobin structure and attitudes, along with status anxiety, are necessary but not sufficient, explanations for the militancy of French students. One has only to read accounts of recent Paris demonstrations in which students have built barricades and done battle with the police to realize that the French revolutionary tradition is not dead.

In sum, a centralized educational administration fosters centralized unions and creates a network of rights and expectations that reinforce Jacobin structures. Add to this picture a revolutionary tradition and the status anxiety of teachers, whose prestige has declined significantly in the era of mass education, and of liberal arts students, who realize that the diplomas they seek have been devalued in the marketplace, and one has some understanding of the volatility of French educational politics.

What would be necessary in order to overcome passionate resistance to change in the educational establishment? If, as Jacques Lesourne argues, the inflexible attitudes of teachers and students are the consequences more than the cause of centralization, then one might expect attitudes to evolve if somehow the structure could be decentralized. The trick, of course, is to move very far down that path—farther than the limited decentralization of recent years—without provoking violent protest. Is the corporatism of the educational profession, especially of the FEN, too strong to permit structural change, at least in primary and secondary education? Teachers certainly are "corporatist" in the French sense of defending sectoral interests, but not in the power-sharing sense in which political scientists have used that term in recent years.[75] Although teachers are more highly unionized (over fifty percent) than most other French professions, and are predominantly in one union, the FEN (eighty percent), union membership dropped by over a third from 1979 to 1989.[76] The FEN has an established right to be consulted by the Ministry of Education, yet its policy influence has been very weak on the critical private-school question and quite limited on matters of curriculum and educational structure, partly because the FEN's component secondary teachers' union, the SNES, and elementary teachers union, the SNI, are seriously divided over issues relating to the training, duties, and salaries of teachers at different levels. Only on matters of personnel management is the FEN powerful enough to impose its view, and then only within the established regulations. On important questions of curriculum and educational structure, the power of the FEN is largely negative. It is too divided to impose reforms of its own, but is capable of imposing a high political price on any government that seeks reform. As for student unions, low membership and political divisions severely limit their power, except on those occasions when they take up themes that coincide with the views—or, more often, the anxieties—of the mass of students. Unions are important, but not invincible.

The case of state subsidies to private schools suggests that one key to overcoming the FEN's resistance to change is mobilization of public opinion. A second, I would suggest, is alleviation of some of the status anxiety of teachers and students. Among recent ministers of education, Jean-Pierre Chevènement probably has been most successful at both of these tasks. He repeatedly lauded the teaching profession and sought to raise teachers' salaries while at the same time appealing to the public to support his dual efforts to raise standards and to push a greater number of children through a complete secondary education. Chevènement self-consciously mobilized public support through dramatic appeals in the media for the purpose of pressuring the teachers and their unions to accept change.[77] In contrast, Alain Devaquet was criticized by members of his own conservative majority for failing to explain clearly, either to students or to the public, how and why the government wished to decentralize the universities.[78] To be sure, Chevènement's policy objectives were compatible with the Jacobin tradition and hence much easier to sell than those of Devaquet.

In recent years, French politics has come more and more to resemble the politics of other Western democracies. French educational politics is an exception to this trend in that passion and power on the streets continue to play a vital role in policy formulation. Education is exceptional in good part because it remains one of the most Jacobin sectors of French society, both in structure and in attitudes. But Jacobinism in French education has failed to turn back the assault of the private-school lobby. Jacobinism is struggling *against* decentralization within the core educational establishment, which is defending the narrow interests of teachers, but also *for* a conception of equality that is deeply rooted in French culture and is unlikely to be eradicated.

Notes

1. John S. Ambler, "French Education and the Limits of State Autonomy," *Western Political Quarterly* 41 (September 1988).

2. Alexis de Tocqueville, *The Old Régime and the French Revolution* (New York: Doubleday Anchor, 1955).

3. Rousseau, of course, rejected representative government and proposed rule according to the "general will," normally by the majority of citizens by direct democracy within a city-state.

4. The Jesuits are a special case, since their presumed ultramontane loyalties were viewed as a threat by the Gallicans. The Jesuits were expelled in 1762 under the Bourbon monarchy. They were again forbidden from teaching in 1828, under the Restoration Monarchy, and yet again by the Third Republic in the *lois laïques* of the 1880s. Each time they were allowed to return, usually through lax enforcement of the law. See Antoine Prost, "Pluralisme et rationalisme," in *La Laïcité en Miroir,* ed. Guy Gauthier (Paris: Edilig, 1985), pp. 165 and 192–206; and Joseph N. Moody, *French Education Since Napoleon* (Syracuse, N.Y.: Syracuse University Press, 1978), pp. 5 and 95.

5. *l'Année Politique 1944–45* (Paris: 1946) pp. 156–57.

6. François Goguel, *France Under the Fourth Republic* (Ithaca, N.Y.: Cornell University Press, 1952), p. 152.

7. Duncan McRae, Jr., *Parliament, Parties and Society in France, 1946–1958* (New York and London: St. Martin's Press, 1967), pp. 115 and 132; Goguel, *France Under the Fourth Republic,* pp. 133–36; and Bernard E. Brown, "Religious Schools and Politics in France," *Midwest Journal of Political Science* 2 (May 1958).

8. Gordon Wright, *The Reshaping of French Democracy* (New York: Reynal and Hitchcock, 1948), p. 140.

9. Lapie Commission, Commission chargée de l'étude des rapports entre l'état et l'enseignement privé, *Rapport Général* (Paris: S.E.V.P.E.N., 1979), 49.

10. Joseph N. Moody, *French Education Since Napoleon,* p. 52.

11. Philip M. Williams, *Crisis and Compromise: Politics in the Fourth Republic* (Hampden, Conn.: Archon Books, 1964), pp. 365–66; Duncan McRae, Jr., *Parliaments, Parties and Society in France,* p. 32; and François Goguel, *France Under the Fourth Republic,* pp. 41 and 123–30.

12. Robert Lecourt, *Concorde sans Concordat (1952–1957)* (Paris: Hachette, 1978).

13. Bernard E. Brown, "Religious Schools and Politics in France," pp. 171–172; William Bosworth, *Catholicism and Crisis in Modern France* (Princeton, N.J.: Princeton University Press, 1962), pp. 298–309; *L'Année Politique 1951,* pp. 153–56.

14. William Bosworth, *Catholicism and Crisis,* p. 172.

15. Brown, "Religious Schools and Politics in France," pp. 173–74.

16. *Année Politique 1951,* pp. 201–24.

17. Lapie Commission, *Rapport Général,* p. 61.

18. Aline Coutrot, "La Loi scolaire de décembre 1959," *Revue française de science politique* 13 (June 1963), p. 357.

19. Coutrot, "La Loi scolaire," p. 363.

20. Article 1, in Coutrot, "La Loi scolaire," p. 380n.

21. *Journal Officiel,* National Assembly meeting of December 23, 1959, p. 3608.

22.   The formal reason offered by Boulloche was the government's decision to accept an amendment to Article 1 that placed the right of free education before the obligations of contract schools. The original and amended texts are almost identical in content, as Coutrot's juxtaposition shows, supporting her concludions that Boulloche had more fundamental reservations about the entire proposal. See Coutrot, "La Loi scolaire," pp. 379–80.

23.   Coutrot, "La Loi scolaire," p. 379.

24.   Coutrot, "La Loi scolaire," p. 384.

25.   Former Assistant Secretary General of Catholic Education, Edmond S. J. Vandermeersch, interview with author, April 29, 1986.

26.   Jean-Pierre Chevènement, *Apprendre pour Entreprendre* (Paris: Librairie Générale Française 1985), p. 183; Jean Pierre Chevènement, interview with author, May 23, 1986; and Pierre Daniel, *Question de liberté* (Paris: Desclée de Brouwer, 1986), pp. 160–61.

27.   Daniel, *Question de liberté*, p. 161; and Secrétaire-Général of UNAPEL Jean Catrice, interview with author, July 25, 1984.

28.   In a book published in 1979, Honoré insists repeatedly upon the need for the Church to adapt to a pluralistic society in the spirit of Vatican II. He writes "Le pluralisme étant une des lois de la société moderne et sa reconnaissance par l'Eglise l'une des conditions de l'annonce évangelique, l'Ecole Catholique ne peut être fidèle à sa vocation présente à la fois dans la société humaine et dans l'Eglise qu'en acceptant le pluralisme, moins comme un fait qui la contraint que comme un enjeu qui la dynamise." See Jean Honoré, *Aujourd'hui l'Ecole Catholique* (Paris: Le Centurion, 1979), p. 118. Compare this view with that expressed in a 1977 book published under the name of the Comité National de l'Enseignement Catholique, but written by the Secrétariat of Catholic Education: "Si l'expression 'pluralisme interne' peut séduire momentanément ceux qui rêvent de solutions miracles et d'apaisement qui auraient le mérite passager des formules syncrétiques et sécurisantes, elle ne semble pas pouvoir répondre dans la pratique aux exigences de l'enseignement catholique." See Comité National de l'Enseignement Catholique (CNEC), *l'Enseignement catholique face à l'avenir* (Paris: Le Centurion, 1977), p. 107.

29.   Daniel, *Question de liberté*, pp. 27–29; and Gérard Leclerc, *La Bataille de l'école* (Paris: Denoël, 1985), pp. 88–91.

30.   This phrase was used in interviews with the author by Jean Catrice, General Secretary of UNAPEL, and by Didier Chouat, Socialist deputy from Côtes du Nord. For accounts of the development and demise of the Savary Bill, see Alain Savary, *En Toute liberté* (Paris: Hachette, 1985); Daniel, *Question de liberté;* Leclerc, *La Bataille de l'école;* and John S. Ambler, "Constraints on Policy Innovation in Education: Thatcher's Britain and Mitterrand's France," *Comparative Politics* 20 (October 1987).

31.   Savary, *En Toute liberté*, p. 162.

32.   Ibid., pp. 162–65.

33.   Didier Chouat (Socialist deputy from Côtes du Nord), interviews with author, June 20, 1982, and July 25, 1984.

34.   Chevènement, interview with author, May 23, 1986.

35.   SOFRES, *l'Opinion publique, 1985* (Paris: Gallimard, 1985), p. 44.

36.   *Le Monde, Dossiers et documents: Les Elections législatives du 16 mars 1986* (Paris: Le Monde, 1986), pp. 42–64.

37.   René Rémond, "La Politique et l'Eglise," *l*Express*, May 11–17, 1984, p. 19; and SOFRES, *l'Opinion publique, 1984* (Paris: Gallimard, 1984), p. 187.

38.   SOFRES, *l'Opinion publique, 1985*, p. 309.

39. SOFRES, *l'Opinion publique, 1985*, pp. 34 and 41.

40. Honoré, *Aujourd'hui l'école catholique*, p. 36.

41. Lucie Tanguy, "L'Etat et l'école: l'Ecole privée en France," *Revue française de sociologie* 13 (1972), p. 348n.

42. *Le Monde de l'Education*, June 1987, p. 46.

43. Marie Zimmermann, *Pouvoir et liberté: clés pour une lecture des rapports église-état de Bonaparte à Mitterrand* (Strasbourg: Cerdic, 1981), pp. 74–77.

44. SOFRES, *l'Opinion publique, 1984*, p. 154.

45. Françoise Oeuvrard, "Note sur la clientèle des établissements privés: l'origine social des élèves," *Education et Formation* 6 (October 1983–June 1984). Service de l'information, de gestion, et des statistiques, Ministry of National Education, p. 22.

46. *Le Monde de l'Education*, June 1987, pp. 36–37.

47. Oeuvrard, "Note sur la clientèle"; Robert Ballion, *l'Argent et l'école* (Paris: Pernoud/Stock 1977); and Robert Ballion, *Les Consommateurs d'école* (Paris: Stock/Laurence Pernoud, 1982).

48. Oeuvrard, "Note sur la clientèle."

49. *Le Monde, Dossiers et documents*, p. 30.

50. Ministry of National Education, *Note d'Information*, vol. 11 (1988), pp. 88–11.

51. Fritz K. Ringer, *Education and Society in Modern Europe* (Bloomington, Indiana: Indiana University Press, 1979).

52. Antoine Prost, *l'Eneignement s'est-il démocratisé?* (Paris: Presses Universitaires de France, 1986).

53. Parti Socialiste, *Libérer l'école: Plan socialiste pour l'éducation nationale* (Paris: Beauchesne, 1978), p. 164.

54. Savary, *En Toute Liberté*, p. 10.

55. Chevènement, interview, 1986.

56. Collège de France, *Propositions pour l'enseignement de l'avenir*, élaborées à la demande de Monsieur le Président de la République par les Professeurs du Collège de France (Paris: Collège de France, 1985), p. 25.

57. *Le Monde de l'Education*, January 1988, p. xxxviii.

58. "Bilan du Collège," *Le Monde de l'Education*, May 1988.

59. *Le Monde de l'Education*, January 1988, p. xiv.

60. Savary, *En Toute liberté*, p. 9.

61. Prost, "Pluralisme et rationalisme," p. 105.

62. Hamon and Rotman report that the general secretary of the SNI made that claim regarding René Haby. See Hervé Hamon and Patrick Rotman, *Tant qu'il y aura des profs* (Paris: Editions du Seuil, 1984), p. 228. In an interview with the author, Haby confirmed that, according to his information, the unions had been responsible for his replacement. Christian Beullac, in another interview with the author, said that he probably would not have been reappointed had Giscard won reelection in 1981 because of union displeasure over an order from the Ministry requiring that principals keep schools open during a teachers' strike. See John S. Ambler, "Neocorporatism and the Politics of French Education," *West European Politics* 8 (July 1985); and V. Aubert et al., *La Forteresse enseignante: La Fédération de l'Education Nationale* (Paris: Fayard, 1985).

63. On the victory of Communist over utopian leadership in student unions in the 1970s, see

Gianni Statera, *Death of Utopia: The Development and Decline of Student Organizations in Europe* (New York: Oxford University Press, 1975).

64.   Michel Alliot, interview with the author, July 19, 1976.

65.   Paul Masson, rapporteur for the Commission Sénatoriale sur les Manifestations Etudiantes, *Etudiantes, Police, Presse, Pouvoir* (Paris: Hachette, 1987), p. 58.

66.   Alain Devaquet, *L'Amibe et l'étudiant. Université et Recherche: l'État d'urgence* (Paris: Editions Odile Jacob, 1988), p. 49.

67.   Ibid., p. 97.

68.   Ibid., p. 98.

69.   Erich Inciyan, "Les Universités deviennent majeures," *Le Monde de l'Education* 155 (December 1988), p. 30.

70.   Ministry of National Education, *Note d'information*, p. 89–94.

71.   Laurence Paye-Jeanneney and Jean-Jacques Payan, *Le Chantier Universitaire* (Paris: Beauchesne, 1988), p. 236.

72.   Gauthier, *Laïcité en miroir*, pp. 97–110; and Ballion, *L'Argent et l'école*, pp. 287–95.

73.   Ambler, "Neocorporatism and the Politics of French Education."

74.   Raynaud, 1988.

75.   Ambler, "Neocorporatism and the Politics of French Education."

76.   *Le Monde de l'Education*, January 1989, p. 23.

77.   Chevènement, interview, 1986.

78.   Masson, *Etudiants, Police, Presse, Pouvoir*.

9

Where Have All the Sartres Gone?
The French Intelligentsia Born Again

George Ross

The French intellectual Left has undergone a startling conversion experience. Socialism, Marxism, and other postenlightenment visions of human liberation through political struggle remained prominent in French intellectual life until very recently, far longer, in fact, than in almost any other advanced capitalist society. Yet, by the 1989 *Bicentenaire* of the French Revolution, they had completely vanished from Left political and intellectual discourses.

This essay will explore this conversion by following both the content and social underpinnings of Left intellectual thought since the early 1960s. To do so we will first trace the trajectories of three specific types of intellectuals: elite Parisian social theorists, "artisanal" political sociologists, and generational cohorts of young Left intellectuals. Then we will connect these trajectories to social and political trends. The story falls into three moments: the high Gaullist years until 1969, the years of renascent left politics of the 1970s, and the turning point of the 1980s.

I. The High Years of Gaullism:
Toward The Ideas of 1968

The Vichy period had destroyed the credibility of Right-of-Center elite intellectualization, so that after Liberation reformist and Left-leaning *Socialisant* notions dominated. The coming of the Cold War after 1947 further narrowed things around Communist ideas. Despite the crudely instrumental nature of the "intellectual" positions of the Parti Communiste Français (PCF), the party's political strength gave it considerable power.[1] This Manichaean Cold War situation came to a paroxysmic end in 1956, when the PCF's unwillingness to de-Stalinize and its support of the Soviet invasion of Hungary dramatically undercut its power to compel. In a new environment of peaceful coexistence and economic growth, official Communist thought appeared more and more inadequate to the task of accounting for a rapidly changing French society. Thus Marxism, which had briefly assumed immense importance in high Left intellectual life, fell under siege. And here our story really begins.

None other than Sartre himself took up the tasks of revisionist reconstruction to defend Marxism. Sartre, the very model of the modern intellectual titan, manipulating a huge store of intellectual capital accumulated by the success of existentialism, remained an overpowering presence.[2] But it was neither the militant existentialist nor the Cold War fellow traveler who stepped forward at this point.[3] Instead, the great man offered the existentialist Marxism of *Search for a Method* and, above all, *Critique de la raison dialectique*.[4]

With Sartre thus in the lead, one major Left intellectual vector, stretching well into the 1960s, was an attempt to revise reductionist, mechanical, and politically determined Cold War Marxism toward greater causal complexity and epistemological openness. Important journals like *Arguments* and *Socialisme ou Barbarie* were founded. Their animators—Morin, Lefort, Lefebvre, Castoriadis, etc.— shared Sartre's basic concerns, if not his existentialist predilections.[5] Despite Sartre's *patronage* and involvement, however, the quest for such an open-ended Marxism fell short. Michel Foucault's 1966 comment that the "*Critique de la raison dialectique* is the magnificent and pathetic effort of a nineteenth-century man to think through the twentieth century" was indicative of how younger intellectuals received Sartre's Marxist magnum opus.[6] Sartre's public prominence remained very significant, but more as celebrity and witness, ever eager to champion radical protests, than as a modernizer of Marxism.[7] In a similar vein, most of the "lesser" post-1956 reformulators of Marxism, like the *Arguments* group, were quick to abandon the effort altogether.

As these attempts to reconstruct a new Marxism faded, a new "great," Claude Lévi-Strauss, armed with a new vision, structuralism, climbed to the top of the elite intellectual hill. Beginning the famous "linguistic turn" by analogizing from linguistics to anthropology, Lévi-Strauss and his followers sought deep, transhistorical constants in human experience, buried structural "languages" common to all social life. Structuralism, like Marxism, thus sought to decode social relationships and expose their basic logics. In contrast to Marxism, however, the logics uncovered by structuralism were so profound that they made history disappear altogether. Perhaps more important, proponents of structuralism were quick to denounce what they considered to be the anachronistic historicism in Marxism's focus on the connections between economic dynamics and social conflict. In its purest forms, in the master's own works, structuralism thus made Marxism look relative and ephemeral.[8] The structuralist movement thus "defeated" the old mechanical Marxism of the PCF. More important, it blocked the claims of post-1956 "independent" Marxism, of which Sartre's existentialist Marxism was probably the most important variety, to institutionalize a more subtle Marxist-humanist vision of the world. Of particular interest was the appeal—which was intellectually odd, given its broadsides against historicism—of structuralism to young, "third-worldist" intellectual activists.

Marxism responded in the person of Louis Althusser, who attempted to graft much of the conceptual vocabulary of structuralism onto the body of Marxism itself. Althusser and his acolytes created a "structuralist Marxism" that, while attacking both Marxist humanism and Stalinist economism, managed to devise a "history without a subject," in the words of Pierre Grémion.[9] By burying social causality in deep structures like "mode of production," the Althusserian turn undercut perhaps Marxism's greatest practical appeal, its purported capacity to lay bare the various motors of historical development and make them accessible to rational, progressive human action. The connection between the Althusserian reformulation of Marxism and real politics became ever more tenuous, leading eventually to political and intellectual impasse.[10] Ultimately, Althusserianism proved to be yet another Parisian fad, and it was well in retreat by the mid-1970s.[11]

French thought about state-society relationships, as in other societies, was also carried on by academic specialists working within their disciplines. French political sociology, the "artisanal text" we have chosen to explore, is no exception. Thus in the 1960s there developed a number of *socialisant* sociological visions of state-society relations. Alain Touraine, but one example, worked toward a theoretical model in which class structuration and struggle were the key elements for understanding political behaviors and state actions in quite a *marxisant* way, at least in the abstract.[12] Pierre Bourdieu deployed a similar conceptual vocabulary in his earlier works on reproduction through education.[13] The important contributions of Serge Mallet, Pierre Belleville, Pierre Naville, André Gorz, Cornelius Castoriadis, and others might be added.[14]

More generally, each sociological artisan developed different specific approaches and each developed visions that were profoundly different from orthodox Marxisms, PCF or other.[15] But the basic perception of a society unequally structured into conflicting classes determining political behaviors and state action persisted.[16] Here what was interesting was the contrast between the flight of elite intellectuals into structuralism and artisanal persistence in the use of *marxisant* conceptual categories.

Looking at "generations" of young Left intellectual activists—a particularly fruitful way of thinking about intellectual politics that historians of contemporary France have developed in recent years[17]—provides yet a different map of the evolution of the Left intelligentsia during the high Gaullist years.[18] The Algerian War generation of young Left intellectuals was deeply rifted.[19] One thing did unify it, however. Student and intellectual rejection of the war was much more strident and militant than the official Left wanted to see.[20] The PCF was eager both to protect de Gaulle and to ensure prospects for a postwar alliance of the Left. It thus desired a moderate and circumspect antiwar movement, leading it to respond to the budding radicalism of student protest in ways that caused virtually all segments of the student movement to reject PCF theories and practices.[21] The complicity of French Socialism with the war itself meant that students saw nothing meritorious in the Section Française de l'Internationale Ouvriére (SFIO), either. The more *marxisant* segments of the generation thus sought different "vanguards" from the PCF along with a different, more muscular, Marxism.[22] Youth protest against the Algerian War was also an essential moment in the development of the Left Catholicism whose role would be so important in 1960s and 1970s France.[23]

The Algerian War and May '68 generations were intimately connected. May '68 had its own complex causes and logics, of course.[24] The protest movement, sparked in large part by the day-to-day ineptitude of university administrations, Gaullist ministerial staffs, and the police, had to improvise structure and organizations quickly, practically out of nowhere. The politically proven cadre of the Algerian War generation were available for such tasks. This juxtaposition explains the May movement's strange combination of extreme libertarianism, even anarchism, an Marxist sloganizing. "Imagination" was brought briefly to power, amidst some chaos, to the words of the *Internationale*. The Marxism of May, such as it was, was an anti-PCF Marxism.[25]

Changing Intellectual Structures

The social spaces of intellectuals were reconstructed in the 1960s. A massive postwar demographic upturn coincided with very high economic growth rates, changing lifestyles, and shifting occupational patterns of the onrushing postwar boom. Employment in tertiary areas, those demanding higher educational attainment in particular, increased very rapidly: the number of managers, bureaucrats, and professionals practically doubled from 7.7 percent of the labor force in 1954 to 14.8 percent in 1968, while white-collar workers grew from 10.8 percent to 14.8 percent.[26] Political changes, in particular the priority placed by the Gaullist regime after 1958 on economic modernization, also played their role.

The aftermath of Algeria thus coincided with a dramatic increase in new middle-strata occupations, in the numbers of young French people seeking higher educational credentials, and, more generally, in the population being schooled at all. The total population of students nearly doubled between 1947 and 1968 (737,000 in secondary school in 1946, three million by 1963, and nearly four million by 1968).[27] The population of university students, 150,000 in 1955, had grown to 510,000 by 1967.[28] While roughly one in twenty (4.4 percent) university students earned a *baccalauréat* in 1946, one in ten did so by 1959 (9.7 percent), and 16.2 percent by 1969.[29] In 1952 there were 263,000 teachers at all levels, 615,000 by 1967 (1,200 university teachers in 1946, 8,000 in 1959, 31,000 in 1969).[30] Between 1965 and 1975, 2,500 educational buildings were opened, one for every school day, according to Henri Weber's calculations.

Modernizing capitalist societies needed greater numbers of educated people; more "intellectual" workers in teaching, research and development, and the production of new cultural objects (books, magazines, films, television programs, advertising); more trained managers and bureaucrats; and more social service workers. France, given the unusual speed of its modernization, needed these new people rather rapidly. And in France they burst into a society that still cherished prewar outlooks. Moreover, these stratification changes in France occurred within a rather specific political "envelope." The post-1958 Gaullist regime combined technocratic commitment to economic modernization, authoritarian attitudes toward movements in "civil society," and a socially conservative coalitional base.

In the 1960s, French intellectual institutions, particularly those in education and research, expanded amidst chaotically changing rules, unpredictable expectations and careers, changing professional structures, and shifts in the organization of knowledge itself. And while these things occurred the Gaullist regime reacted to expressions of discontent as with *lèse majesté*. The young felt such changes with greater intensity because they were also living the intergenerational clash between their outlooks and those of their parents.[31] Add to this the traditional *rite de passage* of student *militantisme* and the prodigious amount of intellectual Leftism the Algerian War years had fostered, and one had a good recipe for the social troubles of May–June 1968.

The Meeting of Society and Politics

These trends may begin accounting for the general leftward shift of all kinds of intellectuals in the 1960s, but they do not explain its more precise logics. We need another level of analysis. In the first instance, intellectuals do not create political ideas either for their private pleasure or in direct response to their changing social structural positions. Political ideas are produced primarily to influence a real political world dominated by those who actually "do" politics, their organizations, and institutions.

To begin the more political analysis that we need, let us restate the context of the Algerian War years. The point of departure of our story occurred when the PCF's tenuous Cold War intellectual hegemony came to an end,[32] largely because of the ways in which the party's policies on Algeria alienated radical student and intellectual antiwar activists.[33] The Socialists, with their deep complicity in colonial warfare—one important Left Catholic has labeled SFIO politics in this period a *socialisme expéditionnaire*[34]—and their sordid domestic political record in the Fourth Republic, had little to offer either. In consequence, as of the early 1960s there existed little official Left space for the strong student and intellectual antiwar movement to occupy and influence. Thus, organized largely by the Union Nationale des Etudiants de France (UNEF), the movement went ahead on their own, despite the indifference, hostility, and active sabotage of the official Left.[35] This was the point of confluence of Left politics, Left intellectuality, and the massive social changes touching the intelligentsia and new middle strata that we have summarized. The result was a generational break between major parts of the Left intelligentsia and official Left organizations.

In this context, the structuralist turn of "high" thought plus attempts by non-PCF Marxists to regenerate a workable intellectual Marxism both were efforts to found a progressive intellectuality independent of the PCF. Sociological "artisans" at the same time were busily borrowing categories from *socialisant* political catalogues to describe the modernizing—and occupationally postindustrializing—France that official Left reflection proved unable to confront. These artisans were clearly more attuned to the evolving rhythms of French politics and society in the 1960s than were the *grands intellos,* and were trying quite hard to *influence* the evolution of French Left politics through their work at this critical juncture.[36] Among younger intellectual generations there was an even broader variety of independent Leftisms. There was considerable young activism in the Parti Socialiste Unifié (PSU), overlapping the positions of the artisans. Then, given the decolonizing, national-liberation, nation-building events of the time, there was also a wide variety of *marxisant* "third-worldisms." Here, as with the "artisans," there was an intimate connection between political ideas and political strategies, however naive and far-fetched.

The official French Left, seriously weakened by the Cold War, Algeria, and the change in Republics in 1958, was strategically lost in the early 1960s. This situation was clear to elite intellectuals, artisans, and younger generations alike, and their differentiated production of political ideas was designed to influence it. All of the intellectuals we have thus far reviewed, then, had concluded in their different ways that the official Left was both obsolete and nonresponsive to new concerns and significant social changes. The PCF seemed isolatable, and the non-Communist Left seemed ripe for major reconstruction. The major loser in the situation was a PCF that was unable to see anything in the rise of independent Left intellectualism beyond anticommunism and the agitation of petit bourgeois enemies. In fact, the PCF was really face to face with fundamental changes in France's social map, calling for major revisions in the party's ideas to appeal to burgeoning new middle strata.[37] Such misperceptions involved a self-fulfilling prophecy. By 1968 there thus existed a broad and determined network of anti-Communist Leftist intellectuals. And here our line of argument about the relationships between Left intellectuals and official Left politics rejoins our earlier discussions about the changing social setting of the intelligentsia more generally. For this divorce between the official Left and leading opinion-maker Left intellectuals was occurring in a context in which the broader intelligentsia, growing apace, was clearly engaged in an important "Left turn."

II. Between Two Mays: 1968–1981

Pure structuralism, triumphant in the 1960s, was itself superseded in the 1970s by what Luc Ferry and Alain Renaut have labeled *La Pensée 68,* postmodern and poststructuralist "antihumanism."[38] Figures like Michel Foucault, Jacques Lacan, and Jacques Derrida became the post-1968 kings of the intellectual hill. All shared a profound rebelliousness, if each in a different way. More generally, all were united by a common rejection of enlightenment thought with its historicist postulation of everprogressing rationality and understanding. Marxism was but one target here.

Foucault, a Nietzschean and perhaps the most important poststructuralist in explicitly political terms, explored the genealogies of various human meaning structures as almost serendipitous historical creations that blossomed into long-standing oppressive realities. History, for Foucault, produced underlying discourses that shaped and constrained social behavior, constituting power in the process, but in a virtually random way. "Man" was dead, or at least the "man" of the Enlightenment was—that integral subject moving bravely forward progressive step by progressive step. Enlightenment humanism, including its Victorian subsidiary, Marxism, was deemed parochial. Oppressive power, to Foucault, could not be localized in institutions, but instead resided in the discursive constructs within which such institutions operated. One did not look to *the* state to see power in action, but rather to a "micropolitics" of discursive definitions and constraints. Moreover, one could never be sure of what one saw, given that actors themselves were placed in—even constituted by—webs of discourses.

Resistance to oppressive power was essential, Foucault implied (and himself practiced in a number of different ways, including activism for prisoners' rights, the Indochinese boat people, among other issues).[39] But the historically serendipitous genealogy of discursive structures and the relativized position of actors—the subject itself constantly changed in accordance with its positioning in different discursive constructs—meant that resisters could never be sure what the appropriate object was, what they should aim to change, and whether any set of specific actions would change things for better or worse.[40]

Lacan's revisionism of Freud was analogous, as he dissolved Freud's concept of the subject and undercut Freud's projected rationalist, if tragic, trajectory of psychodynamics, although here into a much more explicitly linguistic universe. Derrida, the Heideggerian, rigorously denounced the metaphysical cores of both humanism (with Sartre the main target) and structuralism itself, proposing instead a hard-nosed deconstructionist hermeneutics in which the "subject" again disappeared.[41] One could make remarks about the nature of Lacan's and Derrida's rebelliousness analogous to those made earlier about Foucault.[42]

Taken together, all three—and we might include a number of other thinkers (Barthes, Baudrillard, Lyotard, Guattari, and the influential feminists Kristéva, Cixous, and Irigaray)[43]—clearly struck responsive chords in post-1968 debates. In the experience of many of the post-1968 generation, rebellious acts that were rooted in rationalistic, Enlightenment-derived schemas for political action, including those of the traditional Left, proceeded from a statist logic that missed the point of real domination. Changing things at state level through legislation would have but limited, perhaps perverse, effects. All of this resonated with poststructuralist thought. Protest was necessary, given the oppressiveness of reality. Yet the diachronic setting of such protest would be impenetrable and its outcome unclear.

If May 1968 and its aftermath brought the ascension of poststructuralism and postmodernism in elite intellectual circles, they had different effects on the "artisan" sociologists. For them there was no dramatic shift analogous to that from structuralism to poststructuralism.[44] To Alain Touraine and his *équipe,* for example, May 1968 "proved" that the conflict relationships characteristic of "industrial societies" were beginning to give way in France to those of "postindustrial" societies.[45] Production-based conflicts over an economistic "historicity" were being transcended by "new social movements" and struggles over the "programming" of society by new technocratic elites. Here the essential was that the form of traditional *marxisant* arguments— arguing from class to politics—was maintained in order better to argue against the usual *content* of such arguments, in particular against the more classical propositions of the official Left. The Bourdieu *boutique* likewise expanded its production on reproduction, with arguments that proceeded from class conflict to various types of behaviors, via the use of the Bourdivin conceptual toolbox of cultural capital, habitat, "field," cultural investment, etc.[46] What happened in the various realms of culture could only be understood in terms of the strategies of various classes either to maintain their superior positions or to challenge their relegation to inferiority.[47]

There was also great expansion in stratification-based *marxisant* contributions from other, less strictly academic sources. Later Eurocommunist and Euroleft reflections (like those of Nicos Poulantzas and Christine Buci-Glucksmann) were significant, for example.[48] Even *autogestionnaire* political sociology, whether associated with the PSU or with the Confédération Française Democratique du Travail (CFDT), tended to follow a neo-Marxist outline, rejecting, of course, statist correlations in the interests of decentralized class actions.[49] And as the 1970s—and the renaissance of the French Left—progressed, the effects of "official" Left intellectualization made important contributions. The elaborations of the theory of state monopoly capitalism by the PCF's Section Economique and Parti Socialiste (PS) discussions about *le Front de Classe*[50] were examples.

The political intellectuality of the "generation" of May was another story. The renaissance of *gauchisme* was but one of its manifestations. There was also a plethora of autonomous "new social movements"—feminism, regionalism, ecology, etc., not to speak of the social movement energies incorporated into the PSU and the Left Catholic trade unionism of the CFDT. A "new culture" side of much of the May generation, whatever specific trajectory one discusses—excepting, perhaps, the *gauchistes*—is also worthy of mention. The conviction that social life, including sexual life, ought to be more relaxed, or at least different from what it had been before, was shared across political divides.[51]

Changing Intellectual Structures Revisited

Structural trends modifying the situation of the intelligentsia continued throughout the 1970s. For every university student in 1960–61 there were four by 1980–81. In consequence, the numbers of teachers and researchers expanded and the percentage of new middle-strata segments of the labor force continued to grow, if at a somewhat slower pace than in the 1960s. By the early 1980s France's "postindustrialization" had been more or less completed. Aggregated, the labor-force percentages of categories like "liberal professionals and *cadres supérieurs*," "*cadres moyens*," and "*employés*" grew from 19.5 percent in 1952 to 41.4 percent in 1982. During the same period the percentage of workers remained roughly the same (33.8 percent in 1952, 35.1 percent in 1982).[52]

Amorphous though they might look—and were, in census terms—primary and secondary teachers, university professors, researchers, public-sector administrators, service workers, liberal professionals, and upper-level white-collar employees were a considerable mass with many common outlooks and practices. The process of gaining educational credentials, which allowed access to new middle-strata jobs, involved a subjection to an important process of socialization. These people learned to manipulate the various literary and mathematical symbols that made them valuable workers and also gained access to a part of French intellectual culture.[53] The larger social composition of the intelligentsia was thus changing rather dramatically. Alongside "working" intellectuals there was a congeries of groups whose work was also "intellectual" and who looked to the Parisian working intelligentsia for cultural guidance. Many, particularly those employed in the public sector, leaned to the Left in electoral terms, but often had quite practical reasons for doing so, sometimes the corporatistic outlook of a professional guild, for example—the behaviors of the Fédération de l'Education Nationale (FEN) were models here.[54] The inadequacy of public-sector structures, schools and universities in particular, fed periodic crises, constant worries about finances, and hopes for the great funding that Left electoral victory would bring. Moreover, by the later 1970s such groups had begun to feel economically insecure, along with much of the rest of the French population.[55]

Changing social settings directly touched the situations of elite intellectuals. The traditional Parisian Left intellectual had been the center of a relatively small world, few in numbers, often recruited from a narrow social base and a small circle of elite schools and reasonably well-connected with provincial "troops" with similar backgrounds and values. By the later 1960s this world had changed beyond all recognition. There were still important elite networks and cliques, to be sure. But there were also thousands of intellectuals spread over France who did not partake of them. There might still be Sartres, but the bulk of French intellectuals could not aspire to be or know one.

The existence of a vastly increased number of academic and research intellectuals also fostered more professional and "American" structures of intellectual association and peer evaluation. For individuals setting out on new careers in a progressively more fragmented world of knowledge and with much less of the universalistic *esprit de corps* that older intellectual elite status had conferred, the changing system established new gatekeepers over cultural creation. Although such things varied greatly from discipline to discipline, it was undoubtedly true that intellectuals immersed in the problem-solving tasks presented by highly specialized and fragmented areas, often connected directly to lively international dialogue, were somewhat less likely to conceive of their own intellectual work as a universalistic prescription for revamping French society, even though they were not any less likely to lean electorally leftward than their predecessors.

Régis Debray and others make another structural argument about what they call "mediacracy" and its effect on intellectual outlooks.[56] A generic version of this argument might go as follows. Television, the "massification" of a new middle-strata reading public (plus increases in literacy of other groups) and the consequent concentration of publishing together reconfigured the cultural products industry. In consequence, the field of incentives within which many intellectuals operated was restructured. Television enhanced rapid turnover in intellectual modes and a foreshortening of historical perspective. In this setting, mass publishing controlled by a few large houses sought quick "coups" that could be widely advertised and rapidly sold. Becoming a "famous French intellectual" thus involved "flexibilization," to borrow a barbaric word from the economists. Aspirants had to write very quickly on very contemporary subjects in ways that would be accessible to wide audiences. Those who succeeded often had to work in a somewhat ephemeral world of current events and be prepared to change swiftly. The rewards for becoming this new kind of intellectual were very great, the argument went, thus many were tempted into careers that involved networking from, say, an academic point of departure, into regular writing for a newsweekly like *Nouvel Obs* and into affiliations with important Parisian publishing houses.[57]

Politics and Society Revisited

These many changes in the structural situations of intellectuals account no better for the content of Left intellectual debate in the 1970s than they did earlier. Once again, the key factor mediating structural trends and intellectual behaviors that best "explains" things is the relationship between the working intelligentsia and the official Left. And in the 1970s the underlying dynamics of this relationship became clear. The official Left was called upon to respond to a rapidly changing situation. To the degree it was capable of opening space, in terms of doctrine and ideas, to intellectuals and the new intelligentsia, some harmony of vision was possible between intellectual concerns and those of the official Left in general. To the degree to which this did not happen the negative effects were likely to be great.

What was at stake was the political outlook of the progressive new middle strata. In most circumstances these new groups were likely to vote for the Left. Even so, were they to become ideologically alienated the consequences for the Left were potentially costly. And, as we have seen, such alienation was well-rooted by the later 1970s. Here strategic contradictions entered in. The official Left had committed itself to the Union de la Gauche. The key actor in this commitment, the PS, had made an extremely shrewd strategic bet in so doing, that by "buying" a set of outlooks from the PCF it would ultimately be able to smother and undercut French Communism. However, the coalitional logic behind this was clearly at odds with the social alliance logic needed to approach the rising new middle strata that had little or no sympathy for Common Program politics.

The 1970s biographies of different segments of the generation of '68 are a good place to continue the narrative of the growing alienation between Left intellectuals and the official Left. French post-1960s "new social movements" never achieved the prominence of those in other advanced societies largely because at the precise moment when these movements arose, the official French Left, which had been out of power for decades, itself began to gather the steam that eventually brought it to power in 1981. Both the Socialists and the Communists were eager to coopt the energies of various post-1968 rebellious currents. The new social movements had therefore to choose between independence and integration into the official Left, an integration that promised a certain amount of political effectiveness at the price of accepting parts of the official Left's politics. The consequence of this situation divided and severely weakened most of the movements. Different fractions made different choices, of course, but the general "vacuum cleaner" effect of the official Left parties was considerable. Those segments of the movement that remained outside the orbit of the official Left (and outside the unions, also important players) themselves rapidly divided into small competing groups whose internecine conflict further undercut the movement's position.[58]

The *gauchiste* sequels of May 1968 were different—here we will follow the trajectories of the Maoists.[59] The passionate *encadrement* of Maoists and others like them in quasi-cult grouplets could not be sustained in an ever more indifferent environment. The feelings of self-deception and personal waste that followed contributed to the creation of an important community of apostates. The so-called "new philosophy" was one manifestation of this apostasy.[60] From naive beliefs in miracle solutions—whether proletarian revolution or *autogestion*!—there first emerged anger that the world was refractory to such visions and then fury at the "straight" Left that, in the 1970s, was capitalizing on French discontents using traditional political programs and methods. A strange, incredibly belated, discovery by the French Left intelligentsia of the unpleasantness of Soviet society and a consequent wave of anti-Sovietism played an important role here.[61] By the mid-1970s the underlying direction that had emerged was that the politics of the "old" Left, embodied in the Union de la Gauche, were both out of date and dangerous. And by the later 1970s, a "new Philosopher" like André Glucksmann could be taken seriously when uttering aphorisms like *concevoir, c'est dominer.*

The separation of important segments of the maturing *soixante huitard* generation from official Left politics was thus reconfirmed even as the justifications for this separation changed dramatically. The new perspectives involved complete rejection of global social thinking plus strong antistatism, given ties to poststructuralist thought and anarchism. The conviction grew that decentralized and democratic, often nonpolitical movements below central-state level were the real bearers of progressive change in France—in the jargon that was to come, "civil society" was the locus of social creativity, not parties and civil servants. Here the ex-*gauchistes* rejoined other, more *autogestionnaire,* segments of the 1968 generation.

Not all of the generation of '68 gravitated towards a radical skepticism of official Left ideas. A large group of *soixante huitards* also found their ways toward the two major parties of the Left. By the early 1970s the reformulating Socialist Party offered young intellectual *militants* new openings to do Left politics within a rapidly changing political organization that might, in the medium term, confer large career rewards. Large numbers of the '68 and Left Unity generations also joined the PCF, motivated by a desire to combine militancy, passion, and career similar to that of their PS *frères-ennemis.*[62]

The most important characteristic of this incorporation of intellectuals into the official Left was its partiality. Those who entered the PCF were rudely removed at the end of the 1970s when the party's strategy changed. For their part, those who joined the PS bought into a profound contradiction between the party's coalitional setting and the social alliance needs to which it had to respond. Opting for the Union de la Gauche involved "dealing" with the PCF in order better to subordinate and weaken French communism. We now know how successful, in electoral terms, this choice turned out to be. But the Union de la Gauche meant compromising with the PCF on program and ideology.[63] This meant a general PS outlook in the 1970s governed by the spirit of the 1972 Common Program, a statist, *dirigiste* platform of reforms that many intellectuals rejected.

Advocates of *autogestionnaire* politics found the Left's chosen "Common Program" strategy unpalatable. Post–1968 *autogestion* thought, stressing decentralized democratic social creativity embedded in a vague antistatist, antitraditional social democratic and, of course, anticommunist feeling, struck deeper roots in the PSU and the CFDT.[64] *Autogestionnaire* segments of the intelligentsia supported the Left electorally, but did not recognize their own political ideas and outlooks in the official political ideas of the Left in the 1970s.[65] Parti Socialiste strategists, François Mitterrand in particular, quickly recognized the problem and moved to include *autogestionnaire* forces into the PS at the autumn 1974 Assises du Socialisme. The PS thus made a commitment to *autogestion,* but the operation was not persuasive since Mitterrand, without really modifying the basic statist and Jacobin line of the party, immediately manipulated the PS's new *autogestionnaires* to his own ends in the party's complicated internal politics.[66] An opportunity was missed, then. *Autogestionnaire* parts of the post-1968 Left intellectual generation were never effectively integrated into the politics of the official Left.

As the official Left moved closer to power, a clear movement of ideological opposition to official Left politics thus crystallized around a "second Left" with immediate roots in the decentralized rebellion of 1968. However, responding to the progressive extinction of rebelliousness, to economic crisis after 1974, and to the wave of intellectual anti-Sovietism of the later 1970s, this Second Left itself began to change its positions. *Autogestion* was decoupled from radicalism. The goal of transcending capitalism disappeared.[67] *Autogestion,* duly deradicalized, became an appeal to de-statize the Left, for decentralized bargaining as an approach to social problems of all kinds, for a revitalized "civil society," and for recognition of the utility, as a decentralized mechanism, of the market.[68] This evolution was accomplished, in part, through the symbiotic fusion of the *autogestionnaires* with another, largely pre-1968, Left intellectual generation of Mendesists. By the 1970s Mendesism had become a variety of technocratic centrism. Not "socialist" in any conventional ways, it explicitly rejected notions about the transcendence of capitalism, recognized the centrality of innovative management, and proposed a "mixed economy" that would acknowledge the market's limits and the role remaining for intelligent intervention. Above all, it stressed the need for conscious and continual efforts to modernize France, and rejected the lyrical, transformative, and exaggeratedly statist rhetoric of the Left Common Program.

As we remarked earlier, the lifestyles and size of the new intellectual middle strata had changed in ways that challenged the traditional Left. The actual politics chosen by these organizations for the 1970s seduced some Left intellectuals but not all of them. This situation "opened" parts of the new middle strata to political influences from outside the official Left. For such groups, *militantisme* and older types of "engagement" gave way to a more synthetic cultural adhesion that political parties were either unable or unwilling to provide.[69]

Media entrepreneurs were quick to perceive the opportunities. *Nouvel Observateur,* a Mendesist weekly, is the most interesting case. In the 1970s *Nouvel Obs* practically became a quasi-party, disseminating trendy cultural material— including a great deal of vulgarized poststructuralism—plus a shrewd combination of "second Left" ideas to undermine the prevailing political discourses of the official Left.[70] *Nouvel Obs* was not alone, either. Concentrated efforts in the same direction by publishing houses—like Editions du Seuil—intensified the effects. Moreover, by the end of the 1970s *Libération,* an important daily newspaper, had come to play an analogous role as quasi-party for the "new culture" segments of the post-1968 Left intelligentsia.

By the later 1970s new dialogues between parts of the Left intelligentsia and such commercially oriented quasi-parties had solidified. The explosion of intellectual anti-Sovietism occurred largely in such dialogues as did, more generally, the breast-beating, anti-Enlightenment apostasy of the "new philosophy." The trials and tribulations of the Union de la Gauche in 1977–78 provided new material about the evils of statism and the inherently manipulative nature of official Left ideas and apparatus, as did the frightening internal crisis of the PCF after 1978.[71]

By 1981, when the official Left, determined to implement its long-standing program, finally came to power, an important impasse had thus been reached. Much of the intelligentsia and many important intellectuals voted to make this political success happen. At the same time, however, substantial parts of the Left intelligentsia were profoundly alienated from the Left's official politics.

III. The Future Is Us! The 1980s

Fate marked the first years of the 1980s. In close proximity a number of once and would-be kings of intellectual Parisiana died—Barthes, Sartre, Aron, Lacan, Foucault. Certain others (Althusser, after murdering his wife, even Derrida, despite his continuing American celebrity) fell into lengthening shadows. The death of Vincennes University, the symbol of post-1968 thought, was equally emblematic.[72] Starting at the same point, poststructuralism began to decline— even though its success as an export product to the English-speaking world kept such news from crossing the Atlantic—wounded by ever more intense critical attack and changing political concerns. Socially, the post-1968 moment of rebellion had ended. Economically, the postwar boom had collapsed into hard-nosed discussions of policy reevaluation. Boat people washing ashore, martial law, the repression of Solidarność in Poland, and the invasion of Afghanistan, among other things, provided additional reasons to reflect on the various radical utopianisms of the 1960s. The rapid policy failure of the French Left after it came to power in 1981 further contributed to a newly sobered environment.

By the turn of the 1990s a "neoliberalism with a human face" had taken stage center from poststructuralism. Growing antistatism fed a resurrection of liberal political philosophizing. To be sure, there were distant lines of kinship between poststructuralism and thus emergent decentralized individualism. Poststructuralism had made it unsound to reify the state as key locus of oppression and central fulcrum for progressive change. Still, poststructuralism had been intent both on identifying the roots of oppression elsewhere and on advocating resistance.[73] And here the break occurred. The new liberalism, if also belligerently antistatist, was infinitely less concerned with localizing sources of oppression and, more important, anything but rebellious.

A number of different intellectual quests converged on the final results. The Marxist operation of reducing the separate dynamics of state and society to one set of causal variables and programming their reconciliation in a utopian, noncontradictory future had been disposed of earlier. To budding new liberals, the use of state power to reduce social oppression created new problems without alleviating those that statist strategies had set out to resolve in the first place. In the new setting, elite intellectuals also found it less and less compelling to use deconstructive techniques to cast doubt on the very possibility of finding meaning in the social and political world; thus it could no longer be a question of positing the constantly shifting, unpredictable but nonetheless omniscient oppressiveness of *both* state and society. The contradictions between these two things seemed, instead, to be permanent, and this was what was most important to confront. The conclusion was that one had to philosophize anew about relationships between state and society.

By the mid-1980s the search was for the theoretical groundings of a policy where state power would be limited and circumscribed, allowing maximum space for democratic individualism while avoiding the undesirable atomizing aspects of Anglo-Saxon utilitarianism. It was a case of looking for America without Reagan and Adam Smith. To find it, there was first of all an Aron renaissance, which grew even more important after the great liberal's death. Once Aron was monumentalized, there followed a massive reexamination of nineteenth-century French liberalism—Constant, Guizot, and, above all, Tocqueville.[74] Simultaneously there was busy translation, and paraphrasing, from the English and American Karl Popper, Friedrich von Hayek, and Hannah Arendt,[75] 1950s and 1960s reflections on pluralism, and more recent liberal reflections on distributive justice, Rawls in particular.

There was a striking new modesty in all this. Elite French Left intellectuals lost their traditional taste for global reflection on the nature of society per se. Instead they turned to a preoccupation with what they perceived to be the eternal problems of all societies—which, by definition, were unsolvable. The new issue was to find humane ways of living with their permanence. In consequence, generalizing conceptualizations that placed their makers in positions of critical externality to what existed—"ideologies," if you will—came to be regarded as intrinsically dangerous. What existed was fundamentally ineluctable, rendering any effort to transcend it futile and hubristic.

The processes by which this happened were almost as interesting as this theoretical shift itself. To be sure, there were semi-spectacular individual forays onto the battlefield like the Renaut and Ferry onslaught on poststructuralism in *La Pensée 68.*[76] Likewise, the controversy about Heidegger's Nazi sympathies, which had as its real target French Heideggerians like Derrida, had significant debunking effects.[77] In general, however, the "new individualism" succeeded without the assistance of any monumental intellectual figures, as the product of an accretion of middle-level individual contributions and the assiduous collective work of intellectual institutions. The job was done by university colloquia and scholarly journals, elite reviews like *le Débat,* middle-brow weeklies like *Nouvel*

Observateur, the efforts of key publishing houses (Editions du Seuil, Grasset), *Libération,* and the Fondation St. Simon.[78] The elite Left intellectuals' flight toward Franco-American individualistic political philosophy thus coincided with an at least momentary decline of the "great man" as archetype.

The situation of Left intellectual artisans also changed dramatically. First of all there was a rapid deflation of artisanal confidence in neo-Marxist stratification-based models of politics, such that by the mid-1980s Marxist concepts had disappeared from the word processors and bookshelves of French social scientists.[79] In the more influential recent works on issues pertaining to social stratification and politics—Luc Boltanski's *Cadres,* for example—one finds an newly phenomenologized sense of the social construction of groups rather than reference to underlying social structures.[80] The centrality of politics itself declined. Alain Touraine, always a bellwether, wrote in 1987 that "politics seemed . . . [as late as] . . . 1981, to be at the center and summit of social life. Now it is only a passageway between the problems of personal life and those of the international economic and military system."[81]

If Left political sociology ceased being "Left" in the older French sense of the term, no single coherent alternative replaced the "old" class-analytical orthodoxy. Nonetheless here, too, there was also new reflection about nineteenth-century French liberal republican political culture and its social bases, paralleling the rise of similar concerns in elite social theory. Tocqueville, retranslated from the American, often replaced Marx.[82] Quite as important, the increasing intellectual prominence of economists and economism erected a new language of constraint and refractory environments.[83] Underlying this, confidence in the state's capacity to reorient social behaviors, to coordinate the economy in equitable ways, to regenerate civic virtue, and so on, disappeared. Much theoretical and methodological attention turned toward individuals and their calculations[84]—aided and abetted by evidence from opinion polls and election studies that showed a rise in individual, as opposed to class, orientations—and to the textures of nonpolitical associative life.[85]

One gets a different picture of intellectual movements and the forces behind them when one chooses the prism of political generations of intellectuals rather than those of the *grands intellos* and "artisans" just discussed. The trajectories of many post-1968 *gauchistes* towards liberal postures was already quite clear before the 1980s, as was the virtual disappearance of "new social movement" activists due to the vacuum-cleaner effects of the Left in the 1970s. Those parts of the post-1968 and Left Unity generations that entered the PCF brought dimensions of the experience of '68 with them and changed the party almost as much as they were changed by it. Up to 1978–79, that is. The PCF's dramatic strategic shift at this point involved nothing less than the surgical removal of these intellectual generations from French Communism altogether.[86] It was rare, subsequently, for the ex-Communists who emerged from this horrendous massacre to follow ex-*gauchistes* and *autogestionnaires* toward apostasy. Rather, they became political orphans, people with very good ideas and no institutional place to express them.

The fate of the 1960s and 1970s Left intellectuals who aligned themselves with the various Socialist *courants* was interesting. To the degree to which the PS became a sophisticated machine for manufacturing political careers, they tended to fight out their various factional battles inside the party. Prior to 1981, when the party finally came to power, such struggles could be justified in terms of the influence on the course of future Left governments, even though in fact they were as much struggles between elite cliques as anything else. After 1981, the entire PS, including intellectuals of all generations and all factional stripes, fell hostage to the experience of Left power. The administrative logic of state managers— which many PS intellectuals either were or had always wanted to be—supplanted that of collective mobilization. And when, after 1982–83, François Mitterrand and parts of his government decided that the time had come to abandon the voluntaristic statist politics of the Union de la Gauche in favor of "accepting the mixed economy" and "modernizing" France, PS intellectuals were obliged to follow.[87]

On the level of Left intellectual generations, by the earlier 1980s a "certain Leftism"—*marxisant* or *socialisant,* statist and hypervoluntarist—about the uses of political power to change economy and society in a radical way had disappeared. It was replaced in differing ways, of course, but there are common themes that now place much greater weight on the importance of creativity and innovation in the social sphere together with much greater skepticism about the capacities of the state to promote social change. And, almost as significantly, the "market" was rediscovered as a part of this creative social world rather than an appendage of politics to be manipulated by the state.[88]

Thus far the narrative is striking. Elite Left intellectual debates and the discussions of artisan sociologists proceeded according to quite different logics until the later 1970s. Basic, rough-and-ready, *marxisant* notions survived and thrived in political sociology, while poststructuralism came to dominate among the *grands intellos.* By the 1980s, however, the two trajectories, if quite remarkably different, were reaching towards analogous conclusions. The end of the poststructuralist vogue and the rise of "political philosophy" in the 1980s elite debate shared certain common concerns with much recent political sociology. Both debates were profoundly skeptical about theoretical perspectives that posited the scientific comprehensibility of the social world. Each became immeasurably more modest even if, France being France, they became more modest in *dramatic* ways. For other reasons, Left intellectual generations, exmilitant *soixante huitards* of all varieties, found themselves marching in the same parade.

Society, Politics, and Ideas

The social trends correlating with *gauchisation* of the intelligentsia in the 1960s and 1970s had almost all changed by the 1980s. One of the major factors for rising unemployment in the "crisis"—beyond demographic pressures, continuing growth in women's participation in the labor force, and France's declining industrial competitiveness—was a distinct leveling off in tertiary-sector job creation.[89] Underneath this lay the fact that the "postindustrialization" of France had reached a mature point that involved a relative stabilization in public service sector and educational jobs after a long period of expansion. Changing economic circumstances also brought a squeeze on social service growth, public-sector salaries, and institutional overhead expenses.

The trends that earlier had counted most for the intelligentsia and intellectuals involved changes in the numbers, social settings, and life prospects of these groups themselves. Schematically, beginning in the 1960s there was an increase in the weight of new middle-strata occupations in the labor force, particularly in the public sector, and an attendant modification of structures of cultural communication "circuits" reflecting the increased weight in the French population of educationally credentialed new middle-class groups. As these processes moved forward—creaking and groaning, to be sure—the class structure of France was ultimately changed, which is, after all, the meaning of "postindustrialization." One could no longer look at French society plausibly using a traditional Marxian model—workers versus capital and its appendages, with, perhaps, a few social oddments tossed in (intermediary "categories").

The central problem that we have been trying to explore is that involving the meaning and significance of such changes for intellectuals of the Left. And here we have repeatedly discovered that the raw significance of these stratification changes could only be clarified by exploring the interaction between the outlooks of official Left political actors and the desires and needs of the emergent new middle strata, which the intelligentsia tended to reflect. Thus the significance of the completion of processes of sociological new middle stratification in the 1980s turned out to be dwarfed by what happened politically.

The official Left came to power in 1981, tried bravely to implement its Common Program-derived reformism, and then ran aground on a totally unfavorable international economic environment. Then, after a brief moment of confusion, the PS, henceforth dominant on the official Left, completely changed the way it viewed the world. In March 1983 *Libération* rather cheerfully and ironically headlined that *Le Mitterrand Nouveau est arrivé*. The "old Mitterrand" was a reformer who talked, at least, about the imperative of redistributing economic and political resources in France away from the wealthy and powerful to ordinary people. In 1981 he announced that "by nationalizing industry [I am doing] what de Gaulle did in the realm of nuclear energy. I am endowing France with an economic *force de frappe*." The "new Mitterrand" talked about the need to increase profits, to allow the market to flourish, to accept the "mixed economy," to "modernize" French industry and society in order better to compete in the international market. The quest to change the domestic balance of resources in France through statist reforms had abruptly given way to a new crusade to free up the resources, primarily economic, necessary to increase the comparative effectiveness of French capitalism and to do so in a largely decentralized, market-centered way. The rest of the 1980s demonstrated that the political and ideological conversion experience of the PS was definitive.

The different strains of official Left politics in the two decades after the end of the Algerian War had never connected in any satisfactory way with important parts of the emerging new intelligentsia. By the later 1970s, as we have seen, much of the Left intelligentsia had developed sets of ideas that were independent of and different from those of the official Left. These ideas lived a thriving parallel existence in the more general universe of Left intellectualism in France, even if they did not impinge decisively on the evolution of official Left politics. In the 1980s, however, the situation was transformed. Left intellectuals and Socialist politicians came to accept *more or less the same ideas*. More interesting still, a goodly portion of these shared ideas came from the intellectual "Second Left."

The subtext? Official Left policy failure after 1982–83 meant ideological and intellectual collapse as well. Older positions no longer worked to mobilize people either programmatically or inspirationally. Without some new presentation of self, the Socialists faced a political disaster. An ideological conversion experience was imperative to avoid political bankruptcy. The PS therefore tried to repair its damaged political position by foraging through the ideological parts-bin of the moment. Some of its new ideas came straight from the vocabularies of state management itself—technocratic realism, proclamations of superior competence. Others came from internationally ambient economism. Many, however, came directly from pirating the vocabularies of the new middle-strata groups that earlier had found the Common Program so rebarbative.

The prevalent neo-Tocquevillean intellectual climate of the second half of the 1980s was in part the consequence, in part the cause, of this pirating. In particular, the PS borrowed as much as it could from the storehouse of "Second Left" ideological and intellectual material that had accumulated outside the corridors of official Left power before the early 1980s. By this point, however, the ideas of these intellectuals had evolved away from the corrosive radicalism of both poststructuralism and *autogestionnaire* thought into the "soft" liberal revisionism that now dominates both the Left political and intellectual scene. By the end of the 1980s, Marxism was dead along with traditional social democracy. Classes and workers had been surgically removed from intellectual and political discourse. Tocqueville was very much alive. A new individualism had emerged triumphant. In all this, Left French intellectuals had come to play a very important reorienting role in the ideological sphere of French Left politics.

Coda: Uses of the Past

The Bicentennial of the French Revolution was celebrated in 1989. For decades prior to the 1980s a "social" approach had dominated, following Jaurès, Mathiez, and Soboul. This approach whose dominance had been in part a function of the relative hegemony of the official Left political discourse, stressed the conflictual interactions of social classes around economic concerns and contended that the events of 1789–94 were the core of the "bourgeois revolution."[90]

By the 1980s this interpretation was under attack from a new professional orthodoxy that emerged from a movement of historians and publicists led by François Furet. An early apostate ex-Communist (he left the party in 1956), Furet was the very model of a "Second Left" intellectual. He followed an impeccable strategy to impose his views both intellectually and politically. Beginning by achieving professional eminence among historical artisans (culminating in public breakthroughs in important essays like *Penser la Revolution Française* in 1978),[91] Furet accumulated resources, acquired in university politicking[92] from his role as one of the founders of the arch "Second Left" Fondation St. Simon in the early 1980s,[93] and ever greater "mediatic" power.[94]

Furet and followers argued first of all that the social approach had profoundly misunderstood what the Revolution was about, and hence had focused on the wrong issues. What counted in 1789 was not class conflict and bourgeois revolution, but intellectual and ideological combat over political institutions and doctrines. Thus, in the years after 1789 one could see the beginnings of the great twentieth-century struggles between liberal democracy and totalitarianism. The initial, good, period of the Revolution had developed timeless arguments for the rule of law, republicanism, and constitutional representation. The Revolution's later years—with Marat, Robespierre, and Saint Just—had brought the enunciation of modern totalitarian innovations, intolerance, and terror. It was from celebration of these later events that much of the Marxist vision of classless utopia through revolutionary transformation had been derived.[95]

As the Bicentennial approached, advocates of what had become the new— and quite obviously "Second Left"—orthodoxy seized the public platform. The politics of the later twentieth-century showed that the revolution was finally over, they claimed, adding that everyone except a few extremists agreed that a democratic republic that institutionalized the rule of law and the rights of man while socializing citizens to tolerate difference was the logical culmination of 1789. The Marxist-Leninist and totalitarian vision of further revolution was abhorrent and had failed. The real lesson of the Great Revolution was that great evil could come from the intellectualization of utopian social goals and from subsequent efforts, often also promoted by intellectuals, to remodel actual social arrangements to conform to these goals.

Here we are confronted with a miniaturized paradigmatic case of the story we have just told: an intellectual operation leading toward the resurrection of nineteenth-century liberal debates in political philosophy, confirming trends we have observed in other intellectual fields. Moreover, we also see a group of Left intellectual artisans trying—successfully—to use their professional preeminence to influence general public discussion against the older orthodoxy of the official Left. In arguing intellectually about the precise contours of a long-ago set of events, the Furetistes and their allies were attempting to shape political debates in the France of 1989.

After the Dreyfus Affair a famous French Left intellectual "type" crystallized. The intellectuals in question sought a particularly unmediated relationship between the creation of ideas as an intellectual vocation and doing politics. They thought and wrote about the structures and dynamics of the world in universal terms, understood this process as one whose purpose was to enlighten the less-informed. They then felt compelled to intervene in the political world to transform these ideas into social reality. Despite substantial changes in their social settings, French intellectuals still *do* politics in relatively unmediated and quite distinctive ways, and—as the Furetiste story and the official Left's substantial borrowing from "second" and other anti-Common Program Left intellectual repertoires after the collapse of 1983 show—with quite remarkable effectiveness. What has changed, compared with earlier periods, however, is that they now do so in the interests of newly humble and modest political ideas.

Notes

1. Jeannine Verdès-Leroux conveys a good sense of what PCF intellectualism was like in this period in *Au Service du Parti* (Paris: Fayard/Minuit, 1983). The turbulent early history of *Les Temps Modernes* amply demonstrated the larger problematic. Bitter struggles occurred first in the immediate founding years between Raymond Aron and Sartre about basic Cold War issues. Sartre and the rest of the equipe resisted Aron's urging to rally to the anti-Soviet side and attempted to maintain an independent existentialist Leftism. Next, after Aron left the journal for Centrist, pro-American limbo, there was a monumental struggle between Sartre and Merleau-Ponty about Communism and the Soviet Union. Some of Sartre's strangest work, including *The Communists and Peace,* followed. Interestingly enough, Merleau had been much to the pro-PCF Left of Sartre in the earlier struggles with Aron. By 1949 he had changed his views, however.

2. On this period, see Pascal Ory and Jean-François Sirinelli, *Les Intellectuals en France, de l'affaire Dreyfus à nos jours* (Paris: Armand Colin, 1986), chap. 8. The Ory-Sirinelli manual is a useful tool for our subject in general. On the PCF and its own intellectuals in this period, see Verdès-Leroux, *Au Service du parti;* and Michel-Antoine Burnier, *Les Existentialistes et la politique* (Paris: Gallimard, 1970).

3. Beginning in the Resistance-Liberation period, Sartre had pursued a faultless strategy to achieve his eminence, combining serious—if somewhat derivative—philosophy ("professional" conquest), literature (novels, plays, and essays to conquer the broader intelligentsia), and a journal, *Les Temps Modernes* (to maintain a constant theoretical and political presence on the battlefield), all in the interests of existentialism. Anna Boschetti's *Sartre et "les temps modernes"* (Paris: Minuit 1985) provides a very useful sociology-of-knowledge review of Sartre's strategies, again in the Bourdieu line. The problem of this, and other, Bourdivine analyses is that in their sociological reductionism they tend to overlook the importance of creativity. See also Annie Cohen-Solal, *Sartre* (Paris: Gallimard, 1985), for additional strategic information.

4. Jean-Paul Sartre, *Critique de la raison dialectique* (Paris: Gallimard, 1960).

5. Here, for a good sampling of *Arguments*, see Christian Biegalski, ed., *Arguments/3, Les Intellectuels, la pensée anticipatrice* (Paris: Gallimard 10/18, 1970). See also Gilles Delannoi, "*Arguments*, 1956–1962, ou la parenthèse de l'ouverture," *Revue Française de Science Politique* (February 1984).

6. Foucault, cited (from *Arts et loisirs*, June 15, 1966) in Didier Eribon, *Michel Foucault* (Paris: Flammarion, 1989).

7. Sartre's support of the Algerian Rebels—here one should reread his preface to Fanon's *Wretched of the Earth* and his articles in *Les Temps Modernes* from the period—was terribly important politically, as was his subsequent advocacy of third-worldist causes and perspectives and, later, various '68-generation ultra-Leftists. Annie Cohen-Solal's biography reviews these matters with great care.

8. See, for example, chapter 9 in Claude Lévy-Strauss, *The Savage Mind* (Chicago: University of Chicago Press, 1966).

9. On the Althusser crusade against Marxist humanism, which was partly an *histoire du boutique* within the PCF—a settling of accounts with longtime house intellectual Roger Garaudy—see R. Geerlandt, *Garaudy et Althusser: Le Débat sur l'humanisme dans le PCF et son enjeu* (Paris: Presses Universitaires de France, 1978). On structuralist Marxism more generally, see T. Benton, *The Rise and Fall of Structural Marxism* (London: Macmillan, 1984). The Grémion citation is from his excellent *Paris-Prague* (Paris: Julliard, 1985).

10. Here see Hervé Hamon and Patrick Rotman, *Génération*, vol. 1 (Paris: Editions du Seuil, 1985), for the full story.

11. This was true even if an "Althusserian" generation of *normaliens* would become front-line actors in May 1968 and constitute the backbone of French Maoism thereafter. As the British Marxist Perry Anderson astutely noted: "Even at the peak of its productivity, Althusserianism was always constituted in an intimate and fatal dependence on a structuralism that both preceded it and would survive it. Lévi-Strauss had peremptorily sought to cut the Gordian knot of the relation between structure and subject by suspending the latter from any field of scientific knowledge. Rather than resisting this move, Althusser radicalized it, with a version of Marxism in which subjects were abolished altogether, save as the illusory effects of ideological structures. But in an objectivist auction of this kind, he was bound to be outbid." Perry Anderson, *In The Tracks of Historical Materialism* (London: Verso, 1983), p. 38.

12. See, for example, Alain Touraine, *Production de la Société* (Paris: Editions du Seuil, 1973).

13. See Bourdieu and J.-C. Passeron, *Les Héritiers* (Paris: Minuit, 1964).

14. Mallet and Gorz, each in his own way, was importing "foreign" Marxism into France, particularly from Italy. See Serge Mallet, *Le Gaullisme et la gauche* (Paris: Editions du Seuil, 1964), and idem, *La Nouvelle Classe Ouvrière* (Paris: Editions du Seuil, 1963); Pierre Belleville, *Une Nouvelle Classe Ouvrière* (Paris: Julliard, 1963); and Andre Gorz, *Stratégie Ouvrière et Néocapitalisme* (Paris: Editions du Seuil, 1963). Castoriadis continued, until just before 1968, to put out *Socialisme ou barbarie* and to animate the S+B group, which included a number of other important writers, like Daniel Mothe. *Socialisme ou barbarie,* with a Trotskyist edge to its analyses, was explicitly anti-statist and *autogestionnaire* before its time. Important Left journals like *Les Temps Modernes* and *France Observateur* were willing regular vehicles for such ideas.

15. Touraine began to outline a schema of societal evolution that posited that classically Marxist notions of class and class conflict were at least a solid beginning toward an understanding of political and state behavior in "industrial" societies, but that a very different set of class actors, goals and state-society relationships would emerge in the transition to a "post-industrial" society that was in the wings. Bourdieu, in strong contrast, presented no picture of the direction of history, instead positing

a never-ending process of elite strategizing to maintain predominance over popular groups in the multiplicity of arenas where "reproduction" (of power, status, privilege) went on, presumably including the political arena.

16. It is worth adding here that as new theorizing about state-society relations developed apace in the 1960s (and here one might also trace the ledger of political science), there were numbers of important figures of lesser clout than those already mentioned on the liberal side (Bourricaud, for example) and on the *marxisant*. On the Left, which, once again, had pride of place in the general debates, there were, for example, a number of former Communists *en rupture de bans* also busily constructing product-differentiated models of class and class-conflict theories of state-society relationships (Serge Mallet, Cornelius Castoriadis, and others) and even one or two genuine Communists (Garaudy, for example).

17. See *Les Cahiers de l'Institut d'Histoire du Temps Présent*, no. 6, November 1987, for a good introduction. The IHTP *Bulletin Trimestriel* 31 (March 1989) provides an extensive "generational" bibliography. Hervé Hamon and Patrick Rotman's massive, two-volume *Génération* (Paris: Seuil, 1985 and 1988) popularized the notion and uncovered many of the problems it posed. See also Jean-François Sirinelli, "Le hasard ou la nécessité? Une histoire en chantier: l'histoire des intellectuels," *Vingtième Siècle* (January–March 1986); and Michel Wincock, "Les Générations d'intellectuels," *Vingtième Siècle* (April–June 1989). This whole issue is devoted to the theme of generations.

18. The "older" generation at the time of the early 1960s, post-1956 Marxist revisionists, and the Mendesists had already established a precedent of dissociation from the Left partisan orthodoxies that surrounded them. We have already discussed the Marxist revisionists as elite intellectuals. They were also activists. The Mendisists were largely a group of civil-servants and intellectual young turks and their followers that surrounded Pierre Mendès-France in the early 1950s. France's first modern newsweekly, *l'Express,* provided Mendesism with a powerful public voice in the mid-1950s. They rejected the ideological rigidities and transformative pretensions of the official Left, the conservatism of the Right, and the statism of both in the interests of what Mendès-France himself called the *République Moderne.* See Jean-François Sirinelli, "Les intellectuels et Pierre Mendès-France," in Jean-Pierre Rioux, ed. *Pierre Mendès-France et le Mendèsisme* (Paris: Fayard, 1985). Generations have biographies, since they are essentially networks of likeminded individuals seeking to reshape their political environment. What is for our purposes important to note about the Mendesist generation is that its influence and ideas rose fell and rose again with great regularity in more recent years. Mendesism was an essential component in the "club" movement of the mid-1960s, became one of the many families of the PSU, and, later, if in transmogrified form, found its way in the 1970s into the PS.

The third "ancestor" generation contained the post-1956 *deçus* of PCF Marxism. Here there was cacophony from the start, if initially from a roughly similar neo-Marxist score. This group worked first to erect a non-PCF and less schematic Marxism in ways that made a real dent in the already dented hegemony of Communism over intellectuals, and legitimated thenceforth the existence of an independent Marxism in France. In terms of personnel, there was the existentialo-Marxist Sartre and followers, and the *Arguments* group, of which we have already spoken, along with the important number of ex-Communists who made their way into the PSU and, coming from a slightly different trajectory, the *Socialisme ou Barbarie* collective.

19. This is evident from the IHTP's marvelous set of essays "La Guerre d'Algerie et les Intellectuels," *Cahiers de l'IHTP* 10 (November 1988). To be sure, as political trends in the 1980s make painfully clear, there was a strong right-wing side of this generation (Le Pen, et al., Occident, Ordre Nouveau, and the like).

20. See Hervé Hamon and Patrick Rotman's excellent *Les Porteurs de Valise* (Paris: Albin Michel, 1979) for a thorough overview of this.

21. The PCF, persistently unable to cope with any mobilizations from the Left that it could not control, acted forcefully to constrain and denigrate UNEF, the national students' union that assumed

the lead in antiwar activities, and other student protest vehicles. This left a profoundly bitter aftertaste for an entire generation of Left-politicized students for whom anti-PCF Leftism became a virtuous necessity. The effects of PCF policy were felt equally strongly by those young people who actually entered the PCF's youth organizations during the Algerian War. When tensions developed between these young people, drawn toward the protest activism of the moment, and the party leadership, the leadership responded with heavy-handed repressive tactics. The consequence of this was to create a generation of very able ex-Communist young intellectuals who, given their baptism under fire by the PCF's organizational harshness, became profoundly anti-PCF.

22. This sometimes led to Trotskyism (as in the trajectories of Alain Krivine and Henri Weber) and sometimes, prodded by identification with the FLN, to romantic involvement with other Third World revolutionary movements. Hamon and Rotman, *Génération* 1, does a wonderful job in showing this trajectory as well.

23. Thus the older Cold War pattern, typified by the trajectories of worker priests and fellow-traveling Catholic unionists, of "choosing the side of the party of the working class" would be largely broken. If one was a militantly reformist or revolutionary Catholic from this point onward—and many young people were such—one had to seek out a form of Leftist vocabulary and project different from that of official Communism.

24. We have already mentioned the huge contemporary debate about such things prompted by the "revisionism" of Renaut and Ferry, which insists that the deeper sense of 1968 was the emergence of a new individualism among students. A list of the more conventional explanations would include the following: the strains and tensions of modernization were evident in the university along with the patent incapacities of the Gaullist regime to cope with them. Then, in France as elsewhere, a deep wave of anti-authoritarianism was sweeping through the nation's youth. Moreover, the generation of 1968 held an honorable place in an international contagion of protest from students and the intelligentsia. The psychologically inclined saw the 1968 coming out of intergenerational conflict of a psychic kind, from a new "youth culture," from the contradictions of bureaucratizing advanced capitalism and democratic ideology. Henri Weber, at least a credible witness, in recent work for the twentieth anniversary of May, sees May–June as proceeding from the confluence of three "deep movements": a libertarian-democratic one, directed against various forms of authority; a "hedonist-communitarian" one, directed against both the austerity of *la France profond* and the isolation of consumer society; and a romantic-messianic movement against the "loss of meaning" in advanced capitalism. Henri Weber, "Le Travail de mai," chap. 5 of *Mai 1968: Vingt Ans après* (Paris: Editions du Seuil, 1988).

25. May 1968 Marxism was also frenetic in its search for a new, more viable and militant "vanguard" for the *damnés de la terre*, whether Trotskyism, Maoism, role-modeling on *El Che,* or whatever agencies Herbert Marcuse may have had in mind.

26. Serge Berstein, *La France de l'expansion* (Paris: Editions du Seuil, 1989), p. 190. Chapter 6 of this book provides an excellent quick overview of socioeconomic changes from 1958 to 1969. The French census category for white-collar workers—*employés*—includes a large number of simple operatives, store clerks, and other such occupations. Even with these groups subtracted, however, growth was impressive.

27. Jean Fourastié, *Les Trente glorieuses* (Paris: Fayard, Editions Pluriel, 1979) Table 24, p. 112.

28. See Weber, *Mai 1968; Vingt Ans Après.* See also Antoine Prost, *l'Ecole et la famille dans une société en mutation* (Paris: Nouvelle Librairie de France, 1982); and Desiré Calderon, "Enquête sur les intellectuels," *Révolution* (February 1984).

29. INSEE, *Les Données Sociales 1987,* p. 553.

30. Fourastié, *Les Trente glorieuses,* p. 284.

31. Weber, *Mai 1968: Vingt ans après,* makes a great deal of this generational notion of May 1968.

32.   Here we hasten to note that the PCF's hegemony over Left intellectuality was relative and limited, as well as brief. Circumstances of the Cold War, in particular the willingness of French Socialism to assume the critical role of the pro-American pivot in majorities after 1947, a willingness that obliged the SFIO to jettison any serious reformist intentions, left the PCF in de facto control of Left legitimacy in general. This legitimacy, extended to intellectuals, was essentially *political*. The PCF was never able to develop a convincing theoretico-ideological posture, and its Marxism was always a pastiche of Soviet ideas and homilies derived from French politics of the day. The party's political position may have compelled intellectuals listen to it, whether to accept or reject it, but it provided few convincing ideas for intellectuals to deploy professionally. The hegemony of the PCF was thus vulnerable to the change in the general political situation that occurred in the later 1950s.

33.   In these years the party was trying simultaneously to protect de Gaulle and to begin seducing the Socialists and non-Communist union organizations toward an eventual Union de la Gauche, objectives that, taken together, promoted a certain moderation. In the aftermath of Algeria, when a generation of energetic younger Communists tried to change the party from within, this generation was abruptly purged. The first volume of Hamon and Rotman's *Generation* discusses this well. Philippe Robrieux's *Notre Génération Communiste* (Paris: Fayard, 1977) gives a fascinating account of Robrieux's own experiences as a PCF student leader in this period, which is essential not only to understand PCF-intellectual relationships, but the ultimate decline of the PCF more generally.

34.   The term is Michel Winock's; see his *La République se meurt* (Paris: Editions du Seuil, 1978).

35.   On UNEF, see Alain Monchablon, *Histoire de l'UNEF de 1956 à 1968* (Paris: Presses Universitaires de France, 1983).

36.   They thus scurried energetically from club to caucus to journal spouting out their latest schemes, both "doing" their scientific political sociology and trying to provide intellectual frameworks for the "new" Left that they hoped to help emerge. But, given the Left's history and traditions, a *marxisant* or at least *socialisant* vocabulary was *de rigueur,* even if one's ultimate intentions might be to undercut this history and these traditions.

37.   Here there is a counterfactual model, of course. The Italian Communist Party, obviously different from the PCF in many ways, managed to change its approaches and its self-presentation to intellectuals and succeed much more in maintaining its plausibility and the salience of its ideas in the intellectual world.

38.   Luc Ferry and Alain Renaut, *La Pensée 68: Essai sur l'anti-humanisme contemporain* (Paris: Gallimard, 1985).

39.   See *Le Monde,* October 13, 1989, for reportage on a conference on Foucault's politics, including his own political activities; the article by Catherine De la Campagne is particularly good. The recent journalistic biography of Foucault by Didier Eribon talks a great deal about such things as well. Didier Eribon, *Michel Foucault* (Paris: Editions du Seuil, 1989).

40.   It is worth reproducing here Jean-Marie's Domenach's commentary on this (Domenach was at the time editor of *Esprit*): "Doesn't a system of thought which introduces both the constraints of the system and discontinuity in the history of the mind undercut the foundations of any progressive political intervention? Doesn't it eventuate in the following dilemma: Either acceptance of the system or else calls for "wild" events, an eruption of external violence which is alone able to upset the system?" Cited in Eribon, *Foucault,* p. 190.

41.   For a "quick read" on the social theories of Foucault and Derrida, see the David Hoy (Derrida) and Mark Philip (Foucault) chapters in Quentin Skinner, ed., *The Return of Grand Theory in the Social Sciences* (Cambridge: Cambridge University Press, 1985). On Lacan, see Sherry Turkle, *Psychoanalytic Politics* (Cambridge: MIT Press, 1981).

42.   We are here schematizing in the interests of brevity. Foucault and Derrida disagreed rather

profoundly about the prospects for protest. Foucault, of course, believed that discursive constructs causing oppression really existed, even if their appearance historically could not be analyzed in terms of laws, and even if their replacement by other such constructs could not be predicted. Derrida was extremely skeptical, almost ot the point of nihilism, about his analysis. Foucault's opinions on Derridean deconstruction were strongly voiced; he called it a "pedagogy which teaches the student that nothing exists outside the text . . . and which gives to the voices of masters the kind of sovereignty without limits which allows it to restate the text indefinitely." Cited in Eribon, *Foucault,* pp. 146–47, from Foucault, *Histoire de la folie à l'age classique* (Paris: Plon, 1961), p. 602.

43.   The so-called (usually by Anglo-Saxons) "French feminists," such as the three mentioned and others (Antoinette Fouque and Catherine Clément, for example), present us with an interesting subplot. The French women's movement emerged from the student rebellion of the 1960s in much the same way as the new feminism exploded in other societies. The fate of the French women's movement proved very different from those of new feminist movements in Anglo-Saxon societies. The ultimate result of these complicated processes was that important postmodern feminist thinkers like those we have mentioned acquired only the most limited audience in France—they never became "titans" in our sense of the word. On the other hand, they have become extremely important figures in the academic and other debates of Anglo-Saxon, and particularly North American, feminism.

44.   Aronian, Crozierian, and other liberal perspectives survived. Each wrote his treatise on 1968, for example, one that conformed to his earlier theories. See Raymond Aron, *La Révolution introuvable* (Paris: Julliard, 1968); and Michel Crozier, *La Société bloquée* (Paris: Editions du Seuil, 1969).

45.   See Alain Touraine, *Le Mouvement de Mai ou le communisme utopique* (Paris: Editions du Seuil, 1968) and *La Société postindustrielle* (Paris: Denoel, 1969).

46.   See Pierre Bourdieu, *Homo Academicus* (Paris: Minuit, 1985), published much later, but initially put together in the aftermath of May.

47.   Bourdieu's actual conclusions were redolent of the Frankfurt School's pessimism about the eternalization of domination, but the neo-Marxist flavor of the argument was what counted. *Distinction,* published in 1979 (Paris: Editions du Minuit), is where this affinity is most obvious. See also *La Noblesse d'état* (Paris: Editions de Minuit, 1988).

48.   Poulantzas's efforts in *Classes in Contemporary Capitalism* (London: New Left Books, 1965) and *State, Power and Socialism* (London: New Left Books, 1971) had, of course, a powerful impact not only in France, but also on the "theory of the state" debate in Anglo-Saxon countries.

49.   In the aftermath of 1968, the CFDT very rapidly changed its doctrinal vision of the world from Left Catholic reformism to genuine radicalism, in the process adopting a commitment to "socialist transformation" and belief in the class struggle (official commitments voted at its 1970s Congress). See, for example, Pierre Rosanvallon, *L'Age de l'autogestion*. Rosanvallon was, at the time, head of research for the CFDT. Guy Groux and René Mouriaux, *La CFDT* (Paris: Economica, 1989), chap. 3, goes into considerable detail about this. The PSU, alas, is a much less chronicled body. See nonetheless Charles Hauss, *The New Left in France* (Boulder, Colo.: Greenwood, 1978).

50.   I have talked about such matters in George Ross, "Marxism and the New Middle Classes: French Critiques," *Theory and Society* 5 (March 1978): and, more recently, in idem, "Destroyed by the Dialectic: Politics, the Decline of Marxism, and the New Middle Strata in France," *Theory and Society* 16 (January 1978):

51.   The discovery of Freud, via Lacan, by the post-May generation is undoubtedly connected with personal searches for different ways of organizing individual identity.

52.   J. and G. Bremond, *l'Economie française* (Paris: Hatier, 1985). We are well aware that these gross figures exaggerate the point about new middle stratification that we are making. One would have to go through subcategories and subtract inappropriate groups, particularly in the "employees" group. Even at that, however, the change is impressive.

53.   Bourdieu's *La Distinction,* whose data base stops in the middle 1970s, is crystal clear about these changes.

54.   See Veronique Aubert et al., *La Forteresse enseignante* (Paris: Fayard, 1985), especially pt. 4, chap. 3.

55.   The actual differences in outlook between public and private sector new middle-strata groups is explored in an important new book by François de Singly and Claude Thélot, *Gens du privé, gens du public* (Paris: Dunod, 1989).

56.   See Régis Debray, *Teachers, Writers, Celebrities: The Intellectuals of Modern France* (London: Verso, 1981); and Régis Debray, *Le Scribe* (Paris: Grasset, 1980). For a succinct version of a similar argument, see Claude Sales, "L'Intelligentsia, Visite aux artisans de la culture," in *Le Monde de l'Education,* February 1977. From a very different point of view, and on a much higher theoretical plane, see Raymond Boudon, "L'intellectual et ses publics: les singularités françaises," in *Français, qui êtes-vous?* (Paris: Documentation Française, 1981).

57.   We feel guilty about constantly citing the works of Hervé Hamon and Patrick Rotman here, because some do not consider them "serious" enough. But the best book on this Parisian world of interlocking cultural cliques is their *Les Intellocrates* (Paris: Ramsay, 1981).

58.   Were we to have had more space we would have focussed more specifically on the fate of the French women's movement. The best source we know on this subplot is Jane Jenson, "Ce n'est pas un hasard: The Varieties of French Feminism," in Jolyon Howorth and George Ross, eds., *Contemporary France,* 3 (London: Frances Pinter, 1989).

59.   The Romain Goupil film, *Mourir à Trente Ans,* suggests that similar things might apply to the Trotskyists of the *Ligue* as well.

60.   "New Philosophy," of course, accused big-think social theory, the enlightenment, and Marxism as bearing "totalitariansim." It was more than coincidental that the new philosophers were granted an extensive public hearing during the run-up to the 1977–78 electoral season (when the Center-Right majority was in considerable danger). What made their splash even bigger was the objective collusion that developed between the interests of the Right establishment in using the "new philosophy" to undercut a rising Left and certain sectors of the Left itself that disagreed with the logic of Left Union. The open-arms welcome that older left-of-center institutions dominated by Mendesiste-style modernists like *Nouvel Observateur* demonstrated how the politics of different important generations could cumulate.

61.   Here the fracas around the publication of *Gulag Archipelago* and Solzhenitsyn's subsequent departure, amidst immense publicity, was the critical beginning. The attitudes of Left French intellectuals to the Soviet Union after 1945 merit monographic review on their own. One can only speculate why the revelations of 1956, which had been so thoroughly amplified at the time, had been so easily forgotten.

62.   Membership in the PCF skyrocketed in the mid-1970s, with a large part of the new recruitment coming from the new middle strata and intellectuals. The complex processes and battles around the "Eurocommunication" of the party from 1973 to 1979 preponderantly involved intellectuals who were, to varying degrees, the bearers of propositions about inner-party reform involving greater internal democracy, attenuation of ties to the Soviet Union and the Soviet model, *autogetion* of a certain kind (decentralized movements for change), and changes in the PCF's theoretical mapping of the social world.

63.   We have discussed these issues at very great length in George Ross and Jane Jenson, "The Tragedy of the French Left," in Patrick Camiller, ed., *The Future of the European Left* (London: Verso, 1989).

64.   Pierre Rosanvallon's writings provide a bellwether for this very large segment of the intelligentsia. See his *L'Age de l'autogestion* (Paris: Seuil, 1976).

65.   For a solid, if biased, overview of major parts of this *autogestionnaire* movement see Hervé Hamon and Patrick Rotman, *La Deuxième Gauche* (Paris: Ramsay, 1982).

66.   Mitterrand seemed to misunderstand the potential importance of the CFDT *autogestionnaires* while using the incorporation of the Rocardians as cannon fodder to isolate Left factions in the PS in order to deal himself a better internal political hand in anticipation of coming to power later.

67.   An interesting document here is Pierre Rosanvallon and Patrick Viveret, *Pour une nouvelle culture politique* (Paris: Editions du Seuil, 1977).

68.   The political evolution in the 1970s of Michel Rocard, the spokesperson of the "Second Left" par excellence, was exemplary. From leadership of the radical PSU after May 1968, Rocard became the challenger to François Mitterrand's Common Program "archaism" in the name of a new "realism" in 1978.

69.   One could present a similar analysis about publishing houses.

70.   There is a very good monograph on *Nouvel Obs*. See Louis Pinto, *L'Intelligence en action: "Le Nouvel Observateur"* (Paris: Anne-Marie Métaillié, 1984).

71.   The same quasi-parties were the "transmission belts" for the profoundly anti-official Left movement of *recentrage* in the CFDT, as well as the Rocardian offensive against Mitterrand and the Union de la Gauche strategic option of the PS in 1979–80.

72.   In fact, the faculty of Vincennes moved to St. Denis, where obscurity and neglect awaited it.

73.   Even if, in Foucault's words, "resistance to power can never situated itself in a position of exteriority in relationship to power itself." Foucault, cited in Jean-Michel Besnier and Jean-Paul Thomas, *Chronique des idées d'aujourd'hui* (Paris: PUF, 1987), p. 41.

74.   Pierre Rosanvallon, *Le Moment Guizot* (Paris: Gallimard, 1985); and Pierre Manent, *Histoire intellectuelle du libéralisme* (Paris: Calman-Levy, 1987).

75.   Popper's *Open Society and Its Enemies* was first translated into French, amidst much clamor, in 1979.

76.   An important issue of *Pouvoirs* commemorating the twentieth anniversary of the events reiterated this analysis, excepting only the refractory Castoriadis. Renaut and Ferry subsequently counterattacked in a new essay appearing after the student revolt of December 1986. See Luc Ferry and Alain Renaut, *68–86, Itineraires de l'individu* (Paris: Gallimard, 1987).

77.   Victor Farias, *Heidegger et le Nazisme* (Paris: Gallimard, 1986).

78.   The Fondation St. Simon emerged in the mid-1980s as a Left-Center elite debating society that subsidized the kinds of discussions and publication that advanced its political views. Rocardian business figures like Roger Fauroux and Alain Minc promoted it, with François Furet assuming the presidency, to be surrounded by intellectuals like Jacques Julliard and Pierre Rosanvallon. For a fascinating, if gossipy, overview of different intellectual networks see "Le Pouvoir intellectuel en France," *L'Evènement du Jeudi*, February 2–8, 1989.

79.   Only Bourdieu, among well-known figures, persisted along such lines, after a fashion.

80.   Luc Boltanski, *Cadres* (Cambridge: Cambridge University Press, 1988).

81.   *Le Monde*, October 8, 1987.

82.   It is not uncommon to find Left-leaning sociologists in Paris these days lamenting that "Bourdieu is all we have left." And indeed the Bourdieu *boutique*, marred by considerable defections, can be seen to be the last remaining bastion of class-analytical perspectives. This is not very comforting to the lamenters, however, given that Bourdieu's class-analytical model is one of deep pessimism about change. What characterizes "reproduction" over time, to Bourdieu, is that the upper classes always win.

83. On the fringes of this movement there also appeared a reborn phenomenological sociology, usually borrowing from American sources (Schutz and Heidegger via Garfinkel and Goffmann?) skeptical of the endeavor of social mapping altogether.

84. Raymond Boudon's work is the leading source of this in French sociology. See, for example, *L'Idéologie* (Paris: Fayard, 1986). For a very good discussion of this approach see Pierre Birnbaum and Georges Lavau, eds., *Sur l'individualisme* (Paris: Presses de la Fondation Nationale des Sciences Politiques, 1986).

85. The mind-boggling devotion of contemporary French political science to polling and elections, almost to the exclusion of everything else, is extraordinary. The French—their political journalists and scientists (with the two categories overlapping more and more)—have become the largest consumers of political opinion polling in the entire world.

86. We have talked about dimensions of this massacre in Jane Jenson and George Ross, *The View From Inside: A French Communist Cell in Crisis* (Berkeley, Calif.: University of California Press, 1985).

87. The history of all this is recounted in Daniel Singer, *Is Socialism Doomed?* (New York: Oxford University Press, 1988). It is treated somewhat more analytically in George Ross, Stanley Hoffmann, and Sylvia Malzacher, eds., *The Mitterrand Experiment* (New York: Oxford University Press, 1987). One additional treatment, from the Left, is George Ross and Jane Jenson, "The Tragedy of the French Left," *New Left Review* 171 (October 1988).

88. The outlooks of new mid-1980s generations, those that came out of the 1986 student movement, for example, and those involved with SOS-racisme, provided interesting illustrations. Two decades earlier such young people would have mobilized under the banner of *marxisant* politics. In the 1980s, the visions that they developed evinced extremely skepticism about national state level politics altogether. Instead there was a paramount concern for maintaining unity around the specific issues of the movements themselves and for couching their appeals in quite simple moralizing self-presentations. What counted was witnessing in civil society, trying to persuade in certain relatively narrow areas rather than connecting with grandiose, state-centered, and global schemas for change.

89. In the boom years a rise in service-sector employment had consistently compensated for declining agricultural and relatively static industrial job creation. This had ceased as of the 1980s.

90. Different lessons followed from this, of course, with some tracing the revolution's lineage to twentieth-century social-democratic republicanism, some to 1917.

91. François Furet, *Penser la Révolution Française* (Paris: Gallimard, 1978).

92. Furet became president of the *Ecole des Hautes Etudes en Sciences Sociales* in 1977.

93. Furet combined forces in the Fondation with Roger Fauroux, Alain Minc, Jacques Julliard, Pierre Rosanvallon, and others of generally Rocardian political sympathies.

94. Thus Furet achieved through his intimate connections with *Nouvel Observateur, Le Débat* (a neo-Mendesist cum "second Left" intellectual bible edited by Pierre Nora), *Le Monde*, and radio and television elites.

95. See François Furet, *Marx et la Révolution Française* (Paris: Flammarion, 1988).

10

The Foreign Policy of the Fifth Republic: Between the Nation and the World

A. W. DePorte

The French people have felt intensely throughout most of their long history that there was an essential connection between their nationhood and the place their nation held in the world. What they were to themselves depended to a very considerable degree on what they were (or thought they were) to others: not masters or aspirants to mastery (except once or twice) but leaders and guides. The French have seen France as the model feudal nation, the model absolute monarchy, the first democratic republic in Europe, and the central source of European intellectual inspiration—Catholic, rationalist, liberal, democratic, socialist, and much else—as also of Romanesque, Gothic, classical, romantic, and modern art.

But, as France's central geographical position precluded any thought of a foreign policy of isolationism, so, not coincidentally, the French never believed that their nation's creative genius was exclusively self-created or for the benefit of themselves alone. Unlike the Chinese, they did not dismiss all others as being outside civilization except to the extent that they gratefully received blessings from their own country and acknowledged its supremacy. They derived much from others. But, uniquely, they gave back as much or more and enhanced or even validated their own civilization by doing so.

The rhetoric of the French language lent itself famously to celebration of this outlook. Who said it all better than Victor Hugo, in 1877, a few years after France had been crushingly defeated by German might?

> To create might may prove Power, but Glory consists in the creation of daylight. France creates daylight. Thence her immense human popularity. To her Civilization owes the dawn. The human mind in order to see clearly turns in the direction of France.

> . . . as light is compounded of seven colors, civilization is compounded of seven peoples. Of these peoples, three, Greece, Italy, and Spain, represent the South; three, England, Germany, and Russia, represent the north; the seventh, and first, France, is at the same time North and South, Celtic and Latin, Gothic and Greek.
> . . . Such is the privilege of this France, she is at the same time solar and starry.[1]

This distinctively "French note" of what we might call philanthropic superiority, exasperating in its arrogance but beguiling in its generosity, was also caught by foreigners, with a mixture of irony and admiration, as in this view of France and the world that Henry James placed in the mind of an old French socialist exiled in England after the Commune:

> He believed the day was to come when all the nations of the earth would abolish their frontiers and armies and custom-houses, and embrace on both cheeks and cover the globe with boulevards radiating from Paris, where the human family would sit in groups at little tables, according to affinities, drinking coffee (not tea, *par exemple!*) and listening to the music of the spheres.[2]

Rhetoric of this kind faded out of French public discourse in the twentieth century. Charles de Gaulle was its last great practitioner. If his use of it seemed strange and irritating to so many (particularly the Anglo-Saxons), that was in part because it was already anachronistic. Even more important, however, was the fact that France after 1940 was so manifestly *not* what he proclaimed it to be. That, of course, was an important reason why he spoke as he did and why his words in this vein, addressed both to his countrymen and to foreigners, were such an important part of his effort to change an unacceptable reality by changing what people thought about it.

The State and Status of France

De Gaulle is by far the dominant figure of the twentieth-century history of France: twice the savior of his country, the father of what has come to be the most broadly accepted constitution it has ever had, and, most important for our present purpose, the alpha—but not, as I shall argue, the omega—of its contemporary foreign policy. If his career seems to be at the center of most discussions of that subject, it is not because what he did was so successful or so enduring. Much of it was neither. But he set the terms of discourse about French foreign policy in ways that have persisted. And he propounded ideas about the links between France's internal life and its place in the world that more than ever deserve consideration at a time when many believe that the old France is being transformed into—what?

De Gaulle raised all these questions in his most celebrated text:

> All my life I have thought of France in a certain way. This is inspired by sentiment as much as reason. The emotional side of me tends to imagine France, like the princess in the fairy stories or the Madonna in the frescoes, as dedicated to an exalted and exceptional destiny. Instinctively I have the feeling that Providence has created her either for complete successes or for exemplary

misfortunes. If, in spite of this, mediocrity shows in her acts and deeds, it strikes me as an absurd anomaly, to be imputed to the faults of Frenchmen, not to the genius of the land. But the positive side of my mind also assures me that France is not really herself unless in the front rank; that only vast enterprises are capable of counterbalancing the ferments of dispersal which are inherent in her people; that our country, as it is, surrounded by the others, as they are, must aim high and hold itself straight, on pain of mortal danger. In short, to my mind, France cannot be France without greatness.[3]

This first paragraph of de Gaulle's war memoirs is an eloquent and classical statement of France's exceptionalism, with which Victor Hugo and many others would have been at home (although Hugo might have left out the Madonna). But it is more than an expression of the traditional love affair that the French of all times have had with their nation (if not with all of their fellow citizens). What the general calls the "positive side" of his mind adds something new and important to that, namely, a policy-generating insight into the relationship between the nation's inner life, its *essence* as France, and its place in the politics of nations. This gave him a guide to a lifetime of political action, at home and abroad, and it gives us a point of departure for reflecting not only on *his* motivations, actions, and achievements but on that relationship as it exists today.

France, he says, is not really itself (I shall abandon his traditional and emotive use of the feminine pronoun for the more austere neuter) unless it is "in the front rank," that is, one of whatever number of great or major powers there may be at any time. De Gaulle does not define the visible signs of that status. But his career suggests that to him they were what they had traditionally been: a great power was one that took part by right in all international decision making that affected itself and also in all decision making affecting others, at least in areas of the world where it had interests of its own—by right, because its power and influence were such that decisions could not be made in its absence. A France that does not do that is, in his view, no longer "really herself." He does not define what this "not France" would be. But he knew it when he saw it. The regime of Vichy, subjugated to a foreign conqueror, was certainly not France. But neither was the regime of the 1930s, abandoning areas of the utmost importance to French interests, and, worst of all, dependent on an undependable ally (in that case, Great Britain) for decisions affecting those interests. As for the Fourth Republic . . . ! And the Fifth Republic of the 1980s . . . ? The "inherent" divisions among the French people are so severe that they can be neutralized (but not, de Gaulle suggests, eradicated) only by "vast enterprises," that is, only if France exercises its role in the front rank and lives the greatness to which he refers. If the French cannot agree on their institutions or domestic policies, at least they can—and must—be rallied to promote the interests of the nation in the world. A critic might say that France in fact has seemed most characteristically itself just when it was *most* torn by deep and diverse internal dissensions—its usual state, at least until very recent years. De Gaulle would presumably have answered that this factionalism was indeed endemic to the country and was the cause and expression of that "mediocrity" of the *French* that so often in modern times has prevented *France* from being in the front rank, that is, great and secure, and thus itself. France was its true self only when these blights were counterbalanced by an assertive foreign policy, as in the periods of his own rule.

De Gaulle took these propositions very seriously and devoted his long political career to addressing their implications. At the risk of oversimplifying a very complex reality, we might sum up his objective by saying that in 1958 he established a constitutional system whose main purpose was to establish a stable executive authority able to conduct a foreign policy that would promote France's interests effectively as a nation among the others in a very dangerous world and, by doing so, give its people, irremediably fractured by their history, that indispensable focus of unity without which their greatness, the condition of their concord and their essence, could not be manifested, to themselves as well as to others. France needed at least *that* degree of unity in order to be strong, needed strength in order to be great, and needed greatness in order to be itself.

De Gaulle's actions in internal and international politics had important effects on France's status in the world, on its domestic polity, and on its sense of itself. So also, of course, did the actions of his successors. How does the nation stand in the world and how does it perceive itself today—almost half a century after he raised the banner of Free France, and thirty years after he founded the Fifth Republic—with respect to the large interrelated concerns that preoccupied him: its security and rank and its internal cohesion, its greatness and its essence as France? Has it engaged with some success in "vast enterprises" on the international scene? Have they counterbalanced the "ferments of dispersal" inherent in its people? Or, as I shall suggest, have the enterprises been (or become) less vast at the same time as the "inherent" divisions have lost some of their venom for reasons, unrelated to France's international rank, that would have surprised de Gaulle?

The Fifth Republic has pursued an active foreign policy in every part of the world and every sphere of international life. It inherited from the Fourth Republic the formal badges of being in the front rank of nations that that regime, in turn, had inherited from de Gaulle's first period of rule in 1944–46: a permanent seat on the United Nations Security Council and a position along with the United States, the Soviet Union, and Great Britain as an occupying power in Germany and Berlin. To these marks of status or rank the present regime has added others. France is one of the five countries of the world (openly) possessing nuclear weapons and one of those that form the inner circle for the management of the international capitalist system (the groups of Seven and Five). If the nations of the world were divided up according to the categories of another time, France would be classified as a member of the second estate rather than the third, among the gentlefolk rather than the masses.

But there was a vast difference between a court noble and a country squire. The particule did not assure power, influence, wealth, or even consideration. The emblems of status that France has acquired since 1958 have no more assured its place in the front rank as defined earlier than did those it won before. Nor can we assume that the French people have believed otherwise, however much they might have wanted to. To form a judgment about both the substance of French status and the nation's perception of that, we have to look at the regime's record in foreign affairs and its rhetoric about them. Then we can consider to what extent these have contributed to its being perceived as a front-rank player, above all by its own leaders and citizens, and the interrelations between their perceptions and the internal cohesion of the country.

The main elements of French foreign policy are interlinked to a notable degree. But, while keeping that in mind, it is convenient to consider them in terms of three sets of relationships: those with the United States and the Soviet Union, those concerning Western Europe, and those with France's now independent former colonies and, more broadly, the countries in what it is customary to call, with more or less accuracy, the developing or third world. These last have always been very important to France's place in the world and its perception of that. But in order to keep this discussion within reasonable limits I will focus mainly on the other sets of relationships, which are central to France's place as a European and Atlantic power.

France Between the Superpowers:
The Fourth Republic

France's relations with the two nations that have rightly been called superpowers throughout the period since 1945 were at the core of its foreign policy under the Fourth as under the Fifth Republic. De Gaulle's primary objective as leader of Free France after June 1940 was not only or mainly to contribute to the liberation of his country from German occupation—something that he knew would happen if, and only if, Great Britain and, later, the Soviet Union and the United States, defeated Germany—but to see to it that France was restored after the victory to its traditional place in Europe and the world as a nation "in the front rank." To him this was a matter of long-term priority (if France was to remain itself) as well as one of more immediate urgency (participation in the building of the postwar order, particularly as concerned France's security needs with respect to Germany). Only the victorious "Big Three" were in a position to satisfy these French needs, by accepting France into their circle of decision making—if they chose, or could be persuaded, or coerced, to do so. French policy was therefore necessarily directed at them with respect to its status claims as well as many other things.

De Gaulle had some formal success in his pursuit of this goal, but in fact he failed in 1944–46 to achieve what he wanted. The postwar world was dominated by the three powers that had defeated Germany. That exclusive club clearly did not include devastated France, which was dependent on the Western allies for its arms and much else that it needed for its daily survival and its hopes for reconstruction. This inferiority was made cruelly clear, to de Gaulle's immense chagrin, by his exclusion from the Yalta and Potsdam conferences in 1945.

The Fourth Republic continued to pursue the goal of status set by de Gaulle. But it was no more successful than he had been. France remained dependent on the United States for its recovery and was soon obliged by circumstances entirely beyond its control to find its security by becoming a member of a U.S.-dominated Western alliance in a polarized Europe. These multiple dependences were plainly and painfully displayed, for example, by its visibly contentious and unhappy acquiescence in American plans for the organization of a new West German state and, soon after, by the rearmament of that state as an increasingly more important member of the Western system. The foreign policy of the Fourth Republic was in many ways skillfully and constructively adaptive to difficult circumstances. But these achievements were mostly overlooked by opinion. What the French people and others perceived was a succession of short-lived cabinets that habitually yielded to imperative American demands on a succession of issues. De Gaulle, who tried and failed as a party leader to change this state of affairs, did not have to look far, in writing his war memoirs in the 1950s, to find a classic example of what he described as the "mediocrity" that reflected and stimulated the "ferments of dispersal" within France and exposed it to "mortal danger" without. Its attempt to buttress its status by holding on to its colonies (the "France of 100,000,000"), begun by de Gaulle himself in 1945, had the reverse effect, leading to humiliating defeat in Indochina after seven years of war. Then, the rebellion in Algeria that the regime could neither win nor end alienated it from the third world and even its allies, and in 1958 brought about its downfall. Ironically, it was this failure of the Fourth Republic to pursue successfully the policies it had inherited from de Gaulle that gave him his extraordinary opportunity to return to power.

De Gaulle's Quest for Status: The Cold War

De Gaulle's international agenda in 1958 was much the same as it had been in 1940 and 1944 because France still was clearly not on a level with the leaders of the two blocs into which Europe and the world were divided. Even within the Western bloc it was a weak "number three," behind the United States and Great Britain, and at risk soon to become "number four" as the Federal Republic grew stronger. De Gaulle understood that France's relations with the superpowers that dominated the international system were necessarily at the heart of its position in the world and that there were, in theory, only two ways it might try to raise its status with respect to them.

On the one hand, France could try to reduce the predominance of the United States and the Soviet Union, particularly in Europe, in order to increase the freedom of action and the influence of the European countries, above all its own. This approach had been tried by France in 1944–47, before the Cold War created the bipolar system in which it could not avoid taking its place on the Western side. In the years that followed, and in 1958, this remained an entirely utopian goal for a country of France's location, dimensions, and resources, which continued to perceive a still serious or renewed threat to its security from the Soviet Union (this was the year when, after the launching of the sputnik in 1957, Khrushchev revived the Berlin question) and could see no way to counter that but by a continued alliance with the United States.

If France had no chance in 1958 and the years that followed to pursue system-revising, then it had to try to enhance its status *within* the Western bloc. This meant, in practice, efforts to induce the United States, as leader of the Western bloc, to confer the desired status by giving France parity with Great Britain as an American ally. This goal, of course, was entirely familiar to de Gaulle, who had worked during and after the war, unsuccessfully, to persuade the "Big Two" Western allies, or coerce them (by threatening to withhold French cooperation), to admit France to the exclusively "Anglo-Saxon" inner circle.

Returning to office at a time when East-West relations were bad, De Gaulle immediately set about doing this. Although it has become customary to think of him as the father of détente in the 1960s, he should also be remembered, along with Konrad Adenauer, as the last of the cold warriors. The proposal which he made to President Eisenhower and Prime Minister Macmillan in September 1958, asking that a three-power directorate be established not within but above the Atlantic alliance to manage Western affairs throughout the world, was cast in the framework of strengthening the West's ability to pursue the Cold War. De Gaulle's courtship of Adenauer's Germany was based on his contention that the United States and the United Kingdom might well abandon German interests, in Berlin and otherwise, to preserve their own interests vis-à-vis the Soviet Union. His decision to proceed with the development of a nuclear deterrent force was justified as a necessary response to the Soviet threat at a time when reliance for security on the United States seemed increasingly uncertain, for military as well as political reasons. As if his creation of a fourth nuclear force was not a sufficient challenge to the predominance of the "Big Three," his refusal to join them in signing the limited nuclear test ban treaty in August 1963 glaringly—and deliberately—separated France from this first concrete step toward arms control and détente.

De Gaulle's defense policy, like his foreign policy in general, was of course aimed not only at the international situation but also at the perception French people had of their country's place in it. The independent deterrent force was central to this. If that happened (as in the short-term it did not) to help France win greater respect and consideration from the United States and Britain, and leadership in Western Europe based on intimate ties with a fearful and grateful Federal Republic—well and good. If it helped the French begin to shed their sense of weakness and dependence on others—even better. De Gaulle was a master at consciousness-raising. His quarrels with the United States, important in order to bring that reluctant superpower to recognize France's status as a major power, were at least as important for his goal of reeducating the French about their rank in the world. His lesson was that they did not have to obey the protecting superpower, first, because it had its own fully sufficient reasons for guaranteeing French security; second, because its guarantee was less and less dependable and effective; and last, because France would be able (when its nuclear weapons plans were implemented) to provide for its own security, whatever the United States did.

The most central French-American dispute concerned nuclear weapons. The United States strongly opposed the creation of the nuclear force, overtly because it feared the consequences, in time of crisis or war, of the dispersal of alliance nuclear decision-making authority, more quietly because it thought this French action (unlike, somehow, Great Britain's earlier decision to the same end) would stimulate nuclear proliferation elsewhere, not least of all in the Federal Republic—a consideration to which de Gaulle was sublimely indifferent. This debate showed that a considerable number of French people did not want to have their consciousness raised or their country's status enhanced in this way. They feared that the nuclear force, and the more assertive aspects of the general's policies in general, would isolate France from its allies and weaken rather than increase its security and influence in an alliance that was still perceived by them, and many others in Western Europe, as necessary to confront a threatening Soviet enemy. De Gaulle's policies eventually *did* change French public thinking in the ways he desired. But the "Gaullist consensus" on defense, and on the appropriateness and feasibility of asserting French national independence (while remaining in the alliance), was a phenomenon that he created but did not himself enjoy in his time.

De Gaulle did not achieve his status goals within the existing international system during the first, "Cold War" phase of his policy-making, which coincided with the four years required for him to end the Algerian war—an immense drain on France's energies, resources, prestige, and morale (and an added motive, although it was not needed, for de Gaulle's assertiveness on the international stage). It is impossible to say how these policies would have fared if the missile crisis of October 1962, coming soon after the end of the Algerian war had freed his hands and reestablished his political authority, had not fortuitously presented him with a dazzling opportunity to pursue far more ambitious goals than that of enhancing France's status *within* the existing system.

Détente, Entente, and Cooperation

After the missile crisis the superpowers began for the first time to seek concrete ways of redefining their competitive relationship so as to limit the risks of future confrontations (which they succeeded in doing, for there has been no crisis or tension of that magnitude since). This new situation, reinforced by a congruent shift in West German politics, allowed De Gaulle to undertake a most ambitious effort—unique in the history of Europe since 1945—to change and eventually replace the postwar bipolar system in Europe.

The Soviet threat was now more than adequately contained by the American preponderance that had been demonstrated in the crisis—so clearly demonstrated, in fact, as to require France (hopefully not alone) to put some distance between itself and the overpowerful and (as the escalating war in Vietnam would soon show) overconfident American colossus. France, in de Gaulle's view, was the obvious and only leader of this effort, for neither Britain, self-bound to the United States, nor the Federal Republic of Germany, divided, non-nuclear, and with a past, could play the role. The European members of the two blocs now had the opportunity, as de Gaulle put it in a series of memorable phrases, to assert their independence of the superpowers, and their own particular interests, at little risk by pursuing "détente, entente, and cooperation" between the divided halves of the continent so as eventually to "overcome Yalta" and build a "European Europe," a new system of state relations that would stretch "from the Atlantic to the Urals."

This French challenge to the postwar international structural status quo did not in the end bring France the benefits de Gaulle had hoped for. But for five years at least it made him, and France, objects of extraordinary—if often exasperated—attention everywhere. In these years France acted as if it were a major power in order to be taken for one, and it was taken for one more nearly than at any other time since 1945.

De Gaulle's most striking moves, in 1966, were to withdraw France from the integrated military system of the alliance (although not from the alliance itself), in order to reassert national control of national defense, and to make a visit, a few months later, to the Soviet Union, where he lectured his hosts, and all of Europe, on the benefits to everyone of reducing the barriers that divided Europe. He provided few details and set no timetable. But it seems fair to judge that he hoped that the example France had set of loosening its own ties to the United States would be followed by others in Western Europe, and that the Soviet Union, facing a diminishing American threat or presence, would then gradually feel willing and able to loosen the ties that constrained its own bloc in order to concentrate its attention on its growing quarrel with China, which de Gaulle saw as Russia's main long-term enemy. Successive moves of this kind on each side would stimulate more on the other. Sooner or later the two blocs would be so transformed, by the progressive withdrawal or ejection of their superpower leaders from their dominating roles, that a new kind of Europe would emerge. The superpowers would no longer dominate their allies as the countries of Western and Eastern Europe (including the two German states) built ever closer ties with each other. France would derive a benefit from being not only the initiator and the architect of this appealing new Europe but also the linchpin of the emerging system. It would be the ally of both the Federal Republic, in dealing with whatever threat to it persisted from the Soviet Union, and of the Soviet Union, in containing whatever threat the two German states, or a reunited Germany, might be thought to pose to its Eastern neighbors. In thus undoing "Yalta" and the structural sequels of World War II, France, although far less populous, rich, and militarily powerful than the superpowers, would reassert its leadership by exploiting the tides of the time with vision and skill.

At the same time, de Gaulle, in a striking and much-publicized series of journeys, encouraged the leaders of the third world—Nasser, Nkrumah, Sukarno, Sihanouk, and Goulart, among others—to avoid satellization in either bloc by following France's example of independence. In this way, he suggested, the global rivalry of the superpowers would eventually dry up as the objects of their covetous attentions refused any longer to play their game. While "Yalta" was being uprooted in Europe, new Yaltas would be blocked outside it. In this process, the superpowers would have to curtail their ambitions, but the independence and security of nearly every other country, in Europe and outside it, would be enhanced.

In all of this ambitious program, in Europe and beyond, both the process and the achievement would redound to the renewed greatness of France. A happy byproduct of that would be the beneficent consequences for France's internal well-being that de Gaulle expected and, it seems, believed could be achieved in no other way.

De Gaulle pointed the direction in which Europe would move in the next decade, although in a way much more modest than his ambitious dream. But he himself did not reach or even see the promised land. The superpowers, as he might have expected, were tenacious of their "hegemonies" (which he increasingly equated, to the chagrin of the United States). The dis-integration of France from NATO's military structure was not imitated in the West nor, even more important, did it meet an encouraging response in the East. The hopes de Gaulle found in the "Prague spring" were dashed by the "Prague summer"—the forceful reassertion of Soviet control over Czechoslovakia in August 1968. France's European allies, and above all the Federal Republic, had already shown themselves to be very reserved about following his example in distancing themselves from the United States. The Warsaw Pact's action did not make them more ready to do so. The General's resignation in April 1969, as a delayed consequence of the student-worker "events" in France of May–June 1968, was thus a postclimax to the failure of his policy in the preceding summer.

Three French Presidents Face the Superpowers

Chastened by the "events," and the economic difficulties that followed, de Gaulle was quite willing just before he resigned to respond positively to the overtures made to him by the new American president, Richard Nixon, and his foreign policy adviser, Henry Kissinger. De Gaulle's successor, Georges Pompidou, followed in that path. His slogan, "continuity with change," meant, in the area of foreign policy, in part a continuation of the themes of de Gaulle's "high" policy of 1963–68, in part a reversion to his earlier phase of status-seeking *within* the Western bloc.

There was still talk of a special French relationship with the Soviet Union and of the importance of eventually overcoming the barriers between the two parts of Europe. But this was no longer the provocative novelty it had been, nor a French "exclusive." "Détente, entente, and cooperation," launched by de Gaulle as an alternative to the policies of the Cold War and the bipolar division of Europe, was now taken up vigorously by both the new American administration and the new Socialist-led government of the Federal Republic. Their goals, however, were very different from his. They sought the amelioration of the structural status quo in Europe rather than its replacement.

France took an important part in the complex negotiations concerning Berlin, the relations between the Federal Republic and the states of Eastern Europe, and the organization of the Conference on Security and Cooperation in Europe (CSCE) held at Helsinki in 1975. But France was neither the leading party in these negotiations nor even the broker. Washington and Bonn, when they judged the time had come, carried on their own negotiations with the Soviet Union, although, of course, in close collaboration with each other, France, and the other allies. And the kind of "détente" that emerged from this process of negotiations was no more like that of which de Gaulle had dreamed than the process itself had been. "Yalta," as he understood it, was not overcome but confirmed.

These negotiations certainly led to a different sort of Europe from that of the Cold War. Tension remained at a lower level than was the case before, and relations of many kinds were built across the post-1945 line of division. Even the return to a higher level of East-West tension in the 1980s was not sufficient to undo these things. But the FRG's *Ostpolitik,* whatever the long-term hopes of some of its advocates, was premised on German (and allied) *acceptance* of the division of Europe and the existence of two German states ("in one nation," as the German phrase was). Indeed, it could not have been otherwise in light of the fact, patent after August 1968, that change in the European situation could not be carried out in spite of the Soviet Union, but only with its cooperation, and that the price for that was reaffirmation of Western acceptance of these divisions, and of the Soviet bloc in Eastern Europe, as facts of international life. The United States, pursuing its own agenda of détente with the USSR, went along. The most conspicuous sign of this acceptance was the diplomatic recognition of the East

German state by the Federal Republic of Germany and its allies, and the admission of the two German states into the United Nations.

At the same time, French-American relations improved noticeably. Nixon gave Pompidou particular marks of his esteem by meeting with him twice to negotiate revisions in the international monetary system (in the Azores in 1971 and at Reykjavik in 1973), as if France was indeed the leader and spokesman for Western Europe. This was a positive, if belated and very partial, response to de Gaulle's formal demand for U.S. recognition of France as an equal ally along with Great Britain. It was accompanied by improved French cooperation with the military activities of the alliance and a termination of American objections to the French *force de dissuasion,* by now a fact of life. This pattern of improved relations was not permanently derailed even by the sharp U.S.-French clash in 1973–74 with respect to the U.S.-initiated "Year of Europe" and the quarrel that coincided with that, in which France found itself isolated, about the Western response to the petroleum crisis that followed the Yom Kippur war. Indeed, the declaration issued by the alliance at Ottawa in June 1974 recognized the contribution of the independent French nuclear force (as well as that of the British) to alliance security—a very different theme from that heard in Washington in the 1960s. French-American relations were never free from disagreements, but cooperation was considerable and public quarrels were few during the presidency of Valéry Giscard-d'Estaing (1974–81), at least until the winter of 1980.

As this state of things developed, French rhetoric calling for the "overcoming of Yalta" in Europe became increasingly rare. On the practical level, French relations with the Soviet Union became thin of substance. But how could it have been otherwise? Nothing happened in those years to suggest that Soviet control of Eastern Europe, which had been reasserted in August 1968, was going to change in any way favorable to the loosening of the Eastern bloc. In face of that, France could scarcely continue with any credibility to preach the loosening of the Western bloc. The European allies were clearly not inclined to follow such an example, and, moreover, France itself was by then drawing back from its more extreme criticisms of the Western bloc as it became the recipient of some of the signs of status recognition by the United States that it had long wanted.

Giscard's term, however, ended as Pompidou's had: with a flare-up of French-American tension after several years of relative mutual accommodation. U.S.-Soviet relations had been deteriorating through most of the Carter administration, and they reached their lowest point in many years following the Russian invasion of Afghanistan in December 1979. Faced at the same time with the Iranian revolution and the detention of American diplomats in the Teheran embassy, the United States sought support from its allies to deal with both the Afghan and the Iranian situations, which, in the heat of the moment, became conjoined in American public and even official perceptions. Much European opinion, on the other hand, feared that the increasing tension would spill over onto their continent (if the United States acted so as to make sure that détente really was, as was said, indivisible) and, at the least, were concerned about growing American irritation toward them ("Where are the allies when we need them?"). Giscard therefore seemed to have good reason, in May 1980, to think that a meeting with Leonid Brezhnev would signal, to the general approval of Europeans, that they did not see the situation as Washington did and wanted to preserve the fruits of détente in Europe notwithstanding events in other parts of the world.

Remarkably, however, this classic if episodic or opportunistic Gaullist response to the overencroachment of the superpowers' quarrels on Europe did not have the effect Giscard expected. No European government endorsed his effort to define a West European "space" between the superpowers. Even more surprising, French opinion did not approve, either.

François Mitterrand, with a better grasp of the evolution of French intellectual and popular opinion in a sharply anti-Soviet direction, did not embark on the kind of "socialo-Gaullist" policy that had been expected by many people when he was elected to the presidency in May 1981. On the contrary, he announced that French relations with the Soviet Union could not be "normal" while Russian forces remained in Afghanistan, thereby conspicuously dropping even the pretence of a special relationship—supposedly so important to French prestige and independence—between the two countries. Even more important, he not only strongly endorsed the alliance's 1979 decision to deploy intermediate-range nuclear forces (INF) in Western Europe (on which the Giscard government had taken no position) but did not hesitate to go in January 1983 to the Federal Republic, where deployment was one burning political issue of an election campaign, and urge German voters to choose a government that would accept the missiles (*not*, that is, the German Social Democrats).

These positions were criticized by very few in France. To the widespread French sentiment of anti-Sovietism was joined a growing fear that rejection of INF deployment by the Federal Republic might be only the first step (as, indeed, some German opponents hoped) toward the loosening of its ties with the alliance and perhaps its eventual self-neutralization. Neither Gaullists nor Socialists saw such a prospect with anything but concern. This attitude meant that France, on this issue so vital to its fundamental—European—security interests, stood squarely with the United States in opposition to the Soviet Union, its former supposedly special friend, and to those elements in the Federal Republic (and some other countries) most opposed to what they saw as the dangers of superpower hegemony in Europe at a time of sharply increasing U.S.-Soviet tension. In these circumstances, France found that continued West German commitment to the security system led by the United States was very much in its own interest.

We do not know, of course, how de Gaulle would have responded to this situation. But if we define as "Gaullist" the general's policy of asserting that France, and Western Europe and Europe as a whole, had distinctive interests of their own in the face of superpower encroachments, then it would be very difficult to characterize by his name Mitterrand's policy of supporting the alliance and European status quo in the circumstances of the early 1980s. Moreover, Mitterrand rarely talked about the building of a new European system, even as a distant prospect. He summed up his position well when he said that anything that would overcome Yalta would be welcome but that no one should mistake the wish for the reality. He certainly has not done that, and, as we can see from the firm consensus that has formed around his policies and outlook, neither have many other people in France.

Mitterrand broke the diplomatic ice a little by visiting the Soviet Union in 1984, and the pace of contacts has increased since. But so have the contacts of other Western countries, including the United States. Indeed, neo-détente has broken out between the superpowers in the last few years. They have signed one important arms control treaty (banning INF in Europe) and are negotiating, it seems seriously, to reduce strategic missiles and, with their allies, also conventional forces in Europe. But France has not been a leader in this process and, in fact, has been somewhat skeptical or concerned about it. It is the West German foreign minister who has made himself the spokesman for those in Europe who want to extend or rebuild détente between the two halves of the continent (although consistent with the now well-established premises of *Ostpolitik,* he does not offer the long-term vision that de Gaulle once did).

France seems more moved by doubts than by hopes about where all this may lead. As usual, it fears superpower détente may be implemented over the heads and at the expense of the European countries. Or, even worse, the Federal Republic may be tempted to weaken, in a period of relaxed tension, the ties that bind it to the West in periods of high tension. Neither the Socialist president of France nor the Gaullist prime minister, during his two years in office (1986–88), seemed very enthusiastic about American leadership toward what may become a new phase of "détente, entente, and cooperation." But they offered no new European version of the process. The presidential campaign fought between them in April–May 1988 offered an excellent opportunity for one or both to propound a particular vision of France's, and Europe's, interests in this evolving situation. But they did not. They seemed content to leave it to Mikhail Gorbachev to reinvoke the dream, in de Gaulle's very words, of creating a Europe "from the Atlantic to the Urals."

Perhaps that French dream of the 1960s now looks to them like a nightmare, and even pursuit of it like an invitation to danger. France's leaders may judge that they would do better to work to improve its position *within* the system they know than to try to replace that system with a looser and more Euro-centered one in which the possible advantages of increased freedom of action for France would be outweighed by the possible costs of increased freedom of action for the Federal Republic. A moment may come again like that in which de Gaulle thought otherwise, but his successors of all political persuasions do not seem to have found it in the 1980s.

France in Europe

Whether French policy has aimed to raise the country's status within the existing international system or, as in 1963–68, attempted to reconstruct and eventually replace that system with another more congenial to France's interests, relations with its European neighbors have been central to its outlook and its actions. At the end of World War II and later, de Gaulle and many others believed that France's weight in international affairs, both Western and global, would be enhanced to the extent that it could represent and speak for the other countries in continental Western Europe. When the Federal Republic of Germany came into being in 1949, it at once became the main target of this French approach.

European "unity" and the French role in promoting it in various forms need to be looked at with precision. Federalism, confederalism, cooperation, union, supranationality, integration—these words are sometimes, and wrongly, used interchangeably. They have particular meanings, however, and give rise to distinctive policies for promoting them.

For France, there have been three imaginable ways to pursue a leadership role in Western Europe, and it has used all of them. First, France could try to set up a system by which it would consult its European associates (whichever chose to take part) and pay attention to their interests but with the object of persuading or inducing them to support French policies in the main and let France speak for them in the world on major issues. De Gaulle preferred this approach—what might be called a hegemonic version of the *Europe des états* of which he spoke— because France, as the one power among the continental states with nuclear arms and a more or less established "great power" rank, would be their recognized leader and would have to be dealt with by the superpowers as such.

De Gaulle failed to achieve this because his prospective partners were alienated both by his openly hegemonic ambitions and by the anti-American and anti-alliance thrust of his policies. Those policies, far from raising their consciousness, as he intended, about the ways in which their interests and those of the United States differed, made them wary of the path he wanted to follow even if they were not also wary of accepting French leadership in any case. His manner did not help him either. His spectacular veto of Great Britain's application for membership in the European Communities, in January 1963, and his attack on Community institutions in 1965–66, completed that alienation. The most he could accomplish, in January 1963, was the signature of a treaty of cooperation and consultation with the Federal Republic. This has proved to be of considerable symbolic and substantive importance. But the Bundestag made clear, when ratifying the treaty, that it was not to be taken as signifying any distancing between the Federal Republic and the alliance.

Second, the French and other governments of Western Europe could agree to negotiate among themselves until they arrived at common or concerted policies on as many specific issues as they could. As the number of such issues increased, so, in theory, would the cohesion and influence of this "confederal" European grouping. France, however, would not be the one leader or sole spokesman for the group in this version of the *Europe des états* but would have to share influence on its decision making with the Federal Republic of Germany and, once it entered the system, Great Britain.

Such a system has in fact existed since Georges Pompidou, after improving France's relations with the United States and ending its isolation in Europe by lifting the veto on British accession to the European Communities (EC), reached agreement with the other members of the EC to establish a consultative political council. Actual policy coordination, however, has been slight when compared to the need proclaimed on every side, over many turbulent years, for more and better. Anyone who doubts this should study the successive phases of maneuvering and negotiating about advancing the Middle East peace process. The American role is always prominent. That of the Soviet Union seems to be growing. Where is Western Europe's input? And yet no countries have more reason to be interested in the affairs of that region than those of Western Europe.

Third, France, together with other countries, could agree to delegate some part of its national decision making authority (a more expressive formulation than "to give up sovereignty") to a supranational or federal authority whose members would be designated by the member states but which would be empowered to make decisions by other than unanimous vote that would be binding on them all. To Americans of the 1950s and 1960s such a development seemed familiar, and appealing, in that it would resemble that by which the United States, in the 1780s, moved from the Articles of Confederation to the federal constitution.

This was, in fact, part of the European policy of the Fourth Republic, beginning with Robert Schuman's highly creative proposal, in May 1950, to set up a supranational coal-steel community. Some elements of supranationality are also to be found in the European Communities. But the treaties of Rome (March 1957) provided for less "federalism" than did the coal-steel community, and the relevant provisions of those treaties are far, in any case, from having been fully implemented.

De Gaulle was a sworn enemy of all international institutions that threatened to curtail France's right to make its own policies in every sphere. He thought such limitations were dangerous in themselves to French interests because they allowed foreigners to decide France's affairs and also prejudicial to his efforts to re-inspire the French people with confidence in their right and ability to manage their own affairs. Nevertheless, he allowed the European Economic Community and Euratom to be implemented in 1959, because he understood that France's relations with the Federal Republic of Germany, above all, and its economic interests as well, did not allow him to do otherwise. But in 1965–66 he succeeded in blocking the prescribed evolution of the communities toward a greater degree of supranational or federal decision making. By refusing to take part in community business (the "empty chair" policy), he forced the other members to agree that the treaty provisions calling for weighted majority voting on certain issues would *not* go into effect at the scheduled time. In what was called the "Luxembourg compromise," they had to acquiesce in a French interpretation that called for negotiations among the members on those policy issues that any of them considered to be of major importance to itself to continue until unanimity was achieved among them.

The other members of the communities yielded to de Gaulle reluctantly and with the hope that, once he had disappeared from the political scene, movement toward supranationality might be renewed. It is remarkable, however, that two decades after his departure decision making on major matters by less than unanimous agreement among the member states—the hallmark of supranationality—has not been resumed. Apart from the administration of established policies, community decision making can most accurately be described as a kind of permanent negotiation on a wide range of subjects.among the members, negotiation that, on most issues, goes on until the major states, at least, are satisfied.

Was de Gaulle's action, at the critical moment of decision in the mid-1960s, the cause of this? Did his example unleash or at least legitimize nationalist responses in other countries that have perpetuated his work? Is it possible, even, that Georges Pompidou's decision to allow Great Britain (along with Ireland, Norway (had it not declined), and Denmark) to join the communities contributed to this result? Has Britain, never an enthusiast for European federalism despite American hopes to the contrary in the 1960s, been de Gaulle's willing successor in the role of blocking further integration—an ironic outcome he might have relished? Or is it that the first steps in the direction of European integration were the easiest and that no French government, and no government in any of the other large members, was likely to agree to let major decisions respecting its economy and society be made against its will by the authorities of Brussels or a majority of the other member governments? However that may be, they have not agreed to this day, notwithstanding the enlargement of the membership, the direct election of the European parliament since 1979, and the bold plans to carry through, beginning in 1992, the true common market projected by the treaties of Rome.

The 1980s would seem to have been an ideal decade for a significant increase in common decision making among the European states, whether by closer coordination or more structured means. The Europeans were profoundly affected and concerned by *both* the swings in superpower relations (which veered from an upsurge of tension early in the decade to summitry and arms control negotiations) *and* the profound difficulties of the international capitalist system, which often placed the United States and its allies in antagonistic positions with respect to trade problems, interest rates, and exchange rates, among many other issues. We might have thought that the Europeans, beginning with France, would see in this situation powerful reasons to try to enhance their influence on all these issues by speaking increasingly, in one way or another, with a single voice.

Mitterrand has, in fact, identified himself with the idea of "Europe" and has spoken often and eloquently about the necessity for Europe to cease being "the mute witness and passive stake of East-West relations." Gaullists and others on the Right now use much the same language. The debate about "Europe" in French politics, which de Gaulle encouraged and relished, seems to be over. But, as noted earlier, France's concern with the Soviet threat and the possible loosening of the Federal Republic's ties with the West led the country to align itself with the alliance and the United States as its prime response to the "neo-Cold War" of the first half of the decade. France resolutely rejected, if it even gave any thought to, the idea of trying to take the lead of those forces in Europe, and above all in the Federal Republic of Germany, that were fearful of the dangers for the continent of the superpower confrontation. Such a course, one would have thought, might have had some appeal to both Gaullists and Socialists who were traditionally alert to the differences between the interests of the West European countries and those of the United States, not least in such tense circumstances. Remarkably, it did not. The policies of the Mitterrand government in this respect were not challenged by any substantial group except the Communists (*after* they left the cabinet in July 1984). This broad consensus survived the swing of the superpowers from high tension to serious negotiations in 1985, the change of government in France in March 1986, and the return of a Socialist-led government after Mitterrand's reelection in May 1988.

At the same time, the efforts of French governments in the 1980s to strengthen ties with the Federal Republic have in part reflected, of course, the traditional interest in enhancing France's and Western Europe's influence on American decision making. Even more important, however, has been French concern to reassure the Germans that their security and other interests would be taken care of whatever the vagaries of American policy. Every French leader has called for enhancing these ties. The twenty-fifth anniversary of the Franco-German treaty of January 1963 was celebrated in style, and a joint defense council was established, among other new mechanisms of consultation and cooperation. Particular emphasis, of course, has been put on security cooperation, both bilateral and multilateral, as in the framework of the Western European Union (WEU). The reanimation of that marginal organization (which includes also Great Britain, Italy, and the three Benelux states) was often proclaimed to be urgent and imminent.

The Germans have welcomed such French initiatives as the creation of a Rapid Action Force available on short notice for duty in Central Europe (or elsewhere), joint army maneuvers, increased consultation on security issues, and the common production (bilaterally and with others) of weapons. But the Germans in the 1980s seem no less convinced than they were in the 1960s that nothing that France or the WEU or some other Western European configuration could provide with respect to their security would be able to replace what the United States provides, and that too intense a search for a European "solution" for their security problems might actually impel a most unwelcome U.S. withdrawal.

The French are doctrinally opposed to increasing their conventional forces to replace those the United States might someday decide to withdraw from the continent (even if budgetary and demographic restraints did not also stand in the way). Policy continues to affirm that peace depends on deterrence and that only nuclear weapons can provide it, those of the French and also, it is desired, those of the United States. At the same time, the French have *not,* despite considerable fuzzy rhetoric on the subject, extended a nuclear guarantee to the Federal Republic. Even less have they given any sign that they think the notion of a European nuclear defense system is anything but a dream, for reasons, as Mitterrand has said, both historic and practical. For such weapons require unity of command if their employment and, therefore, their deterrent capability are to be credible, and how is the European government to provide such unity? In any case, it is difficult to imagine any French government turning over to any non-French authority or even sharing with it (if that can be imagined) control of the expensive and painfully acquired nuclear weapons whose possession has been so central to France's sense of security and independence for more than twenty years.

Official statements have increasingly emphasized the importance of the Federal Republic of Germany to France, the likelihood that war in Germany would engulf France also, and the confidence that the Germans should put in France in the event of hostilities. But these assurances have stopped short of promising the Germans that an attack on them, nuclear or conventional, would trigger the French nuclear force in the same way as would an attack on France. Mitterrand said in January 1988 that France will not share with the Germans or anyone its ultimate decision to use—or not to use—nuclear weapons. It seems reasonable to take the French at their word on these matters and to believe that they will avoid, as former prime minister Jacques Chirac put it, "wandering into sterile debates about the eventual extension of our nuclear guarantee." Chancellor Helmut Kohl has explicitly done so.

While these large issues were leading French policy forward, although within narrow limits, with respect to cooperation with other European countries—and particularly with the Federal Republic—on security problems, at the same time American economic policies seriously affected France and the others throughout the decade. But France was never inclined (even if others would have been, including the Federal Republic and Great Britain, which is doubtful) to try to deal with these problems by sinking its own national policy preferences in a common West European policy. Even less was it prepared to grant sufficient authority to the EC institutions to enable them to make joint policy on the members' behalf with the United States and Japan. The European Monetary System ("the snake") has been maintained (without Britain until 1990—a very significant and damaging absence), but mainly as a framework for the necessary synchronization of the monetary policies of France and Germany, each the other's best trade partner. The Communities have been said to be "relaunched" on many occasions, and not least by France, which was fertile in putting forward plans and projects. Some of these have taken on substance (e.g., the Eureka program for technological cooperation). Others give promise of doing so (the "great common market" to be established from 1992 on by the members of a common market whose founding treaty was signed in—1957). Yet others have so far remained vague (e.g., "Europe at two speeds").

Up to now, nothing has changed the fact that the European countries continue to make their own economic and social policies within the limits, more or less wide, still allowed by their increasing—and increasingly visible—interdependence with each other, but also, and perhaps no less important, with the United States, Japan, the newly industrializing countries, and the petroleum producers. Notwithstanding the record of the 1980s, the French government and elites do not seem committed to reviving the old dream, associated with Jean Monnet and Robert Schuman, of progressively transferring decision-making authority to supranational or federal institutions that could make decisions binding on all even without the concurrence of all. In the absence of that, France and its partners continue as best they can to develop their policies in concert with each other in the EC and other institutions, and in concert with the United States and Japan— the role of governments being supplemented by that of central banks and private economic decision makers in an immensely complex process. Whether this maximizes the effective projection on the international scene of France's economic interests, and those of the other European countries, is questionable, which explains the high hopes attached to the EC's plans for 1992 and beyond. Whether these hopes will be realized, and, if so, whether the EC will then be able at last to work out and promote *European* interests, remains uncertain in light of the mixed results achieved since 1957 and the ambivalent motivations that the record suggests with respect to the major governments involved.

The Foreign Policy Consensus

Foreign policy provided many of the most contentious issues in the French politics of the Fourth Republic and of Charles de Gaulle's presidency. Many of the general's major initiatives in that field were strongly opposed by much of the political class. This contentiousness waned sharply during the 1970s, and in this decade it has been replaced by a consensus, designed by the Mitterrand government and changed in only secondary ways by the short-lived government of the Right headed by Jacques Chirac. Debate about the main lines of foreign policy has dwindled so far as to obscure, for some, the fact that the broad consensus that now exists on the subject is *not* as old as the Fifth Republic itself. If foreign policy counts for rather little in French political debate nowadays, that cannot be explained entirely by the fact that the successive presidents of the Republic have had overriding authority in this area. De Gaulle invented that authority and exercised it boldly. But there was no such consensus in his time.

The sources of this consensus are probably just what they seem to be: a realistic sense among France's leaders that the international situation in which their country lives, and the means of action available to it, define its foreign policy choices fairly narrowly. A most important example of this is their response to changes underway in the Soviet Union. The French should wish, and therefore have good human reasons to believe, that these changes foreshadow the waning of Soviet control over Eastern Europe, something that de Gaulle rightly considered the prerequisite for the withering away of both blocs, the eventual "overcoming of Yalta," and the enhancement of France's own independence and freedom of action. In fact, however, the French have been the least convinced by the reality and/or the prospects of success of the Gorbachev regime's reformist policies. They seem at least as convinced as any Europeans that there continues to be an important Soviet threat to Western Europe, perhaps the *more* dangerous because of superpower arms agreement and the prospect that the Federal Republic may respond imprudently to changes in Soviet behavior and image, changes *they* themselves are skeptical of. The French believe that alliance with the United States, among other policies, remains necessary for dealing with both these problems.

These premises are very different from those of the period of "high Gaullism" or "overcoming Yalta," and even of that (before 1963) when de Gaulle was a "good ally" of the United States in the Cold War even as he worked to induce or coerce it to accept his demands for status recognition. On these premises has been built in this decade a consensus on the main lines of policy, one that has resisted both neo-Cold War and neo-détente abroad and a contentious political situation at home.

Some of the policies included in the French consensus can fairly be described as Gaullist:

- The firm assertion of France's right and ability to make its own policies, a position so well established by now that proclamations of greatness and independence are comparatively rare, because they have achieved what can be achieved in this respect both at home and abroad and need not be repeated with the old intensity.

- Maintenance and further expansion of the national nuclear force as the bedrock of national security policy despite much confusing talk by officials and politicians of possible changes in nuclear deterrence policy.

- Continued refusal to return to the Atlantic military declaration, a topic that has ceased to be of much practical concern even for the United States and the alliance, between both of which and France contingency military planning has become a matter of course.

- Promotion of French interests in Europe on the basis of a close relationship with the Federal Republic.

- Preservation of the special relations that de Gaulle established with most of France's former dependencies in North and Black Africa as a powerful prop to France's international influence and its belief in its continuing global role.

Other policies are clearly different from those of de Gaulle:

- Closer cooperation with both the European Communities and the alliance by leaders of both Left and Right who do not fear, so well-established is the belief in France's independence, that they will be denounced for undermining it.
- Closer, although still carefully delimited, cooperation with the Federal Republic and on the European level with respect to defense, notwithstanding that this might seem to infringe on the credibility of France's independence and the credibility of its nuclear deterrent doctrine.
- A willingness to let the once cherished "special relationship" with the Soviet Union fall into abeyance even at the cost of putting on the shelf, at least for a time, France's once and always prospective role of balancing between the superpowers to its greater glory and advantage.
- Correlatively with this, openly close relations with the United States on the overriding issue that binds the two together—the preservation of a strategic balance in Europe—notwithstanding disagreements on many other specific issues.
- Downplaying, even by the Socialists, of efforts to encourage the countries of the Third World to "escape" alignment with one or the other superpower, as Claude Cheysson once put it (poignantly, since such escape was recognized as being beyond France's reach).

The Nation in the World

This brief review of the policies that France has pursued in the 1980s gives us a basis for considering its place in the world, its perception of what that place is, and the interplay of that perception with French politics.

First, is the France of today a great power in the sense de Gaulle indicated? Must it be taken into account when its own immediate interests are being treated on the international stage and also when issues in which it has interests (let us say the problems of Europe, the Middle East, and Africa, and international economic and military matters) are being considered?

My answer to that question is "no." France has substantial influence on the matters referred to. But it is neither objectively the case, nor do the French believe or say that it is, that their influence on matters very important to them can be compared to that of what are, still, the two—and only two—superpowers. There is considerable talk these days about the end of global bipolarity and the oncoming or already arrived multipolarity of the international system, talk that is strikingly similar to that of de Gaulle himself and, for example, the official American concept of a "pentapolar" world propounded in the early 1970s. Yet is this view substantially more valid now than it proved to be fifteen or twenty years ago? Probably not. Those powers that have the capacity to destroy not only themselves but all others occupy a special position that all their accumulated difficulties and relative "decline" as others have gained influence have not undone. This ultimate capability may not be used or usable, but its existence, when added to the many other attributes of power shared (although not equally) by these two countries, gives them a unique place in the international system. Even de Gaulle, an astute observer of the realities of power, however much he might work to elude or conceal some of their implications, must have thought so.

France cannot but recognize, and its leaders do, that the "Big Two" still have the main parts in the strategic-political script in which it, and others, then develop their own parts as best they can, whether to support or oppose, accept or defy. In this there has been great continuity. France, for example, in a period of apparently profound internal disorder and international weakness, could not prevent the formation of the Federal Republic of Germany in 1949 or its being armed in 1955. Now, when France's institutions are far more stable and its influence much greater, could it prevent something as central to its interests as the reunification of Germany if the policies of the two superpowers coincided, for whatever reasons, to that end? The answer seems obvious.

France is also one of the Big Five of the global economic system. But here too it has found—and never more clearly than in the 1980s—that the United States, even in the disarray of its economic policies, and Japan and the Federal Republic, have influence on the world economy, and on the *French* economy, which severely constrains France's ability to make the key decisions affecting itself. It has no comparable impact on *their* economic policy-making.

If this is the case, and if France is not in the front rank in the sense defined by de Gaulle, do we find, as he would have expected, that the "ferments of dispersal" are running wild at home, cause and/or effect of that lack? Remarkably enough, the answer to that is certainly "no." The famous ferments among the French people are considerably less violent, deep, fixed, and obstructive of policy-making, domestic and foreign, than they used to be. Centrist policies seem rampant, based on the evaporation of ideologically based dreams of change, even if the structure of politics remains bipolar (but why not?). At what point, since 1789, have the constitutional system and the Republic itself been challenged by so few citizens, politicians, or intellectuals? When has a strong executive authority been accepted by almost everyone as a necessary instrument of decision-making rather than challenged by many as a harbinger of tyranny?

French history puts us on guard against believing that this comparatively happy state of affairs (which perhaps also has its costs) will necessarily prove lasting. Yet it does seem that France may have gone a considerable distance toward draining some of the poisons from its historic divisions. What is remarkable is that this has taken place at a time when France does not meet the condition with respect to its international position laid down by de Gaulle as essential for its being able to tame its "ferments of dispersal." Internal divisions seem to have been overcome, or their ill effects limited, in the absence of the uniting balm that de Gaulle thought would flow inward from the fact that France was holding its place in the front rank of the nations. France holds no such place as he understood it, French leaders acknowledge the fact, the French people know it, and this state of things is not being challenged, as the 1988 presidential campaign reminded us. Yet French divisiveness has declined and politics has changed for the better as a result.

To those who believe that there has been a fundamental transformation of France's political life (and more), whether in the direction of its becoming more like that of "others" (the Anglo-Saxons?) or at least less like that of France's own past, de Gaulle's ghost threatens to rise up and proclaim that this seemingly happy development is a sham at home and a disguise for the abdication abroad of France's proper position and aspirations. It may be, of course, that French politics and society are less "fundamentally" and/or permanently changed than has appeared to be the case. Perhaps, however, the political system of France is now "better" in a better way than de Gaulle's hypothetical posthumous charge of mediocrity at home and abroad would allow. Perhaps the relative temperance of its political life is not the counterpart of slackness and resignation abroad, as an old-fashioned nationalist might see it (is the scarcity of them in France today a sign of health or disease?), but is, rather, an indication of something more positive: that the country has had the wisdom and confidence both to use the institutional cohesion brought about not by de Gaulle's foreign policies but by the constitutional and political system he devised to reconcile itself to its not inconsiderable place in the international system and to understand that a triumphalist foreign policy (even if conditions in the world were favorable to that) was no longer as necessary to French national unity as he, who did not witness these changes in his own time and did not anticipate them, would have believed.

Ironically, then, de Gaulle may have contributed more powerfully than he knew to French domestic cohesion by means that he believed to be at best indirectly contributory to that end. The strong president established by the Constitution and strengthened further by the political system he fostered was, in his view, to provide the means by which France could pursue the kind of foreign policy required by both its international situation *and* its historically rooted internal divisions. In this way France would be able to stand in the front rank despite its internal divisions, and, by doing so, it would achieve the maximum (and limited) degree of cohesion of which the nation was capable. But neither the French nor we have to agree with him that there were no other ways to do these things. Perhaps it is as well that France no longer has domestic needs that impel it to pursue foreign policy objectives beyond its means and that the French people are at liberty to take a fairly realistic view of their place in the world. If they do they should see that their foreign policies appear to be both reasonable and successful, the premises and consensus on which they are based well-adapted to the international situation in which their country must live. If they regret that France is not still the princess of the fairy tales and the Madonna of the frescoes, the guide for the nations, at the same time solar and starry, they can derive a rational pleasure from the fact that it nevertheless holds an assured, important, and respected place among the nations. To the extent that it has, besides, achieved a degree of internal political cohesion with few precedents in the last century or two, so much the better.

Notes

1. Victor Hugo, *History of a Crime* (New York: Hurst, n.d.), pp. 463–65.

2. Henry James, *The Princess Casamassima* (New York: Harper Torchbooks, 1959), p. 80.

3. Charles de Gaulle, *The Complete War Memoirs of Charles de Gaulle, 1940–1946* (New York: De Capo Press, [1984]), p. 3.

Conclusion: Still Searching for the New France

James F. Hollifield

For decades the accepted view of France was one of a country that had failed to keep pace with changes occurring in the world around it. This failure to "modernize" was a focal point of political controversy throughout the Fourth Republic and the early years of the Fifth. How could France transform its economy from one based on small firms and family farms to one based on economies of scale and the latest techniques of industrial production?

The failure of the French economy to industrialize was but one symptom of a much broader problem. France retained too many of the qualities of "traditional" society. In order for France to change, it would be necessary once and for all to liberate the citizen from the influence of medieval society: to get him or her out of the village, out of the shop, off the farm, into the city and into a factory: in the words of Eugen Weber, to turn "peasants into Frenchmen."[1] But this would entail uprooting many individuals and, more important, changing their worldview. How could such a radical transformation occur without a massive intervention of the state, and without totally transforming traditional authority relations? Would not such change be so destabilizing as to provoke a crisis of legitimacy, thereby undermining the authority of the modernizing state itself?

These questions were resolved during the 1950s by the careful but deliberate policies of a modernizing elite led by individuals such as Jean Monnet.[2] France began to break out of economic underdevelopment during the decade of the 1950s, and the "stalemate society" of the Third Republic crumbled under the weight of economic and social change. Yet France retained an air of traditionalism in politics, which remained in a state of paralysis and semi-crisis, breaking into open confrontation during the Algerian War. Even though France was catching up with other industrial powers, it had yet to resolve some basic problems associated with representative government. What should be the role of the citizen in a democratic society? What should be the relationship between the citizen and the state? What limits should be placed on political authority, and how should these limits be institutionalized?[3]

I should like to thank my colleagues Suzanne Berger, George Ross, Martin Schain, and Aristide Zolberg for their helpful comments on earlier versions of this essay.

Thus the story of our book begins in 1962, when the last of the problems of political change had seemingly been resolved by General de Gaulle. Although the economic legacy of the Fourth Republic was positive, the political legacy was one of stalemate and crisis. Government was carried out by an Assembly composed of warring political factions loosely organized into political parties. When the author of the Constitution of the Fifth Republic, Michel Debré, criticized the Fourth Republic as a "régime des partis," he was leveling an indictment at political parties in general, which, it was believed, were responsible for the paralysis of government and the crisis of legitimacy of 1956–58. Parties took the blame for everything from fomenting revolution and discord on the Left, in the form of a Communist conspiracy, to sponsoring a military coup d'état on the Right, in the name of *Algérie Française*. In effect, political parties, the institutions supposed to ensure political participation and stable, representative government, were accused of undermining the Republic and contributing to a crisis of legitimacy, leaving the citizen confused and incapable of influencing the flow of events. Since the *Assemblée Nationale* was the seat of power of political parties, it was the first institution to be targeted for a reduction of power by the founders of the Fifth Republic.

By concentrating power in the hands of a single individual, the founders of the Fifth Republic hoped that it would be possible to solve problems of participation and create a new relationship between the citizen and the state. The powerful position of president of the Republic would transform the political landscape by focusing the attention of political parties and voters on a single source of power— the executive. By appealing to the Jacobin tradition of direct democracy, de Gaulle and his associates succeeded in pushing through a referendum for the direct election of the president, who from 1958 to 1962 drew his authority from an electoral college composed largely of local notables.[4] In creating a popularly elected executive, de Gaulle was also appealing to the Bonapartist tradition, which led some to describe the institution as a republican monarchy, while others denounced the entire process of institutional reform as a "coup d'état permanent."[5]

If France was to be a "modern" industrial power, it would need a political system in which its leaders could pursue the national interest in a climate of stable government. A presidential system, relying on the traditional powers of the centralized Jacobin state, was deemed most appropriate. As a check on the president, the Assembly was to retain many of the powers of a traditional parliament, even though the prime minister and the cabinet would be subordinate to the president. Almost unwittingly, the link between the legislative and executive branches was set up in such a way as to bring political parties back into the picture. The president would be able to rule with a more or less free hand, so long as he was able to maintain majority control of the Assembly. As Stanley Hoffmann points out in his essay on institutional change in this volume, the true test of these institutional arrangements would not come for almost two decades, with the alternation of power from Right to Left in 1981 and "cohabitation" in

1986–88. Nonetheless, it seems that the institutional reforms set in motion by de Gaulle and the founders of the Fifth Republic have succeeded in creating a more representative and stable political system.

Can we therefore conclude that France is now "modern" in every sense, economic, social, and political? Have the experiences of the past three decades succeeded in creating an industrial economy and a consumer society that are comparable to those of other industrial democracies? Is politics no longer characterized by the ideological struggles of the Third Republic, which pitted the authoritarian right against the republican Left, or those of the Fourth and early years of the Fifth Republic, which pitted a nationalist and capitalist Right against a Communist Left? Have we witnessed the advent of a form of centrist, catchall politics, which is supposed to accompany industrial development and the growth of a liberal middle class?[6]

Tocqueville Revisited: Changes in Political Culture

At a time when the notions of catchall and nonideological politics are being questioned in the United States and Britain, when the old model of interest-group liberalism has been challenged by the rise of administrative and regulatory politics, there is *talk* of a "new" pluralism in French politics, which is described as more open and consensual. The power of the state appears to have been reduced by neoliberal reforms and the ongoing integration of France into both Europe and the international political economy; institutions of the Fifth Republic have gained a legitimacy that was often lacking in previous regimes; and political choices are no longer cast in the stark ideological terms of Left versus Right.[7] If these arguments are correct, then the Tocquevillian view of France as a radical republican democracy no longer holds, and we may be witnessing a change in French political culture along the lines described by Tocqueville in his analysis of American democracy:

> I can conceive of a society in which all men would feel an equal love and respect for the laws . . . in which the authority of the government would be respected as necessary, and not divine; and in which the loyalty of the subject to the chief magistrate would not be a passion, but a quiet and rational persuasion. With every individual in the possession of rights which he is sure to retain, a kind of manly confidence and reciprocal courtesy would arise between all classes, removed alike from pride and servility.[8]

In this passage and elsewhere in *Democracy in America*, Tocqueville describes his ideal of a liberal democracy, which he believed he had found in the still young American Republic. This is a statement above all about the practice of democracy and the rise of a distinctive political culture, characterized by the acceptance of certain rules of political behavior and by a willingness to compromise. The American Republic seemed to have solved many of the antidemocratic and alienating tendencies inherent in "modern" society, especially the atomization of the citizenry and the concentration of power in an ever stronger centralized state. This was accomplished, according to Tocqueville, through the creation of intermediary institutions and groups—strong local government and voluntary associations, in particular.

This rather idealized view of American democracy can be contrasted strongly with Tocqueville's view of French democracy, which he describes as being handicapped by an overbearing state with a centralized administration that had hindered rather than helped the development of a "civic culture." The radical egalitarian traditions of direct democracy and popular sovereignty—legacies of the French Revolution—are condemned by Tocqueville as inimical to stable democratic rule.[9] In comparing the two democratic traditions, he states, "I do not hesitate to say that most of the maxims commonly called democratic in France would be proscribed by the democracy of the United States."[10]

Tocqueville's analysis has colored our thinking about the development of democracy in France. One can certainly find strong Tocquevillian overtones in many modern works on French politics and society. To take but one example, writing at the very beginning of the Fifth Republic, Stanley Hoffmann described the pattern of authority relations in France as being the result of "a historical experience which developed both the need for and the fear of authority."[11] It is the dual tradition of a strong, centralized state—a legacy of the Old Regime— and a revolutionary, republican impulse that is the paradox of French political culture, according to Hoffmann. Yet, as we have seen from the essays in this volume, France has undergone dramatic changes since the end of the Second World War. Most scholars recognize these changes, which have eliminated the stalemate society of the Third Republic and replaced it with something that we are struggling to define.[12] Can we safely conclude that because of social (and economic) changes, described in the various contributions to this book, that the Tocquevillian view of French democracy is no longer appropriate?

The general perception of change in France, which is reflected in the various essays in this volume, is that France has modernized economically, thereby creating a consumer society. Yet the question remains open: *Has the "modernization" of society and the economy pushed politics inexorably in the direction of pragmatism and greater consensus?* The disappearance of General de Gaulle from the political scene in 1969 and the subsequent decline of Gaullism has forced political parties, particularly those of the Right, to redefine themselves and their policies. Likewise, the precipitous decline of the French Communist Party in the 1970s and 1980s has opened up a new breathing space for the Socialist Party, thereby encouraging a more centrist form of politics on the Left. But, as both Jane Jenson and Martin Schain point out in their essays, neither of these developments seems to have created a solid two-party system or a "catchall" politics. The French electorate remains fragmented, and protest voting, whether in the form of support for the racist and xenophobic Front National or the new *groupuscules* of the Left, such as the *écolos,* remains high.

In the economic sphere, various French governments have pursued policies of "liberalization" since the early 1970s, when economic planning was eliminated as a tool for managing the economy. After a brief return to *étatisme* in the form of nationalizations under the first Socialist government, there has been a general retrenchment of regulatory politics in the 1980s. The apparent rejection of more *étatisme* by the Socialists in 1983 and the advent of the French version of separation of powers (*cohabitation*) in 1986 have led to increased speculation about the demise of the Jacobin state. Yet, as Alain Lipietz points out, neither the Right nor the Left has been able to solve the problem of finding the appropriate niche for the French economy in what is an increasingly interdependent and competitive world economy.

How can we assess the changes that have occurred since 1962 in the relationship between state and society? A shift in political culture certainly entails more than simply a series of policy changes associated with changes of government. On the other hand, a change in political culture is not necessarily revolutionary. With the obvious exception of May 1968, the transformation of French politics and the "modernization" of the economy have not shaken the foundations of the regime, nor have they resulted in the kind of constitutional crises that have been the hallmark of French history. States (and societies) have very long half-lives, which is to say that there is something fundamental that remains constant over time.[13] It is this "constant" that allows us to identify national patterns of political development and to analyze them. Hence we are led, rightly or wrongly, to characterize American politics as traditionally pluralist, and the French as Jacobin or radical republican.[14] What gives meaning to these categories? How do we know when state-society relations have changed to the point that such categories are no longer meaningful? What role does economic change play in reshaping political systems and political cultures? The arguments presented in this volume paint a picture of the scope of change in France over the past thirty years. They also portend a new France, one that can no longer be viewed purely in Tocquevillian terms, but that is not wholly disconnected from its revolutionary past.

The Scope of Social Change: From "Stalemate Society" to Interest-Group Liberalism

Michel Crozier and Stanley Hoffmann offer a vivid account of politics and society in Third and Fourth Republic France. They describe society and the political system in terms of a stalemate that reflects a delicate balance between modern and antimodern groups, a balance reinforced and maintained by the state.

According to the stalemate argument, the weakness of associational life, the atomization of society (*l'horreur de face à face*), and the overweening power of the administrative state are the keys to explaining the slow pace of social and economic change, as well as the fragility of the political system.[15] It took the experience of defeat and the emergence of a new political class to begin the process of restructuring society. Yet French society was not transformed overnight. Fourth Republic politics reverted to a fragmented process of representation, exacerbated by a weak party system, which was reminiscent of the Third Republic. The old subcultures of peasant-farmers and shopkeepers were weakened by economic change, but they did not simply disappear. Some groups, such as the *notables,* found new institutional niches, while others, such as *petits commerçants,* fought successfully for the protection of their interests.[16] Still other groups were willing and able to make special (neocorporatist) arrangements with the state to protect their interests. The obvious examples are peasant-farmers and teachers.[17]

The short-term beneficiaries of economic modernization were workers and, by extension, the French Communist Party. By the 1960s, France had begun to look more like other industrial societies.[18] However, workers had much greater difficulty than other groups in their efforts to obtain benefits and protection from the state. This is due to the historical weaknesses of the French working class, and the fragmentation of the trade-union movement, which has been unable to develop a united front vis-à-vis employers or the state. Trade unions have consistently been losers in struggles over policy.[19] Class cleavages have been confined by and large to urban areas, reaching only late and haphazardly into the countryside. Class found political expression primarily in the Communist Party and Communist trade unionism. Throughout the nineteenth and much of the twentieth century, French society remained remarkably unchanged, and even sedentary by comparison with the more "dynamic" societies of Britain and Germany.[20]

Given the capacity of the state to pursue strategies of economic modernization in the face of resistance from a range of traditional social groups,[21] the paucity of "peak" interest groups, the weakness of trade unions, and the comparative absence of institutionalized representation of the interests of capital and labor that one finds in Germany and the smaller European democracies, it is difficult to describe the evolution of state-society relations in Fifth Republic France in corporatist terms.[22]

Interest groups in postwar France have had to deal with a relatively autonomous state, and protest has remained a principal avenue of dissent, both for "modern" groups, like workers, and for more traditional groups, such as the Catholic defenders of parochial schools. In his contribution to this volume, René Mouriaux gives a detailed account of the confrontational nature of relations between unions and the state, due in part to the presence of the Right in power from 1962 to 1981. Yet, even under the Socialist governments of the 1980s, unions have had difficulty making their voices heard. In his essay, John Ambler describes the unusual nature of group politics in the area of education, where a love-hate relationship between the powerful teachers' union, the Fédération de l'Education Nationale (FEN), and the Ministry of Education has reinforced the powers of the state, while at the same time making it more difficult for the state to deal with traditional Catholic groups that support parochial schools. It is in the centralized State and uniform political culture of the *corpsards* that Jacobinism still finds its fullest expression.[23]

The special character of interest-group politics in France does not mean that newer forms of political participation are totally absent. There are "social movements" that cut across traditional social cleavages. Although they pale by comparison with similar movements in Germany, Japan, or the United States, peace and environmental groups do exist. But they have yet to emerge as a major feature of French politics, and France cannot be classified as a full-fledged member of the postindustrial club where "citizen politics" is a common form of political participation.[24] Many reasons could be given for the weakness of "postindustrial" politics in France. But it is most likely that the weakness of "citizen" politics is the result of the late development of industrial society in France and the persistence of nationalist and republican ideals, which offer the electorate an entirely different and uniquely French model of political participation and citizenship.[25] France certainly has a tradition of protest and extra-institutional movements, but protest is often associated with the defense of traditional interests or with open, revolutionary defiance of political authority, as in May 1968. More recently, has been a surge in political participation around the issues of immigration, civil rights, and protection of the environment. Pro-immigration, human, and civil rights groups, such as MRAP and SOS-racisme, have been particularly prominent in organizing a segment of the electorate to defend individual rights and *le droit à la différence*.

Jacobin ideals of egalitarianism, direct democracy, and popular sovereignty have played a crucial role in turning "peasants into Frenchmen," and *l'Etat* has been the arbiter of conflict between various subcultures for much of the postwar period. But, in addition to political and civil citizenship dating from the Revolution, we cannot ignore the centrality of the welfare state as a mechanism for political socialization and participation.[26] Douglas Ashford's essay on the *Etat Providence* shows how the growth and institutionalization of the welfare state is driven by a "republican" logic, from its inception under the reforms of radical governments of the Third Republic through the rediscovery of the welfare state by the Socialists in the 1980s. Yet, despite the statist and republican overtones of social policy, it is striking that the French welfare state seems to have grown from the ground up, beginning at the grass-roots level in the *mutualités* and voluntary aid associations, before being overtaken by modernizing political forces in the postwar period.

It is in the area of *le social* that we find the greatest evidence of the development of a kind of *civil* society, which remained outside the control of the state until the Gaullist period. Beginning with the 1967 reform, the political struggles over social welfare take on the air of more classical interest-group politics, with employers squaring off against trade unions for influence. By the 1970s, France looked much like other advanced industrial societies, where social policy and the welfare state are the principal arenas of political conflict and participation. As Ashford notes "social democracy was entering through the back door," because the Right was responsible for institutionalizing social welfare in the postwar period. The Left would have to wait until the 1980s to attempt a more overt construction of social democracy in France, only to face the severe economic conditions of the early 1980s, which prohibited too much tinkering with existing social policies and institutions.

Since 1962, French politics has become more "organized" as various groups in society have been able to take advantage of the new institutional arrangements of the Fifth Republic. Nonetheless, state-society relations have retained a distinctly Jacobin quality, particularly in those policy areas, such as education and immigration, that touch upon what Tocqueville called the "founding myths" of the republican regime. The arrival of millions of ethnically and religiously distinct immigrants, primarily Muslims from North and West Africa, raises questions that strike at the heart of the Jacobin model. This new ethnic cleavage has provoked a crisis of participation, as political parties and the party system struggle to cope with immigration and to assimilate a distinctly foreign population.[27]

Education and Immigration: The Cutting Edge of a
New Pluralism

Two policy areas—education and immigration—have been extremely controversial. Conflicts in these areas have challenged key aspects of the institutional arrangements and ideological foundations of the Fifth Republic. For reasons that are spelled out by John Ambler in his essay, educational policy has had a special place in French politics since the Third Republic, when struggles for control of the schools and their curriculum were almost a perfect reflection of the divisions within French society, between the republican Left and the more authoritarian, conservative, and Catholic Right. While clericalism, anticlericalism, and conflicts over the *école laïque* have receded somewhat in the postwar period, schools have remained a focus of political controversy and are, in many respects, one of the last bastions of Jacobinism in France. Efforts to reform education have provoked some of the most bitter, partisan, and ideologically charged conflicts in contemporary France. May 1968 and the controversies surrounding efforts by Socialist governments in the 1980s to assert greater state control over Catholic schools (through the *loi Savary*) are indicators of the centrality of education in French political development.

As with the institutionalization of the welfare state, attempts to transform the

French educational system were met with resistance from grass-roots Catholic groups, which viewed any intrusion by the state with suspicion. More important, however, was resistance from the entrenched interests of the republican Left, particularly the FEN, which has fought hard throughout the postwar period to protect the autonomy of the entire school system from the encroachment of private (Catholic) influences *and* from efforts by the state to decentralize education policy, particularly at the university level. The result has been to maintain the staunchly republican character of public schools, despite the growth of mass education in the postwar period. Efforts to decentralize education as a way of managing the influx of students and giving greater autonomy to parents and local administrators have been repeatedly thwarted by Jacobin attitudes among teachers and students, while the *Grandes Ecoles* continue to produce a uniform elite imbued with Jacobin ideas. Paradoxically, the gradual resolution of the *querelle scolaire* with the adoption of the Debré law in 1959 and the defeat of the Savary bill in 1984 has helped to push French education in a more pluralist direction by consolidating the position of private, Catholic schools and assuring that they will continue to receive funding from the state, while maintaining considerable independence.

Immigration is another area of state-society relations in which we can see the continuing strength of the Jacobin model. Large-scale immigration in the postwar period has created new cleavages, which have not proven to be cross-cutting. Whereas the immigration of Italian, Belgian, and Polish workers earlier in this century served to reinforce the modern, industrial cleavage of "worker-owner," the immigration of Muslims from North and West Africa has created an ethnic fault. Earlier European immigrations were dealt with in classic Jacobin fashion, for it was not much more difficult to turn Italians or Poles into Frenchmen than it was to turn "peasants into Frenchmen." The schools played an important role in this process of assimilation, which, with some important exceptions, was not dramatically different from the experience of the American melting pot.[28]

In the postwar period, the process of assimilation of Southern European immigrants was in many respects even smoother than in the interwar period, because the old authoritarian, facist Right, which had been so prominent in its opposition to immigration, was for the most part absent from politics. Yet the first signs of trouble and of an impending reaction against immigration could be seen in the early 1970s. The waves of Muslim immigration, which began in earnest after the granting of independence to former colonies in Africa and the settlement of the Algerian conflict, severely tested the Jacobin model. Even though by all accounts only a minority of Muslims living in France are fundamentalists, the presence of an ethnically and culturally distinct minority in society has caused a political crisis.[29] Not surprisingly, the issue of immigration has been redefined in the 1980s as an issue of citizenship, and a polemic has raged over the national and ethnic identities of foreigners, especially Arabs. To complicate matters even more, the old authoritarian Right has reemerged in the form of the Front National and Jean-

Marie Le Pen, who has succeeded in exploiting old sociocultural antagonisms of class, race, and religion for electoral purposes.

The political class and the electorate are divided over how to respond to Le Pen, and the divisions seem to be more along classic lines of the republican Left, including a substantial slice of the right-wing electorate (RPR and UDF), the authoritarian Right (FN), and some type of ill-defined pluralist group, which are most closely associated with the Parti Socialiste (PS). The republican position with respect to the assimilation of the new immigrants is that the North Africans are no different from the Italians, and they too will be turned into Frenchmen by the same processes of national, cultural, and linguistic assimilation operative in the interwar period. This response seems to cut across class and party lines. Nonetheless, the republican consensus is not a solid one, as Le Pen and the FN have been able to capture roughly ten percent of the vote in various elections since 1984, largely on the strength of their anti-immigrant, xenophobic, racist, and nationalist appeals. Despite these gains by the FN, there is considerable evidence of a pluralist breakthrough in the 1980s. Pro-immigrant, civil, and human rights groups have formed in response to the Le Pen phenomenon; and their efforts seem to have had an impact on the policy process via the PS, which has taken a decidedly pluralist stance with respect to such issues as immigrant associations, political participation, and, most recently, the wearing of traditional Islamic garb in the schools. The position of the PS and the Rocard government is nonetheless precarious, because, as we have seen in the area of education policy, there are strong secularist and Jacobin factions within the PS that could undermine the new "consensus."

Clearly, therefore, education and immigration policy are on the cutting edge of a new social and political pluralism in France, and it is in these areas where the Jacobin model will find its greatest (domestic) challenge in the 1990s. The growing interdependence of the European and world economies also represents a challenge to the Jacobin model, and immigration, which is but one indicator of interdependence, is likely to increase rather than decrease in the coming decade.

The Scope of Institutional Change:
Changing Bases of Representation

De Gaulle attempted to use the nationalist, Jacobin tradition to instill more order and discipline in French society and to reduce the influence of political parties. His project was to remake French society through constitutional and institutional reforms by establishing a strong executive authority with a popular mandate and by reducing the number of political parties (via the dual-ballot electoral system). His personal presence and leadership abilities temporarily gave the state the upper hand in controlling and changing society. For the period from 1958 to 1968, the direction of causality in the state-society relationship was clear.

The crises of decolonization were resolved and the project of modernizing the economy picked up speed in the wake of the political consensus surrounding de Gaulle and the new regime.[30] However, the events of May 1968 demonstrated the continuing strength and assertiveness of civil society.

The principal institutional reforms of the Gaullist Republic were a directly elected president, a Parliament that in most circumstances has been subordinate to the president, and a two-bloc party system that has encouraged consolidation of the electorates of the Left and the Right. These institutional reforms have helped to attenuate the compartmentalized nature of French society, breaking down many of the traditional barriers to economic change and eliminating the stalemate society of the Third and Fourth Republics. But the Gaullist reforms were premised on some very traditional aspects of French political culture, namely Jacobinism (direct democracy and the referendum, which in the early years took on a plebiscitarian quality), the *étatiste* tradition (a centralized administrative state with reinforced powers for the *Grands Corps*), and a quasi-republican monarchy (the presidency).[31] The powers of parliament and political parties were drastically reduced compared with what they had been under both the Third and the Fourth Republics.[32]

With the help of Michel Debré and others, de Gaulle created a regime with a new form of representation, which appealed to the Jacobin tradition as a way of accelerating the pace of social and economic change. The irony is that while French society and the economy were evolving at a rapid pace, the new political system was set up to draw on some very traditional, republican instincts. The new institutions, perhaps because of the peculiar combination of a parliamentary and presidential system, seemed to resolve the tension that had long existed in French politics between populist and representative democracy. The executive embodied the populist, Jacobin tradition of direct democracy; the parliament and political parties, although they remained in an unsettled state for the first ten to twenty years of the Fifth Republic, embodied a representative, but not necessarily pluralist, tradition.[33]

De Gaulle used the power of the presidency in combination with the referendum for carrying out reform in the name of the people, hence the plebiscitarian nature of the regime. His successors have been less willing to use the referendum to legitimate governmental decisions. The governments of Georges Pompidou and Valéry Giscard-d'Estaing relied heavily on Jacobin and *étatiste* mechanisms in confronting the economic problems of the 1970s.[34] Likewise, François Mitterrand seems to have succumbed in a variety of ways to the seductive powers of the Jacobin presidency, even though he has been frustrated, like de Gaulle, primarily by the Senate in his efforts to use the referendum as a mechanism for change.[35]

Political parties have reemerged in the Fifth Republic as principal agents of socialization, participation, and representation. Nevertheless, they must operate in the shadows of a powerful presidency, and they are in competition with an administrative state, which they must try to capture and control. This struggle is not unique to France, and in some ways French political parties may be better positioned than American political parties to assert their influence. From an institutional standpoint, one of the most important developments of the past decade is the newfound power of parties and politicians at the local level, following the decentralization of administrative power and the creation of more representative local institutions (via the *loi Defferre*). Decentralization has helped to create alternative bases of power for parties and politicians.[36] However, the decentralization of administrative power and the strengthening of local politics has resulted in the rehabilitation of some traditional groups in French politics, particularly the *notables*. Even though the French political system is not in "danger" of becoming a federal system, the creation and reinforcement of a local politics may weaken the Jacobin tradition.

Cohabitation, another important institutional development of the 1980s, has helped to challenge the powers of the president. The election of a hostile right-wing majority in the Assembly in 1986, while the presidency remained in the hands of the Socialist Mitterrand, was an essential test of the flexibility of the institutions of the Fifth Republic. The experience of *cohabitation* helped to reinforce the viability and the legitimacy of the regime by demonstrating the feasibility of what amounted to a coalition government. But *cohabitation* was not a parliamentary "grand coalition"; rather, the French experiment of coalition government was more akin to the American model, whereby a president of one party is constitutionally obliged to share power with a Congress controlled by the "opposition" party. The experiment, with Jacques Chirac as the right-wing prime minster and Mitterrand as president, lasted barely two years, from 1986 to 1988; nonetheless, for the Fifth Republic this experiment was the constitutional equivalent of crossing the Rubicon.[37] It proved, as Stanley Hoffmann points out in his contribution to this volume, that the regime could accommodate various political *cas de figures*.

Do these new elements of separation of powers mean that the political system of the Fifth Republic is moving irrevocably in the direction of a more consensual and less ideological form of politics? May 1968 and the referendum of 1969 marked a crucial turning point in the history of the Fifth Republic. Gradually, the Gaullist (and Jacobin) disdain for political parties and groups weakened to the point that one political party (the PS) emerged as a centrist "party of government" in the 1980s. Gaullism succeeded in breaking many aspects of the stalemate society, particularly the hold of the formerly republican center and the old authoritarian right, although, with the demise of traditional Gaullism, the latter seems to have made a partial comeback in the form of Jean-Marie Le Pen and the Front National.

Some uncertainty exists as to whether Parliament or the president will emerge supreme from the experience of *cohabitation* and the current situation of "minority" government. The most likely outcome is that neither the president nor the Parliament will go back to playing the roles that they did in the first three decades of the Fifth Republic or in earlier republics. The institutional uncertainty, growing out of the relatively new experience of separation of powers, may serve to weaken the Jacobin tradition in French politics. Nonetheless, it is important to stress the key role of parties and the party system in this process of change. With the decline of Gaullism and the still uncertain rise of "social democracy," parties of the Left and the Right are being reformed and reshaped to respond to postindustrial social and economic developments. In the words of Jane Jenson, parties are searching for a new "societal paradigm" or a new "organizing discourse." In light of the rapidly shifting ideological grounds of French politics and the problems of governing in an interdependent world, it may be difficult to win power or to govern without the backing of an organized political party. Yet one of the main objectives of the founders of the Fifth Republic was to weaken political parties, and the creation of a powerful presidency has led to an electoral dynamic that, while forcing parties of the Right and the Left to cooperate, serves to undermine the capacity of parties to govern.

Changes in the Party System: "Catchall" Politics and Catch-As-Catch-Can

Parties and interest groups are at the heart of politics and the policy-making process in most democracies. They are ordinarily the principal mechanisms of representation, and as such they bear the brunt of criticisms when a regime or government fails to perform adequately. In the French case, owing to a different (more Jacobin) perspective on representation, parties and groups have not played the same central role as in Anglo-American democracies.[38] The traditional weakness of political parties and associational life is not the result of an absence of a representative tradition in French democracy. One need only look at the parliamentary traditions of the Third and Fourth Republics to see the "strength" of representative institutions.[39] Yet, among those institutions that are central to the development of representative government, political parties and the party system must be given special attention, for without broad-based (catchall) parties and cross-cutting cleavages, pluralism is unlikely to flourish. The political party is the modern political system's first line of defence against the rise of new cleavages in society and the incorporation of new groups into the political process.[40]

French parties struggled—some would say unsuccessfully—to cope with the consequences of modernization and industrial development. During the Third and Fourth Republics, only the French Communist Party was capable of offering a coherent response to the processes of social and economic change that were the result of industrialization. Neither the radical-republican center, whose appeal to voters was based on anticlericalism and a defense of republican institutions, nor the authoritarian right, whose principal ambition was to protect traditional society from the ravages of industrialization and the onslaught of secular republicanism, were capable of giving voice to the new industrial classes. Liberal Catholics (the MRP) and social democrats (identified with some segments of the SFIO) never gained the upper hand in efforts to reshape and redefine politics in the Fourth Republic. While their responses to the changes that were sweeping France in the 1950s and 1960s were very different, both the Gaullists (the RPF) and the Communists had distinctive strategies for mobilizing the electorate around the themes of modernization and national grandeur.[41] But in the founding of the Fifth Republic, there was an explicit rejection of party government by the Gaullists, and the PCF was virtually excluded from any role in government. Thus, despite reform of the party system, which was the result, first, of the adoption of single-member districts and majoritarian voting and, second, of the creation of a powerful, directly elected president, political parties were not able to fulfill the same mobilizing and integrative function that one would expect them to play in a pluralist democracy.

In his chapter on the French Right, Martin Schain begins succinctly when he states that the "key to stability of the regime during the Fifth Republic can be found in the party system." Indeed, by refashioning the electoral system and setting up a directly elected president, the founders of the Fifth Republic, and de Gaulle in particular, hoped to reduce the power of political parties. By so doing, they also created the conditions for the reemergence of parties. But parties and the party system of the Fifth Republic would look nothing like those of the Fourth or the Third. Somewhat ironically, Duverger's "law" did take hold, as the new two-bloc party system began to force parties to seek the electoral center and centripetal forces replaced the centrifugal forces of earlier regimes.[42]

The Gaullists were the first political group to benefit from these institutional changes, and they owned the presidency for the first fifteen years of the Fifth Republic. As Schain points out, following Jean Charlot, Gaullism was set to become the "catchall party" that France had never had, garnering support from every corner of the electorate. Yet this was ultimately not to be, because Gaullism contained within itself the seeds of its own destruction. It was built around an antimodern, conservative, and Catholic constituency; its ideological foundations (Jacobinism and Bonapartism) were in many respects equally unmodern, even though it was cosmopolitan, technocratic, and Jacobin at the top. Despite the fact that Gaullism has remained the republican party of the *Rassemblement,* it has been unable to live up to its name, in part because of the survival of old elements of the republican Right—*notables* in the ranks of the republicans and Christian democrats in the ranks of the UDF—and in part because of the reemergence of a populist, authoritarian, and nationalist Right in the form of Jean-Marie Le Pen, and the Front National.[43]

Neither the old republican center nor the newer *marais* could be successfully captured by the Gaullists, who increasingly became simply the party of *the* Right, of big business, shopkeepers, Catholics, and the like. As Schain points out, the continuing decline of Catholicism and the renaissance of the authoritarian Right

under Le Pen have had a devastating effect on the RPR and its hopes of constructing a new catchall majority. As a result, the Right, like the Left, has been
searching for a new "organizing discourse," flirting with some form of Christian
democracy à la Raymond Barre and neoliberalism à la Jacques Chirac; neither
strategy has proven terribly successful, and the business of governing has fallen
to the Left.

The impact of the Fifth Republic on the Left is well documented in Jane
Jenson's chapter. Jenson vividly depicts the dilemmas that the whole process of
modernization poses for the Left, which begins the Fifth Republic under the
banner of the PCF, riding the wave of a new *ouvriérisme*, despite the fact that
the initial impact of institutional reform was to exclude the PCF from the Assembly. Being in the political "ghetto" and playing the tribune role was in 1958–62
a familiar, if not a comfortable, position for the PCF.[44] But the wave was not
going to last. The invigorating experience of Gaullist modernization boosted the
electoral fortunes of the PCF in the 1960s and early 1970s, and held out the hope
that the Party, under a Eurocommunist leadership, might become a viable party
of government.[45] Certainly, the PCF never had the desire to become a catchall
party, and the party's discourse was never that of the ambiguous (pluralist) center.
Rather, in the words of Jane Jenson, Left politics during this period had a peculiar
"*entre-deux-guerres* cast," and the Left "reached the late 1940s in the late 1960s,
just in time to experience the economic crisis that signaled the decline of postwar
economic and social arrangements." In short, the Communists were to suffer the
same fate as the Gaullists, only much worse! The institutional reforms of the
Fifth Republic proved to be especially incompatible with the PCF's brand of
strong party politics and "party" government. If the PCF was ever able to anchor
the Left, it lost this capacity in the economic upheavals of the 1970s.

As the ideological imperatives of Marxism began to wane, the stock of the
French Socialists was rising, slowly at first but with increasing speed by the mid-
1970s. Under the capable and wily guidance of a seasoned Fourth Republic
politician, François Mitterrand, the Socialists would learn how to use the institutions of the Fifth Republic to their benefit. In alliance with the PCF, Mitterrand
launched a new Left politics, which lasted only until 1977, when the PCF broke
away; but it was already too late for the Communists to stop the Socialist/social-
democratic momentum. The new Parti Socialiste was on its way to becoming,
not only the major party of the Left, but the only (modestly) "catchall" party
that could bridge the gap between the recent *modern* past, and the imminent
postindustrial future. There are, of course, many ironies in the rise of the PS from
the ashes of the old SFIO and the ferment of such *groupuscules* as the PSU and
the CERES, not the least of which is the republican traditionalism that still
pervades French socialism. This old-fashioned republicanism tinged with Marxism made the Socialists a conservative force in French politics right up to the
disastrous candidacy of Gaston Defferre in 1969.[46]

The problem for the PS in building a centrist constituency is linked to the

diversity of the Party itself, which is pulled in several directions simultaneously—
Marxist, republican or Jacobin, and liberal or social-democratic. Which of these
factions and which of these ideologies will dominate is still unclear. In Jane
Jenson's phrase, the problem for the Left, including the Socialists and the Communists, was (is) to rethink "categories without falling into the embrace of
American-style pluralism." Indeed, this is a dilemma not just for the Left but for
most political parties in France. While French society and the economy have
moved far away from the stalemate of the Third Republic, party politics in the
post-Gaullist era has gone back, at least partially, to a type of *immobilisme* that
was characteristic of previous regimes.

The coming to power of the Socialists—the much vaunted *alternance*—held
out the hope of radical change. Yet the first Socialist government under Pierre
Mauroy fell back on some of the most traditional instruments of politics and
policy-making: a statist/Jacobin approach to economic management, albeit one
imbued with more "modern" techniques of intervention—viz. nationalizations
and Keynesian stimuli; a thoroughly republican approach to church-state issues,
which led to the Savary bill and one of the largest Catholic demonstrations in
French history; and serious consideration of erecting protectionist barriers (and
possible withdrawal from the European Monetary System) when Keynesian economic policies produced high inflation and a deteriorating balance of payments.
Yet the PS was not pulled only in traditional republican (and Marxist) directions.
There was also a strong liberal, social-democratic pull, which led to a relaxation
of administrative constraints on immigrant groups, and to a whole range of
reforms in the area of civil rights, from abolition of the death penalty and
reinforcement of reproductive rights to greater constraints on police authority and
decentralization of power with respect to the mass media and local government.
With the failures of economic and education policies in particular, the PS lurched
further in the direction of liberalism to embrace a seemingly more open and
pluralist vision of politics and of France's role in Europe and the world. This
lurch in the direction of liberalism came at the expense of more traditional Left
goals of social equity and justice (as embodied in the defunct Common Program),
and at the expense of the Jacobin/statist wing of the party (the CERES). In many
respects, the PS in the 1980s is representative of contradictions that traverse
French political culture, ranging from Jacobinism to neoliberalism.

Does this therefore make the PS a "catchall" party and a harbinger of pluralist
change? It is doubtful. The Party remains fractious from an organizational and
ideological standpoint, but, more important, like the Gaullists it is held hostage
to the powerful presidency and to its leader, François Mitterrand. The true legacy
of Gaullism may very well be the creation of a Jacobin and Bonapartist executive,
which, by its very existence, has a dampening effect on party government.[47] In
this respect the French political system may come more and more to resemble
the American, not because of any dramatic change in political culture (in a
Tocquevillian sense), but because of the workings of an institution—the presi-

dency—that serves to woo the electorate, perhaps into a false sense of security, and to weaken political parties. *Immobilisme* in the late twentieth century seems to be more a characteristic of presidential systems, where parties are weak, than of parliamentary systems, where parties have the potential for playing a greater role in government. If this is accurate, then de Gaulle's legacy is indeed ironic. Having helped to "modernize" the society and economy, the presidential system is now incapable of shaping an agenda for the future.

While "catchall" politics is not immediately evident in France, with the possible exception of the Socialists who seem to be the new party of the center, major political parties are pushed toward the electoral center, not because of any dramatic shift in voting behavior,[48] but because of the electoral logic of the presidential system of the Fifth Republic. The presidency is such a big electoral prize that parties are compelled to put aside many of their ideological disagreements in order seriously to contest a presidential election.

Yet there is something artificial about a system that superimposes a kind of catchall logic on an otherwise weak and fragmented party politics. Apart from the charismatic appeal of the president, what seems to hold parties and the party system together is an elite political culture that is still imbued with Jacobin features. Jacobinism, as expressed in the technocratic training of many members of the *classe politique,* remains a strong undercurrent in party and administrative politics. Politicians still speak in terms of *rassembleur* and *rassemblement* (the traditional language of catchall politics in France), and the attitudes and beliefs of higher civil servants (the *corpsards*) continue to be influenced by the Jacobin nature of their training. Even though the "societal paradigm" has changed, the elite political culture retains many of its Jacobin features.

France—After Modernization?

No consensus has emerged from this book on how to categorize the "new France," just as there is no consensus within France itself. Areas of agreement tend to be limited to changes that have occurred in the social and economic realm: it is clear that society can no longer be described in terms of stalemate, and that the economy, while "modernized," is in a state of flux. It would be wrong to conclude that France has crossed some type of cultural Rubicon.

Each author has struggled to define the new France, and from these struggles the outlines of a picture begin to emerge. France has overcome much of its specificity in the area of the economy—a mass-based consumer society has developed that looks remarkably like that of other advanced industrial societies. With the coming of a consumer society, some of the traditional, sectarian, and nationalist dimensions of politics have receded—the Sorelian and Maurrasian vision of politics and society has little credibility outside the Club de l'Horloge. Likewise, as George Ross demonstrates in his essay on intellectual life, the at times grandiose claims of the Left intellegentisia, from the existentialists to the poststructuralists, have given way to more modest theorizing in social and political history à la François Furet, and there has been a renaissance of interest in French liberal thought, beginning with the latter-day Tocquevillian, Raymond Aron. With the decline of the "intellectual" extremes of Right and Left, one might be tempted to jump to the conclusion that some type of nonideological, classless pluralism is just around the corner. Such a conclusion not only would be premature, but wrong. While we can say with assurance that France has changed, and that these changes have transformed the ideological terrain of French politics, it is much more difficult to place a label on these changes.[49]

Despite the evidence that in policy terms France has come more closely to resemble other democratic societies, political traditions that pre-date Marxism (or whatever variety) and fascism (of the homegrown French variety) are still a part of political discourse. Jacobinism, republicanism, and Catholicism, although greatly weakened by social and economic change, continue to influence both the *classe politique* and the citizenry. Such views of politics and society have come to the fore especially in the decade of the 1980s, which has had an unsettling effect on France. Politicians have experimented with various approaches to economic and social change, and in those areas of greatest controversy, such as education and immigration, we can see quite clearly a struggle between a Jacobin and liberal vision of democracy. In areas of greater consensus, such as social policy and the welfare state, there is a kind of postindustrial, social-democratic trend. Even here, however, disputes among Catholics, republicans, liberals, and social democrats are evident, especially in the sensitive areas of family policy, education, and immigration. Nonetheless, the growth of the welfare state has been a great leveler in French society, as in many other advanced industrial societies.

One of the many paradoxes of French political development is the contradiction between the universalistic, republican discourse of the French Revolution, which has spawned a variety of other universalizing ideologies from Sorel to Sartre and beyond, and the nationalistic pretentions of French politicians, embodied by de Gaulle. Anton DePorte points specifically to the changing French view of France's place in the world, and the more modest foreign policy that has resulted. The new political modesty is attributable in large part to international economic constraints, which may prove to be politically the most inhibiting development of the postwar period. The ongoing political and economic integration of Europe, the apparent end of the Cold War in Europe, and the declining threat of nuclear conflagration have served to undermine many of the nationalist, insular, and sectarian aspects of French politics. France is no longer, if it ever was, the isolated but revolutionary power in Europe that de Gaulle, like other French leaders before him, believed it to be. Cooperation both within Europe and in international relations generally is more imperative (and constraining) than ever before. Ironically, de Gaulle helped to lay the foundation for greater cooperation in Europe by his participation in the construction of a united Europe, albeit admittedly under the political control of the French. In so doing, he helped sow the seeds for a decline of the nationalist policies (*grandeur et gloire*) that he sought to promote. Clearly, European integration has had a liberalizing effect on France, which under the leadership of François Mitterrand has been in the forefront of the political and economic remaking of Europe.

Thus, we are still searching for France, even though *l'Hexagone* is in many respects less mysterious and paradoxical, if no less confusing, than it was thirty years ago, when Stanley Hoffmann wrote that "rarely had Marianne so strongly resembled Janus." As France faces the twenty-first century, it does so with a familiar admixture of the new and the old. To speak of *le citoyen* still evokes memories of 1789. At the same time, in the words of Tocqueville, politics in France in the late twentieth century is more of a "quiet and rational persuasion. With every individual in the possession of rights which he is sure to retain." The French have come to terms with their revolutionary past and they have been able to construct a stable democratic regime, which promises to endure.

Notes

1. See Eugen Weber, *Peasants into Frenchmen* (Stanford, Calif.: Stanford University Press, 1976); and, for a vivid account of *La France profonde* circa 1950, Laurence Wylie, *Village in the Vaucluse* (Cambridge, Mass.: Harvard University Press, 1957.

2. Writing in the early 1960s, Charles P. Kindleberger summarized the ambitions and accomplishments of the modernizing elite in Fourth Republic France. See Kindleberger, "The Postwar Resurgence of the French Economy," in Stanley Hoffmann, ed., *In Search of France* (Cambridge, Mass.: Harvard University Press, 1963), pp. 118–58. Cf. also Alain Lipietz, "Governing the Economy," Chapter 1 in this volume.

3. One can get a sense of the political uncertainties that accompanied the process of social and economic change at the end of the 1950s in the insightful essay by Stanley Hoffmann, "Paradoxes of the French Political Community," in Hoffmann, ed., *In Search of France.*

4. For a discussion of the controversies surrounding the birth of the Fifth Republic and the subsequent reform of the method for electing the president, see Jean Charlot, *The Gaullist Phenomenon* (New York: Praeger, 1971); Nicholas Wahl, "The French Constitution of 1958: The Initial Draft and its Origins," *American Political Science Review* 53 (June 1959): 358–82; and Henry W. Ehrmann, "Direct Democracy in France," *American Political Science Review* 57 (December 1963): 883–902.

5. The latter expression is attributable to the current president, François Mitterrand. On the notion of a republican monarchy, see Maurice Duverger, *Le système politique français* (Paris: PUF, Collections Thémis, various editions).

6. A classic example of this version of the "modernization" argument is to be found in Seymour M. Lipset, *Political Man* (Garden City, N.Y.: Anchor Books, 1959), especially chaps. 2–3. Lipset follows closely the arguments presented in Alexis de Tocqueville's *Democracy in America.*

7. For a good discussion of changes in state-society relations in France, see Ezra N. Suleiman, *Private Power and Centralization in France* (Princeton, N.J.: Princeton University Press, 1987), chaps. 1–2.

8. Alexis de Tocqueville, *Democracy in America,* vol. 1 (New York: Vintage Books, 1945), pp. 9–10.

9. Cf. Alexis de Tocqueville, *The Old Regime and the French Revolution* (Garden City, N.Y.: Doubleday, 1955), especially pp. 32–41 and 61–119. Also *Democracy in America,* 2: 265–78.

10. Ibid., p. 270.

11. Stanley Hoffmann, "Paradoxes of the French Political Community," in Hoffmann, ed., *In Search of France,* p. 9.

12. See, for example, Hoffmann's concluding essay in William G. Andrews and Stanley Hoffmann, *The Fifth Republic at Twenty* (Albany, N.Y.: State University of New York Press, 1981), pp. 281–324; and Michel Crozier, *Etat moderne, état modeste* (Paris: Editions du Seuil, 1987).

13. One *might* call it political culture, but certainly *not* national character, which has been universally rejected as a category of analysis in comparative politics. For a defense of the political-culture argument against the "national character" critique, see Gabriel Almond's forceful essay, "The Intellectual History of the Civic Culture Concept," in Gabriel A. Almond and Sidney Verba, eds., *The Civic Culture Revisited* (Boston: Little, Brown, 1980), pp. 1–36.

14. For a recent attempt to compare "the origins of French and American republicanism," see Patrice Higonnet, *Sister Republics* (Cambridge, Mass.: Harvard University Press, 1988). Cf. also Lucien Jaume, *Le discours jacobin et la démocratie* (Paris: Fayard, 1988).

15. See, for example, Hoffmann's essay, "Paradoxes of the French Political Community"; Michel Crozier, *Le phénomène bureaucratique* (Paris: Editions du Seuil, 1963), and Michel Crozier, *La société bloquée* (Paris: Editions du Seuil, 1970).

16. On localism and the protection of traditional interests, cf. Edgar Morin, *The Red and the White* (New York: Pantheon, 1970); Pierre Grémion and Jean-Pierre Worms, *Les Institutions régionales et la société locale* (Paris: Copédith, 1968); J.-P. Worms, "Le Préfet et ses Notables," *Sociologie du Travail* 7 (July–September 1966): 249–76; Peter Alexis Gourevitch, *Paris and the Provinces* (Berkeley, Calif.: University of California Press, 1980); Suzanne Berger, *Peasants Against Politics* (Cambridge, Mass.: Harvard University Press, 1972); and Suzanne Berger, "Regime and Interest Representation: The French Traditional Middle Classes," in Suzanne Berger, ed., *Organizing Interest in Western Europe* (New York: Cambridge University Press, 1981), pp. 83–101.

17. On the special relationship between farmers, teachers, and the state, cf. John T. S. Keeler, *The Politics of Neo-Corporatism in France* (New York: Oxford University Press, 1987); and John S. Ambler, "Neocorporatism and the Politics of French Education," *West European Politics* 8 (July 1985): 23–42.

18. For an account of these changes, see Bernard Brown, "The French Experience of Modernization," *World Politics* 21 (April 1969): 366–91; Richard Hamilton, *Affluence and the French Worker in the Fourth Republic* (Princeton, N.J.: Princeton University Press, 1967); and Alain Lipietz, "Governing the Economy," chap. 1 in this volume.

19. This is due in part to the fact that social class never achieved the significance in France that it enjoyed in Britain and Germany. The reasons for this peculiarly unmodern feature of French social and economic history have been much studied by historians and sociologists, but the one common feature of their explanation for the weakness of class politics is the strength of traditional society. Cf. the works of Hervé Le Bras and Emmanuel Todd, *L'invention de la France* (Paris: Pluriel, 1981); Hervé Le Bras, *Les trois France* (Paris: Seuil, 1986); and Emmanuel Todd, *La Nouvelle France* (Paris: Seuil, 1988). Both Le Bras and Todd argue that France has retained some important elements of traditional society that help to explain patterns of political development in different regions of the country. For them, family structure (extended versus nuclear) is the best indicator of social modernization, and remains the most salient rift within French society.

20. See Gérard Noiriel, *Ouvriers dans la société française, XIVe–XXe siècles* (Paris, Seuil, 1986); and Serge Mallet, *Essays on the New Working Class* (St. Louis, Mo., Telos Press, 1975).

21. On the ability of the French state to modernize in the face of resistance from social groups, see Stephen S. Cohen, *Modern Capitalist Planning: The French Model* (Berkeley, Calif.: University of California Press, 1977).

22. For an account of the evolution of interest-group politics, cf. Henry Ehrmann, *Organized Business in France* (Princeton, N.J.: Princeton University Press, 1957); Jack Hayward, *Private Interests and Public Policy: The Experience of the French Economic and Social Council* (London, Longmans, 1966); and Ezra Suleiman, *Politics, Power and Bureaucracy* (Princeton, N.J.: Princeton University Press, 1974). John Keeler actually refers to French politics as "partially corporatized," a reflection of the difficulty of generalizing the neocoroporatist argument beyond a few sectors. See Keeler, *The Politics of Neo-Corporatism in France*, and Frank Lee Wilson, *Interest Group Politics in France* (New York: Cambridge University Press, 1987). Keeler and Wilson have carried on a debate over the nature of state-society relations and interest-group politics in France to determine whether they exhibit pluralist or neocorporatist tendencies. See Frank L. Wilson, "French Interest Group Politics: Pluralist or Neo-Corporatist," *American Political Science Review* 77, no. 4 (December 1983): 892–910; and John Keeler, "Situating France on the Pluralism—Corporatism Continuum: A Critique of and Alternative to the Wilson Perspective," *Comparative Politics* 17, no. 2 (January 1985): 229–49. For a description of corporatist practice in other European democracies, see Peter J. Katzenstein, *Corporatism and Change* (Ithaca, N.Y.: Cornell University Press, 1986).

23. On this point, see James Hollifield, "Administration and the French State" in B. Guy Peters and James F. Hollifield, eds., *The State and Public Policy* (Boulder, Co: Westview Press, 1991). For a different interpretation of the evolution of state-society relations in the Fifth Republic, see Suleiman, *Private Power and Centralization*, pp. 299–330. Suleiman views interest-group politics in France as having evolved along lines similar to other industrial democracies. Like Theodore Lowi, he sees the state as being subject to "capture." The French state, he argues, is particularly vulnerable in this regard precisely because of its centralized features. Cf. Theodore Lowi, *The End of Liberalism* (New York: W. W. Norton, 1969).

24. Social movements, which are most closely associated with postindustrial, *citizen* politics, are indeed weaker in France than in other industrial democracies. For a comparative analysis, see Russell J. Dalton, *Citizen Politics in Western Democracies* (Chatham, N.J.: Chatham House, 1988).

25. Jane Jenson argues that post-1968 new Left social movements were "absorbed" into mainstream Left politics. See Chapter 4 of this volume.

26. On civil, political, and social citizenship, see T. H. Marshall, *Class, Citizenship, and Social Development* (Cambridge: Cambridge University Press, 1950), chap. 4, "Citizenship and Social Class."

27. See the author's discussion of the rise of the politics of citizenship in Chapter 5 of this volume.

28. One of the principal differences from the American experience was the role played by the French Communist Party in mobilizing and socializing immigrant workers. While this process of socialization may have served to exacerbate class tensions in the short term, in the long run the PCF helped to complement Jacobin institutions, particularly the schools, and to create a more homogeneous and egalitarian society.

29. See Gilles Kepel, *Les Banlieues de l'Islam* (Paris: Seuil, 1988).

30. One of the best accounts of the history and founding of the Fifth Republic is to be found in Pierre Avril, *La Ve République: histoire politique et constitutonnelle* (Paris: Presses Universitaires de France, 1987). See also Philip M. Williams and Martin Harrison, *Politics and Society in de Gaulle's Republic* (Garden City, N.Y.: Doubleday, 1971).

31. On the importance of these political traditions in the reforms of the Fifth Republic, see

Ehrmann, "Direct Democracy in France"; Francis de Baecque et al., *Administration et politique sous la Ve République* (Paris: Presses de la FNSP, 1980); Pierre Birnbaum, *Les sommets de l'Etat* (Paris: Seuil, 1977); and Jean-Louis Quermonne, *Le gouvernement de la France sous la Ve République* (Paris: Dalloz, 1987).

32. For a comparison of the institutional features of the Third, Fourth, and Fifth Republics, cf. Philip Williams, *Crisis and Compromise: Politics in the Fourth Republic* (Hamden, Conn.: Anchor Books, 1964); Avril, *La Ve République;* and various works of Jean Massot, including *La Présidence de la République en France* (Paris: La Documentation française, 1986) and "Le Parlement français sous trois présidents, 1958–1980," *Revue française de science politique* 1 (1981): 000.

33. In their discussion of "governmental and parliamentary attitudes," Williams and Harrison capture the ambiguities in the quality of French democracy in the early years of the Fifth Republic. They attribute some of the particularly Jacobin features of the regime to Michel Debré, who, although hostile to parties and groups, later would become the champion of "parliamentary government." Cf. Williams and Harrison, *Politics and Society in de Gaulle's Republic*, pp. 184ff., and Michel Debré, "The Constitution of 1958: Its Raison d'Etre and How it Evolved," in Andrews and Hoffmann, ed., *The Impact of the Fifth Republic on France*, pp. 1–14.

34. For a discussion of the use of administrative power in governing the economy during this period, see Peter A. Hall, *Governing the Economy: The Politics of State Intervention in Britain and France* (New York: Oxford University Press, 1986), pp. 164–91.

35. On the way in which the Socialists have used the institutional levers of the Fifth Republic, see Hugues Portelli, *La politique en France sous la Ve République* (Paris: Grasset, 1987); pp. 223ff., Georges Lavau, "The Left and Power"; and Oliver Duhamel, "The Fifth Republic under François Mitterrand," both in George Ross et al., *The Mitterrand Experiment* (New York: Oxford University Press, 1987), pp. 115–27 and 140–60.

36. See Catherine Grémion, "Decentralization in France in Historical Perspective," and Yves Mény, "The Socialist Decentralization," both in Ross, et al., *The Mitterrand Experiment*, pp. 237–62.

37. For more on *cohabitation,* see Maurice Duverger, *Bréviare de la cohabitation* (Paris: Presses Universitaires de France, 1986).

38. For a discussion of the importance of parties and groups in the French political system, see Philip Converse and Roy Pierce, *Political Representation in France* (Cambridge, Mass.: Harvard University Press, 1986); and Frank Lee Wilson, *Interest Group Politics in France.*

39. Cf., for example, Philip M. Williams, *Politics in Postwar France: Parties and the Constitution of the Fourth Republic* (London: Longmans, 1958); and Henry W. Ehrmann, *Organized Business in France.*

40. On this point, see Otto Kirchheimer, "The Transformation of the Western European Party Systems," in Joseph LaPalombara and Myron Weiner, *Political Parties and Political Development* (Princeton, N.J.: Princeton University Press, 1966), pp. 177–200; and the introduction to Seymour Martin Lipset and Stein Rokkan, *Party Systems and Voter Alignments* (New York: Free Press, 1967).

41. For a discussion of these themes from an economic point of view, see the chapter by Alain Lipietz in this volume. For a political perspective on the consequences of modernization, see the chapter by Jane Jenson.

42. The irony is that Maurice Duverger was among the earliest and most vociferous opponents of the new regime. On the connection between electoral and party systems, see Maurice Duverger, *Political Parties* (New York: John Wiley, 1967), pp. 206–80. Cf. also, Anthony Downs, *An Economic Theory of Democracy* (New York: Harper and Row, 1957), pp. 36–74.

43. Some scholars saw the new Gaullist party as holding out hope for a "revitalization" of party

politics. See Frank Lee Wilson, "The Revitalization of French Parties," *Comparative Political Studies* 1 (April 1979): 82–103.

44. See R. W. Johnson, *The Long March of the French Left* (New York: St. Martin's Press, 1981).

45. For a history, see George Ross, *Workers and Communists in France: From Popular Front to Eurocommunism* (Berkeley, Calif.: University of California Press, 1982).

46. For a brief account of the transformation of the Socialists, from a decrepit party of old men (the SFIO) to a relatively effective party of government, see Steven Lewis and Serenella Sferza, "French Socialists between State and Society," in George Ross, et al., *The Mitterrand Experiment,* pp. 100–114.

47. Jean Lacouture, *De Gaulle* (New York: New American Library, 1966); and Charlot, *The Gaullist Phenomenon,* especially chap. 6.

48. As both Jenson and Schain point out, "protest" voting for the political extremes remains high. Whereas in previous decades protest voting was a quasi-monopoly of the Left, many disaffected voters now have shifted their allegiance, at least temporarily, to the Right and to Jean-Marie Le Pen. See Nonna Mayer and Pascal Perrineau, *Le Front National à découvert* (Paris: Presses de la FNSP, 1989); and, on the evolution of protest voting, Daniel Gaxie, *Explications du vote* (Paris: Presses de la FNSP, 1985), *passim.*

49. As Emmanuel Todd is quick to point out, all of the old cleavages of French society were not eliminated by the social and economic reforms of the Fifth Republic, but the ideological terrain *was* transformed. Right and Left no longer mean what they did only a short decade ago, and nationalist ideologies, such as Jacobinism (and perhaps Gaullism too), have lost their appeal in the face of the continuing integration of France into a European and world economy. See Todd, *La Nouvelle France,* especially pp. 243–81.

Bibliography

Adam, Gérard, Jean-Daniel Reynaud, and Jean-Maurice Verdier. *La Négociation collective en France*. Paris: Editions ouvrières, 1972.

Adler, Stephen. *International Migration and Dependence*. Westmead, England: Saxon House, 1977.

Aglietta, Michel. *Régulation et crises du capitalisme*. Paris: Calman-Lévy, 1976. Translated into English as *A Theory of Capitalist Regulation*. London: New Left Books, 1979.

Aglietta, Michel, and Anton Brender. *Métamorphoses de la société salariale*. Paris: Calman-Lévy, 1984.

Allal, Tewfik, et al. *Situations migratoires*. Paris: Editions Galilée, 1977.

Almond, Gabriel. "The Intellectual History of the Civic Culture Concept." In *The Civic Culture Revisited*, edited by Gabriel Almond and Sidney Verba. Boston: Little, Brown, 1980.

Almond, Gabriel, and Sidney Verba. *The Civic Culture*. Boston: Little, Brown, 1965.

Ambler, John S. "Neocorporatism and the Politics of French Education." *West European Politics* 8 (July 1985):

———. "Constraints on Policy Innovation in Education: Thatcher's Britain and Mitterrand's France." *Comparative Politics* 20 (October 1987):

———. "French Education and the Limits of State Autonomy." *Western Political Quarterly* 41 (September 1988):

Ammousson, K. *L'Immigration noire en France depuis 1945*. Université de Paris VIII, 1976. Thèse,

Anderson, Perry. *In the Tracks of Historical Materialism*. London: Verso, 1983.

Andrews, William G. *Presidential Government in Gaullist France*. Albany, N.Y.: State University of New York Press, 1982.

Andrews, William G., and Stanley Hoffmann. *The Fifth Republic at Twenty*. Albany, N.Y.: State University of New York Press, 1981.

Archdeacon, Thomas. *Becoming American: An Ethnic History*. New York: The Free Press, 1983.

Aron, Raymond. *Opium of the Intellectuals*. Garden City, N.Y.: Doubleday, 1957.

———— . *La Révolution introuvable*. Paris: Julliard, 1968.

Ashford, Douglas. *British Dogmatism and French Pragmatism: Center-Local Relations in the Welfare State*. London and Boston: Allen and Unwin, 1982.

———— . *The Emergence of the Welfare State*. Oxford and New York: Blackwell, 1986.

———— . *Policy and Politics in France: Living with Uncertainty*. Philadelphia: Temple University Press, 1981.

———— . "Rhetoric and Reality in the French Welfare State." Mimeo. Bielefeld: Zentrum für interdisziplinäre Forschung, 1989.

Asselain, Jean-Charles. *Histoire économique de la France,* vol. 2. Paris: Seuil, 1984.

Ath-Massoud, Malek, and Alain Gillette. *L'Immigration algérienne en France*. Paris: Editions Entente, 1976.

Aubert, V., A. Bergounioux, J.-P. Martin, and R. Mouriaux. *La Forteresse enseignante: La Fédération de l'Education Nationale*. Paris: Fayard, 1985.

Aupetit, Bernard. *Classes et catégories sociales*. Roubaix: Edires, 1985.

Auspitz, Katherine. *The Radical Bourgeoisie: The Ligue de l'Enseignement and the Origins of the Third Republic, 1866–1885*. Cambridge: Cambridge University Press, 1982.

Avril, Pierre. *La Ve République: histoire politique et constitutionelle*. Paris: Presses Universitaires de France, 1987.

Baecque, Francis de, et al. *Administration et politique sous la Ve République*. Paris: Presses de la F.N.S.P., 1980.

Ballion, Robert. *L'Argent et l'école*. Paris: Pernoud/Stock, 1977.

———— . *Les Consommateurs d'école*. Paris: Stock/Laurence Pernoud, 1982.

Barjot, Alain. "L'Evolution de la sécurité sociale (juin 1960–juin 1966)." *Revue Française des Affaires Sociales* 25 (June 1971): 61–79.

Barou, J. *Travailleurs africains en France*. Grenoble: Presses Universitaires de France, collection *Actualités recherches,* 1978.

Barrot, Odilon. *De la décentralisation et de ses effets*. Paris: Didier, 1870.

Bauchet, Pierre. *La Planification française*. Paris: Editions du Seuil, 1966.

Beer, Samuel. *Britain Against Itself: The Political Contradictions of Collectivism*. New York: W. W. Norton, 1982.

Bell, Daniel. *The Coming of Post-Industrial Society*. New York: Basic Books, 1973.

———— . *The End of Ideology: On the Exhaustion of Political Ideas in the Fifties*. Glencoe, Ill.: Free Press, 1960.

Belleville, Pierre. "Les Enseignements de la grève des mineurs." *Perspectives Socialistes* 59 (April 1963): 2–19.

———— . *Une Nouvelle classe ouvrière*. Paris: Julliard, 1963.

Bellon, Bertrand. *L'Interventionisme libérale: La Politique économique de l'administration fédérale américaine*. Paris: Editions du Seuil/Economica, 1986.

Benton, T. *The Rise and Fall of Structural Marxism.* London: Macmillan, 1984.

Berger, Suzanne. *Peasants Against Politics.* Cambridge, Mass.: Harvard University Press, 1972.

———. "Regime and Interest Representation: The French Traditional Middle Classes." In *Organizing Interest in Western Europe,* edited by Suzanne Berger. New York: Cambridge University Press, 1981.

Bergeroux, Noel-Jean. "L'U.D.F. à la recherche du parti du président." *L'Election présidentielle de mars 1978.* Paris: Dossiers et Documents du Monde, 1978.

Berstein, Serge. *La France de l'expansion.* Paris: Editions du Seuil, 1989.

Bertrand, Hugues. "Le Régime central d'accumulation de l'après-guerre et sa crise." *Critiques de l'Economie Politique* 7–8 (April 1979):

Besnier, Jean-Michel, and Jean-Paul Thomas. *Chronique des idées d'aujourd'hui.* Paris: Presses universitaires de France, 1987.

Besson, Jean-Louis, Maurice Comte, and Paul Rousset. *Compter les chômeurs.* Lyon: Presses universitaires de France, 1981.

Bideberry, P. *Le Chômage des travailleurs étrangers.* Paris: Inspection Générale des Affaires Sociales, 1974.

Biegalski, Christian, ed. *Arguments/3, Les Intellectuels, la pensée anticipatrice.* Paris: Gallimard 10/18, 1970.

Birnbaum, Pierre, *Les Sommets de l'Etat.* Paris: Editions du Seuil, 1977.

Birnbaum, Pierre, and Jean Leca, eds. *Sur l'individualisme.* Paris: Presses de la Fondation Nationale des Sciences Politiques, 1986.

Blum-Girardeau, C. *Les Tableaux de la solidarité.* Paris: Economica, 1981.

Boltanski, Luc. *Cadres.* Cambridge: Cambridge University Press, 1988.

———. *The Making of a Class: Cadres in French Society.* Cambridge: Cambridge University Press/Editions de la Maison des Sciences de l'Homme, 1987.

Bon, Frédéric, and Jean-Paul Chaylan. *La France Qui Vote.* Paris: Hachette, 1988.

Bonacich, Edna. "The Split Labor Market: A Theory of Ethnic Antagomism." *American Journal of Sociology* 37 (1972): 1050–87.

Bonnechère, M. "Conditions de séjour et d'emploi en France des travailleurs africains." *Revue Pratique de Droit Social* 392 (December 1977): 379–389.

Bonnet, J.-C. *Les Pouvoirs publics français et l'immigration dans l'entre-deux-geurres.* Lyon: Centre d'histoire économique et sociale de la région lyonnaise, 1976.

Bonety, René, et al. *La C.F.D.T.* Paris: Editions du Seuil, 1971.

Boschetti, Anna. *Sartre et "les temps modernes.".* Paris: Minuit, 1985.

Bosworth, William. *Catholicism and Crisis in Modern France.* Princeton, N.J.: Princeton University Press, 1962.

Boudon, Raymond. *L'Idéologie.* Paris: Fayard, 1986.

———. "L'Intellectuel et ses publics: Les Singularités françaises." In *Français: Qui êtes-vous?* Paris: Documentation Française, 1981.

Bourcier de Carbon, P., and P. Chaunu. "Un Génocide statistique: On recherche 1,893,000 étrangers disparu dans les ordinateurs de l'INED." *Histoire, Economie et Société* 1 (1986):

Bourdieu, Pierre. *La Distinction*. Paris: Editions du Minuit, 1979.

————. *Homo Academicus*. Paris: Minuit, 1985.

————. *La Noblesse d'état*. Paris: Editions du Minuit, 1988.

————. *Questions de Sociologie*. Paris: Minuit, 1980.

Bourdieu, Pierre, and J.-C. Passeron. *Les Héritiers*. Paris: Editions de Minuit, 1964.

Boutmy, Emile. *The English People: A Study of their Political Psychology*. Translated by J. E. Courtney. London: Unwin, 1904.

Boy, Daniel, et al. *1981: Les Elections de l'alternance*. Paris: Presses de la F.N.S.P., 1986.

Boyer, Robert. *The Influence of Keynes on French Economic Policy: Past and Present*. Paris: CEPREMAP, Série Orange, no. 8404, 1984.

Boyer, Robert, and Jacques Mistral. *Accumulation, inflation, crises*. Paris: Presses Universitaires de France, 1983.

Braudel, Fernand. *L'Identité de la France*. Paris: Flammarion, 1986.

Bremond, J., and G. Bremond. *L'Economie française*. Paris: Hatier, 1985.

Brinton, Crane. *The Jacobins: An Essay in the New History*. New York: Macmillan, 1930.

Brown, Bernard E. "The French Experience of Modernization." *World Politics* 21 (April 1969): 366–91.

————. "Religious Schools and Politics in France." *Midwest Journal of Political Science* 2 (May 1958): 160–78.

Brubaker, Rogers, ed. *Immigration and the Politics of Citizenship in Europe and North America*. Lanham, MD: The German Marshall Fund of the U.S. and the University Press of America, 1989.

Bunel, J., and J. Saglio. "Le C.N.P.F. et la politique d'immigration." *Economie et Humanisme* 221 (January 1975): 41–50.

Burnier, Michel-Antoine. *Les Existentialistes et la politique*. Paris: Gallimard, 1970.

Bussery, H. "Incidence sur l'économie française d'une réduction durable de la main-d'oeuvre immigrée." *Economie et statistique* 76 (March 1976): 37–46.

Calderon, Desiré. "Enquête sur les intellectuels." *Révolution* (February 1984):

Cameron, David. "Stability and Change in Patterns of French Partisanship." *Public Opinion Quarterly* 36 (1972): 19–30.

Campbell, Bruce. "On the Prospects of Polarization in the French Electorate." *Comparative Politics* 8 (January 1976): 282–87.

Capdevielle, Jacques, and René Mouriaux. *Approche politique de la grève en France (1966–1988)*. Paris: CEVIPOF, Cahiers no. 3, 1989.

————. *Mai 68: L'Entre-deux de la modernité: Histoire de trente ans*. Paris: Presses de la F.N.S.P., 1988.

Carré, Jean-Jacques, et al. *French Economic Growth*. Stanford, Calif.: Stanford University Press, 1975.

Casassus, Cecilia, et al. *Stratégies industrielles et politiques d'emploi*. 2 vols. Paris: GST-CRESST, 1984.

Castells, Manuel. "Immigrant Workers and Class Struggles in Advanced Capitalism: The West European Experience." *Politics and Society* 5 (January 1975): 33–66.

Castle, Stephen, and Godula Kosack. *Immigrant Workers and Class Structure in Western Europe*. London: Oxford University Press, 1973.

Catrice-Lorey, Antoinette. *Dynamique interne de la sécurité sociale*. 2d ed. Paris: Economica, 1982.

Cayrol, Roland, and Pascal Perrineau. "La Défaite du politique." In *Le Guide du pouvoir*, edited by Roland Cayrol and Pascal Perineau. Paris: Editions Jean-François Soumic, 1988.

Cerny, Philip G. "The Political Balance." In *French Politics and Public Policy*, edited by Philip G. Cerny and Martin Schain. New York: St. Martin's, 1980.

————. "The New Rules of the Game in France." In *French Politics and Public Policy*, edited by Philip G. Cerny and Martin Schain. New York: St. Martin's, 1980.

Charlot, Jean. "Exposé introductif: l'evolution de l'image des parties politiques en France." Paper presented at the Congress of the International Political Science Association, Paris, July 1985.

————. *The Gaullist Phenomenon*. New York: Praeger, 1971.

Chevalier, Louis. "La Population étrangère en France d'après la recensement de 1962." *Population* 19 (January 1964): 569–78.

Chevènement, Jean-Pierre. *Apprendre pour entreprendre*. Paris: Librairie Générale Française, 1985.

Claise, Guy. "Voyage à travers les électorats." In *Le Dossier de legislatives 1978*, edited by Frédéric Bon. Paris: Le Matin, 1978.

Clark, Peter. *Liberals and Social Democrats*. Cambridge: Cambridge University Press, 1978.

Cohen, Stephen S. *Modern Capitalist Planning: The French Model*. Berkeley, Calif.: University of California Press, 1977.

Cohen-Solal, Annie. *Sartre*. Paris: Gallimard. 1985.

Collège de France, *Propositions pour l'enseignement de l'avenir*, élaborées à la demande de Monsieur le Président de la République par les Professeurs du Collège de France. Paris: Collège de France, 1985.

Comité National de l'Enseignement Catholique (CNEC). *L'Enseignement catholique face à l'avenir*. Paris: Le Centurion, 1977.

Commissariat Général du Plan. "Premier rapport de la Commission de la Main-d'oeuvre (octobre 1946)." In *Documents relatifs à la première session du Conseil du Plan, 16–19 mars 1946*. Paris: Imprimerie Nationale, 1946.

————. *Rapport de la Commission Emploi (Préparation du VIè Plan)*. Vol 2. Paris: Documents Françaises, 1971.

————. "Rapport général de la Commission de la Main-d'Oeuvre (IIIe Plan)." *Revue Française du Travail* 20 (April–June 1958): 40–73.

————. "Rapport général de la Commission de la Main-d'Oeuvre du Ve Plan." *Revue Française du Travail* 28 (January–March 1966): 90–132.

Converse, Philip E., and Roy Pierce. *Political Representation in France*. Cambridge, Mass.: Belknap Press of the Harvard University Press, 1986.

Costa-Lascoux, Jacqueline. *De l'immigré au citoyen*. Paris: Documentation française, 1989.

Courault, Bruno. *Contribution à la théorie de l'offre de travail: Le Cas de l'immigration en France, 1946–78*. Thèse. Paris: Université de Paris I, Panthéon, Sorbonne, 1980.

Courlet, Claude, et al. *Etudes sur les politiques industrielles locales dans le cadre de la promotion des PME*. Mimeo. Grenoble: Report IREP/CNEPP, 1987.

Coutrot, Aline. "La Loi scolaire de décembre 1959." *Revue Française de Science Politique*, 13 (June 1963): 352–88.

Cross, Gary S. *Immigrant Workers in Industrial France*. Philadelphia: Temple University Press, 1983.

Crozier, Michel. "Les Angoisses existentielles des intellectuels français: Réflexions sur vingt années de révolution culturelle." *Commentaire* (Summer 1979):

————. *The Bureaucratic Phenomenon*. Chicago: University of Chicago Press, 1964.

————. *Etat moderne, Etat modeste*. Paris: Fayard, 1987.

————. *The Stalled Society*. New York: Viking Press, 1973.

————. "Western Europe." In *The Crisis of Democracy*, by Michel Crozier, Samuel Huntington, and Joji Watanuki. New York: New York University Press, 1975.

Dahl, Robert. *A Preface to Democratic Theory*. Chicago: Chicago University Press, 1956.

Dalton, Russell J. *Citizen Politics in Western Democracies*. Chatham, N.J.: Chatham House, 1988.

Daniel, Pierre. *Question de Liberté*. Paris: Desclée de Brouwer, 1986.

De Lary de Latour, Henri. "Le Particularisme du contrat de travail pour les travailleurs immigrés." *Droit Social* 5 (May 1976): 63–72.

Debré, Michel. "The Constitution of 1958: Its Raison d'Etre and How it Evolved." In *The Impact of the Fifth Republic on France*, edited by William G. Andrews and Stanley Hoffmann. Albany, N.Y.: State University of New York Press, 1981.

Debré, Regis. *Le Scribe*. Paris: Grasset, 1980.

————. *Teachers, Writers, Celebrities: The Intellectuals of Modern France*. London: Verso, 1981.

Debré, Robert, and Alfred Sauvy. *Des Français pour la France: Le Problème de la population*. Paris: Gallimard, 1946.

Delannoi, Gilles. "*Arguments, 1956–62, ou la parenthèse de l'ouverture.*" *Revue Française de Science Politique* (February 1984):

Delorme, Robert. "A New View of Economic Theory of the State: A Case Study of France." *Journal of Economic Issues* 18 (September 1984):

Delorme, Robert, and Charles André. *L'Etat et l'économie.* Paris: Editions du Seuil, 1983.

Derfler, Martin. *Alexandre Millerand: The Socialist Years.* The Hague: Mouton, 1977.

Dérouin, H., et al. *Traité et pratique d'assistance publique.* Paris: Sirey, 1914.

Derthick, Martha. *The Politics of Social Security.* Washington, D.C.: The Brookings Institution, 1979.

Devaquet, Alain. *L'Amibe et l'Etudiant. Université et Recherche: L'Etat d'Urgence.* Paris: Editions Odile Jacob, 1988.

Domanget, Maurice. *Vaillant: Un grand socialiste, 1840–1915.* Paris: Table Ronde, 1956.

Donzelot, Jacques. *L'Invention de social.* Paris: Fayard, 1984.

Downs, Anthony. *An Economic Theory of Democracy.* New York: Harper and Row, 1957.

Drescher, Seymour. *Tocqueville and Beaumont on Social Reform.* New York: Harper, 1968.

Dubois, Pierre. *Grèves revendicatives ou grèves politiques?* Paris: Anthropos, 1976.

————— . *Mort de l'Etat-patron.* Paris: Editions ouvrières, 1974.

Duhamel, Olivier. "The Fifth Republic under François Mitterrand." In *The Mitterrand Experiment,* edited by George Ross, Stanley Hoffmann, and Sylvia Malzacher. New York: Oxford University Press, 1987.

Dupoirier, Elisabeth, and Gérard Grunberg. *Mars 1986: La Drôle de défaite de la gauche.* Paris: Presses universitaires de la France, 1986.

Duran, P., and J. Herault. "*Aide Sociale* and French Decentralization." In *Discretionary Politics: Intergovernmental Social Grants in Seven Countries,* edited by Douglas Ashford. Greenwich, Conn.: Jai Press, 1990.

Durand, Claude, and Pierre Dubois. *La Grève.* Paris: Presses de la Fondation Nationale des Sciences Politiques, 1975.

Duverger, Maurice. *Bréviare de la cohabitation.* Paris: Presses Universitaires de France, 1986.

————— . *La Ve république.* Paris: Presses universitaires de France, 1960.

————— . *Political Parties.* New York: W. W. Norton, 1955; New York: John Wiley, 1967.

————— . *Le Système politique français.* Paris: Presses universitaires de France, Collections Thémis, various editions.

Ehrmann, Henry W. "Direct Democracy in France." *American Political Science Review* 57 (June 1963): 883–902.

————— . *Organized Business in France.* Princeton, N.J.: Princeton University Press, 1957.

Eribon, Didier. *Michel Foucault*. Paris: Flammarion, 1989.

Ewald, François. *L'Etat providence*. Paris: Grasset, 1986.

Eymard-Duvernay, François. "L'Emploi au cours du VIè Plan." *Economie et Statistique* 74 (January 1976): 40–52.

Farias, Victor. *Heidegger et le Nazisme*. Paris: Gallimard, 1986.

Ferry, Antoine. "La Sécurité sociale depuis les ordonnances de 1967." *Revue d'Economie Politique* 82 (October 1972): 983–97.

Ferry, Luc, and Alain Renaut. *La Pensée 68: Essai sur l'anti-humanisme contemporain*. Paris: Gallimard, 1985.

———. *68–86 Itinéraires de l'individu*. Paris: Gallimard, 1987.

Fisher, H.A.L. "Thoughts on the Influence of Napoleon." In *Studies in History and Politics*. Oxford: Oxford University Press, 1920.

Flora, Peter, and Arnold Heidenheiner. *Development of Welfare States in Europe and America*. New Brunswick. N.J.: Transaction Books, 1981.

Fouet, Monique, et al. "Dernière sortie avant l'inflation." *Observation et Diagnostique Economiques* 27 (April 1989):

Fourastié, Jean. *Les Trente glorieuses*. Paris: Fayard, Editions Pluriel, 1979.

Frears, John. "France: the 'Cohabitation' Election of 16th March 1986." Paper presented at the Annual Meeting of the British Political Science Association, Nottingham, England, April 1986.

Freeman, Gary P. *Immigrant Labor and Racial Conflict in Industrial Societies: The French and British Experiences, 1945–1975*. Princeton, N.J.: Princeton University Press, 1979.

Fridenson, Patrick, and André Strauss, eds. *Le Capitalisme français: Blocages et dynamismes d'une croissance*. Paris: Fayard, 1987.

Furet, François. *Marx et la Révolution Française*. Paris: Flammarion, 1988.

———. *Penser le Révolution Française*. Paris: Gallimard, 1978.

Galant, Henri. *Histoire politique de la sécurité sociale en France, 1945–1952*. Paris: Colin, 1955.

Gani, Léon. *Syndicats et travailleurs immigrés*. Paris: Editions Sociales, 1972.

Garson, Jean-Pierre, and Yann Moulier. *Les Clandestins et la régularisation de 1981–1982 en France*. Geneva: International Labor Office, working paper, May 1982.

Gaudemar, Jean-Paul de. *Mobilité du travail et accumulation du capital*. Paris: Maspero, 1976.

Gaulle, Charles de. *The Complete War Memoirs of Charles de Gaulle, 1940–1946*. New York: De Capo Press, [1984].

———. *Memoirs of Hope: Renewal and Endeavor*. New York: Simon and Schuster, 1969.

Gauron, André. *Années de rêves, années de crise (1970–1981)*. Paris: La Découverte, 1988.

Gauthier, Guy. *La Laïcité en Miroir*. Paris: Edilig, 1985.

Gaxie, Daniel. *Explications du vote.* Paris: Presses de la F.N.S.P., 1985.

Geerlandt, R. *Garaudy et Althusser: Le Débat sur l'humanisme dans le PCF et son enjeu.* Paris: Presses universitaires de France, 1978.

Girard, Alain, "Le Problème démographique et l'évolution du sentiment public." *Population* 5 (1950): 338–410.

Girard, Alain, and Jean Stoetzel. *Français et immigrés: Travaux et Documents.* INED Cahier 19. Paris: Presses Universitaires de France, 1953–54.

Girard, Alain, et al. "Attitudes des français à l'égard de l'immigration étrangère: Nouvelle enquête d'opinion." *Population* 29 (1974): 1015–64.

Giscard-d'Estaing, Valéry. *Démocratie française.* Paris: Fayard, 1976.

Glyn, Andrew, et al. "The Rise and Fall of the Golden Age: An Historical Analysis of Post-War Capitalism in the Developed Market Economic." In *The Golden Age of Capitalism: Lessons for the 1990s,* edited by Steven Marglin. Oxford: Oxford University Press.

Goguel, François. *Chroniques électorales: La Cinquième République du général de Gaulle.* Paris: Presses de la F.N.S.P., 1983.

——— . *France under the Fourth Republic.* Ithaca, N.Y.: Cornell University Press, 1952.

——— . "Géographie des élections sociales de 1950–51." *Revue Française de Science Politique* 3 (April 1953): 246–71.

Gorz, André. *Stratégie ouvrière et néo-capitalisme.* Paris: Editions du Seuil, 1964.

Gourevitch, Peter Alexis. *Paris and the Provinces.* Berkeley, Calif.: University of California Press, 1980.

Granotier, Bernard. *Les Travailleurs immigrés en France.* Paris: François Maspero, 1973.

——— . *Histoire économique et sociale de la Ve République.* 2 vols. Paris: La Découverte, 1983 and 1988.

Green, Diane. "The Seventh Plan—The Demise of French Planning?" *West European Politics* 1 (1978): 60–76.

Greenleaf, W. H. *The British Political Tradition: The Ideology Heritage.* London and New York: Methuen, 1983.

Grémion, Pierre. "Crispation et déclin du jacobinisme." In *La Sagesse et le désordre,* edited by Henri Mendras. Paris: Gallimard, 1980.

——— . *Paris-Prague.* Paris: Julliard, 1985.

Grémion, Pierre, and Jean-Pierre Worms. *Les Institutions régionales et la société locale.* Paris: Copédith, 1968.

Groux, Guy, and René Mouriaux. *La CFDT.* Paris: Economica, 1989.

Grunberg, Gérard. "L'Instabilité du comportement électoral." Paper presented at the Congress of the International Political Science Association, Paris, July 1985.

Hall, Peter A. *Governing the Economy: The Politics of State Intervention in Britain and France.* New York: Oxford University Press, 1986.

Hamilton, Richard. *Affluence and the French Worker in the Fourth Republic.* Princeton, N.J.: Princeton University Press, 1967.

Hammer, Tomas, ed. *European Immigration Policy: A Comparative Study.* New York: Cambridge University Press, 1985.

Hamon, Hervé, and Patrick Rotman. *La Deuxième Gauche.* Paris: Ramsay, 1982.

———. *Génération.* 2 vols. Paris: Editions du Seuil, 1985.

———. *Les Intellocrates.* Paris: Ramsay, 1981.

———. *Les Porteurs de Valise.* Paris: Albin Michel, 1979.

———. *Tant qu'il y aura des profs.* Paris: Seuil, 1984.

Hanley, David L., and Anne P. Kerr, eds., *May '68: Coming of Age.* London: Macmillan, 1989.

Hauss, Charles. *The New Left in France.* Boulder, Colo.: Greenwood Press, 1978.

Hayward, Jack. *The One and Indivisible French Republic.* New York: W. W. Norton, 1973.

———. *Private Interests and Public Policy: The Experience of the French Economic and Social Council.* London: Longmans, 1966.

Hénneresse, Marie-Claude. *Le Patronat et la politique française d'immigration: 1945–1975.* Thèse. Paris: Institut d'Etudes Politiques, 1978.

Hentillä, Seppo. "The Origins of the *Folkhem* Ideology in Swedish Social Democracy." *Scandanavian Journal of History* 3 (1978): 323–45.

Higgens, Winton. "Ernst Wigforss: The Renewal of Social Democratic Theory and Practice." In *Political Power and Social Theory,* edited by M. Zeitlin. Greenwich, Conn.: Jai Press, 1985.

Higonnet, Patrice. *Sister Republics.* Cambridge, Mass.: Harvard University Press, 1988.

Himmelfarb, Gertrude. *The Idea of Poverty: England in the Early Industrial Age.* New York: Random House, 1985.

Hoffmann, Stanley. *Decline and Renewal: France Since the 1930s.* New York: Viking Press, 1974.

———. *Le Mouvement poujade.* Paris: 1956.

———. "Paradoxes of the French Political Community." In *In Search of France,* edited by Stanley Hoffmann. Cambridge, Mass.: Harvard University Press, 1963.

Hoffmann, Stanley, ed. *In Search of France.* Cambridge, Mass.: Harvard University Press, 1963.

Hollifield, James F. *Immigrants, Markets, and States.* (Cambridge, Mass.: Harvard University Press, 1991).

———. "Immigration and the French State: Problems of Policy Implementation." *Comparative Political Studies* 23 (April 1990): 56–79.

———. "Administration and the French State." In *The State and Public Policy,* edited by B. Guy Peters and James F. Hollifield. (Boulder, Co.: Westview Press, 1991).

———— . "Migrants ou citoyens: la politique de l'immigration en France et aux Etats-Unix." *Revue Européenne des Migrations Internationales* (Spring 1990): 159–183.

Honoré, Jean. *Aujourd'hui l'école catholique*. Paris: Le Centurion, 1979.

Hugo, Victor. *History of a Crime*. New York: Hurst, n.d.

Huiban, Jean-Pierre. "La Contre proposition industrielle comme élément de stratégie syndicale (1973–1980)." In *1968–1982. Le Mouvement ouvrier français: Crise économique et changement politique*, edited by Mark Kesselman and Guy Groux. Paris: Editions ouvrières, 1984.

Inglehart, Ronald. *Culture Shift in Advanced Industrial Society*. Princeton, N.J.: Princeton University Press, 1990.

———— . *The Silent Revolution*. Princeton, N.J.: Princeton University Press, 1977.

Inglehart, Ronald, and Avram Hochstein. "Alignment and Dealignment of the Electorate in France and the United States." *Comparative Political Studies* (1972):

Institut d'Histoire du Temps Présent. *Bulletin Trimestriel* 31 (March 1988).

———— . *Les Cahiers de l'Institut d'Histoire du Temps Présent* 6 (November 1987).

———— . *Les Cahiers de l'Institut d'Histoire du Temps Présent* 10 (November 1988).

Jackson, Robert J., Michael M. Atkinson, and Kenneth D. Hart. "Constitutional Conflict in France: Deputies: Attitudes Toward Executive-Legislative Relations." *Comparative Politics* 9 (July 1977):

Jaffré, Jérôme. "L'Affrontement des notables de droite." In *Le Dossier des legislatives 1978*, edited by Frédéric Bon. Paris: FNSP, 1980.

James, Henry. *The Princess Casamassima*. New York: Harper Torchbooks, 1959.

Jaume, Lucien. *Le Discours jacobin et la démocratie*. Paris: Fayard, 1988.

Jenson, Jane. "Ce n'est pas un hasard: The Varieties of French Feminism." In *Contemporary France: An Interdisciplinary Review*, edited by Jolyon Howorth and George Ross. London: Frances Pinter, 1989.

———— . "Changing Discourse, Changing Agenda: Political Rights and Reproductive Policies in France." In *The Women's Movement of the United States and Western Europe: Consciousness, Political Opportunity and Public Policy*, edited by Carole Mueller and Mary Katzenstein. Philadelphia: Temple University Press, 1987.

———— . " 'Different' but not 'Exceptional': Canada's Permeable Fordism." *Canadian Review of Sociology and Anthropology* 26 (Winter 1989):

———— . "From *Baba Cool* to a *Vote Utile:* The Trajectory of the French *Verts*." *French Politics and Society* 7 (Fall 1989):

———— . "Gender and Reproduction: Or Babies and the State." *Studies in Political Economy* 20 (Summer 1987):

———— . "Paradigms and Political Discourse: Protective Legislation in France and the United States Before 1914." *Canadian Journal of Political Science* 22 (1989):

Jenson, Jane, and Alain Lipietz. "Rebel Sons: The Regulation School." *French Politics and Society* 5 (Fall, 1987).

Jenson, Jane, and George Ross. "The Uncharted Waters of De-Stalinization: The Uneven Evolution of the Parti Communiste Français." *Politics and Society* 9 (Autumn 1980).

————. *The View from Inside: A French Communist Cell in Crisis* (Berkeley, Calif.: University of California Press, 1985.

Johnson, R. W. *The Long March of the French Left*. New York: St. Martin's Press, 1981.

Kastoryano, Riva. *Etre turcque en France*. Paris: L'Harmattan, 1986.

Katzenstein, Peter J. *Corporatism and Change*. Ithaca, N.Y.: Cornell University Press, 1986.

Keeler, John T. S. *The Politics of Neo-Corporatism in France*. New York: Oxford University Press, 1987.

————. "Situating France on the Pluralism-Corporatism Continuum: A Critique of and Alternative to the Wilson Perspective." *Comparative Politics* 17 (January 1985): 229–49.

Kent, Christopher. *Brains and Numbers: Elitism, Comtism and Democracy in Mid-Victorian Britain*. Toronto: University of Toronto Press, 1978.

Kepel, Gilles. *Les Banlieus de l'Islam*. Paris: Editions du Seuil, 1988.

Kesselman, Mark, and Guy Groux, eds. *The French Workers' Movement*. London: Allen and Unwin, 1984.

Kesselman, Mark, and Joel Krieger, eds. *European Politics in Transition*. Lexington, Mass.: D.C. Health, 1987.

Kindleberger, Charles. *Europe's Postwar Growth: The Role of Labor Supply*. Cambridge, Mass.: Harvard University Press, 1967.

————. "The Postwar Resurgence of the French Economy." In *In Search of France*, edited by Stanley Hoffmann. Cambridge, Mass.: Harvard University Press, 1963.

Kirchheimer, Otto. "The Transformation of the Western European Party Systems." In *Political Parties and Political Development,* edited by Joseph LaPalombara and Myron Weiner. Princeton, N.J.: Princeton University Press, 1966.

Kuisel, Richard. *Capitalism and the State in Modern France*. Cambridge: Cambridge University Press, 1981.

Lacouture, Jean. *De Gaulle*. New York: New American Library, 1966.

Lafay, Nicole, and Kinh Tran. *Rapport sur l'immigration en France en 1980*. Paris: OECD, SOPEMI, 1981.

Lagrange, François. "Social Security in France from 1946 to 1986." In *Nationalizing Social Security in Europe and America*, edited by Douglas Ashford and E. W. Kelley. Greenwich, Conn.: Jai Press, 1986.

Lancelot, Alain, and Marie-Thérèse Lancelot. "The Evolution of the French Electorate." In *The Mitterrand Experiment*, edited by George Ross, Stanley Hoffmann, and Sylvia Malzacher. New York: Oxford University Press, 1987.

Lapie Commission. Commission Chargée de l'étude des rapports entre l'état et l'enseignement privé. *Rapport Général*. Paris: S.E.V.P.E.N., 1979.

Laurent, Emile. *Le Paupérisme et les associations de prévoyance*. Paris: Guillaumin, 1865.

Lavau, Georges. "The Left and Power." In *The Mitterrand Experiment*, edited by George Ross, Stanley Hoffmann, and Sylvia Malzacher. New York: Oxford University Press, 1987.

Lawson, Kay. "The Impact of Party Reform on Party Systems: The Case of the RPR in France." *Comparative Politics* 13 (July 1981): 401–21.

Le Bras, Hervé. *Les Trois Frances*. Paris: Editions du Seuil, 1986.

Le Bras, Hervé, and Emmanuel Todd. *L'Invention de la France*. Paris: Pluriel, 1981.

Le Pen, Jean-Marie. *Les Français d'abord*. Paris: Editions Carrère, 1984.

Le Play, M. F. *La Réforme sociale en France*. Paris: Plon, 1864.

Le Pors, Anicet. *Immigration et développement économique et social*. Paris: Documentation Française, 1976.

Lebon, A. *Le Point sur l'immigration et la présence étrangère en France*. 1986–1987: Paris: La Documentation française, 1988.

——— . "Sur une politique d'aide au retour." *Economique et Statistique* 193 (July–August 1979): 37–46.

Lebon, A., and X. Jansolin. *Rapport sur l'immigration en France en 1978*. Paris: OECD, SOPEMI, 1979.

Lebon, A., and O. Villey. "L'Immigration et la politique de la main-d'oeuvre." *Economie et Statistique* 113 (July–August 1979): 25–80.

Leclerc, Gérard. *La Bataille de l'Ecole*. Paris: Denoël, 1985.

Lecourt, Robert. *Concorde sans Concordat (1952–1957)*. Paris: Hachette, 1978.

Lefranc, Georges. *Grèves d'hier et d'aujourd'hui*. Paris: Aubier-Montaigne, 1970.

——— . *Les Organisations patronales en France*. Paris: Payot, 1976.

Lemert, Charles. *French Sociology: Rupture and Renewal Since 1968*. New York: Columbia University Press, 1981.

Lequin, Yves, ed. *La Mosaïque France: Histoire des étrangers et de l'immigration*. Paris: Larousse, 1988.

Levasseur, E. *Questions ouvrières et industrielles en France sous la Troisième République*. Paris: Rousseau, 1907.

Leveau, Rémy, and Dominique Schnapper. "Religion et politique: Juifs et musulmans." *Revue Française de Science Politique* 37 (December 1987):

Lévi-Strauss, Claude. *The Savage Mind*. Chicago: University of Chicago Press, 1966.

Lewis, Steven, and Serenella Sferza. "French Socialists Between State and Society." In *The Mitterrand Experiment*, edited by George Ross, Stanley Hoffmann, and Sylvia Malzacher. New York: Oxford University Press, 1987.

Linden, and Georges Weill. *Le Choix d'un deputé*. Paris: Editions de Minuit, 1974.

Lindenberg, Daniel, and Pierre-André Meyer. *Lucien Herr: Le Socialisme et son déstin*. Paris: Calman-Lévy, 1977.

Lipietz, Alain. "An Alternative Design for the XXIst Century." *Couverture Orange*. Paris: CEPREMAP, no. 8738., 1987.

————. "Aspects séculaires et conjoncturels de l'intervention économique de l'Etat." *Couverture Orange*. Paris: CEPREMAP, 1986.

————. *L'Audace ou l'enlisement*. Paris: Maspero, 1984.

————. *Le Capital et son espace*. Paris: Maspero, 1983.

————. *Choisir l'audace*. Paris: La Découverte, 1989.

————. "The Conditions for Creating an Alternative Movement in France." *Rethinking Marxism* 1 (Fall 1988):

————. *Crise et inflation: pourquoi?* Paris: Maspero, 1977.

————. *Mirages and Miracles*. London: Verso, 1987.

————. "Reflections on a Tale." *Studies in Political Economy* 26 (1988).

Lipset, Seymour M. *Political Man*. Garden City, N.Y.: Anchor Books, 1959.

Lipset, Seymour M., and Stein Rokkan. *Party Systems and Voter Alignments*. New York: Free Press, 1967.

Lochak, Danièle. *Etranger de quel droit?* Paris: Presses Universitaires de France, 1986.

Logue, William. *From Philosophy to Sociology: The Evolution of French Liberalism, 1871–1914*. Dekalb, Ill.: Northern Illinois University Press, 1983.

Lowi, Theodore. *The End of Liberalism*. New York: W. W. Norton, 1969.

Luethy, Herbert. *France Against Herself*. New York: Praeger, 1955.

Lutz, Vera. *Central Planning for the Market Economy*. London: Longmans, 1969.

Macrae, Duncan, Jr. *Parliament, Parties and Society in France, 1946–1958*. New York: St. Martin's; London: Macmillan, 1967.

Macridis, Roy, and Bernard E. Brown. *The De Gaulle Republic*. Homewood, Illinois: Dorsey, 1960.

Madison, James. *Federalist no. 10*. in Alexander Hamilton, James Madison and John Jay, *The Federalist Papers*, New York. New American Library, 1961.

Mair, Peter. "Party Politics in Contemporary Europe: A Challenge to Party?" *West European Politics* 7 (October 1984):

Mallet, Serge. *Essays on the New Working Class*. St. Louis: Telos Press, 1975.

————. *Le Gaullisme et la gauche*. Paris: Editions du Seuil, 1964.

————. *La Nouvelle classe ouvrière*. Paris: Editions du Seuil, 1963.

Manent, Pierre. *Histoire intellectuelle du libéralisme*. Paris: Calman-Lévy, 1987.

Marrus, Michael. *Politics of Assimilation: A Study of the French Jewish Community at the Time of the Dreyfus Affair*. Oxford: Clarendon Press, 1971.

Marshall, T. H. *Class, Citizenship, and Social Development*. Cambridge: Cambridge University Press, 1950.

Martin, Gérard. "Social Services, Job Creation and New Technologies." Paper delivered at the European Center for Social Welfare Training and Research, New York, 1986.

Masson, Paul. *Etudiants, Police, Presse, Pouvoir*. Paris: Hachette, 1987.

Massot, Jean. "Le Parlement français sous trois présidents, 1958–1980." *Revue Française de Science Politique* 1 (1981):

———. *La Présidence de la République en France*. Paris: La Documentation française, 1986.

Mauco, Georges. *Les Etrangers en France*. Paris: Colin, 1932.

Mayer, Nonna. "Pas de chrysanthèmes pour les variables sociologiques." In *Mars, 1986: la drôle de defaite de la gauche*, edited by Elisabeth Dupoirier and Gérard Grunberg. Paris: Presses universitaires de France, 1987.

Mayer, Nonna, and Pascal Perrineau. *Le Front National à découvert*. Paris: Presses de la F.N.S.P., 1989.

McBriar, A. M. *An Edwardian Mixed Doubles: The Bosanquets Versus the Webbs: A Study in British Social Policy, 1890–1929*. Oxford: Clarendon, 1987.

McIntoch, Alison C. "The Rise of Twentieth-Century Pronatalism." *International Journal of Politics* 12 (Fall 1982): 42–57.

Mercier, Christian. *Les Déracinés du capital*. Lyon: Presses Universitaires de Lyon, 1977.

Miller, Mark. *Foreign Workers in Western Europe: An Emerging Political Force*. New York: Praeger, 1981.

Milza, Pierre, ed. *Les Italiens en France de 1914 à 1940*. Rome: Ecole française de Rome, 1981.

Minc, Alain. *L'Après crise est commencée*. Paris: Gallimard, 1982.

Ministère de l'Education Nationale (MEN). *Note d'Information*. Issued approximately fifty times per year. The first number indicates the year and the second the issue number.

Mioche, Philippe. "Syndicats et CNPF dans le plan: L'Amorce d'un consensus." In *La Planification en Crise*. Paris: Editions CNRS, 1987.

Monchablon, Alain. *Histoire de l'UNEF de 1956 à 1968*. Paris: Presses Universitaires de France, 1983.

Le Monde, Dossiers et Documents, Les Elections Législatives du 16 mars 1986. Paris: Le Monde, 1986.

Montesquieu, Baron de. *The Spirit of the Laws*. New York: Hafner Press, 1949.

Moody, Joseph N. *French Education since Napoleon*. Syracuse, N.Y.: Syracuse University Press, 1978.

Morin, Edgar. *The Red and the White*. New York: Pantheon, 1970.

Mouriaux, Marie-Françoise. *L'Emploi en France depuis 1945*. Paris: Colin, 1972.

Mouriaux, René. "Le Bilan social d'un quinquennat (15 juin 1969–2 avril 1974)," *Etudes* (June 1974): 869–77.

———. *La C.F.D.T. face à la flexibilité de l'emploi, 1985–1987*. Paris: CEVIPOF, 1987.

———. *Les Stratégies syndicales aux lendemains de mai 1968*. Paris: CEVIPOF, 1987.

———. *Syndicalisme et politique*. Paris: Editions ouvrières, 1985.

————. *Le Syndicalisme face à la crise*. Paris: La Découverte, 1986.

Mouriaux, René, and Catherine de Wenden. "Syndicalisme français et Islam." *Revue Française de Science Politique* 37 (December 1987): 794–819.

Murswieck, Axel. "Health Policy-Making." In *Policy and Politics in the Federal Republic of Germany*, edited by K. von Beyme and M. Schmidt. New York: St. Martin's, 1985.

Guy Neouannic. "L'Heure des choix." *Enseignement Public* 58 (June 1989).

N'Guyen Van Yen, C. *Droit de l'immigration*. Paris: Presses universitaires de France, Thémis, 1986.

Nicol, J. "Les Incidences économiques de l'immigration." *Problèmes Economiques* 1583 (July 26, 1978): 3–7.

Noiriel, Gérard. *Le Creuset français, histoire de l'immigration XIXe–XXe siècles*. Paris: Editions du Seuil, 1988.

————. *Longwy, immigrés, et prolétaires, 1880–1980*. Paris: Presses universitaires de France, 1984.

————. *Ouvriers dans la société française, XIVe–XXe siècles*. Paris: Editions du Seuil, 1986.

Notat, Nicole. "Le 19 septembre: un grand rendez-vous social." *CFDT–Magazine*, July–August 1989.

Notter, Nikolaus. "Le Statut des travailleurs étrangers en Allemagne Fédérale." *Droit Social* 4 (April 1973): 223–30.

Organisation for Economic Cooperation and Development OECD. "Manpower Policy in France." *Reviews of Manpower and Social Affairs* 12 (1973): 22–28.

OFCE. "Plan pour l'emploi du gouvernement." *Liaisons Sociales* 8488 (September 15, 1988).

Oeuvrard, Françoise, "Note sur la clientèle des établissements privés: l'origine sociale des éleves." *Education et Formation* 6 (October 1983–June 1984): 32–38.

Ory, Pascal, and Jean-François Sirinelli. *Les Intellectuels en France, de l'affaire Dreyfus à nos jours*. Paris: Armand Colin, 1986.

Oualid, William, and Charles Picquenard. *Salaires et tarifs, conventions et grèves: La Politique du Ministère de l'Armement et du Ministère de Travail*. Paris and New Haven, Conn.: Presses Universitaires de France/New Haven, Conn.: Yale University Press, 1928.

Parti Socialiste. *Libérer l'Ecole: Plan Socialiste pour l'Education Nationale*. Paris: Flammarion, 1978.

Paye-Jeanneney, Laurence, and Jean-Jacques Payan, *Le Chantier Universitaire*. Paris: Beauchesne, 1988.

Pederson, Mogen. "Changing Patterns of Electoral Volatility in European Party Systems, 1948–1977: Explorations in Explanation." In *West European Party Systems*, Beverly Hills, Calif.: Sage Publications, 1983.

Pelling, Henry. *The Labour Governments*. London: Macmillan, 1984.

Percheron, Annick, and Kent Jennings. "Political Continuities in French Families." *Comparative Politics* 13 (July 1981):

Perrineau, Pascal. "Front National: la drôle de defaite." In *Elections législatives 1988*, edited by Philippe Habert and Colette Ysmal. Paris: Figaro/Etudes Politiques, 1988.

Petit, Pascal. "La Fin des politiques de plein-emploi." *Les Temps Modernes* 501 (April 1988):

————. "Problems of the State in Dealing With the System of Wage/Labour Relations: The Case of France." In *The Search for Labour Market Flexibility: The European Economies in Transition*, edited by Robert Boyer. Oxford: The Clarendon Press, 1988.

Pierce, Roy. *French Politics and Political Institutions*. New York: Harper and Row, [1968].

Pinto, Louis. *L'Intelligence en Action: "Le Nouvel Observateur"*. Paris: Anne-Marie Métaillié, 1984.

Piore, Michael. *Birds of Passage: Migrant Labor in Industrial Societies*. Cambridge: Cambridge University Press, 1979.

————. "Economic Fluctuation, Job Security, and Labor-Market Duality in Italy, France, and the United States." *Politics and Society* 9 (no. 4 1980): 379–407.

Portelli, Hugues. *La Politique en France sous la Ve République*. Paris: Grasset, 1987.

Poulantzas, Nicos. *Classes and Contemporary Capitalism*. London: New Left Books, 1965.

————. *Pouvoir politique et classes sociales*. Paris: Maspero, 1968.

————. *State, Power and Socialism*. London: New Left Books, 1978.

Poussou, J.-P., and F. Malino. "De la grande nation au Grand Empire." In *La Mosaïque France: Histoire des étrangers et de l'immigration*, edited by Yves Lequin. Paris: Larousse, 1988.

Prost, Antoine. *L'Ecole et la famille dans une société en mutation*. Paris: Nouvelle Librairie de France, 1982.

————. *L'Enseignement s'est-il démocratisé?* Paris: Presses Universitaires de France, 1986.

————. "Les Grèves de mai-juin 68." *L'Histoire* 110 (April 1968): 34–46.

————. *Histoire de l'enseignement en France, 1800–1967*. Paris: A. Colin, 1968.

————. "Pluralisme et rationalisme," in Guy Gauthier, *La Laïcité en miroir*. Paris: Edilig, 1985.

Provent, D. "Le Travail manuel dans la société industrielle: Recherche des conditions de sa revalorisation à travers l'analyse des structures de travail et d'emploi." *Revue Française des Affaires Sociales* 2 (April–June 1976): 85–144.

Quermonne, Jean-Louis. *Le Gouvernement de la France sous la Ve République*. Paris: Dalloz, 1987.

Rapport, Anotelli. *Journal Officiel, Débats Parlementaires*. 1930: 526–29.

Rapport Belorgey. "Rapport de la commission des affaires sociales." *Journal Officiel*, Assemblé Nationale, session ordinaire de 1985–86, December 20, 1985.

Rapport Boulin. *Pour une politique de la santé*. Report prepared for the Ministry of Public Health and Social Security. Paris: La Documentation Française, 1971.

Rapport Buisson. "Rapport fait au nom de la commission de travail et des affaires sociales." *Journal Officiel*, Annexes, no. 554. Assemblée Consultative Provisoire, July 24, 1945.

La Rapport Calvez. "La Politique de l'immigration." *Avis et Rapports du Conseil Economique et Social* (May 23, 1975): 349–75.

Rapport Friedel. "Commission d'études des structures de la sécurité sociale." Mimeo. Paris: Prime Minister's Office, 1966.

Rapport Mottin. "Rapport relatif aux travaux de la commission chargée d'étudier le projet d'ordonnance relatif à l'organisation de la sécurité sociale." Mimeo. Paris: July 9, 1945.

Rapport, Théry. "La Place et le rôle de secteur associatif dans le développement de la politique d'action éducative, sanitaire et sociale." *Journal Officiel*, Conseil Economique et Social, 1986 session, July 29, 1986.

Rémond, René. "La Politique et l'église," *L'Express*, May 11–17, 1984, pp. 18–22.

Reynaud, Jean-Daniel. *Les Syndicats, les patrons, et l'Etat*. Paris: Editions ouvrières, 1978.

Richardson, Jeremy, and Roger Henning. *Unemployment: Policy Responses of Western Democracies*. London: Sage, 1984.

Rioux, Jean-Pierre. *La France de la Quatrième République*. Paris: Editions du Seuil, 1980.

Robrieux, Philippe. *Notre génération communiste*. Paris: Fayard, 1977.

Rosanvallon, Pierre. *L'Age de l'autogestion*. Paris: Editions du Seuil, 1976.

————. *La Crise de l'état providence*. Paris: Editions du Seuil, 1981.

————. *Le Moment Guizot*. Paris: Gallimard, 1985.

Rosenvallon, Pierre, and Patrick Viveret. *Pour une nouvelle culture politique*. Paris: Editions du Seuil, 1977.

Ross, George. "Destroyed by the Dialectic: Politics, the Decline of Marxism, and the New Middle Strata in France." *Theory and Society* 16 (Fall 1987):

————. "Marxism and the New Middle Classes: French Critiques." *Theory and Society* 5 (March 1978).

————. "The Perils of Politics: French Unions and the Crisis of the 1970s." In *Unions, Change and Crisis: French and Italian Union Strategy and the Political Economy, 1945–1980*, edited by Peter Lange, George Ross, and Maurizio Vannicelli. London: Allen and Unwin, 1982.

————. *Workers and Communists in France: From Popular Front to Eurocommunism*. Berkeley, Calif.: University of California Press, 1982.

Ross, George, Stanley Hoffmann, and Sylvia Malzacher, eds. *The Mitterrand Experiment*. New York: Oxford University Press, 1987.

Ross, George, and Jane Jenson. "Crisis and France's 'Third Way.' " *Studies in Political Economy* 11 (Spring 1983):

———— . "Postwar Class Struggle and the Crisis of Left Politics." *The Socialist Register, 1985/86,* edited by Ralph Miliband et al. London: Merlin, 1986.

———— . "The Tragedy of the French Left." In *The Future of the European Left,* edited by Patrick Camiller. London: Verso, 1990.

———— . "The Tragedy of the French Left." *New Left Review* 171 (September–October 1988):

Rousseau, Jean-Jacques. *Du Contrat social.* Paris: Editions Garnier Frères, 1954.

———— . *A Discourse on Political Economy.* New York: Dutton, Everyman's Library, 1973.

———— . *The Government of Poland.* New York: Bobbs-Merrill, Library of Liberal Arts, 1972.

Sartre, Jean-Paul. *Critique de la raison dialectique.* Paris: Gallimard, 1960.

Sauvy, Alfred. "Besoins et possibilités de l'immigration en France." *Population* 2–3 (1950): 209–434.

Savary, Alain. *En Toute Liberté.* Paris: Hachette, 1985.

Schain, Martin. "Immigration and Change in the French Party System." *European Journal of Political Research* 16 (1988): 597–621.

———— . "The National Front in France and the Construction of Political Legitimacy." *West European Politics* 2 (April, 1987):

Schnapper, Dominique. "Le Juif errant." In *La Mosaïque France: Histoire des étrangers et de l'immigration,* edited by Yves Lequin. Paris: Larousse, 1988.

———— . *Juifs et israélites.* Paris: Gallimard, 1980.

Schor, Ralph. *L'Opinion française et les étrangers, 1919–1939.* Paris: Publications de la Sorbonne, 1985.

Scott, John. *Republican Ideas and the Liberal Tradition in France.* New York: Columbia University Press, 1951.

Secretary of State for Immigrant Workers. *La Nouvelle politique de l'immigration.* Reprinted in *Droit Social* 5 (1975):

Shonfield, Andrew. *Modern Capitalism.* Oxford: Oxford University Press, 1965.

Singer, Daniel. *Is Socialism Doomed?* New York: Oxford University Press, 1988.

Singly, François de, and Claude Thélot. *Gens du privé, gens du public.* Paris: Dunod, 1989.

Sirinelli, Jean-François. "Le hasard ou la nécessité? Une Histoire en chantier: L'Histoire des intellectuels." *Vingtième Siècle* (January–March 1986):

———— . *Pierre Mendès-France et le mendésisme.* Paris: Fayard, 1985.

Skinner, Quentin. "Meaning and Understanding in the History of Ideas." *History and Theory* 8 (1969): 3–53.

———— . *The Return of Grand Theory in the Social Sciences.* Cambridge: Cambridge University Press, 1985.

————. "Some Problems in the Analysis of Political Thought." *Political Theory* 2 (1974): 277–303.

SOFRES. *L'Etat de l'opinion: clés pour 1987.* Paris: Seuil, 1987.

————. "L'Image de Jean-Marie Le Pen et de l'extrême droit à l'approche des élections Européenes." Paris: SOFRES, May 1984.

————. *L'Opinion Publique, 1984.* Paris: Gallimard, 1984.

————. *L'Opinion Publique, 1985.* Paris: Gallimard, 1985.

Sorlin, Peter. *Waldeck-Rousseau.* Paris: Colin, 1966.

Statera, Gianni. *Death of a Utopia: The Development and Decline of Student Organizations in Europe.* New York: Oxford University Press, 1975.

Steffen, Monica. "Régulation politique de stratégies professionelles: Médecine liberale et émergence de Centres de Santé." Doctoral dissertation, Université des Sciences Sociales de Grenoble II, 1983.

Stoffaes, Christian. *Politique industrielle.* Paris: Cours de droit, 1984.

Stone, Judith. *The Search for Social Peace: Reform Legislation in France, 1890–1914.* Albany, N.Y.: State University of New York Press, 1985.

Suleiman, Ezra N. *Politics, Power and Bureaucracy.* Princeton, N.J.: Princeton University Press, 1974.

————. *Private Power and Centralization in France.* Princeton, N.J.: Princeton University Press, 1987.

Tanguy, Lucie, "L'Etat et l'école: l'école privée en France." *Revue française de sociologie* 13 (1972): 325–75.

Tapinos, Georges. *L'Immigration étrangère en France.* Paris: Presses Universitaires de France, 1975.

Thévent, Amadée. *L'Aide sociale aujourd'hui après la décentralisation.* 6th ed. Paris: Editions EDF, 1986.

Thomson, David. *Democracy in France.* London: Oxford University Press, 1969.

Tocqueville, Alexis de. *Democracy in America.* New York: Vintage Books, 1945.

————. "Memoir on Pauperism," with an introduction by Gertrude Himmelfarb. *Public Interest* 70 (Winter 1983): 102–120.

————. *The Old Regime and the French Revolution.* New York: Doubleday Anchor, 1955.

Todd, Emmanuel. *La Nouvelle France.* Paris: Editions du Seuil, 1988.

Touraine, Alain. *Le Mouvement de Mai ou le communisme utopique.* Paris: Editions du Seuil, 1968.

————. *Production de la Société.* Paris: Editions du Seuil, 1973.

————. *La Société post-industrielle.* Paris: Denoël, 1969.

Tournerie, J.-P. *Le Ministère du Travail: Origines et premiers développements.* Paris: Cujas, 1971.

Truman, David. *The Governmental Process.* New York: Alfred A. Knopf, 1951.

Turkle, Sherry. *Psychoanalytic Politics*. Cambridge: MIT Press, 1981.

Ullmo, Yves. *La Planification française*. Paris: Dunod, 1974.

Vedel, Georges. *La Dépolitisation: mythe ou réalité?* Paris: Presses de la F.N.S.P., Cahier 120, 1962.

Verdès-Leroux, Jeannine. *Au Service du parti*. Paris: Fayard/Minuit, 1983.

Vieuguet, André. *Français et immigrés, le combat du P.C.F.* Paris: Editions Sociales, 1975.

Villey, O. "Le Redéploiement actuel de la main-d'oeuvre étrangère passé le premier choc de la crise." *Travail et Emploi* 8 (April–May 1981): 47–55.

Wahl, Nicholas. "The French Constitution of 1958: The Initial Draft and its Origins." *American Political Science Review* 53 (June 1959): 358–82.

Weber, Eugen. *Peasants into Frenchmen*. Stanford, Calif.: Stanford University Press, 1976.

Weber, Henri. *Mai 1968: Vingt ans après*. Paris: Editions du Seuil, 1988.

Weil, Patrick. *L'Analyse d'une politique publique: La Politique française d'immigration, 1974–1988*. Thèse. Paris: Institut d'Etude Politique, 1988.

Weiss, John. "Origins of the Welfare State: Poor Relief in the Third Republic." *French Historical Studies* 13 (Spring 1983): 47–78.

Wenden, Catherine Withol de. *Les Immigrés et la politique*. Paris: Presses de la F.N.S.P., 1988.

Williams, Philip M. *Crisis and Compromise: Politics in the Fourth Republic*. Hamden, Conn.: Archon Books, 1964.

——— . *Politics in Postwar France: Parties and the Constitution of the Fourth Republic*. London: Longmans, 1958.

Williams, Philip M., and Martin Harrison. *Politics and Society in de Gaulle's Republic*. Garden City, N.Y.: Doubleday, 1971.

Wilson, Frank L. *The French Democratic Left, 1963–1969: Towards a Modern Party System*. Stanford, Calif.: Stanford University Press, 1971.

——— . "French Interest Group Politics: Pluralist or Neo-Corporatist." *American Political Science Review* 77 (December 1983): 892–910.

——— . "The French Party System Since 1981." *Contemporary French Civilization* (Fall–Winter 1983–84):

——— . *Interest Group Politics in France*. New York: Cambridge University Press, 1987.

——— . "The Revitalization of French Parties." *Comparative Political Studies* 1 (April 1979): 82–103.

Winock, Michel. "Les Générations d'intellectuels." *Vingtième Siècle* (April–June 1989):

——— . *Histoire politique de la Revue 'Esprit,' 1930–1950*. Paris: Seuil, 1975.

——— . *La République se meurt*. Paris: Editions du Seuil, 1978.

Wisniewski, J. "Travailleurs migrants dans le bâtiment et les travaux publics." *Hommes et Migrations* 885 (June 1975): 3–19.

Worms, Jean-Pierre. "Le Préfet et ses Notables." *Sociologie du Travail* 7 (July–September 1966): 249–76.

Wright, Gordon. *France in Modern Times, 1760 to the Present.* Chicago: Rand McNally, 1962.

————. *The Reshaping of French Democracy.* New York: Reynal and Hitchcock, 1948.

Wright, Vincent. "Les Préfets d'Emile Ollivier." *Revue Historique* 487 (July–September 1968): 115–38.

Wylie, Laurence. *Village in the Vaucluse.* Cambridge, Mass.: Harvard University Press, 1957.

Ysmal, Colette. *Le Comportement électoral des français.* Paris: La Découverte, 1986.

Zimmermann, Marie. *Pouvoir et Liberté: Clés pour une lecture des rapports église-état de Bonaparte à Mitterrand.* Strasbourg: Cerdic, 1981.

Index

Accumulation regime 19, 22, 23, 88
Acquired Immunity Deficiency Syndrome (AIDS) 40, 75
Adenauer, Konrad 164, 256
Affaire Bull. see Bull Affair
Affaire des foulards 139–140
Affaire Dreyfus. see Dreyfus Affair
Afghanistan 234, 261, 262
African Americans 136
Agence Nationale pour l'Emploi (ANPE) 163
Agence pour la Maîtrise de l'Energie 38
Agence pour la Valorisation de la Recherche 38
Aide sociale 165
Albert, Michel 184
Algeria 5, 10, 44, 54, 93, 121–123, 129, 245n, 255
Algerian immigration 120, 123, 126, 283
Algerian War 4, 28, 48, 51, 62, 122, 174, 176, 223–225, 238, 244n, 257, 275, 283
Algérie française 52, 276
Alliance Nationale pour l'Accroisement de la Population Française 117
Allocation de salaire unique 160–161
Allocation minimum de base 161
Allocation supplémentaire d'attente (ASA) 182, 184
Alsace 158
Alternance 6, 48, 290
Althusser, Louis 223, 234
Ancien régime. see Old Regime
Arendt, Hannah 235
Aron, Raymond 234, 235, 292
ASSEDIC 184
Assemblée Nationale. see National Assembly
Assises du Socialisme 233

Association pour l'Ecole Libre (APEL) 195, 196
Association Parlementaire pour la Liberté de l'Education (APLE) 196
Atelier movement 153
Auroux Laws 32, 187
Autogestion 97, 98, 99, 178, 213, 231, 239
Autogestionnaires 100, 107, 111n, 228, 232–233, 236, 248n

Baccalauréat 201, 207, 215, 224
Balance of payments 86
Balladur, Edouard 37
BAPSO 162
Barangé Law 196
Barre, Raymond 30, 31, 68, 79, 103, 139, 183–184, 289
Barthes, Roland 234
Belgium 140, 267
Belleville, Pierre 223
Bérégovoy, Pierre 35
Bergeron, André 188
Berlin 260
Beullac, Christian 204, 219n
Beveridge Plan 164
Blanc, Jacques 76
Bloch-Laîné, François 165
Blocked society. see *Société bloquee*
Blondel, Marc 188
Blum, Léon 166
Bobigny 134
Bonapartism 44, 52, 276, 288
Bordeaux 177
Bouches du Rhône 78
Boulloche, Robert 197
Bourbon monarchy 217n

321

Bourdieu, Pierre 223, 228, 242n, 248n
Brezhnev, Leonid 262
Buci-Glucksmann, Christine 228
Budget national 151
Budget social 151
Bull Affair 176
Bundestag 264
Bureau d'Assistance Publique 152, 155
Bureaux de Bienfaisance 155

Caen 177
Caisse des Allocations Familiales 158
Caisse primaire 158
Canada 137
Canard Enchainé 180
Carte de séjour 115
Carter, Jimmy 261
Castoriadis, Cornelius 223
Catchall politics 278–279, 287–291
Catholic church 69, 211
Catholic education. see Catholic schools
Catholic schools 95, 193–202, 211–212, 280–
   281, 282–284
Catholic universities. see Catholic schools
Catholicism 288, 292
Centre Démocratie et Progrès (CDP) 66
Centre des Démocrates Sociaux (CDS) 78, 80
Centre d'Etude, de Recherches, et d'Education
   Socialistes (CERES) 98, 100, 101, 104,
   164, 289, 290
Centre National de la Recherche Scientifique
   (CNRS) 37, 156
Centre National des Indépendants et Paysans
   (CNIP) 25, 26, 62
Centrism 81
Centrists. see Centre Démocratie et Progrès
   (CDP)
Chaban-Delmas, Jacques 50–52, 66, 103, 161,
   163, 178, 180
Chapot, Jean 199
Charléty incident 96
Charlot, Jean 288
Chevènement, Jean-Pierre 32, 33, 35, 198,
   200, 204, 216
Cheysson, Claude
China, People's Republic of 258
Chirac, Jacques 30, 37, 39, 45, 49, 50, 66–
   68, 75–78, 79, 103, 131, 139, 178, 181–
   183, 186, 205, 210, 214, 268, 269, 286,
   289

Chouat, Didier 200
Christian Democratic Party (Germany) 49
Christian Democratic Party (Italy) 49
Church schools. see Catholic schools
Churchill, Winston 169n
Circulaire Fontanet 128–129
Circulaire Gorse 130
Circulaire Marcellin 130
Citizenship 113, 142n
Citizenship law 139
Civic culture 278
Classes préparatoires 202
Code de la Nationalité. see Citizenship law
Cohabitation 7, 48–51, 160, 276–277, 279,
   286
Colbertism 105
Cold War 4, 5, 8, 12, 221, 257, 260, 292
Collège de France 204
Collège Gabriel-Havez 139
Collèges d'Enseignement Secondaire (CES)
   202, 205, 213
Comédie Française 156
Commissariat Général du Plan (CGP) 117,
   119, 125, 142n, 184
Commission Pédagogique 206
Comité Interministériel pour l'Amènagement
   des Structures Industrielles (CIASI) 183
Comité National d'Action Laïque (CNAL)
   196, 198–199, 212
Committee of Public Safety 193
Common Agricultural Policy (CAP) 178
Common Program for a Left Government 8,
   29, 31, 40, 65, 66, 90, 99–101, 103, 183,
   185, 231–233, 239, 240, 290
Communism 231, 236
Communist party. see Parti Communiste
   Français
Communist Party of the Soviet Union (CPSU)
   90
Community work program. see travail d'utilité
   publique
Confédération Française Démocratique du Tra-
   vail (CFDT) 34, 112n, 124, 129, 173–190,
   192n, 203, 213, 228, 232, 246n, 248n
Confédération Française des Travailleurs
   Chrétiens (CFTC) 116, 118, 173–175
Confédération Générale des Cadres (CGC)
   174, 188
Confédération Générale des Petites et Moyen-
   nes Entreprises (CGPME) 133
Confédération Générale du Travail (CGT) 92,

103, 109n, 110n, 112n, 116, 118, 123, 124, 133, 174–190, 192n
Confédération Internationale des Syndicats Libres (CISL) 192n
Conference on Security and Cooperation in Europe (CSCE) 260
Conseil d'Etat 53, 129, 140, 141, 161, 167
Conseil National de la Résistance 92
Conseil National du Patronat Français (CNPF) 131, 132, 163, 176, 178, 188
Conseil Supérieur du Travail 155
Conseils d'administration 159
Conservatives 47
Constant, Benjamin 235
Constitution of 1958 43–49, 52, 54–55
Constitutional Committee 195
Constitutional Council 45, 52, 53, 209
Contrats de solidarité 185
Convention des Institutions Républicaines (CIR) 98
Cornec, Jean 196
Corporatism 42n, 280
Cresson, Edith 36
Crisis of assimilation 114
Crisis of participation 114
Croizat, Ambroise 120, 158
Crozier, Michel 205–207, 212–213, 279
Czechoslovakia 96, 259

Dalle Report 34
Daniel, Pierre 199
Dassault Aviation 177
De Gaulle, Charles 2–5, 7, 12, 14, 15, 25, 26, 39, 43–46, 48–55, 66, 68, 91, 93, 96, 105, 118, 122, 157, 161–162, 178, 197, 223, 251–267, 269–273, 276–278, 284–285, 291–293
Débat 236
Debray, Régis 230
Debré, Robert 117–118
Debré, Michel 43–6, 57, 176, 177, 197, 212, 276, 285
Debré-Giscard Stabilization Plan 28, 176–177
Debré Law (1959) 54, 197–198, 201, 283
Decolonization 122–123
Defferre, Gaston 95, 96, 110n, 203, 289
Defferre Law 286
Deixonne, Maurice 196
Delebarre, Michel 36
Delors, Jacques 12, 32, 103, 178–180
Denmark 266

Department of Population and Migration. see Direction de la Population et des Migrations
Derrida, Jacques 227, 234, 235, 245n
Désir, Harlem 138
Détente 260
Deuxième gauche. see New left
Devaquet, Alain 38, 193, 209, 213
Devaquet Bill 210, 214
Didier, Jean 188
Dijoud, Paul 131
Direction de la Population et des Migrations (DPM) 125, 133
Dirigisme 120
Dotation globale de décentralisation (DGD) 165
Dreyfus Affair 11, 113, 155, 240
Duclos, Jacques 96
Durkheim, Emile 151
Duverger, Maurice 90, 288, 296n

Ecole unique 202
Economic and Social Council (CES) 134
Education Priority Zones (ZEPS) 204
Eisenhower, Dwight David 256
Elysée 49, 50, 56
England. see Great Britain
Etablissement publique 156, 158
Etat providence. see welfare state
Etatisme. see Jacobinism
Ethnic minorities 113–142
Euratom 265
Eureka program for technological cooperation 269
Eurocommunism 101, 228, 289
Europe 17, 22, 54
European Coal and Steel Community (ECSC) 265
European Commission 12
European Economic Community (EEC) 4, 12, 14, 24, 25, 27, 29, 52, 53, 131, 140, 178, 264–269, 271
European Monetary System (EMS) 14, 30, 268, 290
European Parliament 71
European Parliament. Elections 72
Evian Agreements 85
Extreme Left 55, 292
Extreme Right 55, 142, 292

Fabius, Laurent 3–7, 38
Falloux Law 194

Fascism 292

Faure, Edgar 77, 193, 207–208

Faure Law 207–208, 210

FCPE 196, 198

Federal Republic of Germany 31, 45, 49, 52, 54, 130, 134, 137, 140, 164, 214, 255, 258–259–270, 272, 280, 281, 294n

Fédération de la Gauche Démocrate et Socialiste (FGDS) 95–96, 110n

Fédération de l'Education Nationale (FEN) 173, 183, 192n, 198, 205–207, 210, 212–216, 229, 281, 283

Fédération des Syndicats Autonomes de l'Enseignement Supérieur et de la Recherche 209

Fédération Nationale du Bâtiment (FNB) 129, 131, 132

Fête Jeanne d'Arc 78

Fifth Plan 124, 128

Fifth Republic 3, 6–8, 43, 45, 51, 54–56, 57–65, 68, 69, 85, 88, 90, 93, 94, 97, 105, 114, 120, 122–135, 141, 142, 160, 193, 197, 214, 252, 269, 275–278, 280, 282, 285–289, 291

First Empire 193

Fondation pour la Vie Associative (FONDA) 165

Fondation St. Simon 240, 248n

Fonds Industriel de Modernisation 38

Fontanet, Joseph 204

Force de dissuasion 261

Force Ouvrière (FO) 174–175, 188, 192n

Fordism 22–34, 39, 86–87, 91–105

Foucault, Michel 222, 227, 234, 245n

Fougères 177

Foulards. see Affaire des foulards

Fourcade plan 181

Fourth Plan 176

Fourth Republic 2–5, 7, 25, 26, 43, 44, 46, 52–57, 59, 61, 68, 89, 91, 92, 96, 114–122, 133, 141, 142, 151, 160, 195, 197, 212, 225, 252, 254–255, 265, 269, 275–276, 279–280, 285, 287

Foyer, Jean 209

Foyer Bill 209

French Revolution 54, 113, 193, 221, 239, 240, 278, 292

Freud, Sigmund 227

Front National (FN) 8, 9, 37, 40, 46, 55, 72, 74–78, 80, 81, 107, 134, 137–139, 140, 142, 214, 279, 283–284, 286, 288

Front pour la Libération Nationale (FLN) 244n

Furet, François 240, 249n, 292

Gallicans 217n

Garantie de ressources 172n

Gardannes 188

Gauchisme 228

Gaudin, Jean-Claude 76

Gaullism 59, 61, 62, 68, 79, 91, 93, 142, 225, 270, 278, 286–288

Gaullist deputies 65

Gaullist leaders 66, 122, 129

Gaullist party. see also Rassemblement du Peuple Français, Union pour la Nouvelle République, Rassemblement pour la République 47, 49, 60–61, 64, 66, 72, 125, 195, 196, 288, 290

Gaullist policies 270–271, 289

Gaullist voters 61, 65

General Electric 176

George, Lloyd 169n

German Democratic Republic 141

Germany 154, 157, 159, 161, 253, 254–255, 268

Giraudet, Pierre 184

Girondins 140

Giscard d'Estaing, Valéry 30, 45, 49, 50, 54, 55, 62, 66, 67, 100, 103, 111n, 130, 131, 134, 139, 164, 174, 176–177, 181, 183, 189, 208, 219n, 261–262, 285

Glucksmann, André 232

Goguel, François 60

Gorbachev, Mikhail 263, 270

Gorz, André 223

Gramsci, Antonio 18

Grandes écoles 202, 207, 208, 213, 215, 283

Grands corps 56, 285

Grandval, Gilbert 161

Grasse 76, 77

Great Britain 44, 49, 52, 152, 155, 156, 161–164, 213, 253, 254, 256–258, 261, 264–269, 277, 280, 294n

Great Depression 114, 116

Greens 9, 104, 106

Grenelle agreements 28, 32, 97, 102, 125, 126, 134, 178

Grenoble 165

Groupe pour la Renovation de l'Université Française (GERUF) 209

Guermeur law 198

Guiberteau, Paul 199
Guizot, François 234

Haby, René 219n
Haby reforms 202
Hébergement 165
Helsinki 260
Higher education 11
Hirsch, Etienne 26
Holland 140
Honeywell Bull 176, 183
Honoré, Jean 199, 201
Hugo, Victor 250, 252
Hundred Propositions (of Mitterand) 165
Hungary 90, 221

Immigrants, North African 74, 283
Immigration 9, 13, 40, 74, 75, 78, 113–142
Independant Republicans. see Républicains Independants (RI)
Indochina 120, 227, 255
Industrial Modernization Fund 36
Inspection Générale des Affaires Sociales (IGAS) 162
Institut Français d'Opinion Publique (IFOP) 60
Instituts Universitaires de Technologie (IUT) 208
Intermediate-range nuclear forces (INF) 262
Interministerial Committee on Immigration 123, 124
Iran 261
Ireland 266
Italian Communist Party (PCI) 245n
Italy 9, 31, 113, 164, 267
Ivory Coast 123
Ivry-sur-Seine 134

Jacobin dictatorship 193
Jacobinism 56, 111n, 113–115, 122, 125, 127, 135–142, 193, 194, 197, 198, 202–204, 211–213, 215, 233, 276, 279, 281–288, 290–292
James, Henry 251
Japan 31, 268–269, 272, 281
Jaurès, Jean 164, 239
Jeanneney, J. M. 124, 163
Jesuits 217n
Jeunesse Agricole Catholique 27
Jospin, Lionel 200, 205, 207, 211, 214
Joxe, Pierre 199–200

Judicial review 52
Juppé, Alain 78

Keynesianism 93, 96–97, 101, 103, 106, 111n, 290
Kissinger, Henry 260
Khrushchev, Nikita 90, 256
Kohl, Helmut 268
Krasucki, Henri 186

Labour Party (Great Britain) 56
Lacan, Jacques 227, 234
Laïcisme 195, 200, 206
Laignel, André 199–200
Laignel amendments 200
Lapie Commission 196
Laroque, Pierre 157, 161, 162
Laroque plan 159
Le Mans 177
Le Pen, Jean-Marie 17, 55, 59, 72–79, 138, 283–284, 286, 288–289
Lecanuet, Jean 77
Left 17, 24, 29, 31, 32, 46, 49, 54, 57–60, 65–67, 77, 80, 85–107, 125, 134, 194–197, 198, 202, 211, 221–241, 271, 277–279, 282–283, 287, 289
Left Catholicism 224
Left Radicals. see Mouvement des Radicaux de Gauche (MRG)
Léotard, François 76, 78
Lesourne, Jacques 205
Lévi-Strauss, Claude 222
Liberal Democratic Party (Japan) 49
Liberalism 81, 106, 214
Libération 233, 236
Ligue de l'Enseignement 156, 198
Lip 180, 183
Lizop, Edouard 196, 197
Loi d'Orientation 207
Loi Le Chapelier 153
Loi Pasqua 75, 78
Loi Roussel 154
London 44–45
Lorraine 9, 158
Luxembourg 140, 267
Luxembourg compromise 266
Lycées 206

Macmillan, Harold 256
Madelin, Alain 38, 186
Maghrébins 136

Maire, Edmond 184, 186
Malhuret, Claude 76, 77
Mallet, Serge 223
Manifeste de Créteil 101
Maoists 231
Marche des Beurs 138
Marie Law 196
Marseille 78
Marshall Plan 3, 23, 120
Marx, Karl 236
Marxism 89, 95, 104, 221–227, 234, 236, 239, 243n, 289, 292
Massé, Pierre 26
Mathiez, Albert 239
Matignon 49, 50, 56
Mauroy, Pierre 52, 136, 137, 165, 185, 198–200, 290
May 1968, crisis of 28–29, 50, 65, 96, 125–126, 178, 207, 224, 228, 231, 279, 281, 285
Mediacracy 230
Meline Laws 23
Mendès-France, Pierre 25, 93, 96, 98, 108n, 160–161, 243n
Mermaz, Louis 200
Messmer, Pierre 180
Metérologie nationale 188
Mexandeau, Louis 198
Michelin 188
Millerand, Alexandre 155
Ministry for International Trade and Industry (MITI) 32
Ministry of Finance 38
Ministry of National Education 193, 198, 203, 212, 213, 281
Ministry of Interior 203
Ministry of Labor 118, 129, 132
Ministry of Population 118
Ministry of Social Affairs 128, 165
Mirman, Léon 155
Mitterrand, François 7, 9, 12, 29, 31, 37, 45–49, 52–55, 72, 78, 95–96, 98, 100–104, 136, 185, 187, 198–200, 204, 212, 232–233, 237, 238, 248n, 262–263, 267–269, 285–286, 289, 290, 293
Mollet, Guy 196–197
Monnet, Jean 26, 269, 275
Monnet Plan 117, 119
Monod, Henri 155–156
Monory, René 193, 204, 207, 212, 213
Monory Plan 205

Morocco 123
Mouvement contre le Racisme et pour l'Amitié entre les Peuples (MRAP) 281
Mouvement des Radicaux de Gauche (MRG) 183
Mouvement Républicain Populaire (MRP) 25, 47, 95–96, 159–161, 195–196, 288
Mulhouse 177
Mutualités 153, 154

Nantes 175
Napoléon 55
National Assembly 37, 43–51, 52, 58, 61, 62, 64, 72, 138, 199–201, 209, 210, 276, 286, 289
National Employment Agency. see Agence Nationale pour l'Emploi
National Employment Fund 176
National Front. see Front National (FN)
National Office of Immigration. see Office Nationale d'Immigration
National Planning Commission. see Commissariat Général du Plan (CGP)
National Union of Elementary Teachers. see Syndicat National des Instituteurs
Naville, Pierre 223
Neocorporatism 280
Neo-Gaullism. see Rassemblement pour la République (RPR)
Neo-Keynesianism 138
Neoliberalism 10, 80, 107, 277, 289
Neo-Marxism 228
Neo-Radicalism 98
Netherlands 267
New Caledonia 49, 54
New Left 89, 104, 107, 111n
Nixon, Richard 164, 260–261
Noir, Michel 76, 77
North Africa 121, 122, 126, 127, 271, 282, 283
North Atlantic Treaty Organization (NATO) 12, 259
Norway 266
Nouvel Observateur 233, 235–236
Nouvelle société 161
Nuclear deterrence 270
Nuclear test ban treaty 256
Nuclear weapons 253, 257, 268, 292

Office Française de Protection des Réfugiés et Apatrides (OFPRA) 137

Office Nationale de Statistique et de Placement 155
Office Nationale d'Immigration (ONI) 118, 120, 123, 124, 126, 128, 131, 133
Old Left 104
Old Regime 55, 193, 278
Ollivier, Emile 153–154
Ostpolitik 260, 263
Ottawa 261

Palente 180
Papacy 196
Paris 175
Parodi, Alexandre 157
Parti Communiste Français (PCF) 9, 17, 23–26, 29, 31, 34, 40, 44–47, 49, 55, 56, 60, 65, 70, 77, 79, 85–107, 108n, 109n, 111n, 120–123, 133, 136, 137, 141, 177, 183, 194–196, 214, 221–226, 228, 231–232, 236, 243n, 244n, 245n, 247n, 278, 280, 287–290, 295n
Parti Républicain (PR). see also Républicains Indépendants (RI) 68, 76, 78, 80
Parti Socialiste Français (PS) 9, 10, 17, 25, 31, 34, 35, 40, 47, 49, 51, 60, 65, 69, 70, 77, 78, 80, 85–107, 133, 136, 183, 194, 195–198, 200, 203, 212, 214, 231–233, 237–239, 281, 284, 286, 289–291
Parti Socialiste Unifié (PSU) 89, 95, 96, 99, 110n, 226, 228, 232, 289
Pasqua, Charles 75–78
Pension 159
Piaget, Charles 180
Piat, Yann 78
Pinay government 145n
Pleven, René 196–197
Pluralism 56, 193, 277, 284, 287, 290
Poland 113, 234
Political participation 70
Pompidou, Georges 8, 50–52, 54, 66, 68, 103, 125, 126, 129, 130, 146n, 174, 176, 178, 181, 198, 260–261, 265, 266, 285
Pons, Bernard 78
Poor Amendment Act 154
Poor Laws 155
Popper, Karl 235
Populationistes 117–119, 121, 127
Portugal 123, 126, 129
Post-Fordism 105
Potsdam 255
Poujadistes 61

Poulantzas, Nicos 228
Prélèvement obligatoire 166, 172n
Privatization laws 37, 38
Programme Commun. see Common Program
Projets d'Action Educative (PAE) 204
Projets d'Activités Educatives (PACTE) 204
Proste, Antoine 206
Protestants 115
Protocol of Grenelle. see Grenelle agreements
Provisional Government 118

Questiaux, Nicole 164–165
Querelle scolaire. see *question scolaire*
Question scolaire 54, 197–202, 283
Quimper 177

Radical republicans 155
Radicals 47, 66, 77, 130, 194, 196
Rapid Action Force 267
Rapport Anotelli 157
Rapport Boutbien 160
Rapport Buisson 158
Rapport Friedel 162
Rapport Laroque 161
Rapport Mottin 158
Rapport Piketty 163
Rapport Prigent 161
Rassemblement du Peuple Français (RPF) 43, 49, 60, 69, 195, 196, 288
Rassemblement pour la République (RPR) 47, 67, 68, 75–81, 83n, 137, 139, 186, 284, 288–289
Rationalized parliamentarism 45
Reagan, Ronald 8, 162, 235
Redon 177
Réformateurs 65, 66
Régime général 159
Régime complémentaire 158, 166
Régimes spéciaux 158
Renault Billancourt 109n
Républicains Indépendants (RI) 26, 62, 64, 65
Republicanism 290–292
Republikaner 134
Representation of interests 87–88, 279–287
Representation of self 87–88
Resistance 3, 7
Restoration monarchy 217n
Reykjavik 261
Rhodiaceta 177
Rhône-Alpes 177
Right 14, 29, 34, 37, 38, 40, 46, 54, 57–84,

97, 114, 197, 200, 202, 211, 271, 277–
    280, 282, 287–289
Robespierre 193, 240
Rocard, Michel 55, 78, 79, 99, 103, 140,
    141, 160, 187–188, 248n, 284
Rome 196
Rossinot, André 77
Rousseau, Jean-Jacques 56, 113
Rueff-Armand Commission 145n

Saint-Etienne 175
Saint Just 240
Saint-Nazaire 175, 188
Salaire Minimum Interprofessionel de Crois-
    sance (SMIC) 28, 161, 184
Sartre, Jean-Paul 222, 227, 234, 292
Saunier-Séïté, Alice 208
Sauvage Law 209
Sauvy, Alfred 117 118
Savary, Alain 193, 198–200, 203, 205–207,
    212
Savary Bill 199–201, 212, 214, 283, 290
Savary Law 209, 215, 282
Savoie 36
Schengen initiative 141
Schuman, Robert 265, 269
Second Empire 115, 152
Secrétariat d'Etudes pour la Liberté de
    l'Enseignement 196
Secretariat of Catholic Education 199
Secrétariat Professionel International de
    l'Enseignement (SPIE) 192n
Section Française de l'Internationale Ouvrière
    (SFIO) 89, 93–96, 98, 109n, 195, 224,
    225, 245n, 288, 289
Sections Syndicales d'Enterprise 28
Séguin, Philippe 37, 39, 78, 187
Séguy, Georges 181
Senegal 123
Servan-Schreiber, Jean-Jacques 66
Single Europe Act 52, 140, 141
SIVAC-Monory savings account package 184
Sixth Plan 128, 180
Smith, Adam 235
SNECMA 188
Soboul, Albert 240
Social democracy 105, 239, 287
Social Democratic Party (Germany) 56, 156,
    262
Social Democratic Party (Sweden) 163, 164
Social security system 24

Socialism 221, 223, 231, 281
Socialist party. see Parti Socialiste Français
Société bloquée 29, 39–40, 212–213, 279–280
Société Générale d'Immigration (SGI) 115,
    116, 123
Société Nationale de Construction de Loge-
    ments pour les Travailleurs (SONACOTRA)
    134, 136
Solidarnosc 234
SOS-Racisme 138, 281
Stages d'Initiation à la Vie Professionelle
    (SIVP) 37–9, 188, 192n
Structuralism 222–223, 226
Sudreau Report 31
Sweden 154
Syndicat Général de l'Education Nationale
    (SGEN) 206, 209, 213
Syndicat National des Enseignement de Sec-
    ond Degré (SNES) 198, 216
Syndicat National de l'Enseignement Supérieur
    (SNE Sup) 208, 209
Syndicat National des Instituteurs (SNI) 198,
    216, 217n

Taux de régularisation 120, 122, 126, 127,
    129
Taylorism 22, 23, 34
Teheran 261
Tenth plan 187
Thatcher, Margaret 8, 162
Thiers, Adolphe 195
Third Plan 123
Third Republic 3, 6, 25, 34, 37, 43, 46, 52–
    55, 59, 68, 90, 94, 113, 117, 154–158,
    167, 193, 217n, 275, 277–280, 281, 282,
    285, 287, 290
Thorez, Maurice 24, 90, 108n, 110n
Tocqueville, Alexis de 153, 193, 235, 236,
    239, 277–279
Togo 123
Toubon, Jacques 76
Touraine, Alain 223, 228, 236, 242n
Trade union leaders 128
Trade unions 10, 36, 102, 112n, 116, 118,
    119, 121, 124, 126, 130, 133, 173–190
Travail d'utilité publique 165
Treaties of Rome 124, 174, 265–266
Trente glorieuses 2, 9–10, 18, 114, 122–135
Tripartite Government 118, 121, 160
Trotskyism 244n
TUC 36, 38, 192n

Tunisia 123
Turkey 123, 126
Twenty-second Congress of PCF 100

UCNASS 162
UNEDIC 187
UNEF-ID 210
Unemployment Act of 1935 157
Unemployment compensation. see ASSEDIC
    and UNEDIC
Union de la Gauche 55, 67, 72, 77, 90, 98,
    100–101, 209, 231–233, 237
Union des Démocrates pour la République
    (UDR) 59, 66
Union des Républicains de Centre (URC) 77,
    78
Union des Républicains pour le soutien du
    Président (URP) 66
Union du Centre (UDC) 78
Union Nationale pour l'Ecole Libre (UNA-
    PEL) 195, 199
Union Nationale des Etudiants de France
    (UNEF) 210, 225, 243n
Union Nationale Interuniversitaire (UNI) 209,
    213
Union of Soviet Socialist Republics (USSR)
    232, 253–258, 260–263, 265, 270, 271
Union of the left. see Union de la Gauche
Union pour la Démocrâtie Française (UDF)
    47, 67, 68, 75, 77–79, 80, 81, 83n, 137,
    139, 186, 199, 284, 288
Union pour la Nouvelle République (UNR).
    see also Gaullists 59, 60, 61, 63, 67
United Left 102
United Nations 260

United Nation Security Council 243
United States Congress 51–52
United States of America (USA) 5, 12, 49,
    102, 135–137, 148n, 159, 161, 213, 214,
    253–269, 270–272, 277–278, 281
University 28, 38, 193, 207–211, 213, 215,
    283

Vaillant, Edouard 159
Value Added Tax (VAT) 183
Veil, Simone 72, 163, 164
Verts. see Greens
Vichy 4, 117, 142, 194, 221, 252
Vietnam 12, 121
Vincennes University 234, 248n
Von Hayek, Friedrich 235
Vote beur 137
Voter volatility 70–72

Waldeck-Rousseau, René 154, 155
War on Poverty 163
Welfare state 151–168
West Africa 121, 123, 126, 282, 283
West European Union (WEU) 267
Wilson, Harold 163
Wohlfahrtsstaat 152
Women's movement 110n
World War One 53, 157
World War Two 61, 113–116, 259, 278

Yalta 5, 255, 257, 259, 260, 263, 270
Yom Kippur War 181, 261
Yugoslavia 123, 126

Zimmern, Alfred 169n

Contributors

John Ambler is Professor of Political Science at Rice University and author of *Soldiers Against the State, The French Army in Politics* and editor of *The French Socialist Experiment*, as well as numerous articles on French politics.

Douglas Ashford is Professor of Political Science at the University of Pittsburgh and has written widely on the welfare state and social policy, including *Policy and Politics in France, Living With Uncertainty* and *British Dogmatism and French Pragmatism, Central and Local Policymaking in the Welfare State*.

A. W. DePorte, a former State Department expert on Europe, is a research associate at the Institute for French Studies at New York University and author of *Europe Between the Superpowers*.

Stanley Hoffmann is Dillon Professor of the Civilization of France and Chairman of the Minda de Gunzburg Center for European Studies at Harvard University. Hoffmann has written extensively on international affairs and foreign policy, has edited *In Search of France, The Fifth Republic at Twenty* (with William Andrews), and *The Mitterrand Experiment* (with George Ross and Sylvia Malzacher). He is the author of *Decline or Renewal? France Since the '30s*.

James F. Hollifield is Assistant Professor of Politics at Brandeis University and has written extensively on matters of immigration, politics and society, including the forthcoming *Immigrants, Markets, and States*.

Jane Jenson is Professor of Political Science at Carleton University in Ottawa, Ontario, Canada and author of numerous books and articles on Canadian and French politics, including *The View From Inside: A French Communist Cell in Crisis* (with George Ross), *The Feminization of the Labor Force: Promises and Prospects* (with Elisabeth Hagen and Ceilleagh Reddy), *Crisis, Challenge and Change: Party and Class in Canada Revisited* (with Janine Brodie).

Alain Lipietz is a researcher at the Centre D'Etudes Prospectives D'Economie Mathématique Appliquées à la Planification (CEPREMAP) in Paris and author of *l'Audace ou l'enlisement, Mirages and Miracles: Crisis in Global Fordism*, and *Choisir l'audace: Une alternative pour le vingt et unième siècle*.

331

René Mouriaux is *Directeur de Recherches* at the Centre Pour l'Etude de la Vie Politique Française (CEVIPOF) at the Fondation Nationale des Sciences Politiques in Paris, teaches at the Institut d'Etudes Politiques in Paris and is the author of numerous works on the French labor movement, including *La CFDT* (with Guy Groux), *La CGT, Les Syndicats dans la société Française*.

George Ross is Morris Hillquit Professor in Labor and Social Thought at Brandeis University and Senior Associate of the Minda de Gunzburg Center for European Studies at Harvard. Ross has written extensively about the Left and labor in Europe and is the author of *Workers and Communists in France, The View From Inside: A French Communist Cell in Crisis,* and *The Mitterrand Experiment* (edited with Stanley Hoffmann and Sylvia Malzacher).

Martin Schain is Professor of Political Science at New York University. Among his many writings on French politics are *French Communism and Local Power* and *The State and Public Policy in France* (edited with Philip Cerny).